Microsoft®

Excel 97
Developer's Kit

Microsoft Press

PUBLISHED BY
Microsoft Press
A Division of Microsoft Corporation
One Microsoft Way
Redmond, Washington 98052-6399

Library of Congress Cataloging-in-Publication Data
Microsoft Excel 97 Developer's Kit / Microsoft Corporation.
        p.   cm.
    Includes index.
    ISBN 1-57231-498-2
    1. Microsoft Excel for Windows.   2. Business--Computer programs.
    I. Microsoft Corporation.
    HF5548.4.M523M51572   1997
    005.369--dc21   97-2409
                                                            CIP

Printed and bound in the United States of America.

1 2 3 4 5 6 7 8 9   QMQM   2 1 0 9 8 7

Distributed to the book trade in Canada by Macmillan of Canada, a division of Canada Publishing Corporation.

A CIP catalogue record for this book is available from the British Library.

Microsoft Press books are available through booksellers and distributors worldwide. For further information about international editions, contact your local Microsoft Corporation office. Or contact Microsoft Press International directly at fax (206) 936-7329.

Acquisitions Editor: Casey D. Doyle
Project Editor: Maureen Williams Zimmerman

Contents

Introduction

The Microsoft Excel Developer's Kit provides information for software developers who want to develop applications that interact with Microsoft Excel. The Microsoft Excel Developer's Kit is a programming and technical reference. It is not a complete guide to Visual Basic programming and discusses the Microsoft Excel macro language (XLM) only in the context of add-in functionality. It assumes an understanding of Microsoft Excel's capabilities as exposed to the user.

This book contains everything you need to know to use the Microsoft Excel Developer's Kit. It assumes that you already know C and that you are familiar with Microsoft Excel and Visual Basic, Applications Edition (VBA). Visual Basic is described in the *Microsoft Excel Visual Basic User's Guide* and the *Microsoft Excel Visual Basic Language Reference*.

If you plan to develop applications for Microsoft Windows, you should know the basics of Microsoft Windows programming and how to write DLLs.

A CD accompanies this book. It contains examples and sample files to support the topics discussed in the following chapters. For information on the contents of this CD, see "Excel Developer's Kit CD-ROM," later in this chapter.

Because Microsoft Excel includes two macro languages and other extension mechanisms, it is not always easy to determine which parts of Microsoft Excel are best suited for your application. The following sections outline the available components, typical scenarios for use, and advantages and disadvantages of each.

Extending Microsoft Excel

Chapter 1 Provides a strong foundation for writing great add-ins and handling the common issues related to integration with Microsoft Excel. This includes some transitional issues from previous versions along with conceptual frameworks for your add-ins.

Chapter 2 Focuses on real-world Wizards using VBA. This includes a strong structured strategy for handing initialization and validation for your Wizards. The source code example is included on the CD.

Chapter 3 Discusses the transitional issues from Microsoft Excel 5/95 to Microsoft Excel 97 from a developer's perspective. This includes VBA issues, converting the Microsoft Excel Applications Programming Interface (C API) to 32-bit code, and porting guidelines for converting C API applications to use OLE Automation.

Chapter 4 Describes OLE concepts, including early and late binding, in process versus out of process, and the performance and programming implications of each option.

Calling DLLs from VBA

Chapter 5 Provides examples of DLL functions written in C that can be called from Visual Basic in Microsoft Excel. Text and examples show how Visual Basic data types (such as arrays, objects, and variants) are passed to DLL functions from Microsoft Excel.

Chapter 6 Discusses the OLE Automation Interface in the Microsoft Excel 97 context.

Because VBA is more powerful than the Microsoft Excel macro language (XLM), you can often write almost all of your custom functions and procedures in Visual Basic. Even with the added power of Visual Basic, however, it may be faster to perform some tasks from a C-language DLL. You may also need to write an external DLL function in C because you need to call a system-level function with a parameter-passing style or memory-management constraint not supported by Visual Basic.

Examples of tasks that must be performed in C include calls to functions that use arrays of structures contained within an enclosing structure or functions that require dynamic memory allocation. Visual Basic's built-in data types and memory-management systems cannot support these complex tasks; therefore a Visual Basic macro that needs to call these functions must call an intermediate C-language function that builds the structures or manages memory to match the function's calling conventions.

It is also appropriate to write DLL functions that are called from Visual Basic if you need to perform speed-intensive calculations (which is one of the same reasons you'd use the C API). If you need to use Microsoft Excel objects as a part of the calculation, you can use the techniques in Chapter 7 to pass objects and other complex parameters to a DLL function and then use the techniques in Chapter 8 to manipulate the Microsoft Excel objects.

OLE vs. C API

Chapter 7 Describes the OLE versus the C API. The strengths and weaknesses of each are highlighted.

Chapter 8 Is a function reference for the C API.

You can use the C API to create new custom worksheet functions (functions that can be entered into a cell on a worksheet), to create new macro functions (optimized for use from Microsoft Excel XLM macro sheets), and to create add-ins written in C but that use Microsoft Excel commands and functions to perform actions and calculate values.

Although you can write worksheet functions in both Visual Basic and the Microsoft Excel macro language, if the function requires high-speed or data-intensive calculations, it may be more appropriate to write the function in C. The Microsoft Excel C API is the best way to integrate external custom worksheet functions with Microsoft Excel.

Applications that require high-speed data transfer from an external source into Microsoft Excel can use the C API. A typical use of this capability is a macro function that retrieves data from an external database and puts the data on a worksheet. Other examples include a function that retrieves data from an external source, such as a stock ticker, or a calculation-intensive statistical analysis function.

Disadvantages of the C API include the following:

- Because the C API is optimized for use from the Microsoft Excel macro language and the worksheet, it is not a very good mechanism for writing external functions to be used by Visual Basic (although Visual Basic and the C API can be combined into hybrid solutions).

- The C API is not object-oriented (because it is based on the Microsoft Excel XLM macro language). You cannot use the C API to access Visual Basic objects, properties, and methods.

- Because the C API can be used only from a DLL loaded in the Microsoft Excel process, an external application cannot use the C API to control Excel.

- The C API cannot be used unless Microsoft Excel has explicitly called the DLL function in response to a menu, toolbar, cell calculation, or event.

File Format

Chapter 9 Describes the binary interchange file format (BIFF) for workbooks. (Microsoft Excel 97 workbooks include worksheets, macro sheets, and Visual Basic modules.)

Chapter 10 Describes the BIFF for charts (charts are also included in workbooks, but their BIFF records are specific to charts). These chapters can be used to write files from external programs that can be read by Microsoft Excel as native documents.

Appendixes

Appendix A, "Dynamic Data Exchange and XlTable Format" Documents the dynamic data exchange (DDE) formats supported by Microsoft Excel and provides detailed information about the high-performance XlTable DDE format.

Appendix B, "Excel 97 and the Registry" Details the keys and values used with Microsoft Excel for add-ins and many of the program settings that are retained from session to session.

Appendix C, "Displaying Custom Help" Provides information about integrating custom help files for your application.

Appendix D, "Wizard Source Code" Is a complete source code listing for the structured Wizard example provided in Chapter 2.

Excel Developer's Kit CD-ROM

The included CD-ROM contains the following:

- The INCLUDE folder contains the header file XLCALL.H, which must be included in all C source files that call Microsoft Excel functions. The workbook Intlmap.xls in this folder contains the XLCALL.H constants translated into several languages.

- The LIB folder contains the library file XLCALL32.LIB. If you need to call Microsoft Excel functions, this library file is linked to your code. XLCALL32.LIB is a Windows import library; it doesn't contain actual code. You can use IMPORT statements in your linker definition (.DEF) file instead of linking to this library. Also included is XLCALL.LIB, which is the 16-bit version of this library used for DLLs written to be used by 16-bit versions of Excel. Lastly, FRMWRK32.LIB is the compiled library of the framework sample.

- The SAMPLES folder contains several subdirectories with sample source code, which is intended as a learning resource and includes extensive comments. Refer to Samples\ReadMe.txt for a description of each sample.
- The BIFF folder contains the BIFF viewing utility, BIFFVIEW.EXE.
- The HELP folder contains sample files for Appendix C, "Displaying Custom Help."
- The XLM folder contains the Microsoft Excel XLM Macro Function Reference help file.

Microsoft Technical Support

In the event you have a technical question about the Microsoft Excel 97 Developer's Kit, Microsoft offers technical support and services ranging from no-cost and low-cost online information services to annual support plans with a Microsoft technical engineer. Below is a brief description of these services to help you decide which option is right for you.

For more information about this and other services available in the United States and Canada, visit our Web site at:

http://www.microsoft.com/support/

Note The services and prices listed here are available in the United States and Canada only. Services and prices outside these countries may vary.

Primary Support Options:

Online Support

Online support uses Microsoft's own cutting-edge technology to help you access the most relevant technical information and resources to answer your support questions quickly and easily through the following features:

Support Wizard Get step-by-step guidance on how to find the information most relevant to your support question.

Microsoft Frequently Asked Questions Get quick answers to the most common technical issues on your Microsoft product.

Microsoft Knowledge Base Access a comprehensive collection of more than 70,000 detailed articles with technical information about Microsoft products, bug and fix lists, and answers to commonly asked technical questions.

Troubleshooters Take advantage of cutting-edge technologies that help you diagnose and solve technical problems quickly and easily.

Drivers, Patches, and Sample Files Choose from hundreds of free software add-ons, bug fixes, peripheral drivers, software updates, and programming aids for easy downloading at your convenience.

Newsgroup Share information with a worldwide community of other Microsoft customers, technical experts, and hundreds of Microsoft-selected Most Valuable Professionals.

WebResponse Conveniently submit support requests via the Web. Available for developer and Office developer products only.

Technical Information Services

If you don't have access to the Internet or you are more familiar with phone, fax, modem, or mail, you can access these two additional technical information resources beyond the World Wide Web:

Microsoft Download Service (MSDL) Gives you access to Microsoft's electronic technical library containing sample programs, device drivers, patches, software updates, and programming aids. Direct modem access to MSDL is available in the U.S. by dialing (206) 936-6735. The service is available 24 hours a day, 365 days a year. Connect information: 1200, 2400, 9600, or 14400 baud; no parity, 8 data bits, and 1 stop bit. In Canada, dial (905) 507-3022; connect information 1200 to 28800 baud, no parity, 8 data bits, and 1 stop bit.

Microsoft FastTips An automated, toll-free telephone service that gets you quick answers to common technical questions as well as technical articles by telephone, fax, or mail. To access FastTips or to receive a map and catalog, call (800) 936-4300.

No-Charge Phone Support

If you still need answers to your technical questions, Microsoft Primary Support provides no-charge toll-charge phone support with a Microsoft technical engineer as follows:

You will receive a total of two (2) no-charge incidents for development issues involving this product. In the United States and Canada, call (206) 635-7048, 6:00 A.M.–6:00 P.M. Pacific time, Monday through Friday, excluding holidays.

When you call, you should be at your computer and have the appropriate product documentation at hand. Be prepared to give the following information:

- The version of the Microsoft product you use
- The type of hardware you use
- The operating system you use
- The exact wording of any messages that appeared on your screen
- A description of what happened and what you were doing when the problem occurred
- A description of how you tried to solve the problem.

Note If your Microsoft product was preinstalled or distributed with your personal computer or provided by an Internet Service Provider (ISP), the personal computer manufacturer or ISP is responsible for providing your product support. Please contact the manufacturer or ISP from which you obtained your Microsoft product for support information.

Priority Support Options

With Microsoft Priority Support, you can purchase additional access to Microsoft technical engineers. Microsoft Priority Support can be purchased annually in sets of incidents, or you can pay per incident. In addition to round-the-clock access, Microsoft Priority Support includes Priority Response, which jumps you to the head of the queue and provides access to senior technical support engineers.

To purchase Microsoft Priority Support for development issues involving all Microsoft products, you can chose from the following options:

- In the U.S. and Canada, to purchase Priority Support *per incident* for a fee of $95US, call (800) 936-5800, 24 hours a day, 7 days a week. In the U.S. only, you can also call (900) 555-2300. Support fees for the 800# calls will be billed to your VISA, MasterCard, or American Express credit card. Support fees for the 900# calls will appear on your telephone bill.
- In the U.S. and Canada, to purchase an *annual contract* of incidents, or for more information on Priority Support, call (800) 936-3500, 6:00 A.M.–6:00 P.M. Pacific time, Monday through Friday. Technical support is not available through this number.

- In the U.S. and Canada to purchase phone-based *hourly* consulting, call Consult Line at (800) 936-1565 at $195US/hour (minimum charge is for one hour).

- WebResponse allows you to submit service requests via the World Wide Web to Microsoft support engineers who receive the requests and work with you to resolve your technical problem. To submit service requests using WebResponse you must establish a Priority account through one of the options listed above. Once you have established your account, go to **http://www.microsoft.com/support/** and use the Priority Web response pointer.

Premier Support

Premier Support gives you proactive support planning and problem-resolution for Microsoft products, with rapid response times—including immediate, server-down response, 24 hours a day, 7 days a week—and special consulting and planning services. Premier Support is part of Microsoft Service Advantage, a suite of offerings combining direct services from Microsoft with established enterprise service partners, for a total solution for the enterprise customer. For more information on Service Advantage and Premier Support, call (800) 936-3200.

Third-Party Support Options

If you have an existing sales or support relationship with another organization, need multivendor support, or prefer an alternative to obtaining support directly from Microsoft, you can choose from a variety of authorized Microsoft support providers.

Microsoft Solution Provider Program   Microsoft Solution Providers are independent developers, consultants, and systems analysts who offer fee-based technical training and support, industry knowledge, objective advice, and a range of value-added services to companies of all sizes. For the name of a Microsoft Solution Provider near you, in the U.S., call (800) 765-7768, 6:30 A.M.–5:30 P.M. Pacific time, Monday through Friday, excluding holidays. In Canada, call (800) 563-9048, 8:00 A.M.–8:00 P.M. eastern time, Monday through Friday, excluding holidays.

Microsoft Authorized Support Centers   A select group of strategic support providers who offer quality, cost-effective, customizable support services that span the complete life cycle of planning, building, and managing your open environment. For more information on the ASC program, in the U.S., call (800) 636-7544, 6:00 A.M.–6:00 P.M. Pacific time, Monday through Friday, excluding holidays. In Canada, call (800) 563-9048, 8:00 A.M.–8:00 P.M. eastern time, Monday through Friday, excluding holidays.

Additional Information

Customer Service For customer service issues on Microsoft products, upgrades, and services, you can call the Microsoft Sales Information Center at (800) 426-9400 in the United States. In Canada, call (800) 563-9048. Technical support is not available at these numbers.

Text Telephone Microsoft text telephone (TT/TDD) services are available for the deaf or hard-of-hearing. In the United States, using a TT/TDD modem, dial (206) 635-4948. In Canada, using a TT/TDD modem, dial (905) 568-9641.

Support Offerings Worldwide For support offerings outside the United States and Canada, contact the local Microsoft subsidiary in your area. For a listing of worldwide Microsoft subsidiaries connect to:

http://www.microsoft.com/supportnet/InternationalPhoneNumbers.htm

Services and prices may vary outside the United States and Canada. Microsoft Technical Support is subject to Microsoft's then-current prices, terms, and conditions, which are subject to change without notice.

C H A P T E R   1

Writing Great Add-Ins

Microsoft Excel allows you to fully customize, enhance, personalize, and extend almost every aspect of the application. Programming in the Visual Basic for Applications (VBA) macro language is usually the starting point for customization. But as this book will make clear, you can also extend Microsoft Excel by means of C code or other languages that support either OLE Automation or Windows Dynamic Link Libraries (DLLs). This chapter focuses on the VBA portions of your code, and provides the information needed to write high-quality add-ins.

When your development work is finished, you can create an add-in from your program, making it a seamless part of the Microsoft Excel interface. You can add custom functions, automate complex processes, and/or create complete programs that function entirely inside Microsoft Excel. If you desire, you can virtually take over the Microsoft Excel user interface with custom toolbars, menus, and on-sheet controls.

In reality, an add-in is a type of macro, similar to the concept of a square also being a rectangle. This chapter focuses on authoring great add-ins, but nearly all of the concepts presented here apply to any VBA application. The chapter also details the changes that have occurred since the previous version of Microsoft Excel.

Why Make an Add-In?

There are several reasons why you might want to create an add-in from your code. The number one reason is to create a seamless extension to Microsoft Excel. Add-ins also have slightly different error handling attributes than regular VBA macros. This will be covered later in the chapter under the section titled "Error Handling."

Once your add-in is opened (either manually or by using the Add-In Manager), it can appear to be an integral part of the Microsoft Excel environment. If you have created a project containing a number of custom worksheet functions, creating an add-in from the project will make those functions available to all workbooks whenever the add-in is open.

For projects that involve user interaction with worksheets, creating a separate add-in also allows you to take advantage of the principle of modularity. The code that runs the project is contained in a workbook that is completely separate from the one seen by the user. This makes it very easy to update your code, by simply plugging in a new add-in.

Unlike in previous versions of Microsoft Excel, creating an add-in is no longer necessary in Microsoft Excel 97 to protect your code from prying eyes. With Microsoft Excel 97 VBA, you can lock your code for viewing whether or not it is an add-in. This is a very useful feature if you need to allow the user access to any worksheets or chart sheets in your workbook but wish to keep the code of the add-in hidden. Creating an add-in from your project completely hides the workbook from the user. Your add-in workbook is not visible to the user (it opens hidden) and it doesn't appear on the Window menu.

Add-In Changes Since the Prior Versions of Microsoft Excel

The two versions prior to Microsoft Excel 97 were so similar that we will treat them as one version for this discussion, which we'll call *Microsoft Excel 5/95*.

Users and Developers Are Separated

In Microsoft Excel 5/95, macro code was placed in VBA module sheets and dialogs were created on dialog sheets. Both of these sheet types existed alongside worksheets and chart sheets in the Microsoft Excel workbook. While most developers would hide module and dialog sheets from users, if you wanted to you could view all of them together in the workbook.

In Microsoft Excel 97, rather than adding module and dialog sheets to the same window used for worksheets and charts, all programming is done from the Visual Basic Editor (VBE). This allows a much richer programming environment that is separate from the worksheet and chart window. You access the VBE from the Microsoft Excel menu by choosing Tools/Macro/Visual Basic Editor or by using the ALT+F11 keys to toggle between the two windows.

In addition to the standard code modules found in previous versions of Microsoft Excel, UserForms, Worksheets, and the Workbook object all contain modules where you can place code that applies to them. Microsoft Excel 97 also includes the ability to create Class Modules. In this chapter we'll refer to the three modules types as Standard Modules, created when you choose Insert/Module in the VBE; Object Modules, which hold the "code behind objects"; and Class Modules. This is a design enhancement that allows you to modularize your code.

Standard Modules are equivalent to module sheets in Microsoft Excel 5/95. Class Modules are a new type of module that allow you to create custom objects. Object Modules are a specific type of class module associated with certain VBA and Microsoft Excel 97 objects.

Good coding practice suggests that you keep all the code that pertains to a given object in one place, and Microsoft Excel 97 VBA allows you to do this. For example: dialog boxes and Wizards are built from Microsoft Excel 97 UserForms. These UserForms contain an Object Module that handles the code associated with objects placed on the UserForm (and the UserForm itself). This may include dialog initialization, error handling, and control code. Your Standard Modules can then call your dialog code with a single entry point, and the dialog will respond based on the code in its Object Module. If you copy an object, its code in the Object Module is copied as well, so you could copy a User Form and add it to another workbook and its associated code would be included automatically.

It's important to recognize that the Object Module behind a UserForm may also call code in the Standard Modules of your project. Microsoft Excel doesn't force you to place all the associated code in the Object Module, but in most cases this is the best practice.

Scope

A VBProject is the Visual Basic project that includes all the code modules, Microsoft Excel objects, references, and forms contained within a given workbook. In Microsoft Excel 97, public constants, variables, and procedures live in Standard Modules. Constants, variables, and functions declared with the Public keyword in a Standard Module are available to all other code in all VBProjects, unless the module contains the Option Private Module statement, in which case they will only be available to the VBProject that contains that Standard Module.

There are certain differences in the way the Public keyword is used in Object Modules and Class Modules. Here are the key differences:

- Constants, DLL declarations, and fixed-length strings cannot be declared as Public in any Object or Class Module.
- Variables declared as Public within an Object or Class Module become new *Properties* of that object.
- Procedures (functions and subroutines) declared as Public within an Object or Class Module become new *Methods* of that object.

You can create custom properties for an Object or Class Module, using the Property Get procedure. The following example illustrates how this is done:

- Create a new workbook.
- Start the VBE and add one UserForm and one Standard Module.
- Add a ListBox and a CommandButton to the UserForm.
- Name the ListBox lstDemo.
- Name the CommandButton cmdOK and give it the caption OK.

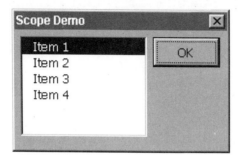

The following procedures should be created in the Object Module for the UserForm:

```
Property Get ListChoice() As String
    ListChoice = lstDemo.Value
End Property

Private Sub cmdOK_Click()
    Me.Hide
End Sub

Private Sub UserForm_Initialize()
    lstDemo.AddItem "Item 1"
    lstDemo.AddItem "Item 2"
    lstDemo.AddItem "Item 3"
    lstDemo.AddItem "Item 4"
    lstDemo.ListIndex = 0
End Sub
```

In the cmdOK_Click event procedure above, the Me keyword is an implicitly declared object variable that refers to the object within which code is currently executing. The next procedure goes in the Standard Module.

```
Sub ShowForm()
    UserForm1.Show
    MsgBox "You chose " & UserForm1.ListChoice
    Unload UserForm1
End Sub
```

Adding the Property Get procedure to the UserForm Object Module actually creates a new property for that UserForm. In this example, the new ListChoice property exposes the choice made in the listbox.

When you run the ShowForm procedure, the UserForm is displayed. Select an item in the listbox and click the OK button. The ShowForm procedure then generates a message box that accesses the ListChoice property of the UserForm to show which item you chose from the list.

The Wizard demo provided later in this chapter (and on the CD) also contains an example of using the Property Get procedure with a UserForm.

Optional Arguments

In previous versions of Microsoft Excel, optional arguments to procedures were required to use the Variant data type. In Microsoft Excel 97 VBA, it is now possible to declare optional arguments to your procedures with a specific data type. If one of these arguments is not passed, however, that argument will not evaluate as missing.

Any optional argument of a specifically declared data type that is not passed by the calling procedure will assume the default value of that data type (0 for integers and longs, an empty string for strings, and so on). Therefore, if you rely on IsMissing you will have to continue to declare optional arguments as type Variant.

You can also provide your own default values for your optional arguments. In the following examples, you'll see different default values depending on which method you use in your code. Here are some simple code fragments to illustrate these differences. All three examples assume that you call this routine without an argument.

Example 1

Implied variant (the same as Microsoft Excel 5/95):

```
Sub MyProcedure (Optional MyArgument)
```

Example 2

Specific type, VBA default:

```
Sub MyProcedure (Optional iMyArgument as Integer)
```

Example 3

Specific type, developer default:

```
Sub MyProcedure (Optional iMyArgument as Integer = -1)
```

Example 1 would pass the argument as a variant. If you tested the argument with IsMissing, it would evaluate to True.

Examples 2 and 3 would both contain a default integer value, either 0 in Example 2 (the VBA default value for integers) or -1 in Example 3. This allows you to provide a specific default if you don't want to use the VBA default value for the data type of your argument.

Custom Dialog Boxes

In Microsoft Excel 5/95, custom dialog boxes were created by adding dialog sheets to a workbook. In Microsoft Excel 97, custom dialog boxes are created with UserForms added to a project in the VBE. Controls are added to UserForms with the Toolbox, in a manner very similar to the way controls were added to Microsoft Excel 5/95 DialogSheets. The most visible difference between UserForms and DialogSheets is that new DialogSheets always had OK and Cancel buttons included on them by default, whereas new UserForms begin as a blank slate. You must add and create code for all controls.

The new ActiveX controls provided with Microsoft Excel 97 and Office 97 are greatly enhanced compared to the simple controls available in earlier versions. You now have much finer control over your custom dialogs and can provide a wider variety of dialog effects. For example, you can easily create wizards, add control tips (similar to tool tips), respond to different events (change, click, mouse over, mouse down, and so on), and provide context-sensitive help.

Unlike DialogSheets, you also have full control over the loading and display of UserForms. There are four UserForm methods that control how a UserForm is handled by VBA. These are Load, Show, Hide, and Unload.

Load   Loads the UserForm in memory, but doesn't display it. This method is useful when your project has complex forms that take a long time to load. The Load method allows you to load these forms into memory at the beginning of the program or at other appropriate times so that they are available without delay when they are needed.

Show   Displays the UserForm. If the UserForm is not already loaded into memory, the Show method will also load it.

Hide   Removes the UserForm from the screen and sets its Visible property to False, but does not remove it from memory. When a UserForm is hidden, all of the properties and methods that it exposes are still available.

Unload Removes the UserForm from memory. When a UserForm is unloaded, its properties and methods are no longer available.

Any UserForms not explicitly unloaded by your add-in can potentially remain in memory until Microsoft Excel is closed. To avoid this, it's a good idea to clean up any loaded UserForms before exiting your add-in. You accomplish this with the UserForms collection. The UserForms collection contains all the *loaded* UserForms in your add-in. Running the following code ensures that all UserForms are unloaded:

```
If UserForms.Count > 0 Then
    For iCount = 1 To UserForms.Count
        Unload UserForms(0)
    Next iCount
End If
```

Events

An *event* is an action that is recognized by an object. In Microsoft Excel 5/95 VBA, there were few events available to the programmer. For instance, most controls responded to only a single event (the OnAction event) which allowed you to specify the procedure that would run when the user selected the control or in some cases typed a character in an edit box.

Microsoft Excel 97 VBA is a highly *event-driven* programming environment. Worksheets, Workbooks, UserForms, and Controls now respond to a wide variety of events. Placing VBA code inside the procedures triggered by various events allows your program to respond to those events.

In Microsoft Excel 5/95, for example, if you wanted to take some action when a workbook was saved by the user, you had to explicitly trap all of the methods by which the user could save the workbook. This included replacing the Save entry on the File menu, the Save toolbar button, and all the different keyboard shortcuts that could be used to save a file (CTRL+S and CTRL+F12 among others). This doesn't include trapping the Save As menu command and keyboard shortcuts, trapping custom toolbars and menus, or other keyboard remappings; it is very difficult to trap every possible save method.

In Microsoft Excel 97, however, the Workbook object has a BeforeSave event. Code placed within the procedure for this event will run automatically when the workbook is saved by any means, including programmatically, allowing you to respond to all workbook saves in a single location.

You may encounter situations in which you need to run code inside an event procedure conditionally, based upon whether the event was fired from the user interface or from some action taken by another procedure in your program. To accomplish this, you can add a new property to the object that owns the event in question, by adding a publicly declared variable to its module. Within a workbook's BeforeSave event, for instance, if you want to run code conditionally based upon whether the user is saving the workbook or your code is saving the workbook, you could do it in the following manner.

```
Public CodeSaved As Boolean

Private Sub Workbook_Open()
    CodeSaved = False
End Sub

Private Sub Workbook_BeforeSave(ByVal _
    SaveAsUI As Boolean, Cancel As Boolean)
    If CodeSaved Then
        MsgBox "Called from code."
        CodeSaved = False
    Else
        MsgBox "Called from UI."
    End If
End Sub
```

The declaration and event procedure shown above would go into the workbook's Object Module. When you save the workbook from another procedure in your program, you would first set the CodeSaved property of the workbook to True and then call the Save method of the workbook.

```
Sub SaveBook()
    wkbBook.CodeSaved = True
    wkbBook.Save
End Sub
```

If the SaveBook procedure will be used in a different project than the one that contains wkbBook, you must establish a reference from that project to the one containing wkbBook.

Working with Events

At the top of the code window of the Object Module for each of the objects that respond to events, there are two drop-downs. The left drop-down contains an object list, while the right one contains a list of event procedures for the selected object. To add code for an object's event procedure, simply choose that object from the left-hand drop-down and choose the event procedure from the right-hand drop-down. An event procedure, to which you can add your custom code, will be automatically generated by VBA. The following figure shows the Object module for a Worksheet with some of the available events in the drop-down.

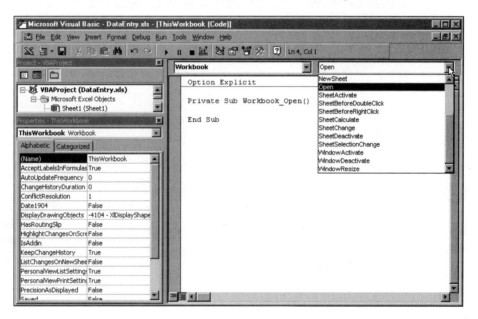

Selecting an object in the VBE Project Window and clicking the View Code button at the top of this window will display the Object Module for the object. Object Modules for all objects other than UserForms can also be accessed by simply double-clicking that object in the VBE Project Window.

Double-clicking a UserForm in the VBE Project Window displays the UserForm itself. Double-clicking anywhere on a displayed UserForm brings up its Object Module and displays the default event procedure for the object that was double-clicked.

Many other objects respond to events in a similar fashion to that described above. Check the online Help for more details.

The AddinInstall and AddinUninstall Events

Microsoft Excel 97 has added two new events, AddinInstall and AddinUninstall, which are fired when the user adds or removes an add-in using the Tools/Addins dialog box. The AddinInstall event should be used to make any modifications to the user interface that the add-in requires. Conversely, the AddinUninstall should be used to remove any modifications to the Microsoft Excel environment made by the add-in.

Object Referencing — The VBE Object Model

In Microsoft Excel 5/95 VBA, you addressed most objects by referring to their collection. For instance, if you needed to get the value of a range on a specific worksheet, you would use the Worksheets collection to address that worksheet, as follows:

```
iNumber = ThisWorkBook.Worksheets("Sheet1") _
    .Range("A1").Value
```

In Microsoft Excel 97, the new VBE object model allows you to reference objects directly by their Name (CodeName) property. In the case of a worksheet, the CodeName property is independent of the name the user sees on the sheet tab. Therefore, you can now uniquely identify worksheets with the CodeName property and not worry about the tab name provided for the user.

Assume that you set the CodeName property of your worksheet to wksMySheet. You can now refer to this worksheet in the following manner:

```
iNumber = wksMySheet.Range("A1").Value
```

If you need to refer to objects in another workbook by name, you must create a reference to that workbook using the Tools/References menu item in VBE. In order to do this, you must give a unique name to the VBProject object for each workbook.

By default, each new workbook you create contains its own VBProject object named VBAProject. You cannot create a reference between two projects whose names are the same. To change the project name, simply select the project in the Project Explorer and type a new name in the name property for that project shown in the Properties window. The following figure shows two VBProjects that have been given unique names.

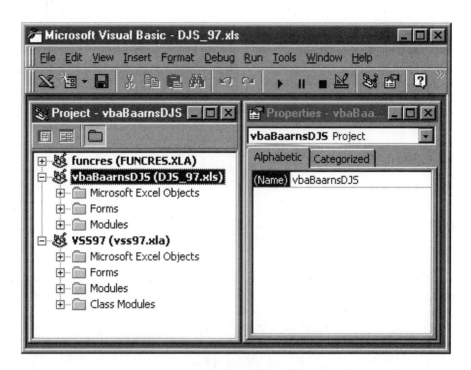

When addressing VBComponents by name in a single-workbook project, the current VBProject name is assumed as a qualifier. For instance, if your VBProject is named vbaMyProject and it contains a VBComponent (in this case, a UserForm) named frmMyForm, the following two lines of code are equivalent:

```
vbaMyProject.frmMyForm.Show
frmMyForm.Show
```

When referring to a VBComponent in a workbook to which you have created a reference, you may use the name of the VBComponent directly if that name is unique (in other words, if there is no VBComponent in the referencing workbook with that name).

If the referencing and the referenced VBProject both have a VBComponent with the same name, then you must use the name of the referenced VBProject as a qualifier. For instance, if the referenced VBProject is named vbaReferenced and both projects contain a worksheet with the CodeName Sheet1, from which you want to get the value in cell A1, you should do it like this:

```
iNumber = vbaReferenced.Sheet1.Range("A1").Value
```

Class Modules

Class Modules are very similar to UserForms except that they have no user interface and do not respond to any user-initiated events. You use Class Modules to create your own custom objects. Code written within the Class Module implements the object's properties and methods. Once you have written the code for your Class Module, you create instances of it by using the New keyword.

The following simple example demonstrates the use of Class Modules to create new objects. In this example, we will create a new object named MyClass, which has two properties, Title and DateCreated, and one method, TitleLength.

Open a new workbook and use the VBE to add one Standard Module and one Class Module. Using the Project Properties window, name the Class Module MyClass. Place the following code in MyClass:

```
Public Title As String
Private datDate As Date

Property Get DateCreated() As Date
    DateCreated = datDate
End Property

Private Sub Class_Initialize()
    datDate = Now
End Sub

Public Function TitleLength() As Integer
    TitleLength = Len(Title)
End Function
```

Now place the following procedure in the Standard Module:

```
Private clsMyClass As New MyClass

Sub CreateMyClassObject()
    clsMyClass.Title = "My Title"
    MsgBox "MyClass Title = " & clsMyClass.Title & _
        Chr(13) & "Title Length = " & _
        clsMyClass.TitleLength & Chr(13) & _
        "Date Created = " & clsMyClass.DateCreated
    Set clsMyClass = Nothing
End Sub
```

When you run the CreateMyClassObject procedure, the code creates a new instance of MyClass assigned to the variable clsMyClass and sets the Title property of the new object. The code then uses a message box to display the Title and DateCreated properties, as well as the TitleLength method of the object.

The Command Bars Object Model

In Microsoft Excel 97, the CommandBars object model replaces both the Toolbars and MenuBars object models from Microsoft Excel 5/95. This allows you to combine text, buttons, or both on any of your menus or toolbars, giving you much greater flexibility than in previous versions of Microsoft Excel. Because Microsoft Excel still displays a command bar with menus and a set of command bars containing toolbar buttons, you generally want to follow the same interface design for your custom add-ins.

The following procedure demonstrates how to add a new menu item to the Tools menu of the Worksheet Menu Bar command bar:

```
Sub AddMenuItem()
    Dim oMenu As CommandBarPopup
    Dim oItem As CommandBarPopup
    Dim oSub1 As CommandBarButton
    Dim oSub2 As CommandBarButton
    Set oMenu = CommandBars("Worksheet Menu Bar") _
        .Controls("Tools")
    Set oItem = oMenu.Controls.Add(Type:=msoControlPopup)
    oItem.Caption = "My Menu Item"
    Set oSub1 = oItem.Controls.Add(Type:=msoControlButton)
    oSub1.Caption = "Sub Menu 1"
    oSub1.OnAction = ThisWorkbook.Name & "!Proc1"
    Set oSub2 = oItem.Controls.Add(Type:=msoControlButton)
    oSub2.Caption = "Sub Menu 2"
    oSub2.OnAction = ThisWorkbook.Name & "!Proc2"
End Sub
```

The Menu Editor is no longer available in Microsoft Excel 97. All modifications to existing command bar menus must be made programmatically. You can also create your own custom command bars and attach them to a specific project. These command bars can include both menus and tools, and your code can hide or display the built-in command bars as needed.

Attaching custom command bars is handled via the Tools/Customize menu. You'll find the Attach button on the Toolbars tab. Beyond the first time the workbook is opened on a particular machine, the custom command bar will not hide or show itself automatically. The custom command bar will be available to all other workbooks unless your code explicitly controls its visibility.

Printing a Project

In Microsoft Excel 97, you print your project code from the VBE interface rather than from the Microsoft Excel interface. Choosing File/Print from the VBE allows you to print the current selection, module, or project. You can also print graphic images of your UserForms.

Dual-Stream File Formats

In addition to having the ability to open and save files created by earlier versions of Microsoft Excel, Microsoft Excel 97 offers a new type of file format called a *dual-stream* file format. This is a file format that can be opened in both Microsoft Excel 5/95 and Microsoft Excel 97, and that independently supports the features of each.

This format allows users of previous versions of Microsoft Excel to open your workbooks and sometimes run your code. This depends on the features you use and how you write your project. If you use Save As, with the file format set to Microsoft Excel Add-in, you do *not* get a dual-stream file.

If you use the dual-stream format for your workbooks, you'll notice the following issues:

- Dual-stream files are significantly larger than workbooks saved in one format or the other. (This should be obvious as you are actually saving two versions of the workbook in one file.)

- If a dual-stream workbook is saved using Microsoft Excel 5/95, the Microsoft Excel 97 stream will be lost and all Microsoft Excel 97–specific features will be lost.

For most add-in developers the dual-stream format isn't really an issue. Its primary function is to provide backward compatibility for worksheets. Your add-ins will generally take advantage of the newer features and will be saved in Microsoft Excel 97 format. Add-ins are never dual-stream; the two formats are mutually exclusive. Note, however, that a Microsoft Excel 5/95 add-in will load and run in Microsoft Excel 97.

DisplayAlerts Property

While working in Microsoft Excel 97, various warning dialog boxes are displayed to confirm that you aren't doing something destructive by accident. For example, overwriting an existing file, deleting worksheets, or closing a modified but unsaved workbook all display alert messages asking for a confirmation of your action. Setting the DisplayAlerts property of the Application object to False suppresses these warning dialogs (and many more) that occur during normal use while your procedure is executing.

Unlike in Microsoft Excel 5/95, in Microsoft Excel 97 the DisplayAlerts property is now persistent during cross-process automation. Therefore, when using cross-process automation you must explicitly set this property back to True before your procedure ends.

Creating an Add-In

The process of creating an add-in has been moved from the previous version's Tools/Make Add-in command to the current version's File/Save As command. When you change the File Type to "Microsoft Excel Add-In (*.xla)" your file will be saved as an add-in. This sets the IsAddin property of the Workbook object to True and then saves the file. Unlike in Microsoft Excel 5/95 VBA, however, this does not compile your VBA code, nor does it protect the VBA project. See the section titled "Code Cleaning" for details on compiling your project.

Worksheet Functions

Worksheet functions are an area often overlooked by the Microsoft Excel VBA developer. Microsoft Excel provides over 170 spreadsheet-specific functions that can be accessed from your VBA code. You'll find mathematical, financial, lookup, database, and many other function categories that can speed your worksheet-specific operations. While these functions were originally designed for use in a worksheet setting, many of them are excellent additions to the VBA developer's toolbox.

Referencing functions such as MATCH, VLOOKUP, HLOOKUP, and INDEX, combined with other worksheet functions such as COUNT, COUNTA, MIN, MAX, and SUM, can create very powerful tools for referencing a spreadsheet. Remember that VBA is a generic language that works across the Microsoft Office family (and beyond), but these worksheet functions are specific to Microsoft Excel.

Additionally, worksheet functions that operate on ranges in Microsoft Excel worksheets can be used with VBA arrays. Functions such as MATCH, SUBSTITUTE, INDEX, ISBLANK, VLOOKUP, and SUM can be used in this manner. There is some small overhead compared with VBA functions, but many of the worksheet functions have no VBA counterpart.

In previous versions of Microsoft Excel, worksheet functions were contained in the Application object. In Microsoft Excel 97, a new object called the WorksheetFunction object is used as a container for all the worksheet functions that can be called from Visual Basic.

Online Help has an excellent section, called "Using Microsoft Excel, Worksheet Functions in Visual Basic," which provides details on using these functions. It also has a complete list of functions available by using the WorksheetFunction object. Be sure to skim this list a few times and familiarize yourself with these powerful functions.

The Two Types of Add-Ins

Most Microsoft Excel add-ins can be divided into two broad categories: add-ins that work *with* Microsoft Excel (*committee*), and add-ins that *take over* the complete workspace (*dictators*). Each type of add-in requires unique considerations by the programmer.

Committee add-ins generally provide additional functionality to Microsoft Excel. They make few, if any, changes to the workspace and are used during the normal course of Microsoft Excel operation. All of the add-ins that ship with Microsoft Excel are committee add-ins (that is, Solver, AutoSave, Web Form Wizard, and so forth). They extend the spreadsheet environment and add specialized functionality.

Dictator add-ins are usually special-purpose, custom add-ins that run within the Microsoft Excel environment. These add-ins tend to make extensive changes to the workspace, often to the point that it is not obvious that Microsoft Excel is hosting them. Custom menus and toolbars are standard features with these types of add-ins.

Committee Add-Ins

Committee add-ins work inside Microsoft Excel and fully cooperate with the built-in features and tools provided by Microsoft Excel. They generally add items to menus and/or toolbars and allow the user to continue using all the built-in functionality of Microsoft Excel. Your committee add-in will have to trap for common conflicts that arise during the normal usage of Microsoft Excel. For example, if the user starts your process and happens to be in print preview mode, are you going to beep, display a message, or will an untrapped error occur because you didn't expect to be in this state? The committee add-in has to recover gracefully and provide very strong error handling for both known and unknown error conditions.

At a minimum you need to develop a testing suite that includes some of the more common conflicts that can occur when you're coexisting with Microsoft Excel and other add-ins. All of your entry points (places where the user starts your code via menus, toolbars, keystrokes, and/or events) should contain traps for the most common conflicts. While there's no way to provide for every possible situation that can occur when starting your add-in, you should ask yourself what happens to your code when:

- No workbook is open?
- The workbook can't be opened (it's missing, or the drive, FTP, or Web site is not available)?
- The workbook is password-protected and can't be opened (your user may or may not know the password and you should code for both cases)?
- The workbook has never been saved (some properties of a workbook are different before it's saved; for example, Workbook.Path is null before a document is saved)?
- The worksheet(s) is/are protected (both with and without a password)?
- The worksheet is hidden?
- The user is viewing a print preview of the document?
- An object is selected when your operation expects cells to be selected?
- Cells are selected when your operation expects an object to be selected?
- Hidden rows or columns are included in the user's selection?
- The workbook is in group edit mode before your code starts (multiple worksheets are selected)?
- The user has a multiple selection of cells or objects?

- Calculation is set to manual (or automatic)?
- Worksheet windows are split or frozen?
- Your test installation includes/omits some components of the Microsoft Excel/Office installation?
- Menus and/or toolbars have been customized?

Of course, your error handling may need to be adjusted and/or a test suite developed that tests for as many conditions as possible. As a rule, the committee add-in requires more testing than the dictator add-in because you have less control over the spreadsheet environment. Answering the questions above will reduce the number of conflicts, but the list is not all-inclusive.

The only way to find specific conflicts is with extensive testing. You should consider testing with Standard, Custom, and Run from CD installations. If you're going to skimp on testing, at least test the Standard installation, as this will be the most common installation. If optional Microsoft Excel/Office components are installed, it's possible that some menus will contain more choices than the Standard install.

If you are modifying built-in menus/toolbars, be sure to verify that you are adding and/or removing objects as expected. One of the properties you can specify when adding menus is where your new menu is placed. Rather than blindly using a numerical index to add or delete your menus (and assuming that the user has not customized the existing menus), use the new Microsoft Excel 97 FindControl method to locate an existing menu (called a ControlPopup) before deleting or adding your custom menus.

You may need to have a secondary location as a fallback in case the user has removed or customized the standard menu command bar. Menu customization is easier than ever from the Microsoft Excel interface, and part of your test plan should include non-standard menu and toolbar configurations.

Dictator Add-Ins

Dictator add-ins (often called applications) are much easier to test. (IMPORTANT: "easier" does not necessarily mean "easy"; the term is relative to the committee add-in.) This is because in a dictator add-in you provide the exact functionality your add-in needs and take away all other options.

Dictator add-ins require a heavy emphasis on Microsoft Excel workspace issues. This involves removing or hiding the standard interface items (menus/toolbars) and replacing them with your own. Before doing this, your dictator add-in should save the current workspace. Your add-in can then implement one or more workspaces for its own use and restore the original workspace when exiting.

Here are the steps you take when your add-in loads:

- Take a snapshot of the user's configuration (save workspace).
- Modify interface elements as needed for your add-in.
- Allow the user to run your add-in.
- Trap exiting Microsoft Excel (and provide a way to quit your add-in).
- Return Microsoft Excel to its original state before your add-in ends.

The following is a list of workspace items that a dictator add-in may need to track:

- Workbooks currently open
- Visible CommandBars
- Formula bar
- Status bar
- Sheet tabs
- Scroll bars
- Gridlines
- Calculation mode
- Comment indicator
- Drag-and-Drop
- Link updating mode
- Reference Style
- Current Directory
- Ignore Other Applications

All of these items must be saved so that they can be restored to their original state when your add-in closes; the only question is where they should be saved. There are two commonly used approaches for saving the workspace. The first involves storing workspace settings in variables. The second involves storing them on a worksheet.

In theory, the advantage of using variables is that it makes workspace operations faster. In practice, the time differential may not be large enough to notice. Using array variables does make it much easier to implement multiple workspaces.

Multiple workspaces are useful when you are displaying several different sheets to the user, each of which needs different settings. For instance, you may have a data entry sheet where you wish to suppress the drag-and-drop function, row and column headers, sheet tabs, scroll bars, and the formula bar. You may then build a schedule sheet and an output table where you want different combinations of these settings. If you store all of these workspace settings in an array during startup, you can quickly switch among them at run time.

Most developers will implement this with a user-defined type structure, as shown below:

```
Option Explicit

''' This type structure specifies all of the workspace
''' settings that are being stored.
Type WORKSPACE_STORAGE
    bRowAndColHeaders As Boolean
    bHorzScrollBar As Boolean
    bVertScrollBar As Boolean
    bSheetTabs As Boolean
    bFormulaBar As Boolean
    bStatusBar As Boolean
    ''' Many more settings follow
End Type

''' This variable will be used to store the workspace
''' settings. Note that it is declared as an array so
''' that multiple workspaces can be stored.
Dim muWorkspace() As WORKSPACE_STORAGE
```

Using a Worksheet to Store Workspaces

As an alternative to using type structures, you can add a worksheet to your project and record all the values that you wish to save. Ideally, you would give each cell a descriptive range name. You then read these values when you need to restore the workspace. In theory, it's much slower to read and write values from a worksheet rather than storing values in an array. In practice, there is almost no difference, as the number of items being stored is relatively small.

The advantage of using a worksheet is that the workspace settings will not be lost if something causes your variables to lose their initialization when a project is reset (also known as *state loss*). If you do use variables to store your workspace settings, make sure that your add-in includes reasonable defaults to fall back on if state loss occurs.

The user of your add-in should rarely experience state loss at run time, but during development this occurs every time a module is edited and/or compiled. Microsoft Excel will warn you before state loss occurs if you check the box labeled Notify Before State Loss in the Tools/Options/General dialog box under the VBE (shown below).

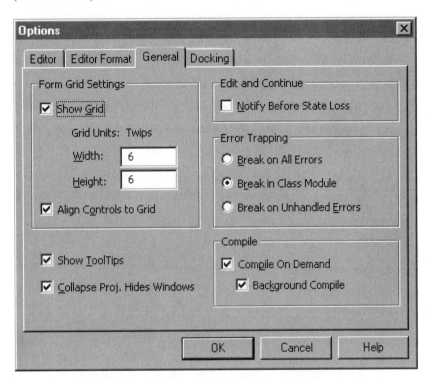

If your add-in is performance-oriented and you need every millisecond, you can implement a dual storage routine. When in the debug mode, write the values to a worksheet. When your add-in is ready for distribution, have your code store the workspace values in an array.

Focused Functionality

While it's simple to take away functionality from the interface (hide standard menus and toolbars), Microsoft Office contains hundreds of keyboard shortcuts, including keyboard shortcuts that exist for backward compatibility with earlier versions of Windows. For example, longtime users of Microsoft Excel may remember that SHIFT+F12 will save their document and CTRL+INSERT will copy a cell or object. Your best defense will be to use any events available in Microsoft Excel first, and then look for the other options available to users.

General Development Recommendations

As stated earlier, if your add-in alters the workspace, always capture the initial settings and then restore them at the end of your program. Don't make the user clean up after your program. If your add-in alters the command bars, for instance, make sure to remove the alterations when your add-in closes. You want to avoid leaving pieces of your add-in hanging around after it is gone. The sections below provide additional ideas for improving your development process.

Use Global or Module Level Constants

Store all values that you might need to change in global or module level constants. Then use the constant instead of the value in your code. If you need to change the value later, you can change it in one place and it will take effect throughout your program. Examples of this include:

- Paths used to access files.
- Messages displayed to your user.
- The names of other workbooks used in your add-in.
- Worksheet names used in your add-in.
- Add-in version number.
- Add-in title for message boxes.
- Starting range addresses for building report sheets.

Store all message strings as global constants in one location. This makes them very easy to modify and translate for international versions of your add-in. Error messages displayed to users should always be in global constants, as the wording of these messages often changes with feedback from users.

Don't assume that an object exists unless you've just created it yourself. When accessing objects that could have been potentially removed by the user, always check to see if they exist before attempting to use them. For example, the following subroutine checks to see if DataBook.xls is open before trying to use it:

```
Sub UseDataBook()
    Dim oBook As Workbook
    On Error Resume Next
        Set oBook = Workbooks("DataBook.xls")
    On Error GoTo ErrorHandler
    ''' The procedure ends here if no data book is found.
    If oBook Is Nothing Then Err.Raise _
        Number:= 999, Description:="Data book not found."
    ''' Continue processing using the oBook variable here.
    Exit Sub
```

```
ErrorHandler:
    MsgBox Err.Description, vbCritical, "My Add-in"
    ''' Do any necessary cleanup here...
End Sub
```

Divide and Conquer

If you find yourself doing the same task in several different procedures, break that task out into a separate procedure and call this new procedure instead of including all the code everywhere you use it. In the event you need to change the way this procedure works, you will now only have to change it in one location rather than in many places throughout your project.

Feedback to the User

Let the user know what is happening while your program is running. Always provide status-bar messages and update them at key points during program execution. Long operations should use percentage complete counters (while running loops) and/or provide ongoing status information. Always remember to reset the status bar when your add-in terminates. Otherwise, your last status bar message will persist until some other action changes it. You can do this with the command:

```
Application.StatusBar = False
```

Improving Performance

We define performance as how fast your add-in runs. The broad idea underlying most performance tips is not to make the VBA engine work any harder than necessary. The less work VBA has to do, the faster it runs.

For instance, you can think of each line of code in your add-in as a step that needs to be completed by VBA when it runs your add-in. If you reduce the total lines of code in your add-in, you generally require VBA to take fewer steps and therefore allow it to run your add-in more quickly. The following are some tips on how to increase the speed of your code.

Declare Once, Use Many Times

If you are going to use an object more than once, declare and use object variables rather than using a fully qualified object reference each time. For instance, in the following example the FillCells2 procedure runs approximately three times as fast as the FillCells1 procedure. This is because the VBA engine doesn't have to resolve the entire object reference each time it runs through the loop.

```
Sub FillCells1()
    Dim iCount As Integer
    For iCount = 1 To 1000
        ActiveWorkbook.Worksheets("Sheet1").Range("a1") _
            .Offset(iCount, 0).Value = iCount
    Next iCount
End Sub

Sub FillCells2()
    Dim iCount As Integer
    Dim oRange As Range
    Set oRange = ActiveWorkbook.Worksheets("Sheet1") _
        .Range("a1")
    For iCount = 1 To 1000
        oRange.Offset(iCount, 0).Value = iCount
    Next iCount
End Sub
```

Don't Do the Two-Step

Don't do something in two steps if there is a method that can do it in one step. For instance, the following example shows two methods you can use to copy a range from one worksheet to another. Method 1 takes almost 10 times as long to execute as Method 2 because of an unnecessary additional step.

Method 1

```
Worksheets(1).UsedRange.Copy
Worksheets(2).Paste
```

Method 2

```
Worksheets(1).UsedRange.Copy _
    destination:=Worksheets(2).Range("a1")
```

Method 2 uses an optional argument of the Copy method to improve performance. Many VBA methods have optional arguments that can significantly improve the performance of code that uses them. Make a habit of highlighting various methods used in your code and pressing the F1 key to access context-sensitive help. If you find an optional argument, take note, as many high-performance optimizations are found in these options. These additional arguments are rarely used by the macro recorder, so you need to seek them out.

Screen Updating

Unless there is a reason for your users to see what a procedure is doing, always turn off screen updating with

```
Application.ScreenUpdating = False
```

This makes your procedures execute much more quickly. Just remember to turn screen updating back on before you display a dialog or a message box. With ScreenUpdating set to False, the screen does not repaint correctly if the user moves the box.

Code Cleaning

As you are writing a VBA program, name spaces and other structures are created invisibly in the background to track and manage your project. As you rewrite and move code and objects, unused structures build up in your project. These development leftovers do not affect the average user, since they don't add up to enough to make a significant difference. But large and/or complex development efforts can benefit from periodic removal of these unused structures. Removing these development leftovers is often called "cleaning your project" or "stripping your code."

Cleaning a project involves saving all of its modules and forms out to text files, deleting the old modules and forms, and then reimporting the modules and forms from the text files. Larger projects may see a 25-percent reduction in file size once you've cleaned them. This reduction in file size may or may not make any real difference in the load time or the run time of your project.

Be sure to recompile your project after this cleaning. The load time saved by the reduced file size can be negated if the modules must re-compile on startup. When you create your add-in using the Microsoft Excel File/Save As menu or setting the IsAddin property of the Workbook object, your add-in is NOT automatically compiled. You compile your project manually from within the VBE by choosing Debug/Compile VBAProject from the VBE menu.

Committee add-ins should minimize their impact on memory and resources. Always clean your code before final testing and shipping. Generally speaking, dictator add-ins may be more forgiving in this area since you are in control of the size of the overall project.

Constant Improvements

Writing high-quality add-ins requires constant vigilance on the part of the developer, as the state of the art continues to advance. Because add-ins are a subset of writing macros, these tips apply to all code development. You can visit the various Web sites dedicated to Microsoft Excel/Office development for additional tips and tricks. Look for examples of real-world code, since samples are often simplified to allow a specific technique or concept to be made obvious.

Error Handling

As a general rule, you should always avoid having a user encounter a Microsoft Excel application error directly when running your add-in. While very helpful during the development process, these error messages tend to confuse nonexpert users. Instead, these errors should be trapped by error-handling code within your add-in and presented to the user in a friendlier manner. Your add-in should then exit or recover gracefully from the error. The bottom line is that a quality add-in will have very strong error handling. This requires care when creating the add-in and a healthy dose of third-party testing to verify your work. The following VBA error-handling features can assist to create a strong, user-friendly add-in.

The Err Object

The Err object is used to obtain information about errors that have occurred during program execution. When a run-time error occurs, the generator of the error sets the properties of the Err object. These properties identify the error and allow you to handle it in your code. The Err object also has a Raise method that allows you to generate your own errors and set the properties of the Err object yourself when you know that something has gone wrong in your code.

The On Error Statement

The On Error statement is used to build error-handling routines for VBA applications. Error handling is set up using an On Error GoTo line, where *line* is the line label at which the error handler begins. The outline of a VBA procedure with basic error handling is shown below:

```
Sub MyProcedure()
    On Error GoTo ErrorHandler
    ''' Procedure code goes here.
    Exit Sub
ErrorHandler:
    MsgBox "Error", vbCritical, "My Add-in"
End Sub
```

There are some cases in which you want a procedure to ignore any errors that occur. You can allow a procedure to bypass errors using the On Error Resume Next statement. When an error occurs, this statement causes program execution to continue at the line immediately following the line that caused the error. If you intentionally turn off error handling, it is recommended that you document the expected errors you are ignoring in your code. This serves you well when you need to upgrade or troubleshoot this section of code in the future. The basic guidelines for turning off errors are:

- Do not do it unless it's absolutely necessary.
- Be aware of the side effects (other errors you weren't anticipating will also be ignored).
- Document the expected errors you are ignoring (for future development).
- Return to a custom error handler as soon as is practical.

If it becomes necessary to disable custom error handling in one of your procedures, you can do this with the On Error GoTo 0 statement. This statement restores standard Microsoft Excel error handling.

Your error-handling code can also be set up to write information to a text file (a log) so that you can analyze errors that occur during testing and/or usage. This strategy is very effective when you are getting bug reports that are tough to reproduce in your test environment.

The following error handling is more real-world and provides a much more realistic view of the process of handling errors. While it's simpler than most real-world code, it's much closer than the previous example. It contains a module level Public variable to pass error messages between procedures, and a function that returns True or False depending on different conditions.

```
Option Explicit
''' Passes error messages between procedures.
Public gszErrMsg As String

Sub ApplicationMain()
    On Error GoTo ApplicationMainError
    ''' This function is used to open the workbook.
    If Not bOpenWorkbook("MyBook.xls") _
        Then GoTo ApplicationMainError
    ''' The rest of your add-in code goes here.
    Exit Sub
ApplicationMainError:
    On Error Resume Next
    ''' Do any necessary clean up operations here.
    MsgBox prompt:=gszErrMsg, Buttons:=vbCritical, _
    Title:="My Add-in"
End Sub
```

```
Function bOpenWorkbook(szName As String) As Boolean
    On Error Resume Next
    Workbooks.Open FileName:=szName
    If Err.Number <> 0 Then
        gszErrMsg = "Error opening workbook '" & _
            szName & "'."
        bOpenWorkbook = False
    Else
        bOpenWorkbook = True
    End If
End Function
```

In real-world code, error handling often needs to address cleanup issues that are beyond the scope of this chapter. Real error handling can be extremely complex due to the nature of stopping in the middle of ongoing code. The ideal learning tool is to view production-quality code available on many Web sites and study the developer's error-handling routines.

Create your Debug Flag

It's a good idea to create a global constant for debugging (for example: Dim Constant bDEBUG = True|False) and set up your error handling so you can turn specific error trapping on or off depending on the value of your constant. Before sending your add-in to be tested, you can set the constant to False and your project will handle errors in the exact manner your users will see. Sometimes a second flag is appropriate if you wish to turn on or off logging functions embedded in your code, and you want this code to run in both the debug and non-debug mode.

The use of a bDEBUG flag has many other applications. You can display developer-only message boxes, write to development-only log files, and/or control other operations you may wish to have available conditionally during development.

Trapping User Cancels

By default, the user can halt the execution of your VBA code by pressing either the ESC key or CTRL+BREAK. You can trap this action by using the EnableCancelKey property of the Application object. Using the statement

```
Application.EnableCancelKey = xlErrorHandler
```

causes the ESC or CTRL+BREAK keys to generate an error which will be trapped by the error handler set in your most recent On Error statement. The Err.Number generated by a user cancel is 18. Have your error handler check for this code and exit gracefully if it occurs.

You can also completely disable the user's ability to cancel program execution with

```
Application.EnableCancelKey = xlDisabled
```

You should be very careful when using this setting, however, because it prevents canceling program execution in the event of an endless loop. In practice, you'll want to explicitly set the EnableCancelKey depending on whether you're ready to ship production code or you're testing.

During testing it makes sense to be able to stop loops (endless or otherwise). But allowing the user to interrupt your code in the middle of a routine is not practical. Either you'll disable the cancel key or set it to your own handler, which will stop at the next appropriate point and/or clean up as needed. This cancel key setting is also an excellent candidate for using your bDEBUG flag.

Break on All Errors

As in Microsoft Excel 5/95 VBA, if the user has the Break on All Errors setting checked, any error handling in your project is disabled. There is still no programmatic method of disabling this feature. However, since it must be set in the VBE interface in Microsoft Excel 97, users may be less likely to have it set. This setting does not affect error handling in add-ins. In other words, once it's saved as an add-in, you don't have to worry about how the user sets this option. But you still need to provide graceful error handling of your own.

Code Security

For security reasons, you can password-protect your add-ins and workbooks. You can also make your code very difficult to interpret.

Password-Protecting Code

The best security that you have for your add-in is locking it with password protection. You lock your project by choosing Tools/VBAProject Properties from the VBE menu. Select the Protection tab in the Project Properties dialog box and check the Lock Project For Viewing option. Enter a password in the text boxes provided, and your code will be inaccessible to anyone who doesn't know the password.

Warning   Your code will also be inaccessible to you if you forget this password, so take care when you are using this method of protection.

Password-Protecting the Workbook

You can also password-protect add-in workbooks so that a password is required before your add-in can be opened. This is accomplished through the File/Save As menu item in Microsoft Excel. Note, however, that password-protected add-in workbooks cannot be loaded using the Add-In Manager. These workbooks can only be loaded manually, which potentially allows the user to turn off all your macros using the virus-protection dialog. Most add-ins are useless without their macros!

Stripping the Code

A way to provide an added level of security for your code is to remove all comments, indents, and blank lines from it. Doing this will make interpretation of the code very difficult, even if someone is successful at gaining access to it.

In many of the code samples in this chapter, you will notice that code comment lines are preceded by three apostrophes rather than just one. This is a good practice to follow because it allows you to quickly strip all comments from your code using the built-in VBE find-and-replace function. If you use only one or two apostrophes to designate comments, this function will not be able to distinguish between apostrophes that designate comment lines and those that are embedded in your code for other purposes.

Some developers go as far as changing the routine names, variable names, and anything else that provides a clue to the intent of a routine. This makes it even more difficult to understand and reverse-engineer a project, but it creates a maintenance issue for you. Be sure to save backup copies of your projects before stripping and cleaning your code.

Installation

There are several ways to install your add-in. You can have the user open the add-in just like any other workbook. This is most appropriate in situations where you do not want or need to have your add-in installed in the AddIns collection (that is, dictator add-ins). The user will be presented with the virus protection dialog if they have virus protection turned on (the default). See the upcoming Macro Virus Protection section for details concerning the virus protection.

You can also have the user open a "loader" application (workbook) that in turn opens your add-in. This method can be used to run your add-in, as well. The loader can also use the Add method of the AddIns collection and the Installed property of the AddIn object to load your add-in using the Add-In Manager. Installation through the Add-In Manager is most suitable for committee add-ins.

A third option is to load your add-in into the AddIns collection directly by setting all the correct registry entries using the Win32 API. This is a highly sophisticated task and should be undertaken only with a thorough understanding of programmatic registry manipulation. Generally speaking, it's much simpler to have a workbook that handles the installation and calls the appropriate methods provided by Microsoft Excel.

Macro Virus Protection

Microsoft Excel 97 includes built-in macro virus protection. This protection is enabled by default during installation. With macro virus protection active, whenever the user opens a workbook containing macros, Microsoft Excel displays a warning dialog box. This dialog box gives the user the option to not open the file, open the file but disable its macros, or open the file with macros enabled. If the user chooses to open the file with macros disabled, all macros in that file are completely disabled, not simply the Auto_Open routine.

All workbooks, including add-ins, opened by the user are subject to the macro virus protection feature. There is no way to programmatically disable it. Workbooks and add-ins opened programmatically and add-ins loaded using the Add-In Manager are not affected. This means that you could create a small add-in that simply adds a menu or tool to one of the built-in bars and have that command open your project. This prevents the user from being presented with the macro virus protection warning dialog box each time your add-in is opened.

References

If you have created references between workbooks in your project, you must do one of three things to ensure that the references are maintained correctly. Either the relative paths between the *referencing* and the *referenced* workbooks must be maintained (you must open the referenced workbook(s) prior to opening the referencing workbook(s)), or you must have the AddIn in the AddInPath. The AddinPath is a registry key value that indicates the search path for Addins.

```
HKEY_CURRENT_USER\Software\Microsoft\Office\8.0\Excel\_
    Microsoft Excel\AddIn Path.
```

The value for this entry is of type string, with a format like:

```
c:\msoffice\excel\library; c:\msoffice\excel\library\solver
```

The ';' character delimits each directory in the path.

By default, Office 97 setup sets the AddIn path to include the Library subdirectory of the Office subdirectory that contains Excel.exe. So you may want to recommend that users copy your add-in into that directory (Application.LibraryPath).

When the workbooks are closed, you must close them in the opposite order. Microsoft Excel does not allow a referenced workbook to be closed while the referencing workbook is still open. The referencing workbook must be closed first, followed by the workbooks that are referenced. This applies to both add-ins and normal workbooks.

Object Referencing—The Microsoft Excel Object Model

Many Microsoft Excel VBA programming problems arise from a misunderstanding of how to correctly reference and navigate Workbook, Sheet, and Range objects using the Microsoft Excel object model. This section reviews the most common methods and their proper usage.

Workbook Objects

There are three common methods of the Application object that are used to access a workbook object from the Microsoft Excel object model.

ThisWorkbook

Refers to the workbook within which the code is currently running. This is most commonly used when referring to objects within the AddIn.

ActiveWorkbook

Refers to the workbook that is currently active in the Microsoft Excel interface. Use this method only when your intention is to reference whatever workbook happens to be active.

Workbooks(*nameindex*)

Uses the Workbooks collection to identify a specific workbook by name or by index number within the collection. Workbooks referenced using this method need not be active.

Sheet Objects

Similarly, there are two common methods of the Workbook object that are used to access Sheet objects from the Microsoft Excel object model. Note that neither of these two methods is object-type–specific. Both return either a worksheet object, a chart object, or any of the Microsoft Excel 5/95 legacy sheet objects, such as DialogSheets and XLM sheets.

ActiveSheet

Refers to the sheet that is currently active in the Microsoft Excel interface.

Sheets(*name|index*)

Uses the Sheets collection to identify a specific sheet by name or by index number within the collection. Sheets referenced using this method need not be active.

Navigating Range Objects

There are several special properties and methods that can be used to navigate ranges on worksheet objects. The most basic of these is the Range property. This property has two variations. The first is used to reference a range directly by its address. In the following example, this syntax is used to enter the value 10 into the range A1:B4 on Sheet1 of the active workbook:

```
Worksheets("Sheet1").Range("A1:B4").Value = 10
```

This syntax also accepts a named range as its argument:

```
Worksheets("Sheet1").Range("Sales").Value = 10
```

The second syntax references a range by using the upper-left cell and the lower-right cell of the range as arguments:

```
Worksheets("Sheet1").Range("A1", "B4").Value = 10
```

This syntax can take as its arguments addresses, range names, or any property or method that returns a valid single-cell range object or address. However, a common mistake when using properties or methods as arguments for the Range property is to not fully qualify the arguments. For example, the code shown below fails if Sheet1 is not the active sheet:

```
Worksheets("Sheet1").Range(Range("a1"), _
    Range("b4")).Value = 10
```

This is because the Range property defaults to the active sheet if no sheet is provided to qualify it. If Sheet1 is not active at run time, the outer Range property and the inner Range property will be referring to different sheets. The correct way to handle this is shown in the following example:

```
With Worksheets("Sheet1")
    .Range(.Range("a1"), .Range("b4")).Value = 10
End With
```

Now all the Range properties are qualified with a reference to the same worksheet, so it no longer matters what the active sheet happens to be.

The Offset and Cells methods are used to refer to ranges located some distance away from some starting point. The following example shows how to use each of these methods to get the value of the cell that is two columns to the left and two rows down from the currently active cell:

```
MsgBox ActiveCell.Offset(2, 2).Value
MsgBox ActiveCell.Cells(3, 3).Value
```

Both lines of code above refer to the same cell. The difference between the two methods is that the Offset method has a base index of zero and accepts negative numbers as arguments, allowing you to reference ranges above and to the left of the current range. The Cells method has a base index of 1 and will not accept negative numbers as arguments.

The End method allows you to move to the end of the current data range. It mimics the functionality of holding down the END key on the keyboard while pressing one of the directional arrows. The End method takes one of four predefined constants as an argument, corresponding to the four directions in which you can move. These constants are xlUp, xlDown, xlToLeft, and xlToRight. In the following example, the End method is used to get the value of the bottom cell of the column of data that begins with cell A1:

```
MsgBox Worksheets("Sheet1").Range("a1").End(xlDown).Value
```

Note, however, that the End method will stop at the cell above the first empty cell it encounters, regardless of whether or not that is truly the last cell. In other words, the End method moves in a specific direction until it finds a blank cell.

Integrating Your Add-In with Microsoft Excel

As discussed earlier, your add-in is really just a specialized macro that's running in Microsoft Excel. It's very important that you write quality code, test it well, and maximize your maintainability by using efficient coding techniques. VBA doesn't force you to use any standards, but adopting the principles adapted from developers with years of experience can make your project much easier to build and maintain.

From the user's perspective, it is very important that your add-in integrate cleanly with Microsoft Excel. Your menus should mimic Microsoft Excel's built-in menus, and your toolbars should look and feel as if they came from Microsoft. Always provide shortcut keys (also known as *accelerators*) in dialog boxes.

Your interface design (UserForms as dialog boxes) should look and feel as if it were a built-in part of Microsoft Excel. For all dialog box design considerations, try to find an existing Microsoft Excel dialog box to use as a model. For example, where do you put the OK and Cancel buttons? Microsoft Excel generally places them in the upper-right part of the dialog box, but multistep Wizards have them across the bottom. Be sure your design is as close to a built-in dialog box as possible.

While you should use good coding techniques and write efficient code, your final work tends to be judged by your user interface. This is not always fair or accurate, but the user can't see the care taken behind the scenes. The combination of a great interface with great code in the background adds up to an outstanding add-in. Plan on using the techniques outlined in this chapter, but be sure you also do plenty of interface testing. This care and optimization provides a cleaner solution and a stronger foundation for future growth.

C H A P T E R   2

Writing Great Wizards

Wizards are the user interface of choice for multistep processes, and Microsoft Excel 97 makes it simple to create one. From a user's perspective, a Wizard appears as a set of dialog boxes asking a series of questions. Throughout the questioning, you explain concepts, request input, validate input, and guide the user as they provide information for your process. When information gathering is finished, you use the set of inputs to drive your process. This section focuses on creating the most common type of Wizard using the new Microsoft Excel 97 UserForms.

Developing great Wizards is a superset of developing great dialog boxes. Most of the issues related to Wizard development are the same as those involved in building single dialog boxes, but on a larger scale. Instead of initializing and validating one dialog, you'll initialize a set of dialogs (or pages that appear as separate dialogs). Both initialization and validation can become much more complicated because the number of controls increases and the interrelationships between them can become more complicated. Strategies for managing these complexities are discussed in the upcoming examples. Before looking at a specific example, it is a good idea to study some of the Wizards that ship with Microsoft Excel 97.

Microsoft Excel 97 ships with quite a few Wizards. Some of them are built into the Microsoft Excel 97 executable, but many of them are *add-ins* created in VBA. You'll see that they can range from very simple to rather complex. The step-by-step Wizard format makes them easy from a user's perspective.

One of the many interesting Wizards provided with Microsoft Excel 97 is the Web Form Wizard shown in the following figure. If you don't see this Wizard on the Tools Wizard menu, you may need to add it through Setup.

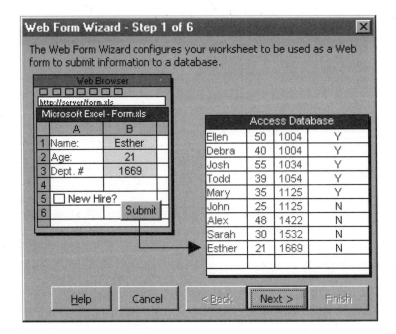

The Web Form Wizard walks users through the process of creating a Microsoft Excel 97 form that gathers information and transfers it to a database attached to a Web server. This is a great idea for an Intranet application and shows some of the synergy between Microsoft Excel 97 and the Web. It also happens to be a great Wizard example, so you should explore it before and during your Wizard development projects.

Explaining the specific details required to produce a Web Form from scratch would require a steep learning curve for most users. The Wizard makes the process much simpler, as the complexities are handled by the Wizard code. The user simply provides appropriate inputs, and the Wizard handles the grunt work of producing the various files needed to create a complete Web solution.

To Show Tabs or Not to Show

From a developer's perspective, standard Wizards are a minor variation of a "tabbed dialog." A classic tabbed dialog is a single dialog box with multiple pages, all accessible by means of a set of tabs at the top. The following figure shows the Microsoft Excel 97 Format Cells tabbed dialog box.

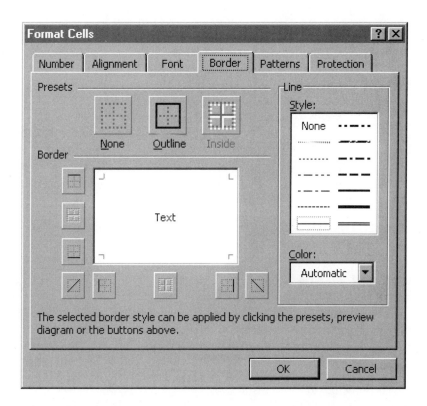

Tabbed dialogs allow random access to a group of pages, each containing a related group of controls. Wizards walk your user though a series of pages in a developer-defined order. In the development process, you'll generally create a tabbed dialog and then hide the tabs after the Wizard is tested and debugged. Wizard users move between the pages using your controls (for example, the Next and Back buttons) rather than selecting pages by using the tabs.

In previous versions of Microsoft Excel, developers created Wizards by building a set of dialog boxes (using multiple dialog sheets) and then displaying them one at a time. Unless you're producing a very complex Wizard, in Microsoft Excel 97 you could create one dialog box and use the new MultiPage control to host all the pages for your Wizard. This makes the process of moving forward and backward trivial—you increment or decrement the Value property of the MultiPage control to display different pages. The Value property has a zero-based index, so you set this property to zero to display the first page.

Compared to a standard dialog box, Wizards generally:

- Contain detailed instructions and explanations.
- Use graphics when possible to show concepts.
- Contain fewer controls and more text per page.

Building Your Wizard

In the process of building your Wizard, you'll deal with two primary areas—the physical layout of your controls on the pages, and VBA code to implement the functionality of your Wizard.

Before looking at the example in detail, we will discuss some of the procedural issues related to laying out a Wizard.

The Physical Layout

Laying out a Wizard can take a tremendous amount of time and energy. Most Wizards go through quite a few interface iterations between initial concept and final deployment. Interface design is both an art and a science. A complete discussion of dialog/Wizard design is beyond the scope of this book. For our purposes, you can consider the following list a starting point for the physical layout of a Wizard:

- Gather a list of all the input needed for your process.
- Gather the text needed to support the inputs.
- Order the inputs logically.
- Decide which controls to use for each input.
- Group controls in related logical functions.
- Establish the number of pages needed to house your control groups.
- Place all controls and text on the pages.
- Test your design with your users and make modifications where needed.

While most of these steps are obvious, "Decide which controls to use for each input" requires additional explanation where lists of data are concerned. The three main choices for presenting lists are radio button groups, list boxes, and drop-downs.

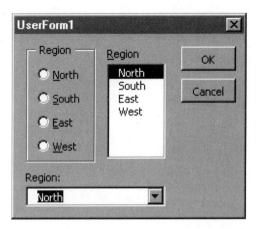

If you stick with radio buttons because your user tells you, "We haven't added any regions in 35 years," you may be forced to do a redesign if the user's boss decides to add "All Regions" or any other unexpected options. The list boxes allow you to update the lists without having to redesign the page layout. You can save yourself quite a bit of future headache by not using radio buttons to present lists.

The VBA Support Code

As stated earlier, you'll be scaling up the code required for simple dialog boxes to handle the additional complexity of your Wizard. While all Wizards vary, we'll focus our attention on the code to handle the following standard issues:

- Displaying your Wizard.
- Handling the Cancel button.
- Initializing your controls and/or pages.
- Validating individual controls and/or pages.
- Code for individual controls as events occur.
- Navigation code for your control buttons (Next, Back, and so on).
- Code for your specific process after the Finish button is chosen.

Rather than discuss each of these issues in a vacuum, it's easier to see the concepts in action by looking at real code. The WizDemo.xls workbook (included on the CD) contains code that addresses all of these issues and more.

Your VBA support code will be divided between two or more modules. One module will be a Standard Module and another will be the Object Module behind your UserForm. The Standard Module will call a UserForm function (in our example, bWizardRun) which will start the Wizard. The UserForm contains all the code for initializing, validating, navigating, and any other routines needed while your Wizard is displayed. Here's the code fragment contained in the mEntry module (a Standard Module) for starting the Wizard.

```
''' Call Object Module routine to display the Wizard
    ''' Wizard was NOT cancelled.
    If frmWizardDialog.bWizardRun Then
        ''' more processing here if needed...
        ''' After your procedure runs remove the
        ''' userform from memory
    Else    ''' User cancelled the Wizard
            '''  Code for any needed cleanup due to cancel
    End If
```

The frmWizardDialog.bWizardRun is a Public routine in the frmWizardDialog Object Module that displays the dialog and returns True if the user completes the Wizard and False if the user cancels. The complete function is listed below:

```
''' Function:    bWizardRun
''' Returns:     True if user completes the Wizard
''' Comments:    Shows the Wizard and Unloads it if the
'''              user cancels
Public Function bWizardRun() As Boolean
''' initialize the Wizard assuming the user will cancel
    mbUserCancelled = True
    frmWizardDialog.Show
    bWizardRun = Not mbUserCancelled
End Function
```

Calling the Show method of a dialog box automatically fires the Initialize event. In other words, the routine above actually runs all the initialization code, displays the dialog box, validates input, and then runs the code to handle the Wizard results. This occurs because all the code for the Wizard is stored in the UserForm Object Module. When it's finished, it returns a True or False based on your user completing or canceling the Wizard.

The WizDemo Example

The CD included with this book contains a Wizard example workbook with complete source code (WizDemo.xls). This simple Cell Input Wizard provides a framework and contains many of the elements needed for real-world development. Here's an overview of the three-step example Wizard:

1. Explain the Wizard and ask for the user's name or address (the exact input is irrelevant).
2. Ask the user to enter a destination range as their input.
3. Allow the user to select among different font attributes.

The Wizard places the user input into the destination cells and formats the font of the specified range based on the check boxes selected. While this example is straightforward, the code needed to handle the real world can be much more complicated than most users would suspect. VBA makes Wizard creation much easier than it would be in another language, but you should not confuse "easier" with "easy." Great Wizard development often requires extensive initialization, data validation, and/or error handling. Before discussing these areas in detail, let's take a look at the Wizard's pages for this example.

The first step gives the user an introduction to the Wizard and asks the user for a name or an address.

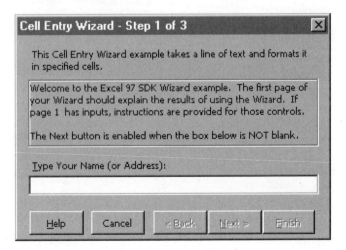

The second step asks the user for a destination for the text provided in Step 1. The edit box is a RefEdit control, meaning that the user can use the mouse to point and click to select the destination range. The user could also type a range—or mistype a range—so the validation code verifies the selection before allowing the user to move to Step 3.

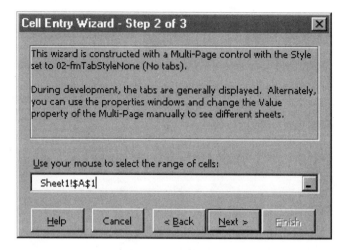

Step 3 allows the user to select font attributes; these attributes are applied to the text after it is written to the worksheet.

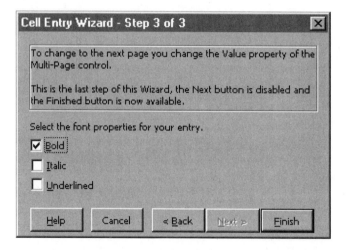

After your Wizard is finished and hidden, you may need to get some additional information from the UserForm. You do this by creating a custom property for the UserForm with a Property Get procedure. In the demo, the Property Get procedure, szSelectedRangeR1C1, takes the range selected in Step 2 and converts it to a text string using R1C1 notation for the reference. The routine ShowWizard in the Standard Module displays this value in a message box.

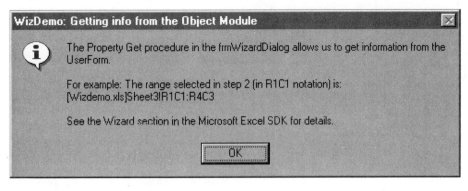

```
'''   Property Get: szSelectedRangeR1C1
'''   Arguments:   None
'''   Comments:    Property Get allows you to get information
'''                from the Object Module in other modules.
'''        This example takes the range the user selects
'''        in step 2 of the wizard, converts the range
'''        to R1C1 notation if needed.  This string is
'''        displayed in a message box called in the mEntry
'''        module.
'''
'''        To use this new property, use the following syntax:
'''        frmWizardDialog.szSelectedRangeR1C1
'''        (UserFormName.Property)
'''
'''        IMPORTANT: This property is NOT available after the
'''        form has been unloaded.
Property Get szSelectedRangeR1C1() As String
    '''   Create an address string in R1C1 notation.
    With Application
        If .ReferenceStyle = xlA1 Then      '''  convert
            szSelectedRangeR1C1 = .ConvertFormula( _
                refEntryRange, xlA1, xlR1C1)
        Else
            szSelectedRangeR1C1 = refEntryRange.Text
        End If
    End With
End Property
```

The Developer's View

While it's not obvious from the preceding figures, this Wizard is really a single UserForm with a three-page MultiPage control. This control covers the complete dialog except for the row of buttons at the bottom. These buttons are common to all pages of the Wizard. The Next and Back buttons set the Value property of the MultiPage to display a specific page. By managing this single property, you can display any page in the Wizard.

During the development process, it is generally easier to work with the page tabs showing. MultiPage controls with their tabs hidden don't show the outline of the pages, so only the page displaying can be seen (all other pages are hidden behind it). With the tabs showing, you can quickly move between pages for control layout and fine-tuning. It's also helpful to have the tabs showing while testing the Wizard, so you can quickly see which page is shown as your code sets the Value property of the MultiPage control.

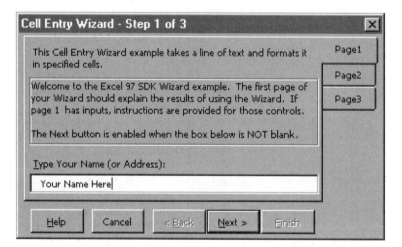

Showing or hiding the tabs is accomplished by setting the Style properties for the MultiPage control. Setting the TabOrientation property to fmTabOrientationRight allows the layout of your dialog to remain fixed, even when you hide the tabs. After hiding the tabs, simply readjust the right side of the dialog box to eliminate the extra space. The following figure shows the property window and the two properties needed to set up your MultiPage control as shown in the preceding figure.

The buttons on the Show Demo worksheet call the demo subroutine (ShowWizard) with an optional flag, and the tabs are displayed when the flag is set. In practice, you'll generally leave the tabs showing during development and testing and then hide them manually before shipping to your users.

Initialization and Validation

Initialization and Validation, known as IV (pronounced "Eye-Vee"), are often the toughest parts of a Wizard (not including actually performing the task your Wizard is designed to handle for your user). Putting some thought into the design of these routines can save you both development time and testing headaches.

Both initialization and validation operate at two major levels, *control level* and *page level*. Control-level IV occurs when an event from one control initializes/validates another control. This can be as simple as enabling the Next button when text is entered into an edit box. Page-level IV applies to a set of controls and occurs on a page change, rather than within the same page. There is not always a strict separation between the two; frequently, page-level IV is just a superset of control-level IV for all the individual controls on a page plus some setup for the next page.

Initialization Overview

In a single dialog box, you generally initialize all controls before the dialog is displayed and validate all input when the user dismisses the dialog (page-level IV). More sophisticated dialogs may initialize and/or change the contents of some controls based on choices made with other controls (control-level IV). For example, choosing a specific state in one list could cause another list to refresh with related ZIP Codes.

In a Wizard, the same interrelationships can occur between controls on a single page as well as between pages. When you develop a Wizard, you need to answer the following questions:

- When do you initialize all controls on a page?
- When do you initialize common controls (Back, Next, and Finish buttons, and so on) and/or the dialog caption (Step x of y)?

Here are some options to choose from:

- Before the Wizard starts.
- Before each page displays.
- Every time a specific page displays.
- After the user provides input by using a control.

The simple choice is to do all initialization before any page displays and page-level validation as the user moves to the next page. In practice, this is nearly impossible because you are often handling many interdependencies.

In reality, most Wizards need combinations of all these choices. Before the Wizard starts, you will do some initialization. Between each page, you update some controls based on the user selection in a previous page. Between pages, you check for the beginning or end of your Wizard so you can enable/disable the Back button and the Finish button as needed. Both moving forward and moving backward require you to update the dialog caption. Proper Wizard initialization can become complicated without a well-defined system for initializing based upon specific points in Wizard program execution.

Page-Level Initialization

The initialization routine below is a master routine that combines all the page-level controls needed for most Wizards. While it is written in the context of the example found on the CD, it is designed to cover the most common issues you'll need in your Wizards. It is called before the Wizard displays for the first time and also between each page, when the Next button is selected.

```
''''''''''''''''''''''''''''''''''''''''''''''''''''''
''' Subroutine: InitWizard
''' Arguments:  iInitPage - Integer: Page being initialized
''' (-1 is special case: First time dialog displayed)
''' Comments:   Initializes all pages of the wizard
''' Contains 4 Initialize sections:
''' SECTION 1: Before initial dialog display
'''     (iInitPage = -1)
''' SECTION 2: Before any page is displayed
'''     EXCEPT the first time
```

```
''' SECTION 3: Common code on any page display,
'''     no exceptions
''' SECTION 4: Page specific code
''' Date           Developer          Action
''' -------------------------------------------------------
Public Sub InitWizard(iInitPage As Integer = -1)
    ''' SECTION 1: Before initial dialog display
    If iInitPage = -1 Then
        ''' Set the module-level step variable,
        ''' set first page: MultiPage control.
        miCurrentStep = 0
        mpgWizardControl.Value = miCurrentStep
        cmdBack.Enabled = False
        cmdNext.Enabled = False
        cmdFinish.Enabled = False
    ''' SECTION 2: Before any page EXCEPT during
    ''' initial display
    Else
        If miCurrentStep = miMAX_PAGE_INDEX Then
            ''' final page
            cmdFinish.Enabled = True
            cmdNext.Enabled = False
        Else
            cmdFinish.Enabled = False
        End If
        If miCurrentStep > 0 Then
            ''' not first page
            cmdBack.Enabled = True
        Else
            cmdBack.Enabled = False
        End If
    End If
    ''' SECTION 3: Common code for all displays
    ''' Set dialog caption
    Me.Caption = mszBASE_DIALOG_CAPTION & miCurrentStep + 1 _
        & " of " & miMAX_PAGE_INDEX + 1
    ''' SECTION 4: Code for page specific initialization
    Select Case iInitPage    ''' if -1 (first time), handled
                             ''' as special case above
        Case 0      ''' Page 1
            If txtCellEntry.Text = "" Then
                cmdNext.Enabled = False
            Else
                cmdNext.Enabled = True
            End If
        Case 1      ''' Page 2
            If refEntryRange.Text = "" Then
                cmdNext.Enabled = False
            Else
                cmdNext.Enabled = True
```

```
                End If
                    refEntryRange.SetFocus
            Case 2
                ''' Page 3 (none in this example)
        End Select
End Sub
```

The routine is designed to group all your page initialization together in one routine. It expects to be called before the Wizard is displayed (passing a "−1" argument) and as you move between pages.

As you develop your own Wizard, you can copy this code and keep the sections while removing the example-specific code. Of course, you will need to adjust the code to reflect the number of pages in your Wizard, but the basic structure can remain unchanged.

Validation Overview

Validation verifies that the input provided by the user is appropriate for your procedure. If you are expecting the user to select a single cell and multiple cells are selected, you should alert the user to the oversight and require them to correct this error before moving on to the next page. Validation can become complicated, but it's critically important, because bad input can cause problems when your Wizard attempts to complete its procedure. Let's look at the same types of questions we discussed in the initialization sections.

When should you consider running your validation code?

- When a control loses focus.
- When a control gains focus.
- While the user is using the control (for example, typing in a text box, selecting items in a drop-down, and so on).
- When the user chooses the Next button to move to the next page.
- When the user chooses the Finish button.
- Any combination of the above.

As is the case with initialization, validation doesn't come in a "one size fits all" for Wizards. Your Wizard may require combinations of these validation techniques. A basic strategy is laid out in the example Wizard (detailed below). Generally, you do the validation as soon as is practical. In most cases, this is when the user moves to the next page. If the validation fails, immediately notify the user and continue on the same page rather than moving forward. Ideally, you'll also set the focus to the control at which the first validation failed (if there is more than one control to be validated).

Validation exists in the same two flavors as initialization code: *control level* and *page level*. Control-level validation attempts to eliminate gross errors and is attached to specific controls using events. It is often much less strict than page-level validation. Page-level validation is run when the user attempts to move to the next page, and it is generally much stricter. Let's take a look at both types in order to compare and contrast the two levels.

Control-Level Validation Code

This is the control-level validation code used in our example:

```
'''  Subroutine:  refEntryRange_Change
'''  Comments:    Enables the Next button if the box contains
'''               text (the bValidate routine validates the
'''               range.
'''  Date         Developer            Action
'''  -------------------------------------------------------
'''
Private Sub refEntryRange_Change()
    If refEntryRange.Text = "" Then
        cmdNext.Enabled = False
    Else
        cmdNext.Enabled = True
    End If
End Sub
```

This simple code is called by the Change event of the text box. It enables or disables the Next button as the user types into the text box. If the text box contains any text, it enables the Next button. This is very loose validation, since it doesn't check to be sure that the text is valid or makes sense within the context of your Wizard. It does prevent users from blatantly skipping required input. In this specific case, we are really looking for a range, not just any text. The change event fires on every character entered into the text box, and it's not practical to validate a range until the user has completed the input. This type of validation is usually done at the page level. When the user attempts to move to the next page, the stricter page-level validation code is run.

Page-Level Validation Code

The page-level validation routine shares many concepts with the initialization routines. It's divided into logical sections so that it can be adapted to a wide range of Wizards. If you look at the validation code for Page 3, you'll see the stricter page-level validation being applied to the control that was used in our preceding control-level validation example. In this specific case, it is checking to see if the user happens to be in R1C1 mode and makes the appropriate conversion before testing the range. The control-level validation simply looked for any text in the control, and the page-level validated the text as a valid range. The two validations working together create a stronger validation mechanism than either one alone.

Here's the complete listing for the bValidate function:

```
''' Function:    bValidate
''' Comments:    Used to validate a single page or all pages
'''              of the Wizard. In WizDemo the -1 flag (all
'''              pages) is NOT used, but would be if you were
'''              validating all pages when the finish button
'''              is chosen. There are 2 major sections:
'''              SECTION 1: Code for All Pages Only
'''              SECTION 2: Code for each page of your Wizard.
''' Arguments:   iValidatePage - validate the page passed
'''              (0 based index) If nothing is passed, default
'''              is: validate all pages (-1)
''' Returns:     True if the page validates
''' Date         Developer           Action
''' --------------------------------------------------
'''
Private Function bValidate(Optional iValidatePage As _
    Integer = -1) As Boolean
    Dim bIsAllPages As Boolean  ''' true if -1 is passed
    Dim szTrash As String   ''' used to hold temp values
    ''' Set function to True. If any validation doesn't pass
    ''' it will be changed to False.
    bValidate = True
    ''' set IsAll flag if -1 is passed.
    bIsAllPages = iValidatePage = -1

    ''' SECTION 1: All pages additional code
    If bIsAllPages Then
    ''' placeholder for additional coded needed if dialog
    ''' is being validated as a batch process when Finish
    ''' button is pressed.
    End If
    ''' SECTION 2: Page specific
    ''' if page 1 or all pages (-1)
    If iValidatePage = 0 Or bIsAllPages Then
        If Len(txtCellEntry.Text) < 3 Then
            MsgBox mszNAME_TOO_SHORT, vbOKOnly + _
                vbExclamation, mszERROR_TITLE
            txtCellEntry.SetFocus
            bValidate = False
        End If
    End If
    ''' page 2 or all pages
    If iValidatePage = 1 Or bIsAllPages Then
    ''' Turn off error handling while testing the range.
        On Error Resume Next
        With Application
```

```
            If .ReferenceStyle = xlR1C1 Then    ''' convert
                szTrash = .ConvertFormula(refEntryRange, _
                    xlR1C1, xlA1)
                ''' next statement will throw error if
                ''' selection isn't a valid range
                szTrash = .Range(szTrash).Address
            Else    .
                ''' next statement will throw error if
                ''' selection isn't a valid range
                szTrash = .Range(refEntryRange).Address
            End If
        End With
        If Err <> 0 Then
            ''' will only happen if range is not valid
            MsgBox mszBAD_SELECTION, vbOKOnly + _
                vbExclamation, mszERROR_TITLE
            refEntryRange.SetFocus
            bValidate = False
        End If
    On Error GoTo 0 ''' reinstate standard error handling
        ''' In a production app,
        ''' reinstate custom error handler
    End If
    ''' if page 3 or all pages (-1)
    If iValidatePage = 2 Or bIsAllPages Then
        ''' Page 3 validation goes here...
        ''' no validation needed in WizDemo
    End If
End Function
```

This routine is much easier to follow when viewed in the Microsoft Excel 97 VBE, because the comments stand out and the individual sections are much clearer.

If you're an experienced spreadsheet developer, you may have noticed that the validation doesn't check the worksheet range (from Step 2) to guarantee that the range is unprotected. Because the demo adds a new worksheet to the workbook and the demo workbook is unprotected, this is a reasonable assumption for example code. In production, the Wizard would require an error handler to trap for the user moving to another workbook and selecting a locked range. This is an intentional omission for this demo, but because the structure is strong, adding additional tests would be very simple.

Guidelines for Wizard Development

Because the applications of Wizards vary so widely, it's impossible to create absolute rules. The following guidelines should be observed, unless you have a compelling reason to do something different:

- Model your Wizard after one that ships with Microsoft Excel.
- Step 1 describes the results of using the Wizard.
- Step 1 generally has limited choices and controls.
- All pages are generally the same size.
- Enable and disable the appropriate navigational buttons.
- The title should include "Step X of Y" to provide a sense of location.
- All title text should be implemented with constants.
- Gather as much input as possible, and then batch process the results after the user has pressed the Finish button.
- Input should be validated as a user leaves a page.
- The Next button shouldn't be enabled if essential input is not provided.
- Minimize processing between pages.
- If possible, provide default values for all inputs and enable the Finish button as soon as is practical.
- Initialize as many pages and controls as possible before the Wizard displays.
- Provide a browse button if file-name information is required.
- Use drop-down and/or list controls instead of radio buttons.
- Provide extensive instructions and/or use graphics to explain concepts.

Constructing Your Wizard

Wizards are the interface of choice for multistep processes. In this chapter, we discussed creating the most common type of Wizard using the MultiPage control and a single UserForm. We detailed the toughest development issues, including initialization and validation, and provided strategies to simplify their development.

Very complex Wizard development may break some of the guidelines discussed in this chapter. For example, the Microsoft Excel Chart Wizard combines MultiPage controls with multiple UserForms. This type of Wizard requires a slightly different implementation, but the strategies remain the same.

The WizDemo.xls file on the CD provides a working copy of the Wizard discussed in this chapter. It provides an excellent foundation for developing your own Wizards. The example doesn't solve every issue or fit all cases, but it was developed to scale up or down to suit your needs. It's designed to provide your Wizard development with a huge jump-start that will save you many hours of design work and coding.

C H A P T E R 3

Transition Issues

Overview

As an Office developer, you will find that Microsoft Excel 97 is a major upgrade of the product, with a greatly enhanced development environment. Starting with the introduction of Visual Basic for Applications version 5.0 and continuing with the evolution of the object model, developers will find any number of reasons to begin using the product as quickly as possible. Great effort has been taken to minimize the conversion effort from previous versions of Microsoft Excel.

In spite of the grand scope of the enhancements, many existing Microsoft Excel 95 applications will work without conversion in Microsoft Excel 97. In most instances, the newest features in Microsoft Excel have not made obsolete the functionality they replace. For example, Microsoft Excel 97 offers developers Visual Basic forms with which to construct custom dialogs. However the dialog sheets introduced in Microsoft Excel 5.0 will still work, and for that matter, the dialog tables used through Microsoft Excel 4.0 will also work. This chapter provides you with both a conversion guide and a reference document.

Note Not all of the new functionality of Microsoft Excel 97 will be covered here, only the areas of concern to Office developers who are interested in getting their applications running in Microsoft Excel 97.

A few of the major new features in Microsoft Excel will be briefly mentioned here, but you should remember that we are offering a number of resources to help you make the transition to Office 97. Some of these include:

- Office Developer Web Site (http://www.microsoft.com/officedev/)
- Microsoft Developer Network
- TechNet
- Mastering Office 97 Development, a multimedia training CD
- TechEd 97, which will feature courses on migrating applications to Office 97

Analyze Your Application

A conversion, like any other software development project, should begin with a complete analysis of the requirements and an understanding of the development tools.

The first question to consider is whether your application or add-in needs to be converted at all. Most applications will run just fine in Microsoft Excel 97. Others may be completely replaceable without code by new features of the product. For example, it is common for custom applications to perform data validation of some sort using the OnEntry property of the Application object. Microsoft Excel 97 has a great data-validation feature built into it, so old validation routines may not be needed at all. Microsoft Excel 97 also offers conditional formatting, so you don't need to use code for that purpose anymore.

There are a few features that have changed significantly, so applications using them should be evaluated carefully:

- Routines that use 16-bit API calls must be rewritten to use 32-bit calls.

- Applications that access external data sources should be closely evaluated to determine if one of the newer data-access methods like DAO or RDO should be implemented.

- Applications that use custom menus will require slight modification and should be evaluated to determine that they behave as expected.

The first item will be addressed here. The other two will be discussed later in this document.

Converting 16-bit API Calls

Migrating to Microsoft Excel 97 implies that you are running a 32-bit operating system. If your application was designed for a 16-bit operating system and makes use of 16-bit Windows API calls, these calls will have to be converted to 32-bit calls. An application with adequate error handling may mask calls to the incorrect API, so you should check that all your API calls are "wrapped" to make them operating system independent.

The following routine checks the operating system version and sets a variable to identify it. The second routine uses the OSBitness variable to call the appropriate API:

```
Function OSBitness() As Integer
    If InStr(Application.OperatingSystem, "32") > 0 Then
        OSBitness = 32
    Else          'default is 16 bit
        OSBitness = 16
    End If
End Function

Sub ReadIni()
If OSBitness = 16 Then
        nReturn = GetPrivateProfileString16("Reports",
"ReportNumberSelected", "", sGetINIValue, 255, sINIFile)
Else
    nReturn = GetPrivateProfileString32("Reports", _
        "ReportNumberSelected", "", sGetINIValue, 255, sINIFile)
    gnReportNumSelected = Val(Left$(sGetINIValue, nReturn))
End Sub
```

For more information about the Win32 API and migrating from 16-bit to 32-bit, see "Calling the Win32 API" in *Porting Your 16-Bit Microsoft Office-Based Solutions to 32-Bit Microsoft Office*, at http://www.microsoft.com/officedev/techinfo/porting.htm#Calling.

Architectural Changes

This section outlines the major architectural changes in Microsoft Excel 97. While none of these will likely break your application, they are important to note.

Modules Now Reside in the Visual Basic Editor

While it may appear that your module sheets are missing, your code is now located in the Integrated Development Environment (IDE) of Visual Basic for Applications 5.0. To view your modules, simply open the Visual Basic Editor (on the Tools menu, point to Macro and then click Visual Basic Editor) and look in the Project Explorer (if you have folders displayed, look in the Modules folder).

File Format Changes

The file format has changed with Microsoft Excel 97, but we have added some options to help you with the transition. You may save in any of the following formats:

- Microsoft Excel Workbook (the native Microsoft Excel 97 format)
- Microsoft Excel 5.0/95 Workbook (the prior file format)
- Microsoft Excel 97 & 5.0/95 Workbook (a dual format)

Leaving Files in the Original Version of Microsoft Excel

If your application does not require functionality that is specific to Microsoft Excel 97, files may be left in their original version of Microsoft Excel. You will still need to check your applications to make sure they run properly in Microsoft Excel 97.

If your applications are written in the Microsoft Excel 4.0 macro language, this is a good time to upgrade them to Visual Basic.

Generally, applications that are not used often or those requiring a complicated rewrite would be candidates for this treatment. Note that saving applications in prior versions of Microsoft Excel may be a useful option while an organization is in the process of rolling out Microsoft Excel 97.

Saving a File in Microsoft Excel 95 and 97 Formats

If users with different versions of Microsoft Excel must share an application or a file, the developer may choose to save a file with *both* file formats. Be aware that Microsoft Excel files saved in this manner will be larger because they contain both file formats.

The general rule of thumb for using this dual format is to use it when a Microsoft Excel 97 user has edited a file with a feature available only in Microsoft Excel 97 (such as conditional formatting) and Microsoft Excel 95 users need to read the file, but do not need to save changes. If both users must be able to edit and save this file, it should be saved in the Microsoft Excel 5.0/95 Workbook format. You must weigh the use of the dual-file format against the option of adding code to an application to mimic the Microsoft Excel 97 functionality. For example, an "On.Entry" routine that formats the values in cells could emulate the conditional formatting that is built into Microsoft Excel 97.

Batch-File Conversion

Once users have migrated to Microsoft Excel 97, many administrators will want to convert all older files so end users don't have to do it one file at a time. A batch-file converter that is provided with Microsoft Excel 97 will convert entire directories of files to the Microsoft Excel 97 format. This File Conversion Wizard is installed on the Wizard submenu of the Tools menu if the user chose to install this Wizard in Custom Setup.

Backward Compatibility

Microsoft Excel 97 still supports running Microsoft Excel 4.0 (XLM) macros with few changes. While Microsoft Excel 4.0 macros still run in Microsoft Excel 97, the Microsoft Excel 4.0 macro language has not been updated to reflect the expanded object model and you can no longer record macros in the Microsoft Excel 4.0 macro language. Correspondingly, support for the XLM macro language will grow increasingly difficult to come by (documentation is no longer provided with Microsoft Excel), so you may want to consider upgrading XLM applications to Visual Basic.

CommandBars Replace MenuBars and ToolBars

The MenuBars and ToolBars familiar to users of previous versions of Microsoft Excel have been upgraded to CommandBars, an object common throughout all the Office 97 applications. CommandBars let you include both menus and buttons on the same bar. While we have sought to ensure that this new feature does not break existing code, it will impact your development going forward. Specifically, ToolBars and MenuBars are both modified using the CommandBar object model.

Microsoft Excel 97 allows you to store custom menu bars and toolbars with the workspace or with the workbook. When the user quits Microsoft Excel 97, the toolbars in the workspace are automatically saved in the file Username8.xlb (where Username is the current user's logon name). Alternatively, if the user isn't logged on, the file name is Excel8.xlb. The toolbars saved in a workbook are stored in the workbook file.

Eliminated MenuBars

A number of menu bars have been eliminated from Microsoft Excel 97 to make Microsoft Excel more consistent with the rest of Office. If your code refers to MenuBars or MenuItems that no longer exist, Microsoft Excel will provide a non-error return value so your code will run without generating errors. Note that this is an instance where you will not be alerted by an error that Microsoft Excel 97 does not support the desired functionality. Also, be aware that the changes that you've made to the old menu bars will of course not appear.

The eliminated MenuBars are:

- Worksheet (XL4)
- Chart (XL4)
- No Docs Open
- Info
- Worksheet (XL4, short)
- Chart (XL4, short)
- Visual Basic Module

Menu Editor of Microsoft Excel 95/5.0

The Microsoft Excel 95 Menu Editor let you control the menus in Microsoft Excel without writing code by using a dialog to change the settings. When the workbook with the edited menu structure is loaded, the menu changes take effect. When the workbook is closed, the menu changes are reset. In Microsoft Excel 97, CommandBar customization through the user interface is at an application-level setting.

One of the most useful compatibility features of Microsoft Excel 97 is the ability to save Menu Editor changes into files that are saved in Microsoft Excel 97 format. In other words, while the Menu Editor does not exist in Microsoft Excel 97, the edits that have been built with the Menu Editor will be honored in Microsoft Excel 97. Remember that changes made to the CommandBar during a session with a file with Menu Editor customization will be lost when the file is closed.

There is, however, no backward compatibility for CommandBars. CommandBar changes are not saved when Microsoft Excel 97 saves a file in Microsoft Excel 95 format. This is consistent with CommandBar edits being at the application level.

Toolbars

Microsoft Excel 97 will continue to run your Visual Basic code that edits toolbars. Routines that modify Microsoft Excel 95 toolbars will continue to work. Be aware, though, that Microsoft Excel 97 introduces new toolbars, and that these toolbars will not be affected by code written for Microsoft Excel 95. For example, the following routine hides all toolbars in Microsoft Excel 95:

```
Sub HideAllToolbars()
    Dim i
    With Application
        For i = 1 To Application.Toolbars.Count
            Application.Toolbars(i).Visible = False
        Next i
    End With
End Sub
```

In Microsoft Excel 97, this routine will hide all of the toolbars that were available in Microsoft Excel 95, but will not affect the toolbars that are new to Microsoft Excel 97, nor will it affect Microsoft Excel 97 custom toolbars. The following routine makes all of the Microsoft Excel 97 command bars not visible:

```
Sub Excel97RemoveCommandBars()
    Dim oBar as CommandBar
    With Application
        For Each oBar in .CommandBars
            .CommandBars(oBar.Name).Visible = False
        Next oBar
    End With
End Sub
```

Accessing ShortcutMenus

The ShortcutMenus method of the Application object will still function as it did in Microsoft Excel 95; however, this method will be hidden, and its use is no longer encouraged.

You now access shortcut menus by their CommandBar name via the CommandBars accessor. The shortcut name will not enumerate out of the CommandBars collection, although it is there. Supply the shortcut name rather than a constant. For example:

```
Application.ShortCutMenus(xlAxis).Delete
```

Should become:

```
Application.ShortCutMenus("Chart Axis").Delete
```

Help Menu Is Now Included in the Menu Bar

In Microsoft Excel 97, the Help menu does not default to the last menu on the CommandBar. In prior versions of Microsoft Excel, omitting the menu-placement argument meant that the custom menu was added directly to the left of the Help menu. In Microsoft Excel 97, this code will result in the custom menu being placed at the far right of the CommandBar.

To make sure your custom menu appears directly to the left of the Help menu:

```
Dim nHelpIndex as integer
Dim cmdbr as commandbar
Set cmdbr =Application.CommandBars("Worksheet Menu Bar")
nHelpIndex= cmdbr.Controls("help").Index
cmdbr.Controls.Add Type:=msoControlPopup, _
        Before:= nHelpIndex
```

Visual Basic Objects

UserForms Versus DialogSheets

In Microsoft Excel 97, DialogSheets have been replaced by UserForms. UserForms are now part of the Visual Basic Editor (VBE) (whereas DialogSheets are part of the workbook), making for a more efficient development environment. DialogSheets will continue to work in Microsoft Excel 97, so there is no reason to immediately convert Microsoft Excel Dialog Sheet to UserForms. Microsoft Excel 97 will also support custom dialogs constructed using the Dialog Editor or the XLM dialog table. You may want to consider converting to UserForms, however, as they are common across all Office products and support the use of custom controls.

Range Method Changes

The Range method has been changed to improve efficiency. Numeric values can now be dimensioned either as integer or double. Note that in Microsoft Excel 95 numeric values resolved into strings where appropriate. This is no longer the case. Therefore, code that concatenates a range containing a number into a text string will generate a "run-time error 13 Type Mismatch" error. To avoid this, you should define a variable as a string and set the value of that string to the value of a cell.

Below is an example where A1 is equal to a number. This code works in Microsoft Excel 95 but will not work in Microsoft Excel 97:

```
Msgbox "The value of Cell A1 =>" & Range("A1")
```

To make this work in Microsoft Excel 97:

```
Dim strCellValue As String
strCellValue = Range("A1")
MsgBox "The value of Cell A1 =>" &  strCellValue
```

Compatibility with Visual Basic for Applications

This section outlines some of the primary changes to Visual Basic for Applications that will likely cause an error in existing Microsoft Excel 95 applications.

Type Library Changes

The type library for Microsoft Excel 97 is able to more specifically type objects. This far-reaching change may cause your application to return "Type Mismatch" errors. The following table illustrates some type library changes that will affect your application.

Code Will Be Compiled Earlier

Microsoft Excel 97 and its strongly typed type library allows the compiler to flag "Type Mismatch" errors. These errors are not caught by the compiler in Microsoft Excel 95. Be aware that code that is not used but still exists in the workbook or code that is "protected" by On Error Resume Next will also prevent compilation if a type mismatch occurs. You must fix the underlying error; there is no way to set the compile warning at a lower level.

Note that the Run method of the Application object will no longer allow mismatched argument types. This type mismatch will be caught at compile time. Here's an example of code that is broken:

```
Sub CallsFunction()
 Dim mv as Variant
 MsgBox Application.Run("MyFunction",mv)
End Sub

Function MyFunction(MyVar1 as Long) as String
 MyFunction = "test"
End Function
```

De-referencing a Typed Object

In Microsoft Excel 95, some objects were typed to return Variant values. For example, you may have used code similar to the following:

```
Sub AddSheet()
    Worksheets.Add (Worksheets(2))
End Sub
```

The type library for Microsoft Excel 97 is able to more specifically type objects. Worksheets are now typed to return an Object rather than a Variant. The parentheses in existing code will cause Visual Basic to attempt to de-reference the returned Worksheet object, which will result in an error.

To work around this problem, specify the object directly without using parentheses. This approach won't cause Visual Basic to try to de-reference the object, and the error will be avoided. The following code will work in Microsoft Excel 97:

```
Sub AddSheet()
    Worksheets.Add  Worksheets(2)
End Sub
```

Automatic Type Coercion in Arrays

Microsoft Excel can no longer declare an array as variant and then pass an item in the array to other functions and receive it as something other than a variant. This requires changing the declaration of the array argument. The following code works in Microsoft Excel 95:

```
Sub CallFunction()
    Dim avData as Variant      'note that avData is a variant
    Dim vItem as Variant
    avData =ThisWorkbook.Worksheets(1).Range("A1:A5")
    vItem = TimesTen avData(1,1)
End Sub

Function TimesTen(iData as Double) as Double      'will no longer work
    TimesTen = iData * 10                         'iData needs variant
End Function
```

For this code to work in Microsoft Excel 97, the argument iData should be re-dimensioned as a variant data type, as in the following example:

```
Sub XL97CallFunction()
    Dim avData as Variant       'note that avData is a variant
    Dim vItem as Variant
    avData = ThisWorkbook.Worksheets(1).Range("A1:A5")
    vItem = XL97TimesTen avData(1,1)
End Sub


Function XL97TimesTen(vData as Variant) as Double
    TimesTen = vData * 10                'vData now variant
End Function
```

OnRepeat Arguments Now Strongly Typed to String

You may have used the OnRepeat property to control what happens when the user clicks Repeat on the Edit menu. If so, Microsoft Excel 95 allows the following undocumented resetting (unassigning of a custom routine) of the OnRepeat property:

```
Sub ResetOnRepeat()
    Joe= Null
    Chris= Null
    Application.OnRepeat Joe, Chris     'Line does nothing
End Sub
```

In Microsoft Excel 97 this will result in the following error: "Run-time error '94': Invalid use of null." The workaround is to use the more common means of resetting an "On..." property, as in the following example:

```
Sub ResetOnRepeat()
    Application.OnRepeat "", ""
End Sub
```

Floating Point to Integer Conversion

When converting a Double or Single in a variant into an Integer, Visual Basic rounds rather than truncates the number. Any code that relies on truncation behavior may be broken. For best results, explicitly truncate floating points using the Int method.

Error Codes in Visual Basic

If your application captures returned error values in prior versions of Microsoft Excel, you will find that Microsoft Excel 97 may not return the same error values. The safest course of action is to not attempt to discern the actual error from the returned error code. As for existing code, we recommend that you examine your code for any references to Err and eliminate code that is conditional upon the value of Err.

ParamArrays Are Always Base 0

ParamArray is an optional argument type that allows you to pass a variant array to your function or subroutine. In Microsoft Excel 95, a function with a ParamArray argument may return different results when called from a worksheet rather than Visual Basic code. In Visual Basic to Visual Basic function calls, ParamArrays are base 0 (the index number of the first element is zero). Calling the same function from a worksheet cell would have the ParamArray always be base 1. Therefore, programmers had to use the LBound method to determine the index number of the first element.

In Microsoft Excel 97, Visual Basic now packages all ParamArrays with a 0 base. This will affect function calls with ParamArray arguments that are expecting the first element to be index one. Therefore spreadsheet functions using ParamArrays will need to be modified to work with base 0 ParamArrays.

ParamArrays Cannot Be Passed by Reference

In Microsoft Excel variables are passed by reference (ByRef) by default; however, you may pass them by value (ByVal). The following code will work in Microsoft Excel 95:

```
Sub Hello()
    x = ShowMessage("hi there", 0)
End Sub

Function ShowMessage(szMessage As String, iButtons As Integer,
ParamArray       vaSubText() As Variant) As Integer
    Dim szFinalMessage As String
    szFinalMessage = SubstituteText(szFinalMessage, vaSubText)
End Function

Function SubstituteText(szMessage As String, vSubText As Variant) As
String
SubstituteText = szMessage
End Function
```

This code will not work in Microsoft Excel 97 as ParamArrays must be passed by value (ByVal). This indicates that the sub or procedure may have access to a copy of the variable but may not change the value of the variable. The workaround for Microsoft Excel 97 is:

```
Function SubstituteText(ByVal szMessage As String, vSubText As Variant)
As String
SubstituteText = szMessage
End Function
```

Parentheses in ParamArray Declaration

Note that when declaring a DLL function with a ParamArray argument, Microsoft Excel 95 allowed the user to omit parentheses next to the argument name. This bug has been fixed in Microsoft Excel 97. Applications with such improperly declared DLLs will generate the following error: "ParamArray must be declared as an array of variant." To correct the problem the developer must simply add the correct parentheses. Thus the following code will not work:

```
Declare Function RunVBA 16 Lib "XLRUN.DLL" Alias "RunVBA" (szMacro As
String, ParmArray args as Variant) as Variant
```

And should be replaced by this code:

```
Declare Function RunVBA 16 Lib "XLRUN.DLL" Alias "RunVBA" (szMacro As
String, ParmArray args() as Variant) as Variant
```

New Global Constants: Checked, Grey, Unchecked

Microsoft Excel 97 claims three new global constants: Checked, Grey, and Unchecked. If you used one of these now-reserved words as a control name, you will get an error. Note that in Microsoft Excel 95, the following code would work for a checkbox named "Checked," while in Microsoft Excel 97, it does not:

```
[Checked].Value = xlOff
```

The best way to work around this issue and to avoid similar issues is to use a naming convention for all variables. Typically, a variable-naming convention uses a prefix that identifies the variable type concatenated to the variable name. For example, an option button formerly named "Checked" could be named "optChecked" (although it should be noted that while Boolean variables are traditionally named as adjectives, to avoid confusion, objects are not).

Methods Returning Worksheets

In Microsoft Excel 95, using the class "Excel.Sheet" as an argument to the CreateObject function, the GetObject function, or the CreateLink method returned a Worksheet object. In Microsoft Excel 97, using this argument with one of these methods returns a Workbook object. Code that uses these methods must be changed accordingly. You should be aware that any customized applications that control Microsoft Excel through OLE Automation will be affected by the changes to CreateObject and GetObject. Note that the following Microsoft Excel 95 code:

```
Set MySheet = CreateObject("Excel.Sheet")
```

Should become the following in Microsoft Excel 97:

```
Set MyBook = CreateObject("Excel.Sheet")
Set MySheet = MyBook.Sheets(1)
```

Code No Longer Runs After the Close Command

In Microsoft Excel 95, Visual Basic will run the code after a Close method is called from within the workbook being closed. The workbook is not really closed until execution of Visual Basic code ends.

In Microsoft Excel 97, execution of Visual Basic code ends with the execution of the Close method. Code that closes the workbook should be in a different workbook so that it can continue to run after it closes the file.

```
Sub CodeRunsAfterClose()
    ThisWorkbook.Close
    MsgBox "hi" ' This line will run in Microsoft Excel 95 but not in
Microsoft Excel 97
End Sub
```

References to Closed Workbook

You may have used the References dialog on the Tools menu to create a reference from one workbook to another. In Microsoft Excel 97, before closing a workbook that has a reference to an object (even if the reference is to a closed workbook) you must first set the object to Null.

Consider the following example in which First.XLA is referenced by Second.XLA, and the code is contained in Third.XLA:

```
Set wbCode = Workbooks.Open "First.XLA"
wbCode.Close
Workbooks.("Second.XLA").Close
```

This code will fail and produce an error message stating that Second.XLA is "Currently referenced by another project and cannot be closed." The workaround is as follows:

```
Set wbCode = Workbooks.Open "First.XLA"
wbCode.Close
set wbCode = Null
Workbooks.("Second.XLA").Close     'Will now close as wbCode = Null
```

RunAutoMacros Called Twice

If you run call RunAutoMacros twice within the same subroutine, the second calling within the same subroutine of the RunAutoMacros method will fail. For example, in the following routine, the message box will not appear:

```
Sub RunAutoCode()
    ThisWorkbook.RunAutoMacros which:=xlAutoOpen
    ThisWorkbook.RunAutoMacros which:=xlAutoClose
    MsgBox "Returned"
End Sub
```

Set SeriesCollection(1).Values = Range("A1")

In Microsoft Excel 95, you could assign a worksheet range directly to a chart series. The relevant code might say:

```
Set ActiveChart.Series(1).Values = wSheet1.Range("A1:A10")
```

This line of code will not work in Microsoft Excel 97. Instead, assign the range to an array, and then assign the array to the chart series.

```
adData = Array(ThisWorkbook.Sheets("Sheet1").Range("A1:A10"))
Set ActiveChart.Series(1).Values = adData
```

Chart Activation Changes Selection

Activating an embedded chart through code in Microsoft Excel 95 does not change the selection from the worksheet. In Microsoft Excel 97, when the developer activates the chart, it becomes the selection. This may cause problems with code relying on the selection before chart activation.

ScreenUpdating Is Not Reset Inside OnSave

If you set ScreenUpdating to False in a routine that has been called by the use of OnSave, Microsoft Excel 97 does not reset the ScreenUpdating property. The result is that it may appear that Microsoft Excel has stopped running.

Check all OnSave routines to ensure that the ScreenUpdating property is set back to True before macro execution halts. Be sure to consider all possible points of exit, including error handling.

Error Handling Ctrl-Break While MsgBox Shown

Microsoft Excel 95 does not produce a run-time error when a message box is showing and CTRL-BREAK is executed (it simply dismisses the box and continues). Because Microsoft Excel 97 will generate a run-time error in this case, you may want to add error handling around your message boxes, or at least be aware that your existing error handling will be called. When doing so, note that under Microsoft Excel 97 there is a difference between Resume and Resume Next. Whereas Resume Next will skip two lines following the line that caused the error, Resume will simply continue. Consider the following example:

```
Sub Excel97MsgBoxExample()
    On Error Goto ERRORHANDLER
    Application.EnableCancelKey = xlErrorHandler
    MsgBox "First"
    MsgBox "Second"      'This line gets skipped if Resume Next used
    MsgBox "Third"
    Exit Sub
ERRORHANDLER:
    MsgBox "Escape Key Hit"
    Resume              'Using Resume here ensures that no lines skipped
End Sub
```

Remember that the condition we are describing here does not apply to dialog boxes or UserForms.

Orienting a Style with xlVertical

A bug in Microsoft Excel 97 does not allow for the proper creation of a style if the orientation of the style is xlVertical. Thus the following code, which will work in Microsoft Excel 95, will not work in Microsoft Excel 97:

```
Sub NewStyle
    Set MyStyle = ThisWorkbook.Styles.Add(Name:="Test")
    MyStyle.Orientation = xlVertical
End Sub
```

Creating a style at run time is not common, and the vertical orientation is probably less so. Nevertheless, developers who create styles at run time should be aware of this bug and the following workaround:

```
Sub VerticalStyleWorkaround()
    With Selection
        .Orientation = xlVertical
        .HorizontalAlignment = xlGeneral
        .VerticalAlignment = xlBottom
    End With
    ActiveWorkbook.Styles.Add Name:="VerticalOrientation"
End Sub
```

Essentially, you must first create the style in a cell, and then add it to the selection (the coding equivalent of manually adding a style "by example").

Copy or Move a Sheet After a Hidden Sheet

Microsoft Excel 97 can not move worksheets to the end of a workbook if the current end worksheet is hidden. Moved sheets will be placed before the hidden sheet.

To work around this, simply reorder all hidden worksheets to the beginning of the workbook.

Copy Hidden Sheets No Longer Selects the Sheet

In Microsoft Excel 95, when you copy a hidden sheet the sheet remains active. In Microsoft Excel 97, the sheet is not active, so code that relies on the ActiveSheet property will fail. An example of code that will not work:

```
Sub CopySheet()
    Sheets("HiddenSheet").Copy Before:=Sheets(1)
    MsgBox ActiveSheet.Name & "Has been copied."
End Sub
```

To work around this:

```
Sub Excel97CopySheet()
    Dim wSheetName as Worksheet
    Sheets(wSheetName).Copy Before:=Sheets(1)
    MsgBox wSheetName & "Has been copied."
End Sub
```

Add-In Names Beginning with '_'

On closing the Add-In Manager, Microsoft Excel 95 would normally attempt to add an "Open=" line to the registry so that installed add-ins will be loaded at startup. Microsoft Excel also looks at the InitCommands and InitMenu registry key values to find additional add-ins that need an "Open=" line.

You should not name an add-in with an underscore in Microsoft Excel 97 because it makes an exception to those registry key values beginning with '_'. It ignores those registry key values and does not automatically add an "Open=" line for them. Add-ins that install a InitCommand or InitMenu registry key value with a '_' prefix will not be opened at startup.

Module Name with Spaces or Other Illegal Characters

Microsoft Excel 97 will read in modules that were created in Microsoft Excel 95 and named with illegal characters. However, Microsoft Excel 97 will not allow you to create, copy, or rename any module to an illegal name. Illegal characters include "!", "." and "..".

Visual Differences

Tahoma Font Used in DialogSheets

Microsoft Excel 97 conforms to the rest of the Office suite and uses the Tahoma font in dialog sheets. The metrics of Tahoma are slightly smaller than those of MSSansSerif or MSSansSerif Bold, the fonts used in Microsoft Excel 95. There may be spacing issues in custom dialog sheets. The best way to work through this issue is to check all dialogs by eye and manually edit those that are affected. If you are developing an application for both Microsoft Excel 95 and Microsoft Excel 97 and want to ensure that your dialogs and dialog controls are correctly sized, you may change dimensions based on the version of Microsoft Excel that is running. For example, the following code discerns the version of Microsoft Excel and then adjusts a label based on the version:

```
Sub SizeByVersion()
    With ThisWorkbook
        If Application.Version <> "8.0" Then     ' Excel 97 is version
8.0
            .DialogSheets("dNames").Labels("lblText").Width = 94.5
        Else
            .DialogSheets("dNames").Labels("lblText").Width = 90
        End If
    End With
End Sub
```

Data Access Objects (DAO) Changes

DAO Upgraded to Version 3.5

Microsoft has upgraded the Data Access Object (DAO) to version 3.5. If your application uses DAO 3.0, you may still reference it. Because DAO 3.5 is designed to work well with applications designed for DAO 3.0, you will not be required to reference the newer version. Of course, applications written in Microsoft Excel 97 with a reference to DAO 3.5 will not reference DAO 3.0 if saved in Microsoft Excel 95 format.

DAO 3.5 Will Be Default if DAO 3.0 Is Not Installed

If DAO 3.0 is not installed, then Microsoft Excel 97 will default to DAO 3.5. You will want to ensure that users of your applications have the appropriate installation of DAO, as there is functionality that is specific to each.

CreateObject Method and DAO

Objects in DAO 3.5 are named slightly differently than their equivalents in DAO 3.0. For example: the DBEngine in DAO 3.0 is referred to as DAO.DBEngine while in DAO 3.5 it is DAO.DBEngine.35. The best way to ensure application portability is to avoid using CreateObject in either Microsoft Excel 95 or Microsoft Excel 97.

DAO and Named Arguments

Although named arguments were never supported by DAO, in some cases they would work. We discouraged the use of this practice, but there may be code that works in Excel 95 that uses named arguments with DAO, so you cannot be sure that these arguments will be correctly identified. For example, this working Microsoft Excel 95 code:

```
Set dbTest = DBEngine.OpenDatabase(Name:="C:\My Documents\MyDB.mdb", _
    Exclusive:=False, _
    ReadOnly:=False) 'Note that the second argument has changed
```

Should become the following in Microsoft Excel 97:

```
Set dbTest = DBEngine.OpenDatabase(Name:="C:\My Documents\MyDB.mdb", _
    Options:=dbDriverComplete, _
    ReadOnly:=False)  'Note the corrected argument
```

Miscellaneous Changes

XlVeryhidden Module Sheets

In Microsoft Excel 95, these very hidden code modules are not visible in the sheet tabs, nor the Unhide dialog box. In Microsoft Excel 97, all modules are moved to the Visual Basic Editor, which essentially hides them from the non-programmer. These modules will not be protected or hidden in the editor; however, you may prevent users from viewing a module sheet by a password protecting it in Microsoft Excel 95.

Tools/Macro Dialog Changes

Microsoft Excel 97 no longer includes the ability to add a macro to the Tools menu via the Macro Options dialog. Correspondingly, the MacroOptions method cannot add a macro command to the Tools menu. Attempting to add the menu item will not generate a run-time error, but the menu item will not be added. The following code example illustrates the proper way to insert a menu item with Microsoft Excel 97:

```
Set NewItem = CommandBars("Worksheet Menu Bar").Controls("Tools") _
    .Controls.Add(Type:=msoControlButton, Before:=6)
With NewItem
    .Caption:= "Pop Message Box"
    .OnAction:="NewMacro"
End With

Sub NewMacro()
    MsgBox "My New Macro"
End Sub
```

F1 in Custom Dialog Boxes

When displaying a custom dialog box in Microsoft Excel 95, the F1 key brings up the custom Help file for the custom dialog. In Microsoft Excel 97, the F1 key brings up the Assistant. However, if there is a Help button in the dialog, that button's OnAction is triggered by the F1 key.

Merged Cells

Microsoft Excel 97 allows users to merge cells, a feature not supported by prior versions of the product. When selecting an area within a group of merged cells, the selected range will be always be rectangular. This means if you use the Select method on a range of a merged set of cells, you will select all of the cells under the merged cell, plus whatever other cells are necessary to make the complete selection rectangular.

Existing code can still access any range, and get or set properties or call methods as usual, with the exception that the Select method imitates the selection in the user interface.

If you have code that depends upon the selection and its address, you may encounter erroneous results, although you would not necessarily encounter a macro error. If your users are unable to merge cells (because of worksheet protection), you will not encounter this problem.

An example of this would be if you merged cells A1, A2, and A3. If you then selected cell A2, through Visual Basic code, and formatted the pattern to be black, you would notice that cells A1, A2, and A3 turned black. Because A2 is part of the merged cell spanning A1, A2 and A3, Microsoft Excel selects all three of the cells when any one of them is selected.

Pasting an Array Formula Over a Copied Cell

Microsoft Excel 95 allowed you to paste an array formula over the copied cell. Microsoft Excel 97 does not. Whereas the following code worked in Microsoft Excel 95, it will not in Microsoft Excel 97:

```
Sub CopyAndPaste()
    With ActiveSheet
        .Range("A1").Copy
        .Range("A1:J1").Select
        .Paste
    End With
End Sub
```

To work around this you must not include the copied cell in the selection to paste to, or to use AutoFill, as in the following example:

```
Sub UseAutoFill()
    Range("A1").Select
    Selection.AutoFill Destination:=Range("A1:J1"), Type:= _
        xlFillDefault
End Sub
```

ERR() Function Returns a Long

In Microsoft Excel 95 there were no error codes that could not be coerced into integers. This is not the case with Microsoft Excel 97. While the following code worked in Microsoft Excel 95, it may return an error in Microsoft Excel 97:

```
Function DemoErr()
    Dim iError As Integer
    On Error GoTo ErrorHandler
    ThisWorkbook.Worksheets("Q1PineManor").Range("Lynn") = 28 / 0
    Exit Function
ErrorHandler:
    iError = Err
    MsgBox "Error Number:" & iError
End Function
```

To restate, you should not rely on the particular error code that Microsoft Excel returns. You may run into an unexpected data type, as in the above case, and even if the data type is correct you may not get the value that you expect.

C API Compatibility

Converting 16-Bit XLLs to 32-Bit

Most of your 16-bit DLL code will not recompile for use in Win32 without a few changes. The following sections discuss the changes required to convert your 16-bit add-ins to 32-bit. Judicious use of conditional compilation will enable you to upgrade your source so that it can be compiled for both Win16 and Win32.

Declaration Changes

One of the first things you will need to change is the declaration of your functions and subroutines. Win32 uses the stdcall calling convention instead of the pascal calling convention. This means that the pascal keyword should be removed from the declaration. Far has no meaning in a 32-bit context and should be removed from the declaration also. The _export keyword has been replaced with _declspec(dllexport). See the next section for issues on using _declspec(dllexport). An example of how conditional compilation can be used to solve this problem follows. Function names are case-sensitive in Win32.

```
#if defined(WIN32)
_declspec(dllexport) __stdcall int WINAPI SuperZoom(int Zoom, LPSTR
UserHelpFile, LONG wCommand, LONG topic)
#else
int far pascal _export SuperZoom(int Zoom, LPSTR UserHelpFile, LONG
wCommand, LONG topic)
#endif
```

An alternative method that you will see used throughout the samples is to use the WINAPI macro. The WINAPI macro is defined as __stdcall under Win32 and far pascal under Win16.

Exporting Correctly

To correctly export functions with Visual C++ you will also need to add definition or a .DEF file to the project. The .DEF file needs to list all the exports that have already been specified with _declspec(dllexport). If this is not done all exports will have C++ style name mangling performed on them. A minimum .DEF file would look like this:

```
LIBRARY DLLNAME
EXPORTS
    FuncName1
    FuncName2
    …
```

Variable Size Changes

Before recompiling your code, closely examine parameters, variables, and return values declared as type int in your C/C++ code. In C/C++ code the size of an int depends on the system and/or compiler. Win16 defined an int to be 16 bits, or the same as a short int or short. In Microsoft Excel the short int code used with REGISTER() is "H" (signed short int) or "I" (unsigned short int). Win32 defines an int to be 32 bits, or the same as a long int or long, and the Microsoft Excel registration code is "J".

Microsoft Excel does not support a system-dependent int parameter or return value type and will have a problem with carelessly written Win16 code that is recompiled for Win32. Plain int parameters and return values are expanded to 32 bits, which effectively changes the registration type code from "H" to "J". Calling an incorrectly declared procedure may result in incorrect results or a protection fault. There are three solutions to this problem:

1. Leave the C/C++ code alone (it still uses system-dependent plain int) and conditionalize your calls to REGISTER() to be aware of the current operating system platform. On Win16 use 16-bit "H" and "I" codes, and on Win32 use the 32-bit "J" value. An example of how to do this would be:

```
=IF(Win16)
=    REGISTER("mydll.dll","StandardFile","PIGGG")
=ELSE()
=    REGISTR("mydll.dll", "StandardFile","PJGGG")
=END.IF()
```

2. Leave the XLM code alone and instead clean up the C/C++ variable declarations. All int parameters and return values are modified to be either a short int or a long int as required. The same REGISTER() type code can then be used on either platform.

3. Use conditional compilation to declare the appropriate C/C++ variable declarations. Change your XLM code to use the appropriate parameter sizes for the appropriate platform. This is somewhat of a combination of options 1 and 2.

String Variables and Unicode

One significant difference between 16-bit and 32-bit environments is in how string data is stored and manipulated. Visual Basic in Microsoft Excel uses ANSI (American National Standards Institute) characters (a single byte represents each character) to store and manipulate strings in both 16- and 32-bit versions. Conversely, 32-bit OLE Automation and the 32-bit OLE 2 API use Unicode (two bytes represent each character) to store and manipulate strings.

Environment	Character Set
Windows 3.1	ANSI
Windows95 API	ANSI
32Bit Object Libraries	Unicode
Windows NT API	Unicode
OLE Automation in Windows NT	Unicode
OLE Automation in Windows95	Unicode

When you pass string data from Visual Basic in Microsoft Excel, the data uses ANSI characters. You can leave the strings in ANSI format if you are simply passing them back to Microsoft Excel or calling a Windows 95 system function, but you may need Unicode characters if you use OLE Automation or you call an OLE 2 API function. You can use the MultiByteToWideChar Win32 API to convert an ANSI string to Unicode, and the WideCharToMultiByte API to convert a Unicode string to ANSI.

In addition, because Microsoft Excel uses ANSI characters in BSTR variables, you cannot use the standard OLE string allocation and reallocation functions (these functions now create Unicode strings). Two new functions, SysAllocStringByteLen and SysStringByteLen, exist to operate on single-byte character strings.

xlGetHwnd

The C-API xlGetHwnd call that retrieves the main window handle of Microsoft Excel can create problems when converting your code. This is because sizeof(HWND) on Win32 is a long but the field used to receive the HWND parameter in the XLOPER structure is a short. Consequently the high word of the actual Microsoft Excel HWND is truncated. To work around this problem call xlGetHwnd to get the low word of the actual hwnd, then iterate the list of top-level windows and look for a match with the returned low word. This code illustrates the technique:

```
typedef struct _EnumStruct {
    HWND    hwnd;
    unsigned short  wLoword;
} EnumStruct;

#define CLASS_NAME_BUFFER    50

/*
**
** Function: EnumProc
**
** Comments: Used to find the hWnd in the Win32 version of Excel.
**           This is the callback routine that checks each hwnd.
**
** Arguments: hwnd - The hwnd of the window currently being looked at
**            EnumStruct * - A structure containing loword of hwnd of
**                    interest and space to return full hwnd.
**
** Returns:   BOOL - indicates success or failure
**
** Date           Developer          Action
** -------------------------------------------------------------
```

```c
*/
BOOL CALLBACK EnumProc(HWND hwnd, EnumStruct * pEnum)
{
    // first check class of the window.  Must be "XLMAIN"
    char szClass[CLASS_NAME_BUFFER+1];

    GetClassName(hwnd, szClass, CLASS_NAME_BUFFER);

    if(!lstrcmpi(szClass, "XLMAIN"))
        {
        // if that is a match, check the loword of the window handle
        if(LOWORD((DWORD)hwnd) == pEnum->wLoword)
            {
            pEnum->hwnd = hwnd;
            return FALSE;
            }
        }
    // no match continue the enumeration
    return TRUE;
}


/*
**
** Function: GetHwnd
**
** Comments: Used to find the hWnd in the Win32 version of Excel.
**           This routine sets up the callback and checks the results.
**
** Arguments: pHwnd - This is actually the returned hwnd
**
** Returns: BOOL - Indicating success or failure.
**
** Date            Developer           Action
** --------------------------------------------------------------
*/
BOOL GetHwnd(HWND *pHwnd)
{
    XLOPER x;

    // Get the loword of the hwnd
    if(Excel4(xlGetHwnd, &x, 0) == xlretSuccess)
        {
        EnumStruct enm;

        // Set up the structure
        enm.hwnd = NULL;
        enm.wLoword = x.val.w;
```

```
// Start the enumeration
EnumWindows((WNDENUMPROC)EnumProc, (LPARAM) &enm);

// Check results
if(enm.hwnd != NULL)
    {
    *pHwnd = enm.hwnd;
    return TRUE;
    }
}
return FALSE;
}
```

LibMain Is Now DllMain

Under Win16 LibMain is supplied by the C run-time libraries. Win32 instead expects to find DllMain. One major way in which DllMain differs from LibMain in that the parameters passed in indicate the reason for which DllMain is being called. DLLMain takes over the functionality of both the LibMain and the WEP function.

The REGISTER Macro Function

The REGISTER macro function and the Declare Visual Basic statement are not equivalent. Using the REGISTER function registers the DLL function only for the macro sheet or the worksheet. You cannot directly call the function from a Visual Basic module without using the Declare statement, even if you have already used the REGISTER function and called the same DLL function from a macro sheet. You can, however, call the function from a Visual Basic module by using the ExecuteExcel4Macro method to call the registered DLL function just as you would call any other Microsoft Excel macro function.

Public functions are those declared without either the Public or Private keywords (or explicitly declared with the Public keyword). If you declare the DLL function as Private, you can call the function only from the Visual Basic module where it is declared.

In addition, the REGISTER and UNREGISTER functions allow you to dynamically load and unload DLL functions. This is not possible in Visual Basic. Once a DLL function is loaded by a Visual Basic module (the first time a declared function in the DLL runs), the DLL remains loaded until you close the workbook that contains the Visual Basic module.

You can use the dynamic loading behavior of the REGISTER and UNREGISTER functions by creating a stub macro on a macro sheet. The stub macro should accept appropriate arguments for the DLL function, register the DLL function, call it, unregister it, and return the return value from the DLL function. You can then use the ExecuteExcel4Macro function to call the stub macro from Visual Basic. The stub macro in turn calls the DLL and returns to Visual Basic. A simple example of this is shown in the CallEvaluateExample in Sample\Example\EXAMPLE.XLS.

Using Strings

When Visual Basic passes a string by reference to a C-language DLL, it uses a special OLE 2 data type called a BSTR. OLE Automation allows BSTR strings to be allocated and freed by any component that supports this data type.

In most cases, a BSTR can be treated like a pointer to a null-terminated string. In general, it's best if your C-language code does not directly manipulate the string data. You can de-reference the pointer to copy data from the BSTR, however.

Using Arrays

OLE 2 provides a special data type for arrays passed from Visual Basic to a DLL. This data type, called a SAFEARRAY, allows both Visual Basic and the DLL to allocate, free, and access array data in a controlled way. SafeArrays are the equivalent of xltypeMulti XLOPERs for VBA.

Type Libraries

Type libraries are quasi-replacements for XLL add-ins. The type library can contain constant and function declarations and other information about the DLL. Once you have created a type library, you can use the References command on the Tools menu in Microsoft Excel to load the type library. Once loaded, the constant and function declarations are available in Visual Basic without using Declare statements. For more information on creating type libraries see the *OLE Programmer's Guide Volume 2* or MSDN.

Visual Basic in Microsoft Excel does not support user-defined data-structure declarations in type libraries (user-defined data structures are those declared with the Visual Basic Type statement or the C/C++ struct statement). To use the structures in your Visual Basic code, you will have to add their declarations to the module.

C H A P T E R   4

Using OLE Automation

With the introduction of Visual Basic for Applications (VBA) in Microsoft Excel 5.0, a new method of communicating with Microsoft Excel was provided: OLE Automation. VBA is not an intrinsic part of Microsoft Excel. It is implemented as a series of DLLs and uses Automation to communicate with Microsoft Excel. This provides maximum reusability among the various pieces of Microsoft Office.

OLE Automation provides a mechanism for a controller (VBA) to interact with an object (Microsoft Excel). This is a two-way interaction. Because OLE Automation is a protocol, any automation controller can use every automation object, and any automation object can be used by every automation controller. This communication is typified by calling "methods" and setting "properties." Methods equate to function calls, and properties equate to setting the value of a variable.

This chapter focuses on OLE Automation from a Microsoft Excel and a Visual Basic point of view. The concepts discussed also apply to OLE Automation controllers built in C/C++, but the actual details of building these controllers are beyond the scope of this book.

Early and Late Binding

There are two different ways of implementing OLE Automation: VTBL (virtual method table, pronounced V-Table) binding, and the IDispatch (pronounced EYE-Dispatch) interface. Using VTBL binding is similar to programming the speed dialer on your phone. You look up the number once and program it into the phone. Once you verify that it's valid, a single button dials the number. All the work of looking up the phone number is handled long before you use the phone number. Using the IDispatch interface is similar to looking up the phone number in a phone book before *each* call, and then dialing the phone. Both will get the intended results, but the speed dialer is much more efficient when you need to make the call. However, looking up the number each time verifies its correctness.

Early Binding: VTBL Binding

A VTBL is a data structure containing the addresses (pointers) for the methods and properties of each object in an Automation server. Using the VTBL is generally known as *early binding* in VBA. Frequently, early binding requires type information provided in the form of a type library. This type information allows VBA to perform compile-time syntax and type checking. At run time, this type of binding is faster, as the entry points for the Automation server are already known and the data types and syntax have already been verified.

Late Binding: The IDispatch Interface

Using the IDispatch interface is a way to call member functions within an object without knowing the exact location of their entries in the VTBL. An IDispatch implementation is frequently referred to as *late binding*. With IDispatch, VBA has no preexisting information about the server it will be calling. It assumes during its compile phase that the code is correct. It then attempts at run time to execute the code and trap for run-time errors. This is much less elegant and represents a step backward from the familiar syntax and type checking we have come to expect from VBA. An IDispatch call also requires both the client and the server to marshal their arguments into a consistent form that is understood by both. In most cases, this means that arguments are copied into and out of variants. This not only slows down IDispatch, but it also limits the data types that can be passed using this technique. In all future discussions VTBL binding will be referred to as *early binding* and IDispatch as *late binding*.

What does this mean to you as a developer using VBA? If possible you should attempt to early bind when using Automation objects from VBA. Early binding not only increases performance, but you get syntax and type checking at compile-time. If you can't early bind you must use late binding, which is slower and doesn't allow you to catch simple errors (such as type mismatches) until run time.

Early binding should be used whenever possible. However, there are programming situations in which late binding is preferred. If you are implementing polymorphic code (one call can represent multiple different objects), then late binding is required. For example, you can create three classes —widgets, gidgets, and gadgets—all with a Create method. By defining your variable as an object, you can call the Create method for any of the three classes based on run-time conditions.

When testing this type of late-bound strategy, it's generally best to test a single object, early bind to get the syntax and type checking, and then switch to late binding after you've tested each object individually.

Binding in VBA

What does early binding versus late binding look like in VBA? The main difference is in how you declare your variables. The following code snippet declares an object variable that refers to an instance of Microsoft Word. This example represents late binding, since we have used the generic Object data type. VBA doesn't know what type of object it is and will use late binding at run time to handle it. This is like running to the phone book before dialing the phone.

```
Dim wrd as Object
```

In the following code snippet, we declare the same object variable and specifically type it as Word.Application. This can be done only after we have referenced the Microsoft Word type library using Tools/References. Since VBA knows about the type of this object, it attempts to use early binding when dealing with it.

```
Dim wrd As Word.Application
```

How you declare the object variable is the factor that determines whether an object is early or late bound. How you create the object has no bearing on the type of binding VBA does, but it does have some performance implications.

To create an object, you can use either the New keyword or the CreateObject method. The CreateObject method is typically used when you don't know the Program ID (ProgID) of the object you are going to create until run time. Excel.Application is an example of a ProgID. Typically, a ProgID is composed of the application name followed by a period and then the class name (for example, Application.Class). To arrive at the ProgID for a particular object, use this method and then look at HKEY_CLASSES_ROOT in the registry to verify that you are correct. If you are correct, the ProgID should show up in this hive as a key. It's often assumed that if you use CreateObject you are using late binding, but this is not always the case. The declaration of the object variable is the overriding factor. CreateObject does have a slight performance disadvantage when compared to New. CreateObject assumes there is no reference to the object it is trying to instantiate and loads all the type information from the registry. This process is slower than using the type information available in a type library.

The New keyword has two syntaxes. The following example declares and instantiates the object in separate lines:

```
Dim wrd As Word.Application
Set wrd = New Word.Application
```

This is the recommended syntax. The following example shows how New can be used to declare and instantiate an object at the same time:

```
Dim wrd As New Word.Application
```

This ensures that `wrd` always contains a valid instance of Word.Application. You don't have to worry about checking to see if `wrd` has been initialized yet. But there is a minor penalty for this, since the VBA compiler adds some overhead to be sure the object was loaded. This is transparent to you, but your compiled code will be slightly larger compared with the previous syntax.

CreateObject can also be used, and it retrieves the type information for Word.Application from the referenced type library. The results of the following are identical with but slightly slower than using the similar construct with the New keyword:

```
Dim wrd as Word.Application
Set wrd = CreateObject("Word.Application")
```

New is the recommended method for instantiating objects if you have access to the object's type library.

In-Process vs. Cross-Process

OLE Automation objects are instantiated in two different manners: *in-process* and *cross-process*. An in-process Automation object is loaded as a DLL into the process space (the memory of the application) of the controller. This has a distinct performance advantage, since the controller and object are in the same process space and direct function calls may be made between them. However, there are some drawbacks. When loading servers in-process, each controller must load its own copy of the object. There is no sharing of objects between processes. When an object is in-process, a bug in the object can bring down both the controller and the object. Despite the pitfalls, in-process object communication is fastest and is typically the method you want to use.

Cross-process objects load in separate process spaces and use remote procedure calls (RPC) to communicate. There is a certain amount of overhead involved in cross-process RPC, and as a result this method is typically slower than the in-process implementation. It does, however, have the advantage of partitioning the processes, and it allows a single object to be shared by multiple controllers.

Benchmark: Excel Calling Visual Basic 4.0

As an example of the above discussions, the CD contains samples of two VBA objects (with source code). These objects are called from VBA in early-bound and late-bound fashion as well as in-process and cross-process. The objects accept three string parameters, concatenate them, and return the result. The VBA source code listing is shown at the end of this chapter.

To create a meaningful benchmark, the code loops a variable number of times. The following results were obtained from running the code for 10,000 iterations.

	In-Process	**Cross-Process**
Early Bound	0 seconds	13 seconds
Late Bound	3 seconds	32 seconds

The actual times are not important, as these can vary from machine to machine, depending on its configuration. The ratio between the times is the important factor. As the table above shows, the most important consideration when looking at this performance data is whether the object runs in-process versus cross-process. This single change can yield a 10x to 13x performance increase. Performance due to early versus late binding is not affected nearly as much, on the order of 3x in this test.

All this must be kept in perspective. If your code isn't running a loop and makes a single call or two, the difference between the two methods is often insignificant.

Benchmark Source Code

The companion CD to this book contains all the source code needed to run and/or build the automation examples in this chapter. Both the Microsoft Visual Basic 4.0 Automation servers (InProc and OutProc folders) and the VBA source code (UsingOle.xls) are included. The complete VBA code is listed below:

```
Sub Button1_Click()
    ''' Early bind to objects
    Dim cOutProc As clsOutProc
    Dim cInProc As clsInProc
    ''' Late bind
    Dim oOutProc As Object
    Dim oInProc As Object
    Dim dStart As Date
    Dim dEnd As Date
    Dim iIter As Integer
    Dim iCount As Integer
    Dim szString1 As String
    Dim szString2 As String
    Dim szString3 As String
    Dim szRes As String
```

```
''' Instantiate objects
Set cOutProc = New clsOutProc
Set cInProc = New clsInProc
''' Get number of iterations and strings
With ThisWorkbook.Sheets(1)
    iIter = .Range("Iterations").Value
    szString1 = .Range("String1").Value
    szString2 = .Range("String2").Value
    szString3 = .Range("String3").Value
End With
''' Show what we are doing
Application.StatusBar = "Early Bound InProc Running..."

''' Get start time. This is subject to the granularity
''' of Excel's Now() function.
''' This is accurate only to the second
''' You may have to increase the iterations
''' to get relevant comparisons
dStart = Now()

''' Loop and call the object
For iCount = 1 To iIter
    szRes = cInProc.ConcatStrings(szString1, _
        szString2, szString3)
Next
''' Record ending time
dEnd = Now()

''' Display difference
ThisWorkbook.Sheets(1).Range("EarlyInProcTiming") _
    .Value = DateDiff("s", dStart, dEnd)

''' Display what we are doing
Application.StatusBar = "Early Bound OutProc Running..."

''' Get next start time
dStart = Now()

''' Loop and call the object
For iCount = 1 To iIter
    szRes = cOutProc.ConcatStrings(szString1, _
    szString2, szString3)
Next

''' Record ending time
dEnd = Now()
```

```
''' Display difference
ThisWorkbook.Sheets(1).Range("EarlyOutProcTiming") _
    .Value = DateDiff("s", dStart, dEnd)

''' now do the late bound versions
''' Instantiate objects
Set oInProc = CreateObject("EDKInProcess.clsInProc")
Set oOutProc = CreateObject("EDKOutProc.clsOutProc")

''' Display what we are doing
Application.StatusBar = "Late Bound InProc Running..."

''' Record starting time
dStart = Now()

''' Loop and call the object
For iCount = 1 To iIter
    szRes = oInProc.ConcatStrings(szString1, _
 szString2, szString3)
Next

''' Record ending time
dEnd = Now()

''' Display difference
ThisWorkbook.Sheets(1).Range("LateInProcTiming") _
    .Value = DateDiff("s", dStart, dEnd)

''' Display what we are doing
Application.StatusBar = "Late Bound OutProc Running..."

''' Get next start time
dStart = Now()

''' Loop and call the object
For iCount = 1 To iIter
    szRes = oOutProc.ConcatStrings(szString1, _
 szString2, szString3)
Next

''' Record ending time
dEnd = Now()

''' Display difference
ThisWorkbook.Sheets(1).Range("LateOutProcTiming") _
    .Value = DateDiff("s", dStart, dEnd)
```

```
            ''' Clear the status bar
            Application.StatusBar = False

            ''' Release the objects
            Set oOutProc = Nothing
            Set oInProc = Nothing
            Set cInProc = Nothing
            Set cOutProc = Nothing
End Sub
```

C H A P T E R 5

Using DLLs from Visual Basic

Using DLL functions from Visual Basic Applications Edition in Microsoft Excel is very similar to using DLL functions from Visual Basic. Chapter 24 of the *Microsoft Visual Basic Programmer's Guide* for version 3.0 of Visual Basic provides detailed guidelines and examples for calling DLL functions from Visual Basic. This chapter provides more specific information about using DLL functions from Visual Basic in Microsoft Excel.

The examples in this chapter were prepared and tested with Microsoft Visual C++ version 4.2b and run on Microsoft Windows 95 and Windows NT Workstation 4.0. Visual C++ version 4.2b includes the OLE 2 header files and libraries required to create DLLs using variants, strings, objects, and arrays as described in this chapter.

You can use another C compiler and linker if they are capable of creating DLLs. In this case, you must also have the Microsoft Win32 SDK to create DLLs using variants, strings, objects, or arrays.

In addition to the Help provided with Visual C++ and the Win32 SDK, Chapter 6 in Volume 2 of the *OLE 2 Programmer's Reference* provides valuable information about the functions used in the examples in this chapter.

Using the Declare Statement

Before you can call a DLL function from Visual Basic, you must use the Declare statement to identify the function, the name of the DLL where it is located, and its argument types. Once the function is declared in a Visual Basic module, you can call it just as if it were part of your code.

For example, the following C-language function calculates the circumference of a circle given the circle's radius:

```
double WINAPI DoubleArg(double dRadius)
{
    return dRadius * 2 * 3.14159;
}
```

In Windows 95 and Windows NT, DLL functions use the __stdcall calling convention. The examples in this chapter were written to run on 32-bit Microsoft Windows (Win32).

The _export keyword has been replaced by __declspec(dllexport). If you use __declspec(dllexport) without also exporting each function via the .DEF file, you will find that Visual C++ has decorated the names of all your functions. Export each function via the .DEF file to prevent this. Win32 includes a predefined constant WINAPI that contains the __stdcall directive. Our code examples will make use of this shortcut.

This Visual Basic code uses the DoubleArg C function to display a table of circumference values:

```
Declare Function DoubleArg Lib "debug\ADVDLL.DLL" _
    (ByVal radius As Double) As Double

Sub CircumferenceTable()
    Dim i As Double

    Worksheets(1).Activate
    Range("a1:b11").Clear
    Cells(1, 1) = "Radius"
    Cells(1, 2) = "Circumference"
    For i = 1 To 10
        Cells(i + 1, 1) = i
        Cells(i + 1, 2) = DoubleArg(i)
    Next
    Columns("a:b").AutoFit
End Sub
```

The Declare statement uses the ByVal keyword because the argument is passed by value. DLL functions declared as public functions in a Visual Basic module can be called from any Visual Basic module in the workbook, but cannot be called from an XLM macro sheet or worksheet. Public functions are those declared without the Private keyword (or explicitly declared with the Public keyword). If you declare the DLL function as Private, you can call the function only from the Visual Basic module where it is declared. Visual Basic loads a DLL the first time a declared function in the DLL runs, and the DLL remains loaded until you close the workbook that contains the Visual Basic module.

Passing Arguments by Reference

By default, Visual Basic passes arguments by reference, rather than by value. If your function expects a pointer, you should pass ByRef; otherwise pass ByVal. Strings are an exception to this rule. When you pass a string ByVal you are passing a pointer to the string. If you pass a string ByRef you are passing a pointer to a pointer to a string.

For example, this C-language function modifies its argument by multiplying it by two. The function returns False if the argument is less than zero.

```
BOOL WINAPI PointerArg(short *pn)
{
    if (*pn < 0)
        return 0;    // False in Visual Basic

    *pn *= 2;
    return -1;       // True in Visual Basic
}
```

The Visual Basic declaration for this function does not include the ByVal keyword. You may include the ByRef keyword, but it isn't necessary. It is a good idea to explicitly include the ByRef keyword for clarity. Most problems with declarations have to do with a confusion over whether to pass ByRef or ByVal.

```
Declare Function PointerArg Lib "debug\ADVDLL.DLL" _
    (ByRef d As Integer) As Boolean

Sub TestPointerArg()
    Dim n As Integer
    Dim r As Boolean

    n = CInt(InputBox("Number?"))
    r = PointerArg(n)
    MsgBox n & ":" & r
End Sub
```

Using Variants

Passing an argument of Variant data type is very similar to passing any other argument type. In the DLL, you can use the VARIANT data structure to access the data contained in the argument. See Chapter 5 in Volume 2 of the *OLE 2 Programmer's Reference* for descriptions of the VARIANT data type.

The VARIANT type is a C-language structure containing a single member for the variable type, three reserved members, and a large named union that is used to access the variable data depending on the type.

For example, this C-language function determines the data type contained in the VARIANT argument passed by Visual Basic:

```
short WINAPI VariantExample(VARIANT vt)
{
    if (vt.vt == VT_DISPATCH)        // variant is an object
        return -1;
    else if (vt.vt == VT_BSTR)       // variant is a string
        return _wtoi(vt.bstrVal);
    else if (vt.vt == VT_I2)         // variant is an integer
        return vt.iVal;
    else                             // variant is something else
        return -3;
}
```

This Visual Basic code declares and calls the VariantExample function:

```
Declare Function VariantExample Lib "debug\ADVDLL.DLL" _
    (ByVal v As Variant) As Integer

Sub VariantArgTest()
    MsgBox VariantExample(Worksheets(1))    ' -1
    MsgBox VariantExample("25")             ' 25
    MsgBox VariantExample(5)                ' 5
    MsgBox VariantExample(3.2)              ' -3
End Sub
```

You could use this information to implement a function that accepts either a Range object or a text description of a range. If the argument contains an object, you can use IDispatch to access properties and methods of the object directly. If the argument contains a string, you can use IDispatch to create an object and then access its properties and methods.

Visual Basic in Microsoft Excel does not support all the data types supported by the VARIANT structure. The following table shows the allowed data types and their value constants. Microsoft Excel never returns a variant with a data type not shown on this list.

Data Type	Variant Constant
Boolean	VT_BOOL
Currency (scaled integer)	VT_CY
Date	VT_DATE
Double (double-precision floating-point)	VT_R8
Integer	VT_I2
Long (long integer)	VT_I4
Object	VT_DISPATCH
Single (single-precision floating-point)	VT_R4
String	VT_BSTR

Variants and Objects

The VariantExample function shows how you declare and call a DLL function with a Variant passed by value. A Variant passed by reference would be declared in C as a pointer to a VARIANT structure.

```
void VariantByRef(LPVARIANT *pvar)
```

While it is possible to pass an object as a Variant, it is also possible to specifically declare a function that accepts only an object. An object is passed as a dispatch pointer, either by value:

```
void ObjectByVal(LPDISPATCH pdisp)
```

or by reference:

```
void ObjectByRef(LPDISPATCH *ppdisp)
```

When you pass a variant or object by reference, you receive a pointer. If you change what the pointer is pointing to, remember that your DLL code must free any allocated object, string, or array first. Failure to free allocations results in memory leaks. More information about freeing allocated strings and arrays appears in the following sections, and the ReleaseVariant function example that appears in Chapter 6 shows how this can be done for a variant variable.

Return Values

When your function returns an object, it is declared as returning a dispatch pointer:

```
LPDISPATCH ReturnsObject(void)
```

Returning a Variant is simple:

```
VARIANT ReturnsVariant(void)
```

Using Strings

When Visual Basic passes a string by reference to a C-language DLL, it uses a special OLE 2 data type called a BSTR. OLE Automation allows BSTR strings to be allocated and freed by any component that supports this data type. In Excel 97, BSTRs now contain UNICODE strings. This is a change from Excel 95 and earlier, so be careful when porting your code.

In most cases, a BSTR can be treated like a pointer to a null-terminated string. In general, it's best if your C-language code does not directly manipulate the string data. You can de-reference the pointer to copy data *from* the BSTR, however.

Instead of directly manipulating BSTR data, OLE provides several functions that should be used to allocate, free, and reallocate BSTR values. These functions are listed in Chapter 6 in Volume 2 of the *OLE 2 Programmer's Reference.* Microsoft Excel still passes all strings as ANSI, even though string APIs under Win32 are typically UNICODE. This can cause problems when dealing with the BSTRs that Microsoft Excel passes to your DLL. The OLE functions for dealing with BSTR values under Win32 assume the BSTRs contain UNICODE strings. There are a few functions that will deal with byte-oriented strings, and you should make sure to use these functions. For example, instead of using SysStringLen() on a string from Excel, you should use SysStringByteLen().

When you pass a string by reference, your C-language function should declare the argument as a pointer to a BSTR. The pointer will never be NULL, but if the Visual Basic string is unassigned (that is, created with the Dim statement but not assigned a value), the BSTR pointed to will be NULL. If the string is assigned but empty, the first character will be a null character and the string length will be zero.

The pointer may also reference a NULL pointer if the original variable was created as a variant but not assigned. Visual Basic would coerce the variant to a string when it called the DLL; but because the variant is empty, it behaves like a declared—but unassigned—string.

The following code example tests for these conditions:

```
short WINAPI SType(BSTR *pbstr)
{
    if (pbstr == NULL)   // pointer is null; will never happen
        return 1;
    if (*pbstr == NULL)  // string (or variant) is alloc by VB
                         // with Dim statement,
                         // but not yet assigned
        return 2;
    if (*pbstr[0] == 0)  // string is allocated
                         // and assigned to empty string ("")
        return 3;
    // string has a value; this value can be accessed at *pbstr
    return 4;
}
```

This Visual Basic code declares and calls the SType function:

```
Declare Function SType Lib "debug\ADVDLL.DLL" _
    (s As String) As Integer

Sub STypeTest()
    Dim s As String

    MsgBox SType(s) 'displays 2
    s = ""
    MsgBox SType(s) 'displays 3
    s = "test"
    MsgBox SType(s) 'displays 4
End Sub
```

Allocating BSTR Values

You should always use OLE functions to operate on BSTR values. If you need to change a BSTR value, first test the BSTR to see if it is already assigned. If it isn't, you may use the SysAllocStringByteLen function to assign a value to the BSTR. If the BSTR is already assigned, you must free the current assignment (with the SysFreeString function) before you can use SysAllocStringByteLen. You cannot use the SysReAllocString or SysReAllocStringLen function to reallocate the string (these functions automatically free the initial assignment) because they do not have a byte version for dealing with the ANSI strings that Microsoft Excel is passing into the code.

For example, the following C-language code copies some number of characters from one BSTR into another. Notice that this example tests the second BSTR to see if it is already assigned. If it is, the example uses the SysReAllocStringLen function to free the existing string before replacing it.

```c
short WINAPI StringArgs(BSTR *pbstrArg1,
    BSTR *pbstrArg2, short cch)
{
    BSTR *pbstrTemp;

    // Return error code if requested characters
    // less than zero, or input string is unassigned
    // or has too few characters.
    // Use ByteLen since string is not unicode
    if (cch < 0 || *pbstrArg1 == NULL ||
        (short)SysStringByteLen(*pbstrArg1) < cch)
        return -1;

    if (*pbstrArg2 == NULL)
    {   // String is unassigned;
        // we can allocate a new one.
        // Use ByteLen since string is not unicode
        *pbstrArg2 = SysAllocStringByteLen((LPSTR)*pbstrArg1, cch);
        if (*pbstrArg2 == NULL)
            return -2;
    }
    else
    {   // Argument string is already assigned;
        // we must reallocate.
        *pbstrTemp = SysAllocStringByteLen((LPSTR)*pbstrArg1, cch);
        // Did it fail?
        if (pbstrTemp == NULL)
            return -3;

        SysFreeString(*pbstrArg2);
        *pbstrArg2 = *pbstrTemp;
    }

    return 0;
}
```

The calls to the SysAllocStringByteLen function use the dereferenced BSTR pointer *pbstrArg1 to access the characters in the first argument. This is permitted when you are reading the characters, but you should not write to the dereferenced pointer.

This Visual Basic code declares and calls the StringArgs function:

```
Declare Function StringArgs Lib "debug\ADVDLL.DLL" _
    (inpStr As String, outStr As String, ByVal n As Integer) As Integer

Sub StringArgsTest()
    Dim newStr As String
    Dim x As Boolean

    ''' First code path
    x = StringArgs("abracadabra", newStr, 5)
    MsgBox x & ":" & newStr

    ''' Second code path
    x = StringArgs("abracadabra", newStr, 4)
    MsgBox x & ":" & newStr
End Sub
```

Using User-Defined Data Structures

The Type statement in Visual Basic can be used to create user-defined data structures. For example, the following Visual Basic data type and C-language structure are equivalent.

In Visual Basic:

```
Type ARG
    i as Integer
    str as String
End Type
```

In C:

```
typedef struct
{
    short i;
    BSTR str;
} ARG;
```

User-defined data types cannot be passed by value; they must be passed by reference. Your C function should declare the argument as a pointer to the structure. If the structure contains BSTR values (as this example does), the rules discussed above apply to those values; you must test the BSTR before you reassign it (and free it if it is already allocated). You should not manipulate it directly.

For example, this C-language function fills a structure with a string and the length of the string:

```
short WINAPI StructArg(ARG *parg, char *szArg)
{
    BSTR bstr;

    if (parg == NULL)
        return -1;

    // allocate a local string first; if this fails,
    // we have not touched the passed-in string

    if ((bstr = SysAllocString((BSTR)szArg)) == NULL)
        return -1;

    if (parg->bstr != NULL) // string is already assigned
        SysFreeString(parg->bstr);

    parg->i = SysStringByteLen(bstr);
    parg->bstr = bstr;

    return parg->i;
}
```

Declared and called from Visual Basic:

```
Declare Function StructArg Lib "debug\ADVDLL.DLL" _
    (a As ARG, ByVal s As String) As Integer

Sub StructArgTest()
    Dim x As ARG
    MsgBox StructArg(x, "abracadabra")
    MsgBox x.str & ":" & str$(x.i) 'displays string and length
End Sub
```

Using Arrays

OLE 2 provides a special data type for arrays passed from Visual Basic to a DLL. This data type, called a SAFEARRAY, allows both Visual Basic and the DLL to allocate, free, and access array data in a controlled way.

Your DLL should always use OLE Automation functions to allocate and access SAFEARRAYs. These functions are described in Chapter 6 in Volume 2 of the *OLE 2 Programmer's Reference.* When OLE Automation passes a SAFEARRAY to your DLL, you receive a pointer to a pointer to the array itself. Like BSTR pointers, a SAFEARRAY pointer may point to a NULL array if the array has been declared but not yet dimensioned:

```
Dim a() as Integer
```

The pointer itself will never be NULL, however.

The following example determines the upper and lower bounds of an array and then loops through the array producing the sum of the elements in the array:

```
short WINAPI SumArray(
    LPSAFEARRAY *ppsa, long *plResult)
{
    short iElem;
    long lLb, lUb, l, lResult;

    if (*ppsa == NULL) // array has not been initialized
        return -4;

    if ((*ppsa)->cDims != 1) // check number of dimensions
        return -5;

    // get the upper and lower bounds of the array

    if (FAILED(SafeArrayGetLBound(*ppsa, 1, &lLb)) ||
            FAILED(SafeArrayGetUBound(*ppsa, 1, &lUb)))
        return -1;

    // loop through the array and add the elements

    for (l = lLb, lResult = 0; l <= lUb; l++)
    {
        if (FAILED(SafeArrayGetElement(*ppsa, &l, &iElem)))
            return -2;
        lResult += iElem;
    }

    *plResult = lResult;
    return 0;
}
```

Declared and called from Visual Basic:

```
Declare Function SumArray Lib "debug\ADVDLL.DLL" _
    (a() As Integer, r As Long) As Integer

Sub SumArrayTest()
    Dim n(5) As Integer
    Dim result As Long
    For i = 0 To 5
        n(i) = 2
    Next
    x = SumArray(n, result)
    MsgBox x & ":" & result
End Sub
```

Visual Basic does minimal type checking and enforcement on array element size. Because this function was declared as accepting only an array of integers, it is safe to use an integer element in the call to the SafeArrayGetElement function in the DLL. If the function was declared as accepting an array of any type, however, the Visual Basic code might pass an array of long values; in this case, the C-language function would produce incorrect results. If your DLL function must accept an array of any type, you should use an array of variants and check the variant type in the DLL.

Static Arrays

If you declare and dimension an array:

```
Dim x(5) as String
```

The pointer you receive in your C function points to a static array (the fFeatures element of the SAFEARRAY structure has the FADF_STATIC flag set). You can read the array, but you cannot redimension the array or modify the pointer, and you cannot copy over the array. If you need to modify the array in the DLL (to create a new one, for example), you must not dimension it in Visual Basic or pass a variant containing a SAFEARRAY. In the latter case, you can then free the SAFEARRAY and redirect the variant to a new SAFEARRAY created by your DLL.

Allocating Arrays

Your DLL can create new SAFEARRAYs. When you create a new array, you should use a local variable rather than modify a passed-in array pointer. Once the allocation and any subsequent operations on the array are successful, you can assign the passed-in pointer to the local pointer and return from the function.

The following example accepts an array pointer and creates an array containing 10 integer elements:

```
short WINAPI NewArray(LPSAFEARRAY *ppsa)
{
    LPSAFEARRAY psa;
    SAFEARRAYBOUND sa;

    sa.lLbound = 1;
    sa.cElements = 10;

    if (*ppsa == NULL) //array not yet initialized
    {
        if ((psa = SafeArrayCreate(VT_I2, 1, &sa)) == NULL)
            return -2;
        *ppsa = psa;
    }

    if ((*ppsa)->cDims != 1) // check array dimensions
        return -1;

    else    return -3;

    return 0;
}
```

Declared and called from Visual Basic:

```
Declare Function NewArray Lib "debug\ADVDLL.DLL" _
    (a() As Integer) As Integer

Sub NewArrayTest()
    Dim a(1) As Integer
    Dim b() As Integer

    MsgBox NewArray(a) & ":" & LBound(a) & ":" & UBound(a)
    MsgBox NewArray(b) & ":" & LBound(b) & ":" & UBound(b)
End Sub
```

Destroying Arrays

Like BSTRs, SAFEARRAYs must be freed before they can be destroyed. When Visual Basic passes an existing array to your DLL, it is passed as a static array that cannot be destroyed. Your DLL can create its own arrays, however. When you no longer need an array, it should be destroyed.

You must be careful when you destroy an existing array. Freeing the array frees only the array memory; if the array contains any pointers (such as BSTR values), these will not be freed. In this case, you must free each BSTR element individually and then free the array. If you do not know what the array contains, you should probably not free or redimension the array.

Using Arrays of Strings

SAFEARRAYs can contain elements of any allowable type, including BSTRs and user-defined data structures. BSTRs inside arrays should be manipulated with the same OLE Automation functions as ordinary BSTRs. Always remember to free any existing BSTR before allocating a new one, or use the reallocation function. Do not directly modify BSTR data.

The following example creates or redimensions an array of strings. Any existing BSTR data in the array is freed before new data is copied into the array.

```
short WINAPI StringArray(LPSAFEARRAY *ppsa)
{
    unsigned long l;
    BSTR bstr;
    LPSAFEARRAY psa;
    SAFEARRAYBOUND sa;
    HRESULT hr;

    sa.lLbound = 0;
    sa.cElements = 3;

    if (*ppsa == NULL) // array not yet initialized
    {
        if ((psa = SafeArrayCreate(VT_BSTR, 1, &sa)) == NULL)
            return -2;
        *ppsa = psa;
    }
    else
        {
        if ((*ppsa)->cDims != 1) // check array dimensions
            return -1;

        }

    // loop through the array; get each element and free
    // any existing string, then allocate the new string
    // and put it in the array
```

```
    for (1 = sa.lLbound; 1 < sa.cElements; 1++)
    {
        if (FAILED(SafeArrayGetElement(*ppsa, &1, &bstr)))
            return -4;
        SysFreeString(bstr);
        if ((bstr = SysAllocString((BSTR)"test string")) == NULL)
            return -5;
        if (FAILED(SafeArrayPutElement(*ppsa, &1, bstr)))
            return -6;
    }

    return 0;
}
```

Declared and called from Visual Basic:

```
Declare Function StringArray Lib "debug\ADVDLL.DLL" _
    (s() As String) As Integer

Sub StringArrayTest()
    Dim s() As String
    Dim t(1) As String

    t(1) = "Original String"
    MsgBox StringArray(s) & ":" & UBound(s) & ":" & s(1)
    MsgBox StringArray(t) & ":" & UBound(t) & ":" & t(1)
End Sub
```

Using Arrays of Data Structures

You cannot use the SafeArrayCreate function to create a new array of user-defined structures. Instead, you must use the SafeArrayAllocDescriptor function to create the array descriptor, then use the SafeArrayAllocData function to allocate space for the array data, and finally use the SafeArrayAccessData function to return a pointer to the data. The SafeArrayAccessData function locks the array data; when you are done with the array, you should call the SafeArrayUnaccessData function to unlock it.

You cannot replace an existing array, so if your Visual Basic code passes a dimensioned array, you must redimension it. Remember to free any existing BSTR pointers in the array before overwriting them.

The following example creates or redimensions an array of data structures and then copies an array of strings into the structures, adding the string length to each structure. Any existing BSTR data in the array is freed before new data is copied into the array.

```c
short WINAPI StructArray(LPSAFEARRAY *ppsaArg,
    LPSAFEARRAY *ppsaStr)
{
    ARG *parg;
    SAFEARRAY *psa;
    BSTR *pbstr;
    unsigned long i, cElements;
    #define BUFF_SIZE 1024
    TCHAR szBuff[BUFF_SIZE];

    if (*ppsaStr == NULL)
        return -1;

    cElements = (*ppsaStr)->rgsabound[0].cElements;

    if (*ppsaArg == NULL) // create a new array
    {

        if (FAILED(SafeArrayAllocDescriptor(1, &psa)))
            return -3;

        // set up the SAFEARRAY structure
        // and allocate data space

        psa->fFeatures = 0;
        psa->cbElements = sizeof(ARG);
        psa->rgsabound[0].cElements = cElements;
        psa->rgsabound[0].lLbound = (*ppsaStr)->rgsabound[0].lLbound;

        if (FAILED(SafeArrayAllocData(psa)))
        {
            SafeArrayDestroyDescriptor(psa);
            return -4;
        }

        // get a pointer to the new data

        if (FAILED(SafeArrayAccessData(psa,
                (void HUGEP* FAR*)&parg)))
        {
            SafeArrayDestroy(psa);
            return -5;
```

```
        }
    }
    else // fail since we can't redimension
    {
            return -6;

        // get a pointer to the old data

        if (FAILED(SafeArrayAccessData(*ppsaArg,
                (void HUGEP* FAR*)&parg)))
            return -7;
    }

    // get a pointer to the string array data

    if (FAILED(SafeArrayAccessData(*ppsaStr,
            (void HUGEP* FAR*)&pbstr)))
        return -8;

    // allocate strings in the structure array and
    // fill them with strings from the string array.
    // free any old BSTRs in the structure

    for (i = 0; i < cElements; i++)
    {
        SysFreeString(parg[i].bstr);//SysStringByteLen(pbstr[i])
        MultiByteToWideChar(CP_ACP, MB_PRECOMPOSED, (LPSTR)pbstr[i], -1,
            szBuff, sizeof(szBuff));
        parg[i].bstr = SysAllocString(szBuff);
        parg[i].i = SysStringLen(parg[i].bstr);
    }

    // release pointers and move the structure
    // array pointer to the new array if we created one

    SafeArrayUnaccessData(*ppsaStr);

    if (*ppsaArg == NULL)
    {
        SafeArrayUnaccessData(psa);
        *ppsaArg = psa;
    }
    else
        SafeArrayUnaccessData(*ppsaArg);

    return 0;
}
```

Declared and called from Visual Basic:

```
Declare Function StructArray Lib "debug\ADVDLL.DLL" _
    (x() As ARG, s() As String) As Integer

Sub StructArrayTest()
    Dim x() As ARG
    Dim s(1 To 4) As String
    s(1) = "yellow"
    s(2) = "orange"
    s(3) = "blue"
    s(4) = "green"
    n = StructArray(x, s)
    If n = 0 Then
        Worksheets(1).Activate
        Range("a1:c25").Clear
        For i = LBound(x) To UBound(x)
            Cells(i + 1, 1) = i
            Cells(i + 1, 2) = x(i).str
            Cells(i + 1, 3) = x(i).i
        Next
    Else
        MsgBox "StructArray failed, returned" & n
    End If
End Sub
```

You will note in this code that we use MultiByteToWideChar on the string before we place it into the structure. This is the one exception to the rule that Excel passes and returns ANSI strings. Strings returned to Excel inside a structure must be UNICODE. This function converts the strings to UNICODE before creating a BSTR to place in the structure.

Using the C API and Visual Basic

When you call a DLL function from Visual Basic in Microsoft Excel, the DLL function can use the Microsoft Excel Applications Programming Interface (C API) functions to call back into Microsoft Excel. You cannot use the C API across processes. The DLL using the C API must be called from Visual Basic running in Microsoft Excel (a DLL called from Microsoft Project or Microsoft Visual Basic or another Microsoft Office application cannot call the C API). In addition, the C API can be called only after Microsoft Excel has called the DLL. This qualification is met when Visual Basic in Microsoft Excel calls the DLL, and the DLL in turn calls the C API. When the DLL function is called by an external event (such as a DDE command from another application or a Windows timer), the DLL function cannot call the C API.

For more information about using the C API, see Chapter 7, "The Microsoft Excel Applications Programming Interface" and Chapter 8, "Applications Programming Interface Function Reference."

Type Libraries

You can create a type library for your DLL. The type library can contain constant and function declarations and other information about the DLL. A type library can be compiled into your DLL as a resource. Once you have created a type library, you can use the References command on the Tools menu in Microsoft Excel to load the type library. Once loaded, the constant and function declarations are available in Visual Basic without Declare statements.

Visual Basic in Microsoft Excel does not support user-defined data-structure declarations in type libraries. (User-defined data structures are those declared with the Visual Basic "Type" statement or the C/C++ "struct" statement.) To use the structures in your Visual Basic code, you will have to add their declarations to the module.

For more information about creating type libraries, see Chapter 7 in Volume 2 of the *OLE 2 Programmer's Reference.*

CHAPTER 6

Using the OLE 2 IDispatch Interface

Microsoft Excel exposes its objects as OLE Automation objects. OLE 2 allows another application, called an *OLE Automation Controller,* to access the exposed objects and use their properties and methods with the IDispatch interface or by means of vtbl binding. This chapter describes techniques you can use to write an OLE Automation Controller in standard C that can be used to manipulate objects, properties, and methods in Microsoft Excel.

In Chapters 7 and 8, you will see how an application can use the C API interface to call into Microsoft Excel. The C API interface exposes Microsoft Excel macro-language functions and commands. The OLE 2 IDispatch interface allows an application to call Microsoft Excel and manipulate any object, property, or method that can be called from Visual Basic.

This chapter does not discuss techniques for implementing an OLE Server (an application that creates new OLE objects and exposes their properties and methods using an IDispatch interface) or techniques for using vtbl binding. Microsoft Excel operates as both an OLE Server (Microsoft Excel creates objects that can be accessed by other applications) and as an OLE Automation Controller (Visual Basic in Microsoft Excel can access objects in other applications that support OLE Automation, and in fact, Visual Basic uses OLE Automation to call Microsoft Excel properties and methods). Vtbl binding requires an application to support dual interfaces that can be used by either IDispatch or vtbl calls. Of the 193 interfaces in Microsoft Excel, only 19 of them are marked as dual and can be used for vtbl binding. Becuase of the relatively low number of interfaces, which does not include the Range object, it is doubtful that many developers will eschew IDispatch for vtbl binding.

The examples in this chapter were built and tested with Microsoft Windows 95 and Windows NT Workstation version 4.0 (SP2), using Microsoft Visual C++ version 4.2b. Visual C++ version 4.2b includes the OLE 2 header files and libraries required to create OLE Automation Controller applications. If you use another C compiler, you will also need the Microsoft Win32 SDK.

In addition to the Help provided with Visual C++ and the OLE 2 SDK, Volume 2 of the *OLE 2 Programmer's Reference* provides detailed information about OLE Automation and the IDispatch interface. This chapter focuses mainly on implementation details for using the IDispatch interface with Microsoft Excel. You should use the *OLE 2 Programmer's Reference* with this chapter to understand the IDispatch interface.

IDispatch Step by Step

Using IDispatch to access exposed OLE Automation objects involves the following steps:

1. Initialize OLE using the OleInitialize function.

2. Create an instance of the object you wish to access using the CoCreateInstance function.

   If the object's application is not yet running, OLE starts it and initializes the object. Note that if OLE starts the application, it may not be visible. With Microsoft Excel, you must set the Visible property for the application to make it visible.

3. Obtain a reference to the object's IDispatch interface using the QueryInterface member function.

   With Microsoft Excel, you can combine steps 2 and 3 and obtain the IDispatch reference directly from the CoCreateInstance function.

4. Use the GetIDsOfNames member function to obtain the DISPID values for the desired method or property exposed in the object's IDispatch interface.

5. Use the Invoke member function to access the method or property.

6. Terminate the object by invoking the appropriate method in its IDispatch interface.

7. Uninitialize OLE, using the OleUninitialize function.

Complete information about accessing OLE Automation objects appears in Chapter 3 in Volume 2 of the *OLE 2 Programmer's Reference*.

C++ and C Programming

While the examples in the *OLE 2 Programmer's Reference* were written in C++, the examples in this chapter were written in standard C. The following list describes some of the differences you will encounter.

- Reference data types (such as REFCLSID and REFIID) must be used in standard C with a prepended ampersand (&). In C++, these data types are often used with C++ references, so the ampersand is not required. Because references do not exist in standard C, an explicit address-of operator (the ampersand) is required.

  For example, the CoCreateInstance function uses both a class ID reference (REFCLSID) and an interface ID reference (REFIID) as arguments. In C++, the call to this function can be written as:

  ```
  CoCreateInstance(CLSID_ExcelApp, NULL, CLSCTX_LOCAL_SERVER,
      IID_IDispatch, &pdispExcelApp);
  ```

  In standard C, however, you must use the address-of operator with the first and fourth arguments:

  ```
  CoCreateInstance(&CLSID_ExcelApp, NULL, CLSCTX_LOCAL_SERVER,
      &IID_IDispatch, &pdispExcelApp);
  ```

- In C++, you can call a class member function directly using the member-selection operator (->). In standard C, classes are defined as structures; each structure contains an lpVtbl element that is a pointer to the table of class functions. You must first access the lpVtbl element of the structure and then call the function using a pointer. In addition, the first argument to the function must be the object pointer itself.

  For example, when you are done with an object you have created with the CoCreateInstance function, you should free it with the Release function. In C++, you can call this function directly:

  ```
  pdisp->Release();
  ```

  In standard C, you call the function using the lpVtbl pointer and pass in the dispatch object as the first argument:

  ```
  (*(pdisp->lpVtbl->Release))(pdisp);
  ```

- In C++, you can use the Microsoft Foundation Class library and the ClassWizard in Visual C++ to access OLE methods and properties as member functions of a base class. This simplifies much of the work required to access OLE objects with the IDispatch interface. For more information about using the ClassWizard, see the Visual C++ documentation.

Microsoft Excel Specifics

This section describes some differences between a generic implementation of an OLE Automation Controller and a controller specifically designed to work with Microsoft Excel.

IDispatch and IUnknown

Because Microsoft Excel supports the IDispatch interface, your application does not need to get the IUnknown interface and then query Microsoft Excel for the IDispatch interface. You can use the CoCreateInstance function to directly access the IDispatch interface because you know Microsoft Excel supports IDispatch.

Passed-in Objects

When Visual Basic in Microsoft Excel passes an object reference to your DLL function, the DLL can go directly to step 4 in the process shown in the section on Idispatch Step by Step and access the IDispatch interface directly from the object reference. The PropertyPut and PropertyGet examples in the following section show how this is done in a DLL.

Variant Data Types

Visual Basic in Microsoft Excel does not support all the data types supported by the VARIANT structure. The following table shows the allowed data types and their value constants. Microsoft Excel never returns a variant with a data type not shown on this list.

Data Type	Variant Constant
Boolean	VT_BOOL
Currency (scaled integer)	VT_CY
Date	VT_DATE
Double (double-precision floating-point)	VT_R8
Integer	VT_I2
Long (long integer)	VT_I4
Object	VT_DISPATCH
Single (single-precision floating-point)	VT_R4
String	VT_BSTR

Microsoft Excel coerces other data types into one of the supported data types.

Exception Handling

When an error occurs during the execution of the IDispatch Invoke function, Microsoft Excel returns an error code or returns the DISP_E_EXCEPTION error and places information about the error in an EXCEPINFO structure. The error code in the exception info structure will be one of the trappable error values listed in the Visual Basic Help topic "Trappable Errors." When the exception info structure is filled in, your application is responsible for freeing the strings in the structure. A memory leak will result if you do not free the strings before reusing the structure or exiting the application.

The ShowException function discussed later in this chapter is an example of an error-handling function for an OLE Automation Controller. Notice that the Invoke function frees the exception-info strings before it returns.

PropertyPut and PropertyGet

The simplest example of a Microsoft Excel OLE Automation Controller is a DLL function that takes an object as an argument, obtains a DISPID for the object's Value property, and then uses PropertyPut or PropertyGet to set or get the value of the object. This simple example does not need the CoCreateInstance and QueryInterface functions, because the function can call the IDispatch interface directly with the object reference.

The CalcCells function is an example of a simple OLE Automation Controller. The function accepts a Range object as its first argument and a variant as its second argument. The function uses the PropertyGet method to obtain the value of the range; if the range contains more than one cell, the value is returned as an array. The function iterates the array, adding the value from each cell to a total (it attempts to coerce any values that are not doubles). Once the total is obtained, the function places the result in the second argument; if the argument specifies another range, the function uses the PropertyPut method to set the range value.

```
SCODE WINAPI CalcCells(LPDISPATCH *ppdsSourceRange,
    VARIANTARG *pvtResult)
{
    HRESULT hr;
    EXCEPINFO excep;
    ULONG cElements, i;
    DISPPARAMS dispparams;
    unsigned int uiArgErr, cDims;
    DISPID dispidValue, dispidPut;
    VARIANTARG vSource, vResult, vTemp, *pvdata;
```

```
        LPOLESTR lpszName = L"Value";

        hr = (*((*ppdsSourceRange)->lpVtbl->GetIDsOfNames))
                (*ppdsSourceRange, &IID_NULL, &lpszName,
                1, LOCALE_SYSTEM_DEFAULT, &dispidValue);
        if (hr != NOERROR)
            goto calc_error;

        // PropertyGet has no arguments

        dispparams.cArgs = 0;
        dispparams.cNamedArgs = 0;

        // Invoke PropertyGet

        hr = (*((*ppdsSourceRange)->lpVtbl->Invoke))
                (*ppdsSourceRange, dispidValue, &IID_NULL,
                LOCALE_SYSTEM_DEFAULT, DISPATCH_PROPERTYGET,
                &dispparams, &vSource, &excep, &uiArgErr);
        if (hr != NOERROR)
            goto calc_error;

        // initialize the result variant

        VariantInit(&vResult);
        vResult.vt = VT_R8;
        vResult.dblVal = 0.0;

        // If there is more than one cell in the source range,
        // it's a variant containing an array.
        // Access this using the SafeArray functions

        if (vSource.vt & VT_ARRAY)
        {
            // iterate the dimensions; number of elements is x*y*z
            for (cDims = 0, cElements = 1;
                    cDims < vSource.parray->cDims; cDims++)
                cElements *= vSource.parray->rgsabound[cDims].cElements;

            // get a pointer to the data
            hr = SafeArrayAccessData(vSource.parray, (LPVOID)&pvdata);
            if (hr != NOERROR)
                goto calc_error;

            // iterate the data. try to convert non-double values to double
        for (i = 0; i < cElements; i++)
        {
```

```
            vTemp = pvdata[i];
                if (vTemp.vt != VT_R8)
                {
                    hr = VariantChangeType(&vTemp,
                        &vTemp, 0, VT_R8);
                    if (hr != NOERROR)
                        goto calc_error;
                }

                // add the data. this is where we could
                // add a more complicated function
                vResult.dblVal += vTemp.dblVal;
            }

        SafeArrayUnaccessData(vSource.parray);
    }
    else
    {
        // only one cell in the source range.
        // if it's not a double, try to convert it.
        if (vSource.vt != VT_R8)
        {
            hr = VariantChangeType(&vSource, &vSource, 0, VT_R8);
            if (hr != NOERROR)
                goto calc_error;
        }
        vResult = vSource;
    }

    // if the result value is an object,
    // get the DISPID for its Value property

    if (pvtResult->vt == VT_DISPATCH)
    {
        hr = (*(pvtResult->pdispVal->lpVtbl->GetIDsOfNames))
                (pvtResult->pdispVal, &IID_NULL, &lpszName,
                1, LOCALE_SYSTEM_DEFAULT, &dispidValue);
        if (hr != NOERROR)
            goto calc_error;

        dispidPut = DISPID_PROPERTYPUT;

        dispparams.rgdispidNamedArgs = &dispidPut;
        dispparams.rgvarg = &vResult;
        dispparams.cArgs = 1;
        dispparams.cNamedArgs = 1;

        // Invoke PropertyPut
```

```
            hr = (*(pvtResult->pdispVal->lpVtbl->Invoke))
                    (pvtResult->pdispVal, dispidValue, &IID_NULL,
                    LOCALE_SYSTEM_DEFAULT, DISPATCH_PROPERTYPUT,
                    &dispparams, NULL, &excep, &uiArgErr);
        if (hr != NOERROR)
            goto calc_error;
    }
    else
    {
        // Result is not an object; it's a variable passed by reference.
        // Must free any existing allocation in the variant.
        // The ReleaseVariant function is in dispargs.c

        ReleaseVariant(pvtResult);
        *pvtResult = vResult;
    }

    return 0;

calc_error:
    return GetScode(hr);
}
```

This is a simple example, but it shows the setup for PropertyPut and PropertyGet and how the range value is returned as an array. You could write a more complex data-handling function around this simple example to implement a specialized DLL function. Remember that any variants your DLL function allocates (strings or arrays) must be freed to prevent memory leaks.

The code for this function is included on the samples disk in the SAMPLES\SDISP directory. This directory also includes the make file and module-definition file required to build SDISP.DLL. Once SDISP.DLL is available, you can call this function from Microsoft Excel, as shown in the following example:

```
Declare Function CalcCells Lib "SDISP.DLL" _
    (source As Range, result As Variant) As Integer

Sub Button1_Click()
    Worksheets(1).Activate
    Range("A4").Clear
    CalcCells Range("A1:B3"), Range("A4")
End Sub
```

Dispargs.c

Method calls more complex than the PropertyGet and PropertyPut examples shown in the preceding section require extensive setup work. Before you can call the Invoke function, each argument must be placed into the argument array. After the Invoke function call, any variant arguments that were allocated (created BSTR or SAFEARRAY values) must be freed. Creating arrays of BSTR values requires repetitive allocation, testing, and error handling.

The functions provided in dispargs.c on the sample disk (in the SAMPLE\AUTOXL directory) were written to simplify these tasks. The following procedure shows how to use these functions:

- Use the ClearAllArgs function to clear and reset the argument array.
- Use the AddArgument*Type* argument-constructor function(s) to set the appropriate argument(s).
- Use the Invoke function to invoke the method (note that this is the Invoke function in dispargs.c, not the Invoke function provided by OLE 2).
- Free any arguments not automatically freed by the Invoke function.
- Free the return value if a return value was requested. Use the ReleaseVariant function to free variant return values and arguments.

The following sections discuss the argument-constructor functions and the Invoke function in more detail.

Argument Information

The argument-constructor functions in dispargs.c place argument information in global arrays.

```
int        g_iArgCount;
int        g_iNamedArgCount;
VARIANTARG g_aVargs[MAX_DISP_ARGS];
DISPID     g_aDispIds[MAX_DISP_ARGS + 1];
LPOLESTR   g_alpszArgNames[MAX_DISP_ARGS + 1];
WORD       g_awFlags[MAX_DISP_ARGS];
```

The Vargs array contains the argument values; the lpszArgNames array contains the argument names (unnamed arguments have NULL names); and the wFlags array contains argument flags (such as NOFREEVARIANT). The information in these arrays is used to build the argument list for an IDispatch interface call. The arrays in dispargs.c are statically allocated to reduce complexity; this places a limit on the number of arguments that can be passed. To remove this limit and manage memory more effectively, the code could be modified to allocate memory dynamically.

When the Invoke function is called, it uses the IDispatch::GetIDsOfNames function to convert the names in the lpszArgNames array into DISPID values for the IDispatch::Invoke function. The resulting DISPID values are placed in the DispIds array. The first element of the DispIds array is the DISPID of the method or property, and the first element of the lpszArgNames array is the method or property name.

Utility Functions

Dispargs.c also includes utility functions used to manage variants and argument arrays. The ClearVariant function sets a variant to zero. This function ignores the current contents of the variant. If you are unsure of the current contents of the variant, you should call the ReleaseVariant function before you clear the variant.

```
void ClearVariant(VARIANTARG *pvarg)
{
    pvarg->vt = VT_EMPTY;
    pvarg->wReserved1 = 0;
    pvarg->wReserved2 = 0;
    pvarg->wReserved3 = 0;
    pvarg->lVal = 0;
}
```

The ClearAllArgs function releases any memory in use by the argument array and resets the argument counters. Because these arrays are static, it is important to call the ClearAllArgs function before you begin to set up arguments.

```
void ClearAllArgs()
{
    int i;
```

```
    for (i = 0; i < g_iArgCount; i++)
    {
        if (g_awFlags[i] & DISPARG_NOFREEVARIANT)
            // free the variant's contents based on type
            ClearVariant(&g_aVargs[i]);
        else
            ReleaseVariant(&g_aVargs[i]);
    }

    g_iArgCount = 0;
    g_iNamedArgCount = 0;
}
```

The ReleaseVariant function releases any memory allocated for a variant (such as a variant containing a string or array). Use this function anytime you set a variant if you are unsure of its current contents. For example, a memory leak will result if you set a variant that currently contains a string without first releasing the string.

This function supports the following data types: integers, Booleans, doubles, objects, strings, and arrays of any of the listed data types.

```
void ReleaseVariant(VARIANTARG *pvarg)
{
    VARTYPE vt;
    VARIANTARG _huge *pvargArray;
    long lLBound, lUBound, l;

    vt = pvarg->vt & 0xfff;      // mask off flags

    // check if an array.  If so, free its contents,
    // then the array itself.
    if (V_ISARRAY(pvarg))
    {
        // variant arrays are all this routine currently knows about.
        // Since a variant can contain anything (even other arrays),
        // call ourselves recursively.
        if (vt == VT_VARIANT)
        {
            SafeArrayGetLBound(pvarg->parray, 1, &lLBound);
            SafeArrayGetUBound(pvarg->parray, 1, &lUBound);

            if (lUBound > lLBound)
            {
                lUBound -= lLBound;

                SafeArrayAccessData(pvarg->parray, &pvargArray);
```

```
                            for (l = 0; l < lUBound; l++)
                            {
                                ReleaseVariant(pvargArray);
                                pvargArray++;
                            }

                            SafeArrayUnaccessData(pvarg->parray);
                        }
                    }
                    else
                    {
                        MessageBox(g_hwndApp, L"ReleaseVariant: Array contains
                            non-variant type", g_szAppTitle, MB_OK | MB_ICONSTOP);
                    }

                    // Free the array itself.
                    SafeArrayDestroy(pvarg->parray);
                }
                else
                {
                    switch (vt)
                    {
                        case VT_DISPATCH:
                            (*(pvarg->pdispVal->lpVtbl->Release))(pvarg->pdispVal);
                            break;

                        case VT_BSTR:
                            SysFreeString(pvarg->bstrVal);
                            break;

                        case VT_I2:
                        case VT_BOOL:
                        case VT_R8:
                        case VT_ERROR:      // to avoid erroring on an error return
                                            // from Excel
                            // no work for these types
                            break;

                        default:
                            MessageBox(g_hwndApp, L"ReleaseVariant: Unknown type",
                                g_szAppTitle, MB_OK | MB_ICONSTOP);
                            break;
                    }
                }

                ClearVariant(pvarg);
            }
```

Argument-Constructor Functions

The argument-constructor functions in dispargs.c are used to set up an argument list before you use the Invoke function. Each argument-constructor function adds a single argument of a specific type to the list of arguments (the global argument arrays). If appropriate, memory may be allocated to represent the argument. This memory will be automatically freed when the ClearAllArgs function is called unless you specify the NOFREEVARIANT flag for the argument. If you specify this flag, it is your responsibility to free the memory allocated for or contained within the argument.

For example, if a method has one Boolean argument and two integer arguments, you would call AddArgumentBool, AddArgumentInt2, AddArgumentInt2. Each AddArgument*Type* function accepts the name of the argument, a flag that tells the function whether the argument should be freed after use, and the value of the argument. Functions are provided for the following data types: integers, Booleans, doubles, objects, strings, and arrays of strings. IDispatch is capable of supporting other data types; you can add an argument handler for a data type by writing the appropriate AddArgument*Type* function and adding argument-release code to the ReleaseVariant function.

Arguments may be named. The name string must be a C-style (null-terminated) string, and it is owned by the caller. If the string is dynamically allocated, the caller is responsible for freeing the string.

All named arguments must be set before any positional arguments. The following example shows a Visual Basic call and its equivalent call using the AddArgumentInt2 function (the flags argument is omitted for clarity). Notice that the arguments are added in reverse order (the last argument is added first).

Visual Basic

```
SomeMethod 5, 2, named1 := 3, named2 := 4
```

Dispargs

```
AddArgumentInt2("named2", 4);
AddArgumentInt2("named1", 3);
AddArgumentInt2(NULL, 2);
AddArgumentInt2(NULL, 5);
```

If you are using PropertyPut, use a NULL name and add the value to be set as the argument.

All argument-constructor functions use the AddArgumentCommon function to set the name and value of the argument and increment the argument count.

```
void AddArgumentCommon(LPOLESTR lpszArgName, WORD wFlags, VARTYPE vt)
{
    ClearVariant(&g_aVargs[g_iArgCount]);

    g_aVargs[g_iArgCount].vt = vt;
    g_awFlags[g_iArgCount] = wFlags;

    if (lpszArgName != NULL)
    {
        g_alpszArgNames[g_iNamedArgCount + 1] = lpszArgName;
        g_iNamedArgCount++;
    }
}
```

Object Arguments

```
BOOL AddArgumentDispatch(LPOLESTR lpszArgName, WORD wFlags,
    IDispatch * pdisp)
{
    AddArgumentCommon(lpszArgName, wFlags, VT_DISPATCH);
    g_aVargs[g_iArgCount++].pdispVal = pdisp;
    return TRUE;
}
```

Integer Arguments

```
BOOL AddArgumentInt2(LPOLESTR lpszArgName, WORD wFlags, int i)
{
    AddArgumentCommon(lpszArgName, wFlags, VT_I2);
    g_aVargs[g_iArgCount++].iVal = i;
    return TRUE;
}
```

Boolean Arguments

```
BOOL AddArgumentBool(LPOLESTR lpszArgName, WORD wFlags, BOOL b)
{
    AddArgumentCommon(lpszArgName, wFlags, VT_BOOL);
    // Note the variant representation of True as -1
    g_aVargs[g_iArgCount++].boolVal = b ? -1 : 0;
    return TRUE;
}
```

Double Arguments

```
BOOL AddArgumentDouble(LPOLESTR lpszArgName, WORD wFlags, double d)
{
    AddArgumentCommon(lpszArgName, wFlags, VT_R8);
    g_aVargs[g_iArgCount++].dblVal = d;
    return TRUE;
}
```

String Arguments

OLE and IDispatch use a BSTR for strings (for more information about BSTR values, see Chapter 6 in Volume 2 of the *OLE 2 Programmer's Reference*). The AddArgumentCString function copies the passed-in C-style string into a BSTR. You must not set the NOFREEVARIANT flag for C-string arguments; the allocated BSTR should be freed by the ReleaseVariant function.

```
BOOL AddArgumentCString(LPOLESTR lpszArgName, WORD wFlags,
    LPOLESTR lpsz)
{
    BSTR b;

    b = SysAllocString(lpsz);
    if (!b)
        return FALSE;
    AddArgumentCommon(lpszArgName, wFlags, VT_BSTR);
    g_aVargs[g_iArgCount++].bstrVal = b;
    return TRUE;
}
```

If you already have a BSTR argument, you should use the AddArgumentBSTR function to avoid making an extra copy of the BSTR. With BSTR arguments, you should set the NOFREEVARIANT flag unless you want the ReleaseVariant function to free the passed-in BSTR. (If you plan to use the BSTR after the Invoke function call, you should set this flag.) Be aware that the BSTR must contain a UNICODE string as opposed to the ANSI string required in Win16.

```
BOOL AddArgumentBSTR(LPOLESTR lpszArgName, WORD wFlags, BSTR bstr)
{
    AddArgumentCommon(lpszArgName, wFlags, VT_BSTR);
    g_aVargs[g_iArgCount++].bstrVal = bstr;
    return TRUE;
}
```

String-Array Arguments

The following function copies an array of C-style strings into a one-dimensional array of string variants. You should allow the ReleaseVariant function to free the allocated strings; do not set the NOFREEVARIANT flag.

```
BOOL AddArgumentCStringArray(LPOLESTR lpszArgName, WORD wFlags,
    LPOLESTR *paszStrings, int iCount)
{
    SAFEARRAY *psa;
    SAFEARRAYBOUND saBound;
    VARIANTARG *pvargBase;
    VARIANTARG *pvarg;
    int i, j;

    saBound.lLbound = 0;
    saBound.cElements = iCount;

    psa = SafeArrayCreate(VT_VARIANT, 1, &saBound);
    if (psa == NULL)
        return FALSE;

    SafeArrayAccessData(psa, & (VARIANTARG _huge *) pvargBase);

    pvarg = pvargBase;
    for (i = 0; i < iCount; i++)
    {
        // copy each string in the list of strings
        ClearVariant(pvarg);
        pvarg->vt = VT_BSTR;
        if ((pvarg->bstrVal = SysAllocString(*paszStrings++)) == NULL)
        {
            // memory failure:  back out and free strings alloc'ed up to
            // now, and then the array itself.
            pvarg = pvargBase;
            for (j = 0; j < i; j++)
            {
                SysFreeString(pvarg->bstrVal);
                pvarg++;
            }
            SafeArrayDestroy(psa);
            return FALSE;
        }
        pvarg++;
    }
```

```
SafeArrayUnaccessData(psa);

// With all memory allocated, set up this argument
AddArgumentCommon(lpszArgName, wFlags, VT_VARIANT | VT_ARRAY);
g_aVargs[g_iArgCount++].parray = psa;
return TRUE;
}
```

The Invoke Function

Once you have set up the argument arrays with the argument-constructor functions, you can use the Invoke function to call a method or to set or get a property.

This function accepts a pointer to the object; the name of the method or property; a pointer to a location for the return value; a flag indicating whether you are calling a method, setting a property, or getting the value of a property; and a flag indicating whether the Invoke function should clear the arguments when it returns.

The Invoke function returns True if the call succeeded and False if an error occurred. A message box will be displayed explaining the error unless the DISP_NOSHOWEXCEPTIONS flag is specified. Errors result from unrecognized method or property names, bad argument names, invalid data types, or run-time exceptions defined by the recipient of the IDispatch call.

After the IDispatch call, the Invoke function calls the ClearAllArgs function to reset the argument list if the DISP_FREEARGS flag is specified. If this flag is not specified, it is up to the caller to call ClearAllArgs.

The return value is placed in the pvargReturn variable, which is allocated by the caller. If no return value is required, this argument should be NULL. It is up to the caller to free the return value (use the ReleaseVariant function).

This function calls IDispatch::GetIDsOfNames every time it is called. This is not very efficient if the same method or property is invoked multiple times, because the DISPID value for a particular method or property will remain the same during the lifetime of an IDispatch object. Modifications could be made to this code to cache DISPID values. If the target application is always the same, you could store the DISPID values at compile time (an application will return the same DISPID values in different sessions). Eliminating the extra cross-process GetIDsOfNames calls can result in a significant time savings.

```
BOOL Invoke(IDispatch *pdisp, LPOLESTR szMember,
            VARIANTARG * pvargReturn,
            WORD wInvokeAction, WORD wFlags)
{
```

```
HRESULT hr;
DISPPARAMS dispparams;
unsigned int uiArgErr;
EXCEPINFO excep;

// Get the IDs for the member and its arguments.
// GetIDsOfNames expects the member name as the
// first name, followed by argument names (if any).
g_alpszArgNames[0] = szMember;
hr = (*(pdisp->lpVtbl->GetIDsOfNames))(pdisp, &IID_NULL,
    g_alpszArgNames,1 + g_iNamedArgCount, LOCALE_SYSTEM_DEFAULT,
    g_aDispIds);
if (FAILED(hr))
{
    if (!(wFlags & DISP_NOSHOWEXCEPTIONS))
        ShowException(szMember, hr, NULL, 0);
    return FALSE;
}

if (pvargReturn != NULL)
    ClearVariant(pvargReturn);

// if doing a property put(ref),
// we need to adjust the first argument to have a
// named arg of DISPID_PROPERTYPUT.
if (wInvokeAction & (DISPATCH_PROPERTYPUT |
    DISPATCH_PROPERTYPUTREF))
{
    g_iNamedArgCount = 1;
    g_aDispIds[1] = DISPID_PROPERTYPUT;
    pvargReturn = NULL;
}

dispparams.rgdispidNamedArgs = g_aDispIds + 1;
dispparams.rgvarg = g_aVargs;
dispparams.cArgs = g_iArgCount;
dispparams.cNamedArgs = g_iNamedArgCount;

excep.pfnDeferredFillIn = NULL;

hr = (*(pdisp->lpVtbl->Invoke))(pdisp, g_aDispIds[0], &IID_NULL,
    LOCALE_SYSTEM_DEFAULT, wInvokeAction, &dispparams, pvargReturn,
    &excep, &uiArgErr);

if (wFlags & DISP_FREEARGS)
    ClearAllArgs();

if (FAILED(hr))
```

```
        {
            // display the exception information if appropriate:
            if (!(wFlags & DISP_NOSHOWEXCEPTIONS))
                ShowException(szMember, hr, &excep, uiArgErr);

            // free exception structure information
            SysFreeString(excep.bstrSource);
            SysFreeString(excep.bstrDescription);
            SysFreeString(excep.bstrHelpFile);

            return FALSE;
        }

        return TRUE;
}
```

The ShowException Function

If an error occurs as the result of an Invoke function call, the ShowException function attempts to display information about the exception. Note that this function uses a global window handle, which must be set before this function can be called.

```
void ShowException(LPOLESTR szMember, HRESULT hr, EXCEPINFO *pexcep,
    unsigned int uiArgErr)
{
    TCHAR szBuf[512];

    switch (GetScode(hr))
    {
        case DISP_E_UNKNOWNNAME:
            wsprintf(szBuf, L"%s: Unknown name or named argument.",
                szMember);
            break;

        case DISP_E_BADPARAMCOUNT:
            wsprintf(szBuf, L"%s: Incorrect number of arguments.",
                szMember);
            break;

        case DISP_E_EXCEPTION:
            wsprintf(szBuf, L"%s: Error %d: ", szMember, pexcep->wCode);
            if (pexcep->bstrDescription != NULL)
                lstrcat(szBuf, pexcep->bstrDescription);
            else
                lstrcat(szBuf, L"<<No Description>>");
            break;
```

```
        case DISP_E_MEMBERNOTFOUND:
            wsprintf(szBuf, L"%s: method or property not found.",
                szMember);
            break;

        case DISP_E_OVERFLOW:
            wsprintf(szBuf, L"%s: Overflow while coercing argument
                values.", szMember);
            break;

        case DISP_E_NONAMEDARGS:
            wsprintf(szBuf, L"%s: Object implementation does not support
                named arguments.", szMember);
            break;

        case DISP_E_UNKNOWNLCID:
            wsprintf(szBuf, L"%s: The locale ID is unknown.", szMember);
            break;

        case DISP_E_PARAMNOTOPTIONAL:
            wsprintf(szBuf, L"%s: Missing a required parameter.",
                szMember);
            break;

        case DISP_E_PARAMNOTFOUND:
            wsprintf(szBuf, L"%s: Argument not found, argument %d.",
                szMember, uiArgErr);
            break;

        case DISP_E_TYPEMISMATCH:
            wsprintf(szBuf, L"%s: Type mismatch, argument %d.",
                szMember, uiArgErr);
            break;

        default:
            wsprintf(szBuf, L"%s: Unknown error occured.", szMember);
            break;
    }

    MessageBox(g_hwndApp, szBuf, g_szAppTitle, MB_OK | MB_ICONSTOP);
}
```

AutoXL: A Detailed Example

AutoXL.exe, included on the sample disk (in the SAMPLE\AUTOXL directory), uses the dispargs functions to implement a more complex OLE Automation Controller. AutoXL uses Microsoft Excel to create a pie chart. It starts Microsoft Excel, adds a new workbook, inserts data into the first worksheet in the workbook, and then uses the ChartWizard method to create a pie chart. The following Visual Basic code shows the equivalent work:

```
Set wb = Application.Workbooks.Add(template := xlWorksheet)
Set ws = wb.Worksheets(1)
ws.Range("A1:D1").Value = Array("North", "South", "East", "West")
ws.Range("A2") = 5.2
ws.Range("B2") = 10
ws.Range("C2") = 8
ws.Range("D2") = 20
Set sourceRange = ws.Range("A1:D2")
Set crt = wb.Charts.Add
crt.ChartWizard source := sourceRange, gallery := xl3DPie, _
    format := 7, plotBy := xlRows, categoryLabels := 1, _
    seriesLabels := 0, hasLegend := 2, title := "Sales Percentages"
wb.Saved = True
' So that Excel won't ask whether to save this document on close.
```

Wincode.c

The code in wincode.c creates the main window and message queue for AutoXL. This is a fairly typical window-management code module; the interesting portion of this code occurs in the WinMain function. Notice that it increases the size of the message queue and that it initializes and uninitializes OLE.

```
int WINAPI WinMain(HINSTANCE hInst, HINSTANCE hPrevInst, LPSTR lpszCmd,
int iCmdShow)
{
    MSG msg;
    int iMsg = 96;

    // for OLE, enlarge message queue to be as large as possible
    while (!SetMessageQueue(iMsg) && (iMsg -= 8));

    // various initialization, including OLE
    g_hInstApp = hInst;
    msg.wParam = FALSE;

    if (!InitApplication(hPrevInst))
        goto ExitApplication;
```

```
        if (!InitOLE())
            goto ExitApplication;

        if (!InitInstance(iCmdShow))
            goto ExitApplication;

        // message loop
        while (GetMessage(&msg, NULL, (unsigned int) NULL, (unsigned int)
            NULL))
        {
            TranslateMessage(&msg);
            DispatchMessage(&msg);
        }

ExitApplication:
        // make sure OLE is cleaned up if init was done
        if (g_fOLEInit)
            OleUninitialize();

        return msg.wParam;
}

BOOL InitOLE()
{
        DWORD dwOleVer;

        dwOleVer = CoBuildVersion();

        // check the OLE library version
        if (rmm != HIWORD(dwOleVer))
        {
            MessageBox(NULL, L"Incorrect version of OLE libraries.",
                g_szAppTitle, MB_OK | MB_ICONSTOP);
            return FALSE;
        }

        // could also check for minor version, but this application is
        // not sensitive to the minor version of OLE

        // initialize OLE, fail application if we can't get OLE to init.
        if (FAILED(OleInitialize(NULL)))
        {
            MessageBox(NULL, L"Cannot initialize OLE.", g_szAppTitle,
                MB_OK | MB_ICONSTOP);
            return FALSE;
        }
```

```
    // otherwise, init succeeded
    g_fOLEInit = TRUE;

    return TRUE;
}
```

AutoXL.c

The code in autoxl.c actually creates the pie chart using the code in dispargs.c as helper functions to set up the Invoke function calls.

The CLSID for Microsoft Excel is unique and is used by OLE to identify the server to start. Instead of hardcoding the CLSID into your application, it is a good idea to obtain the CLSID from the registry using the ProgID. The ProgID for Microsoft Excel is "Excel.Application." The CLSIDFromProgID function looks up the ProgID in the registry and returns the associated CLSID.

```
CLSIDFromProgID(L"Excel.Application", &clsExcelApp);
```

Excel Instance-Management Functions

The StartExcel, ReleaseExcel, IsExcelRunning, and SetExcelVisible functions are used to manage an instance of Microsoft Excel. The StartExcel function uses the CoCreateInstance function to create an instance of Excel. The ReleaseExcel function invokes the Quit method for the Microsoft Excel Application object (this causes Excel to exit), and shuts down the OLE server. The SetExcelVisible function invokes the Visible method for the Application object, making the instance of Microsoft Excel visible.

```
IDispatch * pdispExcelApp = NULL;

BOOL StartExcel()
{
    CLSID clsExcelApp;

    // if Excel is already running, return with current instance
    if (pdispExcelApp != NULL)
        return TRUE;

    // Obtain the CLSID that identifies EXCEL.APPLICATION
    // This value is universally unique to Excel versions 5 and up,
    // and is used by OLE to identify which server to start. We are
    // obtaining the CLSID from the ProgID.
```

```
        if (FAILED(CLSIDFromProgID(L"Excel.Application", &clsExcelApp)))
        {
            MessageBox(g_hwndApp, L"Cannot obtain CLSID from ProgID",
                g_szAppTitle, MB_OK | MB_ICONSTOP);
            return FALSE;
        }

        // start a new copy of Excel, grab the IDispatch interface
        if (FAILED(CoCreateInstance(&clsExcelApp, NULL, CLSCTX_LOCAL_SERVER,
                &IID_IDispatch, &pdispExcelApp)))
        {
            MessageBox(g_hwndApp, L"Cannot start an instance of Excel for
                Automation.", g_szAppTitle, MB_OK | MB_ICONSTOP);
            return FALSE;
        }

        return TRUE;
    }


BOOL ReleaseExcel()
{
    if (pdispExcelApp == NULL)
        return TRUE;

    // Tell Excel to quit, since for automation simply releasing the
    // IDispatch object isn't enough to get the server to shut down.

    // Note that this code will hang if Excel tries to display any
    // message boxes. This can occur if a document is in need of saving.
    // The CreateChart() code always clears the dirty bit on the
    // documents it creates, avoiding this problem.

    ClearAllArgs();
    Invoke(pdispExcelApp, L"Quit", NULL, DISPATCH_METHOD, 0);

    // Even though Excel has been told to Quit, we still need to release
    // the OLE object to account for all memory.

    (*(pdispExcelApp->lpVtbl->Release))(pdispExcelApp);

    pdispExcelApp = NULL;
    return TRUE;
}
```

```
BOOL IsExcelRunning()
{
    return pdispExcelApp != NULL;
}


BOOL SetExcelVisible(BOOL fVisible)
{
    if (!IsExcelRunning())
        return FALSE;

    ClearAllArgs();
    AddArgumentBool(NULL, 0, fVisible);
    return Invoke(pdispExcelApp, L"Visible", NULL, DISPATCH_PROPERTYPUT,
        DISP_FREEARGS);
}
```

SetRangeValueDouble Function

The SetRangeValueDouble function uses PropertyPut to set the value of a range given the cell reference as a string. The CreateChart function calls this function several times to set cell values.

```
BOOL SetRangeValueDouble(IDispatch *pdispWs, LPOLESTR lpszRef, double d)
{
    VARIANTARG vargRng;
    BOOL fResult;

    ClearAllArgs();
    AddArgumentCString(NULL, 0, lpszRef);
    if (!Invoke(pdispWs, L"Range", &vargRng, DISPATCH_PROPERTYGET,
        DISP_FREEARGS))
        return FALSE;

    AddArgumentDouble(NULL, 0, d);
    fResult = Invoke(vargRng.pdispVal, L"Value", NULL,
        DISPATCH_PROPERTYPUT, 0);
    ReleaseVariant(&vargRng);

    return fResult;
}
```

CreateChart Function

The CreateChart function uses the argument-constructor functions and the Invoke function to create a pie chart in Microsoft Excel. The Visual Basic equivalent calls are described in the comments immediately preceding the AddArgument*Type* and Invoke function calls.

```
BOOL CreateChart()
{
    BOOL fResult;
    VARIANTARG varg1, varg2;
    IDispatch *pdispWorkbook = NULL;
    IDispatch *pdispWorksheet = NULL;
    IDispatch *pdispRange = NULL;
    IDispatch *pdispCrt = NULL;
    LPOLESTR apszNames[4] = { L"North", L"South", L"East", L"West" };

    // Set wb = [application].Workbooks.Add(template := xlWorksheet)
    ClearAllArgs();
    if (!Invoke(pdispExcelApp, L"Workbooks", &varg1,
            DISPATCH_PROPERTYGET, 0))
        return FALSE;

    ClearAllArgs();
    AddArgumentInt2(L"Template", 0, xlWorksheet);
    fResult = Invoke(varg1.pdispVal, L"Add", &varg2,
        DISPATCH_METHOD, 0);
    ReleaseVariant(&varg1);
    if (!fResult)
        return FALSE;
    pdispWorkbook = varg2.pdispVal;

    // Set ws = wb.Worksheets(1)
    ClearAllArgs();
    AddArgumentInt2(NULL, 0, 1);
    if (!Invoke(pdispWorkbook, L"Worksheets", &varg2,
            DISPATCH_PROPERTYGET, 0))
        goto CreateChartBail;
    pdispWorksheet = varg2.pdispVal;

    // set up the data labels

    // ws.Range("A1:D1").Value = Array("North", "South", "East", "West")
    ClearAllArgs();
    AddArgumentCString(NULL, 0, L"A1:D1");
    if (!Invoke(pdispWorksheet, L"Range", &varg2, DISPATCH_PROPERTYGET,
            DISP_FREEARGS))
        goto CreateChartBail;
```

```
AddArgumentCStringArray(NULL, 0, apszNames, 4);
fResult = Invoke(varg2.pdispVal, L"Value", NULL,
    DISPATCH_PROPERTYPUT, DISP_FREEARGS);
ReleaseVariant(&varg2);
if (!fResult)
    goto CreateChartBail;

// set up the data series values

// ws.Range("A2") = 5.2
if (!SetRangeValueDouble(pdispWorksheet, L"A2", 5.2))
    goto CreateChartBail;
// ws.Range("B2") = 10
if (!SetRangeValueDouble(pdispWorksheet, L"B2", 10.0))
    goto CreateChartBail;
// ws.Range("C2") = 8
if (!SetRangeValueDouble(pdispWorksheet, L"C2", 8.0))
    goto CreateChartBail;
// ws.Range("D2") = 20
if (!SetRangeValueDouble(pdispWorksheet, L"D2", 20))
    goto CreateChartBail;

// set sourceRange = ws.Range("A1:D2")
ClearAllArgs();
AddArgumentCString(NULL, 0, L"A1:D2");
if (!Invoke(pdispWorksheet, L"Range", &varg2, DISPATCH_PROPERTYGET,
        DISP_FREEARGS))
    goto CreateChartBail;
pdispRange = varg2.pdispVal;

// set crt = wb.Charts.Add
ClearAllArgs();
if (!Invoke(pdispWorkbook, L"Charts", &varg1,
        DISPATCH_PROPERTYGET, 0))
    goto CreateChartBail;
ClearAllArgs();
fResult = Invoke(varg1.pdispVal, L"Add", &varg2,
    DISPATCH_METHOD, 0);
ReleaseVariant(&varg1);
if (!fResult)
    goto CreateChartBail;
pdispCrt = varg2.pdispVal;
```

```
    // crt.ChartWizard source := sourceRange, gallery := xl3DPie, _
    // format :- 7, plotBy := xlRows, categoryLabels := 1, _
    // seriesLabels := 0, hasLegend := 2, title := "Sales Percentages"
    ClearAllArgs();
    AddArgumentCString(L"title", 0, L"Sales Percentages");
    AddArgumentInt2(L"hasLegend", 0, 2);
    AddArgumentInt2(L"seriesLabels", 0, 0);
    AddArgumentInt2(L"categoryLabels", 0, 1);
    AddArgumentInt2(L"plotBy", 0, xlRows);
    AddArgumentInt2(L"format", 0, 7);
    AddArgumentInt2(L"gallery", 0, xl3DPie);
    AddArgumentDispatch(L"source", 0, pdispRange);   // will auto-free
    pdispRange = NULL;
    if (!Invoke(pdispCrt, L"ChartWizard", NULL, DISPATCH_METHOD,
            DISP_FREEARGS))
        goto CreateChartBail;

    // wb.Saved = True
    // ' So that Excel won't ask whether to save this document on close.
    ClearAllArgs();
    AddArgumentBool(NULL, 0, TRUE);
    Invoke(pdispWorkbook, L"Saved", NULL, DISPATCH_PROPERTYPUT, 0);

    fResult = TRUE;

CreateChartExit:
    if (pdispWorkbook != NULL)
        (*(pdispWorkbook->lpVtbl->Release))(pdispWorkbook);
    if (pdispWorksheet != NULL)
        (*(pdispWorksheet->lpVtbl->Release))(pdispWorksheet);
    if (pdispRange != NULL)
        (*(pdispRange->lpVtbl->Release))(pdispRange);
    if (pdispCrt != NULL)
        (*(pdispCrt->lpVtbl->Release))(pdispCrt);
    return fResult;

CreateChartBail:
    fResult = FALSE;
    goto CreateChartExit;
}
```

C H A P T E R   7

The Microsoft Excel Applications Programming Interface

This chapter describes the Applications Programming Interface (API) for Microsoft Excel. You can use the API to develop programs that call Microsoft Excel.

The first part of this chapter discusses writing DLL functions and calling them from a Microsoft Excel worksheet. For information about using DLL functions with Visual Basic, see, "Using DLLs from Visual Basic." The second part of this chapter, "Calling Microsoft Excel from C," discusses the API calls that allow a C-language application to call into Microsoft Excel.

Microsoft Excel exposes its objects as OLE Automation objects. OLE 2 allows another application, called an *OLE Automation Controller,* to access the exposed objects and use their properties and methods. For more information about using the Microsoft Excel OLE Automation interface, see, "Using the OLE Automation Interface."

Depending on your application, you may wish to use the C API, a DLL called from Visual Basic, the OLE Automation interface, or some hybrid combination. The introduction to this book discusses when each of these solutions is most appropriate and gives guidelines for selecting an approach best suited to your application.

Microsoft Excel 97 has two macro languages: the Microsoft Excel 4.0 macro language and Visual Basic for Applications. Throughout this chapter, we use the term "macro language" to mean the Microsoft Excel 4.0 macro language.

Why Use the Excel SDK?

Microsoft Excel 97 offers a very fast, powerful and portable macro language for enhancing Microsoft Excel. You can create user-defined functions, write code that controls Microsoft Excel, and even create entire applications using Microsoft Excel as a platform. Prior to Microsoft Excel 5.0, the only choice for enhancing Microsoft Excel was the Microsoft Excel Macro Language (XLM). This language has fallen out of general use with the introduction of Visual Basic for Applications (VBA) in Microsoft Excel 5.0. Visual Basic for Applications brought a more understandable syntax, dimensioned variables, faster looping, enhanced debugging tools, and a host of programming enhancements found in Visual Basic.

This new power requires a programmer to use a more rigorous coding style. While sophisticated XLM code was frequently self-modifying, VBA code can not modify its source during execution. This presented new complexities and interesting trade-off decisions over when to use one versus the other. Virtually everything could be done in both languages, but certain operations frequently lent themselves to implementation in one language over the other. Because of the many advantages and improvements to VBA since version 5, these discussions have become overwhelmingly one sided toward the VBA camp and now XLM is supported primarily for backward compatibility.

In a similar vein, some operations are more easily implemented in a language other than the VBA provided by Microsoft Excel. Perhaps you already have a large base of code written in C or you feel that a truly compiled language would offer additional speed advantages as well as increased security. The Excel SDK was created just for you! When Excel 4.0 was released a new feature was included, the C API. The C API allowed the programmer to use a high-level, compiled language to extend Microsoft Excel's functionality. The C API allowed a programmer to:

- Create functions and commands in a high-level language such as C.
- Dynamically link and call functions between the macro language and a high-level language.

The C API was based upon the XLM language, and there was a one-to-one correspondence between the functions available in the C API and commands available in XLM. This allowed many developers to greatly extend the capabilities of Excel. With the introduction of VBA in Microsoft Excel 5.0, a second method for extending the functionality of Microsoft Excel via a high-level language was exposed. As it turns out, VBA is not a compiled component of the Excel EXE file. Instead, VBA is implemented as a DLL external to Microsoft Excel. This makes it available as a shared component for all members of the office suite as well as for members of the Office Compatible program.

If VBA isn't internal to Microsoft Excel, how does it communicate with Microsoft Excel? While implementing VBA, the Microsoft Excel developers also implemented a new API for VBA to use to control Microsoft Excel. The API itself was accessed by a relatively new feature called OLE Automation. OLE2 allows an application called an *OLE Automation Controller* to control another application via a set of exposed methods and properties of an *OLE Automation Server*.

Which Should I Use?

When Microsoft Excel 4.0 shipped this was not a question. A developer wishing to extend Microsoft Excel with C would use the C API. The question is not quite so simple any longer. We now have two different extension methods each with their own strengths and weaknesses. Beyond these strengths and weaknesses there is no reason to write to one API vs. the other. If you are starting a new project, OLE Automation is generally the best choice. If you have a lot of existing code implemented using the C API, don't blindly port it to use OLE Automation just because it is the newest of the two APIs. The following discussion focuses on the compromises experienced when selecting one of the APIs over the other.

Synchronous vs. Asynchronous

One of the most frustrating limitations of the C API is the synchronous nature it imposes. Many programmers want to exert control over Excel at arbitrary times. Perhaps the goal is to start a process in Microsoft Excel each time a stock price comes in on the Internet. The C API doesn't enable this scenario. It is necessary for Microsoft Excel to call the developer's code before the developer is allowed to utilize the C API to call functionality within Microsoft Excel. An example of the proper way to use the C API is when a function in your DLL is called as part of recalculation, your DLL utilizes the C API to get additional information and returns. An improper utilization would be to call your DLL as part of recalculation and then have your DLL set a timer and return. When the timer fires, the DLL will attempt to call back into Microsoft Excel. This will not work. The OLE Automation interface doesn't experience this limitation. Whenever Microsoft Excel is in a ready state, OLE Automation calls may be performed on it's methods and properties. There are a few times when Microsoft Excel appears to be in a ready state and will not respond to OLE Automation (for example, when dialogs are showing, menus are pulled down, or macro code is executing). These exceptions are much less limiting than the limits imposed by the C API. If you truly need asynchronous access to Excel you should choose the OLE Automation Interface.

Intended Audience

If the goal of your extension is to provided additional functions for the user to call from a worksheet, you should probably look at using the C API. Using the C API you can build a .XLL that the user can File/Open just like any other workbook. Upon opening the XLL it will be able to automatically register the worksheet functions for your users. This is theoretically a single-file solution. To accomplish this same task with OLE Automation requires at least two files. The first file is the .DLL containing your code. The second file is a workbook containing a VBA module that wraps each of the functions in your DLL with a VBA routine so that they are callable from the worksheet. On the other hand, if your intended audience is composed of VBA developers you should look at using the OLE Automation interface and providing a type library for your DLL. A type library automatically registers all of the functions in your DLL for a VBA developer and eliminates the need for the developer to declare your functions before they call them.

New Functionality

In Microsoft Excel 5.0, all functionality in the XLM language was mirrored in the VBA language. Since the C API is based directly upon XLM, this meant that all functionality in Excel 5.0 was also available from the C API. This continued to be the case with Microsoft Excel 95. Starting with Microsoft Excel 97, however, there is quite a bit of functionality that is not exposed to XLM and consequently the C API. If you need access to some of this functionality from your C code, you will need to use the OLE Automation interface. This trend will continue as new versions of Microsoft Excel are released.

Performance

OLE Automation gained a reputation early on for being slow and unwieldy. This was due to the initial implementation of OLE Automation only supporting late binding. OLE 2.0 currently supports three types of binding:

1. Late Binding
2. ID Binding
3. Early or Vtable Binding

To understand why the various types of bindings perform differently, you need to understand a little bit about the implementation of OLE Automation. OLE Automation controllers use the OLE IDispatch interface to gain access to OLE objects. IDispatch identifies all members (methods and properties) by a number, the Dispatch ID (DISPID). Programmers, on the other hand, know object members by name. The resolving of these names to determine which functions to call (known as *binding*) is the main performance impediment in OLE Automation. Each of the binding types mentioned above implement this binding in different manners.

Late Binding

Late binding is the slowest method and the one that gave OLE Automation a reputation for slowness. In late binding, the OLE Automation controller knows nothing about the object at compile time. At run time, all of the binding information is determined on the fly. The controller determines the DISPIDs by calling the IDispatch::GetIDsOfNames function. After determining the DISPID of the function it wants to call, it then call IDispatch::Invoke specifying the DISPID. In addition to being slow, this method provides no validity or syntax checking at compile time, since the information is determined on the fly at run time.

ID Binding

ID Binding is the next-fastest binding method for OLE Automation. In ID binding a type library is provided for the OLE Automation controller. This type library documents each of the DISPIDs of the various members. At compile time, the DISPIDs are determined and compiled into the application. When calling, the member function only needs to call IDispatch::Invoke, bypassing a call to IDispatch::GetIDsOfNames. This method is almost twice as fast as late binding.

Early/Vtable Binding

Early binding (also known as Vtable Binding) is the fastest OLE Automation method. Early binding totally bypasses the entire IDispatch interface and allows the controller to bind directly to the members in the object. Early binding does not use DISPIDs and will not work on a straight IDispatch implementation. The developer of the object must have provided a dual interface that is a combination of an IDispatch and a VTable interface. At compile time the type library for the object is read to determine the location in the VTable of each member. Code is then generated to directly call the function through the VTable. Early binding provides compile time type checking and, if an in-process OLE server is used, offers significant performance gains over the other binding methods. This is because there is no need to marshal arguments for the IDispatch::Invoke, no indirection through the Invoke call, and no marshaling is required in the server to unpack the various arguments before calling the member. Marshaling is the process of packing and unpacking arguments for a remote procedure call. With VTable binding on an in-process server, each member access equates to a direct function call. On an out-of-process OLE Server (EXE), this process will be slightly slower due to the overhead of the remoting code required to call the function in another process.

An interesting tidbit is that the main communication method for VBA is OLE Automation! Don't let performance be the determining factor in your choice of the C API over OLE Automation. Well-written OLE Automation code can be just as fast as code that uses the C API.

High Level Development Language Choice

The choice of your development language may force you to choose one API over the other. The C API is limited to development languages that can create compiled DLLs with true function entry points. C, C++, and even Pascal are good examples of this. Visual Basic can create DLLs, but these DLLs are termed OLE DLLs. These DLLs do not have true function entry points that can be accessed by direct function calls. Instead, these DLLs implement OLE interfaces that can be called by other applications (including Microsoft Excel). If you develop in Visual Basic, you will need to use the OLE Automation interface.

Why Use the C Applications Programming Interface?

Visual Basic for Applications (VBA) is a fast, powerful, and portable tool for enhancing Microsoft Excel. You can create user-defined functions, write code that controls Microsoft Excel, create new commands, and even create entire applications using Microsoft Excel as a platform. However, VBA is not always powerful enough. You may already have large libraries of code written in another language. You may need the speed and security of compiled high-level languages. Or perhaps you need to interface with external libraries or databases.

The C API can provide all these capabilities for you to use with a compiler for a high-level language. With the tools in this package you can:

- Create functions and commands in a high-level language such as C.

- Dynamically link and call functions between the worksheet and a high-level language.

If you know C and the Microsoft Excel macro language, you'll be able to write add-ins in C. In most cases, translating existing macro code into C is a straightforward task. You will not have to learn a large API in order to use C to develop add-ins. As a benefit, your add-ins will run faster, and they will be able to access functionality available only from C. For example, if you already have large libraries written in C (or any language that can be called from C), you will be able to use them with Microsoft Excel.

Getting Started

There are three possible ways of calling your C code from Microsoft Excel:

- From a Visual Basic module. You write a custom function in C and use the Declare statement to reference the function in the Visual Basic module. For more information about using DLLs with Visual Basic, see Chapter 5, "Using DLLs from Visual Basic."

- From a worksheet. You write a user-defined function in C, which Microsoft Excel users can enter on worksheets and evaluate. Your code is called whenever Microsoft Excel needs to calculate that function.

- From a menu, button, ON function, shortcut key, or toolbar. You write a custom procedure in C, which can be attached to a menu item, to a tool on the toolbar, to an event with an ON function, to a shortcut key, or to a button or other object on the worksheet drawing layer.

There is a difference between user-defined functions, which simply compute values based on their parameters and return the values, and user-defined commands, which actually perform actions. The following section describes calling DLLs from Microsoft Excel. For information on calling Microsoft Excel from your add-ins, see "Calling Microsoft Excel from C" on page 150.

Note Writing DLLs is slightly more complex than writing normal Windows code, which in turn is more complex than writing normal C programs. Make sure you understand both before you begin.

Creating DLL Files in C

The Microsoft Windows DLL examples in this chapter were prepared and tested with Microsoft Windows 95 and Windows NT Workstation 4.0 (SP2) using Microsoft Visual C++, version 4.2b. If you use another compiler, you may also need the Microsoft Win32 SDK.

Creating a Microsoft Windows DLL with Visual C++ is very simple. When you create a new project for your DLL, select "Dynamic-Link library" from the list of project types in the New Project Workspace dialog. For more information, select the Search command from the Help menu and search for the topic "DLL Creation."

When you create a simple DLL with Visual C++, you do not need to write a DllMain function. However, if your DLL must perform some action when it is initialized or unloaded, you will need to implement DllMain (the example DLL in Chapter 8 uses a DllMain function to initialize string byte counts when the DLL is first loaded).

A Simple Example

The CIRCUM.MAK project in the SAMPLE\CIRCUM directory builds a simple Microsoft Windows DLL. The DLL contains a single exported function, called CalcCircum, which takes the radius of a circle as its argument and returns the circle's circumference.

```
double * WINAPI CalcCircum (double *pdRadius)
{
    *pdRadius *= 6.283185308;

    return pdRadius;
}
```

Functions that will be called from Microsoft Excel in 32-bit Microsoft Windows should be declared as __stdcall. The example above uses the WINAPI typed for __stdcall, as well as the other Windows example code in this book.

For more information about using this DLL, see the next section, "Calling the Function from Within Microsoft Excel." For information about calling a DLL from Visual Basic, see Chapter 5, "Using DLLs from Visual Basic."

Calling the Function from Within Microsoft Excel

Once you have created a DLL, you should be able to call the DLL from within Microsoft Excel.

Note The examples in this chapter discuss calling a DLL function from a worksheet or XLM sheet. For information about calling DLL functions from Visual Basic, see Chapter 5, "Using DLLs from Visual Basic." Microsoft Excel 97 has eliminated Macro Sheet as a choice from the "Insert" menu. There are still two remaining methods for getting a macro sheet from the user interface:

1. Press CTRL+F11

2. Right-click on a sheet tab and choose "Insert".

Functions for Linking DLLs

Microsoft Excel uses three key functions to link to DLLs. The first function, REGISTER, establishes a dynamic link to a function that resides in a DLL. The CALL function then calls that DLL function. Finally, the UNREGISTER function breaks the link, allowing the operating system to remove the DLL from memory. For an example, see the following macro.

	A	B
1	fCircum	=REGISTER("CIRCUM","CalcCircum","EE")
2		=CALL(fCircum,100)
3		=UNREGISTER(fCircum)
4		=RETURN()

Cell B1 has the defined name fCircum.

Registering the Function

Cell B1 registers the function CalcCircum, which is exported by a DLL called CIRCUM.DLL. If the function is found, REGISTER returns a number called a *register ID*. That number can then be used as the first argument to the CALL and UNREGISTER functions.

The third argument to the REGISTER function informs Microsoft Excel what data types the CalcCircum function expects and what data type it will return. The first letter is a code describing the return type, in this case, E, meaning a pointer to a floating-point number. The next letter or letters describe all the arguments. The CalcCircum function takes a pointer to a floating-point number as its single argument, so the second letter of the code is E. Microsoft Excel supports several data types, such as integers, floating-point numbers, strings, arrays, and Booleans.

There is even a special code for the Microsoft Excel internal data type, the XLOPER; for more information, see "The XLOPER Data Type" on page 151. All of the recognized data types are described under "REGISTER" on page 219, and in the online Microsoft Excel Function Reference. To find this information, look under the help topic titled "Using the CALL and REGISTER functions."

After the registration, cell B2 calls the function, with an argument of 100. The result becomes the value of B2. Finally, B3 unregisters the function, allowing the DLL to be removed from memory.

Running the Function

Now try running the CalcCircum function. Make sure the name fCircum is defined to refer to B1. To do this, select B1; then choose the Define... command from the Name submenu on the Insert menu, type fCircum and then choose the OK button. To run the macro, choose the Macros command from the Tools/Macro menu, select fCircum, and then choose the Run button. The DLL should load and run the function. A quick way to see all the return values in the macro sheet is to press CTRL+` (accent grave). Microsoft Excel then switches into Display Values mode, and you see something like the following illustration.

	A	B
1	fCircum	-540868608
2		628.3185308
3		TRUE
4		TRUE

The value in B1 is the result of registering the function; in other words, it is the register ID. This value may vary from session to session. The value in B2 is the result of evaluating the CalcCircum function. The values in B3 and B4 indicate that both of the commands in these cells were evaluated successfully. You can press CTRL+` again to switch back to Display Formulas mode.

Registering a Function Automatically

For registering functions you need to use only once, there is a shortcut. You can use an alternate form of the CALL function, which automatically registers and then calls a function. The following illustration shows this form.

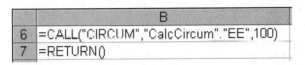

	B
6	=CALL("CIRCUM","CalcCircum"."EE",100)
7	=RETURN()

This shortcut is helpful because it can be entered directly on a worksheet, as well as on a macro sheet. This is one way you can allow worksheets to use functions that are defined in a DLL.

Defining a Name for the Function

Although the preceding methods are effective, you ideally would like to be able to provide "native" functions, which look to the user like ordinary Microsoft Excel functions. To do this, you can use the full form of the REGISTER function on a worksheet. The following illustration shows this form.

	B
9	=REGISTER("CIRCUM","CalcCircum","EE","CalcCircum","radius",1,"Math & Trig")
10	=CalcCircum(100)
11	=RETURN()

In this example, in addition to registering the function, REGISTER defines a
new name so that you can refer to the function directly. To do this, you need
to specify the Microsoft Excel internal name, the names of the arguments, and
the category to which this function belongs. Now, when the user chooses the
Function... command from the Insert menu, the new function appears in the list
under Math & Trig, as shown in the following illustration.

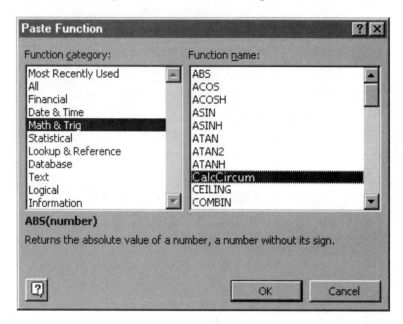

For more information about using the different forms of REGISTER, see
page 219. For more information about using the different forms of CALL,
see page 207.

Calling Microsoft Excel from C

Earlier in this chapter, you learned how to call DLLs from Microsoft Excel.
However, in the CIRCUM example, you didn't actually drive Microsoft Excel;
you just calculated a function and returned the result. Starting with Microsoft
Excel 4.0, it is possible to call internal Microsoft Excel functions directly from
the code in your DLL.

Note The examples in this chapter discuss using the C API to call internal
Microsoft Excel functions. For information about using the OLE Automation
interface to access Microsoft Excel Visual Basic objects, methods, and properties,
see Chapter 4, "Using OLE Automation."

Driving Microsoft Excel from C is straightforward because there is only one function, Excel4, to learn. The following is the function prototype:

```
int _cdecl Excel4(int iFunction, LPXLOPER pxRes, int iCount, ...)
```

The Excel4 function takes three or more arguments:

- The first argument is an integer that identifies which internal Microsoft Excel function you want to call.
- The second argument is a pointer to a buffer where the result is to be stored.
- The third argument is an integer that specifies how many arguments you will be passing to the function.

The third argument is followed by the actual arguments to the Microsoft Excel function. All the arguments to Microsoft Excel functions and their return values must always be specified as pointers to XLOPER data structures, which are discussed in the following section. The return value indicates success or an error code. The keyword `_cdecl` indicates that the function uses the C calling convention.

To use this function, you need to know the following:

- What an XLOPER is and how to construct and examine one.
- How to specify which function or command equivalent you want Microsoft Excel to perform.

The next two sections discuss these two issues. Then you will be ready to start programming Microsoft Excel in C.

The XLOPER Data Type

Microsoft Excel is *polymorphic.* Cells can hold many different types of values: strings, numbers, arrays, error values, or logical values. Internally, this is accomplished by using a special, 10-byte data type called an XLOPER. Every XLOPER has 2 bytes that indicate the type of data and 8 bytes that indicate the actual data. The 8 bytes are used differently, depending on the data type— sometimes they contain a pointer to data that is stored elsewhere.

Note Although the actual size of an XLOPER is 10 bytes, the effective size may vary depending upon the operating system. C compilers and/or CPUs are frequently more efficient when structures are aligned on fixed byte boundaries. Under Win16 the preferred alignment is 2 bytes, and the effective size remains 10 bytes. Under Win32 the preferred alignment is 8 bytes. The best way to handle this is to set the Struct Member Alignment to 8 bytes. This is the default value in Microsoft Visual C++. This increases the effective size of an XLOPER to 16 bytes under Win32.

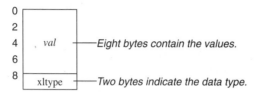

There are 12 different types of XLOPERs. You specify a type by entering a *type constant* in the *xltype* field of the XLOPER. The type constants are defined for you in XLCALL.H and are listed in the following table.

Type constant	xltype	Type of value
xltypeNum	0x0001	Numeric (IEEE floating-point)
xltypeStr	0x0002	String (byte-counted)
xltypeBool	0x0004	Logical (TRUE or FALSE)
xltypeRef	0x0008	General reference (external and/or disjoint)
xltypeErr	0x0010	Error
xltypeFlow	0x0020	Flow control in a macro
xltypeMulti	0x0040	Array
xltypeMissing	0x0080	Missing argument in a function call
xltypeNil	0x0100	None (for example, an empty cell)
xltypeSRef	0x0400	Single rectangular reference to current sheet
xltypeInt	0x0800	Integer (rarely used; use xltypeNum)
xltypeBigData	0x0802	Persistent data storage

The file XLCALL.H contains the definition of the XLOPER structure. In Windows, the definition appears as follows:

```
typedef struct xloper
{
    union
    {
        double num;                 /* xltypeNum */
        LPSTR str;                  /* xltypeStr */
        WORD bool;                  /* xltypeBool */
        WORD err;                   /* xltypeErr */
        short int w;                /* xltypeInt */
        struct
        {
            WORD count;             /* always = 1 */
            XLREF ref;
        } sref;                     /* xltypeSRef */
        struct
        {
            XLMREF *lpmref;
            DWORD idSheet;
        } mref;                     /* xltypeRef */
        struct
        {
            struct xloper *lparray;
            WORD rows;
            WORD columns;
        } array;                    /* xltypeMulti */
        struct
        {
            union
            {
                short int level;    /* xlflowRestart */
                short int tbctrl;   /* xlflowPause */
                DWORD idSheet;      /* xlflowGoto */
            } valflow;
            WORD rw;                /* xlflowGoto */
            BYTE col;               /* xlflowGoto */
            BYTE xlflow;
        } flow;                     /* xltypeFlow */
        struct
        {
            union
            {
                BYTE *lpbData;      /* data passed in */
                HANDLE hdata;       /* data returned */
            } h;
```

```
        long cbData;
    } bigdata;                    /* xltypeBigData */
  } val;
  WORD xltype;
} XLOPER, *LPXLOPER;

typedef struct xlref
{
  WORD rwFirst;
  WORD rwLast;
  BYTE colFirst;
  BYTE colLast;
} XLREF, *LPXLREF;

typedef struct xlmref
{
  WORD count;
  XLREF reftbl[1];        /* actually reftbl[count] */
} XLMREF, *LPXLMREF;
```

Types of XLOPERs

Following are diagrams of the various types of XLOPERs.

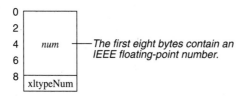

xltypeNum: Declared as double in C

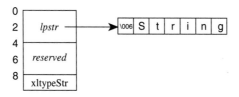

xltypeStr: Points to a byte-counted ("Pascal") string

Caution When you get string XLOPERs from Microsoft Excel, they are not always null-terminated! Do not attempt to pass them directly to C string-handling functions, such as strcpy(), that expect null-terminated strings.

Note Be sure to use an unsigned char or (BYTE) for the byte count. This is important, because otherwise it is possible to create negative string lengths. For example:

```
LPSTR s;
WORD w;

w = s[0];          /* Bad */
w = (BYTE) s[0]; /* Good */
```

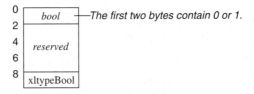

xltypeBool: The logical (Boolean) type

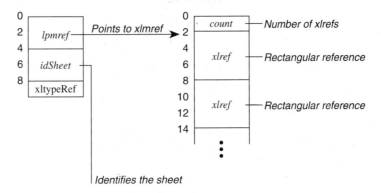

xltypeRef: A general, external, or disjoint reference.
You can use the xlSheetId function to get
the sheet ID number.

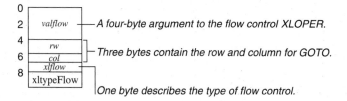

Error Code	Defined Constant	Value
#NULL!	xlerrNull	0
#DIV/0!	xlerrDiv0	7
#VALUE!	xlerrValue	15
#REF!	xlerrRef	23
#NAME?	xlerrName	29
#NUM!	xlerrNum	36
#N/A	xlerrNA	42

The first two bytes contain one of the Microsoft Excel error codes.

xltypeErr: The error type

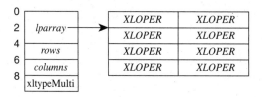

— *A four-byte argument to the flow control XLOPER.*

— *Three bytes contain the row and column for GOTO.*

— *One byte describes the type of flow control.*

xltypeFlow: The type used for flow control functions on macro sheets

For more information, see "Advanced Flow Control in Macro Sheets" on page 191.

XLOPER	XLOPER
XLOPER	XLOPER
XLOPER	XLOPER
XLOPER	XLOPER

xltypeMulti: Contains a pointer to a two-dimensional (row major) array of XLOPERs, and the number of rows and columns in that array

xltypeMissing: A missing argument in a function call. This type can be used only as an argument to a function.

xltypeNil: An empty cell on a sheet

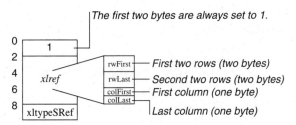

xltypeSref: A single rectangular reference to the current sheet

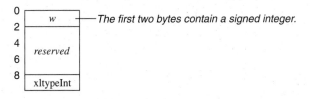

xltypeInt: Integers are rarely used in Microsoft Excel; you will generally use xltypeNum.

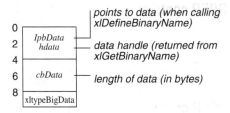

xltypeBigData: Used with defined binary names for persistent data storage.

Examples of XLOPERs in C

The following are some examples showing how to construct various types of XLOPERs in C. As a convention, XLOPER variable names start with a lowercase "x."

To construct an integer XLOPER with value 27

```
XLOPER xInt;

xInt.xltype = xltypeInt;
xInt.val.w = 27;
```

To construct a numeric (floating-point) XLOPER with the value 3.141592654

```
XLOPER xPi;

xPi.xltype = xltypeNum;
xPi.val.num = 3.141592654;
```

To construct an XLOPER containing the string "Excel String"

```
XLOPER xStr;

xStr.xltype = xltypeStr;
xStr.val.str = (LPSTR)"\014Excel String";
/* Notice the octal byte count in front of the string. */
```

To construct an XLOPER containing the logical value TRUE

```
XLOPER xBool;

xBool.xltype = xltypeBool;
xBool.val.bool = 1;
```

To construct an XLOPER containing a zero divide (#DIV/0!) error

```
XLOPER xZeroDivide;

xZeroDivide.xltype = xltypeErr;
xZeroDivide.val.err = xlerrDiv0;
```

To construct an XLOPER containing the array {1,2}

```
XLOPER rgx[2];
XLOPER xArray;

rgx[0].xltype = rgx[1].xltype = xltypeInt;
rgx[0].val.w = 1;
rgx[1].val.w = 2;
xArray.xltype = xltypeMulti;
xArray.val.array.lparray = (LPXLOPER) &(rgx[0]);
xArray.val.array.rows = 1;
xArray.val.array.columns = 2;
```

To construct a bigdata XLOPER

```
XLOPER xData;

xData.xltype = xltypeBigData;
xData.val.bigdata.h.lpbData = lpbData;      // pointer to the data
xData.val.bigdata.cbData = cbData;          // data length in bytes
```

For more information about using bigdata XLOPERs, see "Persistent Storage" on page 175.

Using Reference XLOPERs

References are not only one of the most common features in the XLM language—they are also the most confusing! In the Microsoft Excel XLM language, you have to remember when to use a local reference and when to use an external reference. You also have to remember when to use R1C1 notation and when to use A1 notation. Sometimes references are specified as strings; sometimes they are not. To help keep all this straight, the C API is designed to simplify specifying references. This section describes the different types of references and how to construct XLOPERs that specify them.

The first thing you must do is decide which sheet you want to refer to. There are three possibilities: the current sheet, the active sheet, or an external sheet.

Current Sheet

The current sheet is the sheet that is currently being calculated. This may be a macro sheet (in the case of a running macro) or a worksheet (in the case of a user-defined function). The current sheet is not necessarily the one that appears in front on the screen, as shown in the following example.

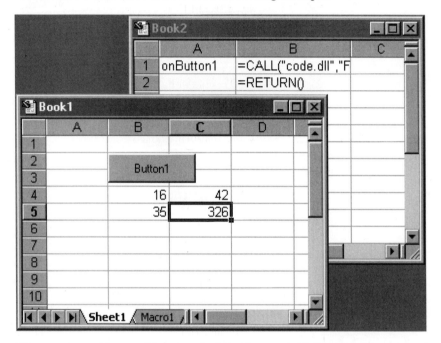

The user is working on Sheet1 and clicks Button 1. This executes a macro in Book2. While that macro is running, it calls your DLL. Macro1 is now the current sheet because it is the one being calculated.

To create a reference to the current sheet, you create an xltypeSRef XLOPER, as shown in the following example.

```
XLOPER xRef;

xRef.xltype = xltypeSRef;
xRef.val.sref.count = 1;
xRef.val.sref.ref.rwFirst  = 0;
xRef.val.sref.ref.rwLast   = 2;
xRef.val.sref.ref.colFirst = 0;
xRef.val.sref.ref.colLast  = 2;
```

This creates a reference to the cells A1:C3 in the upper-left corner of the current sheet. Notice how rows and columns are always zero-based inside Microsoft Excel.

Tips for Creating References

- To create a reference to a single cell, set rwFirst = rwLast and colFirst = colLast.

- To create a reference to an entire column, set rwFirst = 0 and rwLast = 0xFFFF. In versions earlier than Microsoft Excel 97, rwFirst has a maximum of 0x3FFF.

- To create a reference to an entire row, set colFirst = 0 and colLast = 0xFF.

- To create a reference to the entire sheet, set rwFirst = colFirst = 0, rwLast = 0xFFFF, and colLast = 0xFF. In versions earlier than Microsoft Excel 97, rwLast has a maximum of 0x3FFF.

- To create a nonadjacent reference on the current sheet, you must create an external reference. The xltypeSRef type does not support nonadjacent references. For more information see "External Sheet," which follows.

Active Sheet

The active sheet is the sheet that the user sees in front on the screen. For example, in the preceding illustration the active sheet would be Sheet1 in Book1. To create a reference to the active sheet, you need to find out the sheet ID of the active sheet and then construct an external reference to that sheet ID. For more information see the following section, "External Sheet."

External Sheet

Technically, an external sheet is any sheet except the current sheet. This means that the active sheet is an external sheet unless the current sheet and the active sheet are the same. For example, when you are executing a user-defined function during recalculation on a worksheet, the active sheet might be the same as the current sheet. External references are the most common type of reference used in C functions. That is because you need an external reference to refer to the active (front) sheet, which is probably the sheet used to call the DLL. To construct an external reference, you need to find the sheet ID of the sheet you want and build the external reference XLOPER.

To find the sheet ID of the sheet you want, use the xlSheetId function. For more information about how to call the xlSheetId function, see "xlSheetId" on page 254. The xlSheetId function has two forms. If it is called with no arguments, it returns the sheet ID of the active sheet—that is, the sheet that the user sees in front. If it is called with one argument, of type xltypeStr, it returns the sheet ID of the named sheet. The xlSheetId type returns its result by putting the sheet ID in the val.mref.idSheet field of the result XLOPER. For example:

```
XLOPER xRef;

if (xlretSuccess != Excel4(xlSheetId,&xRef,0))
{
    error("No active sheet!");
}


/*
**   Now xRef.val.mref.idSheet contains the
**   sheet ID of the active sheet.
*/
```

If this succeeds, the sheet ID for xRef is filled in. Or, you might want an external reference to a named sheet. The following example shows how to obtain the sheet ID of SHEET1 in BOOK1.XLS.

```
XLOPER xRef, xFileName;

xFileName.xltype = xltypeStr;
xFileName.val.str = "\021[BOOK1.XLS]SHEET1";

if (xlretSuccess !=
    Excel4(xlSheetId, &xRef, 1, (LPXLOPER)&xFileName))
{
    error ("SHEET1 not found");
}
```

The next step is to build the external reference XLOPER. This is an XLOPER of type xltypeRef, which is the most general reference type. The following code constructs a rectangular reference to the active sheet:

```
XLOPER xRef;
XLMREF xlmref;

if (xlretSuccess!=Excel4(xlSheetId,&xRef,0))
{
    error();
```

```
}
else
{
    xRef.xltype = xltypeRef;
    xRef.val.mref.lpmref = (LPXLMREF) &xlmref;
    xlmref.count = 1;
    xlmref.reftbl[0].rwFirst = 0;
    xlmref.reftbl[0].rwLast  = 3;
    xlmref.reftbl[0].colFirst= 0;
    xlmref.reftbl[0].colLast = 3;
}
```

This code generates a reference to 16 cells in the upper-left corner of the active (front) sheet. This would be called !A1:D4 in the macro language. If you want to specify a nonadjacent reference, you can use a different value for count. You will also have to allocate more memory for xlmref. Then, you can fill in reftbl[*n*] for the (*n*+1)th rectangular region. The reftbl[*n*] reference is easily expanded using the XLMREF and XLREF constructs defined in XLCALL.H. Dynamically allocate space for the XLMREF and specify sizeof(XLMREF) + sizeof(XLREF) * (*n*–1), where *n* is the number of nonadjacent references you want to build.

Note As a shortcut, you can use an idSheet number of 0 in your XLOPER to get the current sheet. Microsoft Excel automatically fills in the correct idSheet number. When you get external references from Microsoft Excel, you always get an actual idSheet number, not 0, even if they refer to the current sheet.

Using XLOPERs to Communicate with C Functions

You can use XLOPERs when your function is called by C. This is the most flexible way to communicate with Microsoft Excel. To do this, use the R data type in the third argument to the REGISTER function. For example:

```
=REGISTER("myDLL","myFunc","RR","MyFunc","Value")
```

This would register a function declared as:

```
LPXLOPER myFunc(LPXLOPER px);
```

You can also use data type P in the third argument. The distinction between data types P and R is significant only when the argument being passed is specified as a reference. Type R passes the reference as xltypeRef. The programmer must then coerce the xltypeRef to an xltypeMulti and walk the XLOPER array to obtain the values. Data type P passes the value represented by the reference.

Specifying Microsoft Excel Functions

The Excel4 function is used to call any of the Microsoft Excel functions or command equivalents. These function or command equivalents are the same as those defined in the online Microsoft Excel Online Function Reference. The Microsoft Excel Online Function Reference can be obtained from http://www.microsoft.com.

Of course, many functions in the Microsoft Excel XLM language do not make sense in DLLs. For example, you would never want to call the GOTO function or the ARGUMENT function from a DLL because its behavior wouldn't make sense outside of an XLM macro sheet.

To understand how to specify a function, you need to know something about how Microsoft Excel works internally. Microsoft Excel contains two tables: the *function* table and the *command-equivalent* table. These tables are simply arrays of pointers to internal Microsoft Excel functions.

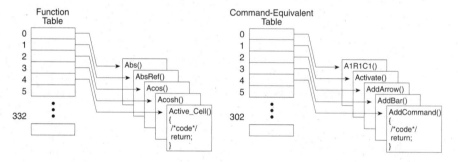

The command-equivalent table is equivalent to the function table, with entries that point to Microsoft Excel command equivalents. When you use Excel4, you will need to know the index of the Microsoft Excel function or command equivalent. These are defined for you in XLCALL.H:

```
#define xlfCount 0
#define xlfIsna 2
#define xlfIserror 3
#define xlfSum 4
#define xlfAverage 5
#define xlfMin 6
#define xlfMax 7
#define xlfRow 8
#define xlfColumn 9
#define xlfNa 10
```

.
.
.

```
#define xlcBeep (0 | xlCommand)
#define xlcOpen (1 | xlCommand)
#define xlcOpenLinks (2 | xlCommand)
#define xlcCloseAll (3 | xlCommand)
#define xlcSave (4 | xlCommand)
#define xlcSaveAs (5 | xlCommand)
#define xlcFileDelete (6 | xlCommand)
#define xlcPageSetup (7 | xlCommand)
#define xlcPrint (8 | xlCommand)
#define xlcPrinterSetup (9 | xlCommand)
```

.
.
.

The name of each function or command equivalent is based on the name in the Microsoft Excel Online Function Reference. Functions are prefixed with "xlf," while command equivalents are prefixed with "xlc." You will also notice that all the command equivalents have their xlCommand bit set, so Microsoft Excel knows whether to use the command-equivalent table or the function table. You can also easily determine whether you have a function or a command equivalent. It is important to distinguish between the two: a function returns a value, and a command equivalent executes some action.

Calling the Dialog Box Forms of Functions

In the macro language, most command equivalents that have dialog boxes can be called either with the dialog box or without. In the *dialog box form* of the function, the name is followed by a question mark. For example, SAVE.AS will not prompt the user with a dialog box, but SAVE.AS? will. To use the dialog box form in C, simply set the xlPrompt bit (defined in XLCALL.H). For example, this code deletes the file BOOK1.XLS:

```
XLOPER xResult, xBook1;

xBook1.xltype = xltypeStr;
xBook1.val.str = "\011BOOK1.XLS";

Excel4(xlcFileDelete, &xResult, 1, (LPXLOPER)&xBook1);
```

The following code displays the Delete dialog box, offering all the *.BAK files as candidates for deletion:

```
XLOPER xResult, xFilter;

xFilter.xltype = xltypeStr;
xFilter.val.str = "\005*.BAK";

Excel4(xlcFileDelete | xlPrompt, &xResult, 1, (LPXLOPER) &xFilter);
```

Using International Versions of Microsoft Excel

So far, you have read about running DLLs on only the U.S. version of Microsoft Excel. However, you may want to create an international DLL. This is a DLL that will work with any international version of Microsoft Excel.

The first argument to the Excel4 function, specifying which function to execute, is universal. Every version of Microsoft Excel uses the same function codes, although the name the user may see for the codes is different in international versions. For example, the SUM function is called SOMME in French Microsoft Excel, but it still uses function code 4. A problem arises only when you need to refer to this function by name; for example, if you want to place a SUM formula in a cell, and you are calling the FORMULA function. In the U.S. version, you could call FORMULA("=SUM(1,2)"), but this would not be understood in the French version.

To get around this problem, you can set the international bit (xlIntl). This tells Microsoft Excel to treat the following command as if it were executed in U.S. Microsoft Excel. As a result, setting the xlIntl bit and calling FORMULA("=SUM(1,2)") has the same effect on any version of Microsoft Excel. The French Microsoft Excel user simply sees =SOMME(1,2) entered on the sheet.

```
int WINAPI InternationalExample()
{
    XLOPER xResult, xSum;

    xSum.xltype = xltypeStr;
    xSum.val.str = "\012=SUM(1,2)";

    Excel4(xlcFormula | xlIntl, &xResult, 2, (LPXLOPER) &xSum,
        TempActiveRef(237,237,1,1));

    return TRUE;
}
```

Excel4

Now that you know all about XLOPERs and specifying functions, you can take a closer look at the Excel4 function:

```
int _cdecl Excel4(int iFunction, LPXLOPER pxRes, int iCount, ...)
```

First, notice that this function is _cdecl. This means that it uses the C calling convention. For more information about calling conventions, see your compiler documentation.

The function takes at least three arguments. The following three arguments must always be present.

- The iFunction argument is the function code. You should always use one of the defined constants from XLCALL.H.

- The pxRes argument is a pointer to an XLOPER that you have allocated for the result of the function. This is where Microsoft Excel will put the result of your function call. If you use 0, Microsoft Excel discards the return value. However, it is a very good idea to check the value of pxRes, as well as the result from Excel4.

- The iCount argument is the number of arguments you are going to pass, from 0 to 30. Microsoft Excel never allows more than 30 arguments in a function call.

Following the iCount argument are the arguments to the Microsoft Excel function itself. These must all be LPXLOPERs, that is, pointers to XLOPERs that you have allocated. As a rule, all arguments to all Microsoft Excel functions and command equivalents are always specified as pointers to XLOPERs. In order to represent a missing (omitted) argument, create an XLOPER of type xltypeMissing, and pass a pointer to that, or use a NULL pointer.

With Microsoft Windows, it is a good idea to always cast these arguments to LPXLOPERs. For example, always write:

```
Excel4(xlfGetCell, &xResult, 1, (LPXLOPER) &xMyXloper);
```

Instead of:

```
Excel4(xlfGetCell, &xResult, 1, &xMyXloper); /* BAD!!! */
```

When you include XLCALL.H, the Excel4 function prototype automatically casts the second argument (the return value) to an LPXLOPER. All the other arguments, starting with the fourth, need to have casts. The cast forces the compiler to create a full 32-bit address for the XLOPER. This is important mainly in the 16-bit world, where the XLOPER could exist in the DS of the DLL. If you consistently cast all arguments past the second you will never run into this problem regardless of platform.

More About Using the Excel4 Function

You should always check the return value from Excel4. If it is not xlretSuccess, something has prevented the call from succeeding. For example, one of the XLOPERs may not be valid; Microsoft Excel may be low on memory; or you may have used an invalid number of arguments. For a list of the possible return values, see "Excel4" on page 214. If Excel4 does not return xlretSuccess, the XLOPER returned (pxRes) will contain a #VALUE! error.

Note The Excel function in the framework library automatically checks the return value to aid in debugging.

Be careful to distinguish between a Microsoft Excel function failing and the Excel4 function failing. When a Microsoft Excel function fails, Excel4 succeeds but pxRes contains one of the Microsoft Excel error codes. When Excel4 fails, it actually returns one of the xlret... failure codes. There is a fine distinction between a failure in Microsoft Excel and a failure in the callback mechanism.

You can call Excel4 only when control has been passed to your code by Microsoft Excel. You are not able to call back into Microsoft Excel anytime you want. In other words, you cannot set up a timer with a callback address, return control to Microsoft Excel, and then in your callback function call Excel4. Neither can you create a DLL that interacts with Microsoft Excel but is loaded and called by another application. To communicate with Microsoft Excel from another application you should use OLE Automation or DDE. For more information about OLE Automation, see Chapter 4, "Using OLE Automation." For more information about DDE, see Appendix A, "Dynamic Data Exchange and XlTable Format."

Important Unless Microsoft Excel has called you, Microsoft Excel will not be ready to handle callbacks.

Note Even though the Excel4 and Excel4v functions are named for Microsoft Excel version 4.0, they work with any version Microsoft Excel later than 4.0. The current Excel4 and Excel4v functions will continue to work even with future versions of Microsoft Excel. This ensures that any add-ins you develop now will still work with future versions of Microsoft Excel.

There is an additional function, Excel4v, which works like Excel4, but it takes an array of LPXLOPERs passed by reference instead of on the stack:

```
int _cdecl Excel4v(int iFunction, LPXLOPER pxRes,
    int iCount, LPXLOPER rgx[]);
```

This function allows you to wrap up Excel4 in another function. For example:

```
int MyExcel4(int iFunction, LPXLOPER pxRes, int iCount, ...)
{
    int result = Excel4v(iFunction, pxRes, iCount,
        (LPXLOPER *) (&iCount+1));
    assert(result == xlretSuccess);
    return result;
}
```

Memory Management

The biggest disadvantage of writing code in a high-level language, instead of the Microsoft Excel macro language, is the problem of dealing with memory management. This section discusses several critical issues in memory management. You should understand this section fully before attempting to write Microsoft Excel DLLs.

Memory Used for XLOPERs

Where is the memory used for XLOPERs allocated and freed? First, consider the simple case in which Microsoft Excel calls a function in a DLL that returns a value. Microsoft Excel allocates and frees the arguments it passes, so you don't have to worry about them.

The only potential problem is the return value. If your function returns a simple value, there is no problem using the normal C return value. However, sometimes your function needs to return an XLOPER. That XLOPER may be contained in 10 bytes as usual, but it might also have pointers to large blocks of data that are stored elsewhere. The simplest way to return such data is to allocate some static memory and return a pointer to the memory. Following is an example for Windows of a simple DLL that returns a string XLOPER.

```
LPXLOPER WINAPI ReturnString(void)
{
    static XLOPER x;

    x.xltype = xltypeStr;
    x.val.str = "\004Test";

    return (LPXLOPER) &x;
}
```

Next, consider the case in which the DLL calls a Microsoft Excel function using Excel4. Again, the caller (the DLL) allocates the arguments. The caller must allocate 10 bytes for the return value XLOPER as well, and a pointer to this XLOPER is passed as the second argument to Excel4 so that Microsoft Excel knows where to place the return value.

This works for simple XLOPERs without any pointers. But what happens when Excel4 must return a string? The XLOPER contains a pointer to memory that has been allocated by Microsoft Excel from its own memory management system. You need to let Microsoft Excel know when you are finished with that data so that Microsoft Excel can free its memory. This is done using the xlFree function, which takes one or more XLOPERs and tells Microsoft Excel that it can free any associated memory.

For example, if the XLOPER is a string, calling xlFree on it frees the string, not the XLOPER itself. Similarly, if the XLOPER is an array of strings, xlFree frees everything except the top-level XLOPER. To summarize, whenever Excel4 returns an XLOPER containing a pointer, you must call xlFree on that XLOPER.

Note In Excel 97 calling xlFree on an XLOPER containing an xltypeMulti will change the xltype of the XLOPER to xltypeMissing. This is a change from previous versions of Excel.

A safe rule is to call xlFree on every return value you get back from Excel4. If you pass xlFree an XLOPER that does not contain a pointer, nothing happens. If xlFree is accidentally called twice on the same XLOPER, Microsoft Excel ignores the second call.

Do not modify XLOPERs that you get back from Microsoft Excel. If you do, the Microsoft Excel memory manager will not be able to free them properly and may crash.

Example of xlFree

The following example uses the xlFree function to return a string.

```
/*
** Use Microsoft Excel to get input from the user,
** then copy it into our own memory space.
*/

XLOPER xQuery, xResponse, x2;
static unsigned char rgchResult[64] = "";
unsigned char i;

xQuery.xltype = xltypeStr;
xQuery.val.str = "\022What is your name?";

x2.xltype = xltypeNum;
x2.val.num = 2;

Excel4(xlfInput, &xResponse, 2, (LPXLOPER) &xQuery, (LPXLOPER) &x2);

if (xResponse.xltype == xltypeStr)
{
    /*
    ** Now Microsoft Excel has allocated memory for the
    ** string in its own memory space. Copy the string out
    ** to our own memory, while converting to a C
    ** (null-terminated) string.
    */

    for (i=1;
            (i <= (unsigned char)xResponse.val.str[0]) && (i < 64);
            i++)
    {
        rgchResult[i - 1] = xResponse.val.str[i];
    }

    rgchResult[i - 1] = '\0';
```

```
}

/*
** Let Microsoft Excel free the string from its memory.
*/

Excel4(xlFree, 0, 1, (LPXLOPER) &xResponse);
```

Returning XLOPERs That Still Need to Be Freed by Microsoft Excel

As explained in the previous section, it is important to call the xlFree function on any XLOPERs that return values from callback functions because Microsoft Excel may have allocated some memory for these values and needs to free this memory. For example, suppose we need a DLL function that returns the name of the current sheet. That DLL function calls GET.DOCUMENT(1) to get the name of the sheet. For example:

```
/*
** BAD!
*/
LPXLOPER WINAPI GetSheetName(void)
{
    static XLOPER xl, xSheetName;

    xl.xltype = xltypeInt;
    xl.val.w  = 1;

    Excel4(xlfGetDocument, &xSheetName, 1, (LPXLOPER) &xl);

    return (LPXLOPER)&xSheetName;
}
```

What's wrong with this code? It calls GET.DOCUMENT(1), which returns a string. This string is then allocated by Microsoft Excel. However, the code never calls xlFree on the return value, so Microsoft Excel loses the memory associated with the string. You can waste quite a bit of memory this way, and it can never be retrieved.

You could try calling the xlFree function on xSheetName before returning it. Unfortunately, the contents of an XLOPER are undefined after xlFree, so that probably wouldn't work. You could allocate your own static XLOPER, with your own, static buffer to keep the string. This would require copying out the data yourself, and would waste static (global) memory.

Microsoft Excel supports a special bit called xlbitXLFree (0x1000). You can turn on this bit in the xltype field of any XLOPER returned from Microsoft Excel. If your function returns an XLOPER in which the xlbitXLFree bit is 1, Microsoft Excel copies out the data it needs from the XLOPER and frees it for you. For example, you could rewrite the preceding function as:

```
/*
** GOOD!
*/
LPXLOPER WINAPI GetSheetName(void)
{
    static XLOPER x1, xSheetName;

    x1.xltype = xltypeInt;
    x1.val.w  = 1;

    Excel4(xlfGetDocument, &xSheetName, 1, (LPXLOPER) &x1);

    xSheetName.xltype |= xlbitXLFree;

    return (LPXLOPER)&xSheetName;
}
```

Microsoft Excel frees xSheetName for you after the function has returned.

Returning XLOPERs That Still Need to Be Freed by the DLL

Another common problem occurs when you want to write a function that returns a very large XLOPER (for example, a large array full of strings) as the return value. As described in "Memory Used for XLOPERS" on page 169, you can simply allocate the space for the return value as your own global memory by declaring it static. This works for small return values. But for very large arrays, this can consume quite a bit of memory.

To address this problem, Microsoft Excel allows you to set the xlbitDLLFree bit (0x4000) in the xltype field of the XLOPERs that you return from your functions. To use it, you allocate any extra memory that you need for your XLOPER using your own memory allocation routines. You then set the xlbitDLLFree bit in the xltype field to true (1). Finally, you return a pointer to the XLOPER to Microsoft Excel using the normal return statement. Microsoft Excel automatically copies out the data in the XLOPER; then, it calls back the DLL to give you a chance to free the memory that was allocated. It does this by calling the xlAutoFree function, which your DLL must provide. Microsoft Excel passes one argument, which is the XLOPER that is ready to be freed. See the following example.

```
LPXLOPER WINAPI GetString(void)
{
    static XLOPER x;

    x.xltype = xltypeStr;
    x.val.str = malloc((size_t)8));

    lstrcpy(x.val.str, "\006Sample");

    x.xltype |= xlbitDLLFree;

    return (LPXLOPER)&x;
}

void WINAPI xlAutoFree(LPXLOPER px)
{
    free(px->val.str);

    return;
}
```

When the GetString function is called from Microsoft Excel, it allocates memory
from the system. Then GetString sets the xlbitDLLFree bit in x.xltype and
returns x. When Microsoft Excel sees that this bit is on, it copies out the data it
needs and then calls xlAutoFree to free the data. (In this code sample, xlAutoFree
is not very robust. In a real application with more than one DLL function, you
may want to write a version of xlAutoFree that actually checks the type of the
LPXLOPER being passed and uses that information to decide how to free it.)
With Windows, make sure that you export xlAutoFree in your .DEF file.

Setting Names in DLLs

You can use DLLs even though no macro sheet is present. However, you may
want to define some names to help you keep data between calls to your DLL. For
example, you may want to call xlfSetName from a DLL even though there is no
macro sheet where you can define the name.

For this purpose, Microsoft Excel has a special, hidden name space that is
accessible only to DLLs. This allows you to store temporary names in Microsoft
Excel. However, it is important to remember that this name space is shared by
all DLLs within the same instance of Microsoft Excel. Therefore, if you want to
ensure that your names do not conflict with names defined by another DLL, be
sure to begin all your names with a unique prefix, preferably the name of your
DLL. For example, if your DLL is called MYDLL.DLL, create names such as
MYDLL_hWnd.

The following is a way you might use the hidden name space:

- You can keep instance-specific static data when running with Windows. For more information, see "Multiple Instances of Microsoft Excel" on page 176.

The hidden name space is not accessible when the DLL is calculating a function on a worksheet. If the DLL function was called as part of a normal recalculation on a worksheet, names refer to the current sheet unless the DLL was registered as a macro type DLL (the data type string contained "#"). However, if the DLL was called from a macro sheet or if the DLL function was invoked through a menu, keyboard shortcut, toolbar, or otherwise, names will refer to the hidden name space.

Persistent Storage

The xlDefineBinaryName and xlGetBinaryName functions provide a mechanism for storing data and referencing it by name. Data with a defined binary name is stored with the workbook when you save the workbook. When the workbook is reloaded, the data is again available to any application that knows the data name.

Your application defines a name by passing the name (a string XLOPER) and a pointer to the data (in a bigdata XLOPER) to the xlDefineBinaryName function. Once the name is defined, you can use the xlGetBinaryName function to return a handle for the data whenever you need it.

Using the Stack

In Microsoft Windows, DLLs must share the same stack space as Microsoft Excel. When a DLL is first called, there is usually about 40K of space left on the stack. When that DLL calls the Excel4 function, Microsoft Excel consumes even more space on the stack. Microsoft Excel tests the amount of available stack space before it runs the function or command specified by the Excel4 function. If the stack would be overrun, Microsoft Excel will not run the command or function, and the Excel4 function call fails. This means that it is very important to use as little stack space as possible. Don't put large data structures on the stack, declare local variables as static if at all possible, and avoid calling functions recursively.

In 16-bit Microsoft Windows, the Excel4 function stack check requires 8.5K of available stack space when the function is called from a DLL called from a macro sheet or in response to an event or button press, and 4K of available stack space when the function is called from a DLL called from a calculating worksheet.

Note Microsoft Excel 4.0 did not perform this stack checking. Microsoft Excel 97 tests for adequate stack space for the most stack-intensive function or command every time you call the Excel4 function. If there is not enough stack space available for the most stack-intensive function or command, your function call will fail, even if it could run with the available stack space. This "worst case" stack check may cause some Excel4 function calls that worked in Microsoft Excel version 4.0 to fail in Microsoft Excel 97.

To help you in debugging, a function called xlStack is provided, which returns the number of bytes left on the stack. If you suspect that you are overrunning the stack, call this function frequently to see how much stack space is left.

Finally, if you desperately need more stack space than the 40K that you normally get, you can use the Windows functions SwitchStackTo and SwitchStackBack. For more information about these functions, see the documentation for the Microsoft Win32 SDK.

Important If you switch stacks using SwitchStackTo, you must make sure you use the original stack when calling the Excel4 function.

Multiple Instances of Microsoft Excel

Windows 16-Bit Only You must consider the possibility that your DLL will be called by more than one running instance of Microsoft Excel. If this happens, remember that your DLL has only one global data segment. For example, consider this code:

```
int i = 0;

int WINAPI test(void)
{
    return ++i;
}
```

This returns successive integers as long as there is only one copy of Microsoft Excel using this DLL. But if there are multiple instances of Microsoft Excel running at the same time and intermittently calling this DLL, there will still be only one copy of the variable i between all the instances. This means that your DLL cannot save state as easily as a normal C program can. What can you do about this, if you need a DLL to maintain a state that is distinct for each instance of Microsoft Excel?

The usual solution is to use a block of memory called an *instance block*. For example, you have a program Zoo with two functions: see_bears and see_fish. You can create an initialization function init_zoo, which allocates an instance block of memory (using LocalAlloc or GlobalAlloc) that contains all of the state that is instance-specific. The function init_zoo returns a pointer (or handle) to this memory. Then see_bears and see_fish take this handle as the first argument. Finally, exit_zoo frees the global memory. The code might look like this:

```
typedef struct tagInstanceBlock
{
    int a;
    int b;
} INSTANCEBLOCK;

HANDLE WINAPI init_zoo()
{
    return GlobalAlloc(GMEM_MOVEABLE, sizeof(INSTANCEBLOCK));
}

void WINAPI see_bears(HANDLE hInstBlock)
{
    INSTANCEBLOCK FAR *pib;

    pib = GlobalLock(hInstBlock);

    // Now use pib->a and pib->b as instance-specific
    // variables

    GlobalUnlock(hInstBlock);
}

void WINAPI exit_zoo(HANDLE hInstBlock)
{
    GlobalFree(hInstBlock);
}
```

There are other ways around this problem. For example, you can store all instance-specific information on sheets, using Microsoft Excel to maintain your state. You can also store the instance handle in a name on the sheet or in the hidden name space. Or you can simply prevent multiple instances of Microsoft Excel from using your DLL. You can call the xlGetInst function to find out the instance handle of the instance that is calling you, so that you can distinguish between different instances.

High Bandwidth Communications

The Microsoft Excel DLL interface has been optimized to maximize performance for the two most common operations: getting values out of cells and putting values into cells. This has been done with two special functions, xlCoerce and xlSet. These are available only from DLLs.

xlCoerce

The xlCoerce function can be used for two different purposes: getting values from cells and converting XLOPERs from one type to another. Although these tasks seem unrelated, they are implemented in the same way.

To understand xlCoerce, consider how Microsoft Excel itself uses this function. Microsoft Excel is polymorphic, allowing a user to pass any type of value to a function; but a function may not understand the data type being passed to it. For example, the SIN function requires a number. The user may enter =SIN("25") in a cell, passing a string argument. Although the user has provided a string, Microsoft Excel knows that the function requires a number, so it uses xlCoerce to coerce the string into a number. The xlCoerce function takes two arguments: an XLOPER to coerce and the target type.

Coercing a String to a Number

The following example shows how to create a string "25" and coerce it to a number:

```
XLOPER xStr, xNum, xDestType;

/* Create the string "25" */
xStr.xltype = xltypeStr;
xStr.val.str = "\002" "25";

/* Create the second parameter (xltypeNum) */
xDestType.xltype = xltypeInt;   /* xDestType is an integer */
xDestType.val.w = xltypeNum; /* Destination is a number */

Excel4(xlCoerce, &xNum, 2, (LPXLOPER) &xStr, (LPXLOPER) &xDestType);
```

You can specify more than one target type. Some functions behave differently based on whether an argument is a string or a number. This is called function overloading. For example, the DELETE.MENU function can take a string or a number as its second argument. To cover this possibility, xlCoerce allows you to specify multiple target types.

Coercing an Unknown to a String or a Number

The following example converts the unknown XLOPER *x* into a string or a number:

```
XLOPER xDestType, xStrOrNum;

xDestType.xltype = xltypeInt;    /* xDestType is an integer */
xDestType.val.w = xltypeStr | xltypeNum; /* String or number */
Excel4(xlCoerce, &xStrOrNum, 2, (LPXLOPER) &x, (LPXLOPER) &xDestType);
```

Using xlCoerce with References

The xlCoerce function works even when the source XLOPER is a reference. Therefore, if you coerce a reference to Sheet1!A1 to a string, xlCoerce looks up the current value of A1 and converts it to a string. In fact, you can coerce a reference to any nonreference type, which has the effect of looking up the value of that cell. This is the fastest way to get the value from a cell. Because this operation is so common, it is the default behavior of xlCoerce. If the second argument (destination type) is omitted, it is assumed that you want to coerce a reference to any nonreference type or, in other words, look up the value of a cell.

Getting a Value from a Cell

The following example shows code for the function LookupCell, which finds the value of any single cell on the active (front) sheet by constructing an external reference and then coercing it.

```
/*
** LookupCell
** Looks up the value of a cell on the active sheet
**
** Arguments:
**
**   LPXLOPER pxResult    Room for an XLOPER to store result
**   int iRow        0-based row
**   int iColumn      0-based column
**
** Returns:
**
**   pxResult
**
** Important! You must remember to call xlFree on pxResult when
** you are done!
*/
```

```
LPXLOPER WINAPI LookupCell(LPXLOPER pxResult, int iRow, int iColumn)
{
    XLOPER xRef;
    XLMREF xlmref;

    /* Get Sheet ID of active sheet */
    Excel4(xlSheetId, &xRef, 0);
    xRef.xltype = xltypeRef;
    xRef.val.mref.lpmref = (LPXLMREF)&xlmref;

    xlmref.count = 1;
    xlmref.reftbl[0].rwFirst=xlmref.reftbl[0].rwLast=iRow;
    xlmref.reftbl[0].colFirst=xlmref.reftbl[0].colLast=iColumn;

    /*
    ** Since there is only one argument to xlCoerce, Microsoft Excel
    ** will coerce to ANY nonreference type
    */

    Excel4(xlCoerce, pxResult, 1, (LPXLOPER)&xRef);

    return pxResult;
}
```

Similarly, you can coerce a rectangular reference. This allows you to look up a rectangular range of cells, all at once, and returns an xltypeMulti (Microsoft Excel array). An example of this is FuncSum in Framewrk\Generic.c. The code from this function follows:

```
__declspec(dllexport) LPXLOPER WINAPI FuncSum(
        LPXLOPER px1,LPXLOPER px2,LPXLOPER px3,LPXLOPER px4,
        LPXLOPER px5,LPXLOPER px6,LPXLOPER px7,LPXLOPER px8,
        LPXLOPER px9,LPXLOPER px10,LPXLOPER px11,LPXLOPER px12,
        LPXLOPER px13,LPXLOPER px14,LPXLOPER px15,LPXLOPER px16,
        LPXLOPER px17,LPXLOPER px18,LPXLOPER px19,LPXLOPER px20,
        LPXLOPER px21,LPXLOPER px22,LPXLOPER px23,LPXLOPER px24,
        LPXLOPER px25,LPXLOPER px26,LPXLOPER px27,LPXLOPER px28,
        LPXLOPER px29)
{
    static XLOPER xResult;   // Return value
    double d=0;              // Accumulate result
    int iArg;                // The argument being processed
    LPXLOPER *ppxArg;        // Pointer to the argument being processed
    XLOPER xMulti;           // Argument coerced to xltypeMulti
    WORD i;                  // Row and column counters for arrays
    LPXLOPER px;             // Pointer into array
    int error = -1;          // -1 if no error; error code otherwise
```

```
//
// This block accumulates the arguments passed in. Because FuncSum is
// a Pascal function, the arguments will be evaluated right to left.
// For each argument, this code checks the type of the argument and
// then does things necessary to accumulate that argument type. Unless
// the caller actually specified all 29 arguments, there will be some
// missing arguments. The first case handles this. The second case
// handles arguments that are numbers. This case just adds the number
// to the accumulator. The third case handles references or arrays.
// It coerces references to an array. It then loops through the
// array, switching on XLOPER types and adding each number to the
// accumulator. The fourth case handles being passed an error. If this
// happens, the error is stored in error. The fifth and default case
// handles being passed something odd, in which case an error is set.
// Finally, a check is made to see if error was ever set. If so, an
// error of the same type is returned; if not, the accumulator value
// is returned.
//

for (iArg = 0; iArg < 29; iArg++)
   {
   ppxArg = &px1 + iArg;

      switch ((*ppxArg)->xltype)
      {

         case xltypeMissing:
            break;

         case xltypeNum:
            d += (*ppxArg)->val.num;
            break;

         case xltypeRef:
         case xltypeSRef:
         case xltypeMulti:
            if (xlretUncalced == Excel(xlCoerce, &xMulti, 2,
               (LPXLOPER) *ppxArg, TempInt(xltypeMulti)))
               {
               //
               // That coerce might have failed due to an
               // uncalced cell, in which case, we need to
               // return immediately. Microsoft Excel will
               // call us again in a moment after that cell
               // has been calced.
               //
```

```
                        return 0;
                }

        for (i = 0;
            i < (xMulti.val.array.rows * xMulti.val.array.columns);
            i++)
        {

            // obtain a pointer to the current item //
            px = xMulti.val.array.lparray + i;

            // switch on XLOPER type //
            switch (px->xltype)
            {

                // if a num accumulate it //
                case xltypeNum:
                    d += px->val.num;
                    break;

                // if an error store in error //
                case xltypeErr:
                    error = px->val.err;
                    break;

                // if missing do nothing //
                case xltypeNil:
                    break;

                // if anything else set error //
                default:
                    error = xlerrValue;
                    break;
            }
        }

        // free the returned array //
        Excel(xlFree, 0, 1, (LPXLOPER) &xMulti);
        break;

    case xltypeErr:
        error = (*ppxArg)->val.err;
        break;

    default:
        error = xlerrValue;
        break;
    }

}
```

```
if (error != -1)
{
    xResult.xltype = xltypeErr;
    xResult.val.err = error;
}
else
{
    xResult.xltype = xltypeNum;
    xResult.val.num = d;
}

return (LPXLOPER) &xResult;
}
```

xlSet

When you buy an airline ticket, you generally have to choose between a full-fare ticket with no restrictions and a much cheaper ticket with restrictions. The cheaper ticket might be nonrefundable or require a Saturday night stay.

Similarly, in Microsoft Excel there are two ways to enter information into cells. The usual way, available in the macro language, is to use the FORMULA function, called xlcFormula from C. This is the expensive, unrestricted way. It takes a long time, but you can put almost anything anywhere and, if you don't like the result, you can undo it by calling xlcUndo.

However, there is a much faster function called xlSet. It is available only from the C API, and comes with four restrictions:

- You can enter only constants, not formulas, into cells. This allows Microsoft Excel to skip recomputing the internal formula dependency tree.

- You cannot undo with the xlSet function. This saves time, since Microsoft Excel does not have to record the information required to undo the action.

- You are limited by the maximum array size in Microsoft Excel. Ranges larger than approximately 5,460 cells may fail.

- A function that is called from a worksheet cannot call xlSet. It is a command equivalent function. In other words if the function in the DLL was called as part of recalculation, xlSet will fail.

In spite of these restrictions, xlSet is very useful. In most database access scenarios, you need to write a large table of constant values into a rectangular range of cells. This can all be done with one call to Microsoft Excel.

Note Because xlSet is a command-equivalent function, it does not work in user-defined functions.

The following code creates a large array and places it into the active sheet, in one step:

```
int i,j;
static XLOPER rgx[10][10], xArray, xRef;
XLMREF xlmref;

if (xlretSuccess != Excel4(xlSheetId, &xRef, 0))
    return;

xRef.xltype = xltypeRef;
xRef.val.mref.lpmref = (LPXLMREF) &xlmref;
xlmref.count = 1;
xlmref.reftbl[0].rwFirst  = 0;
xlmref.reftbl[0].rwLast   = 9;
xlmref.reftbl[0].colFirst = 0;
xlmref.reftbl[0].colLast  = 9;

for (i=0; i<10; i++)
{
    for (j=0; j<10; j++)
    {
        rgx[i][j].xltype = xltypeNum;
        rgx[i][j].val.num = i * 10 + j;
    }
}

xArray.xltype = xltypeMulti;
xArray.val.array.lparray = (LPXLOPER) &rgx;
xArray.val.array.rows = xArray.val.array.columns = 10;

Excel4(xlSet, 0, 2, (LPXLOPER) &xRef, (LPXLOPER) &xArray);
```

By using xlCoerce and xlSet, you can speed up data transfer dramatically.

Creating Stand-Alone DLLs (XLLs)

Up to this point, only DLLs that are registered and called from macro sheets have been discussed. However, Microsoft Excel 4.0 and greater also supports stand-alone DLLs. These are DLLs (or code resources) that the user opens by choosing Open from the File menu and selecting a DLL file or by using the Microsoft Excel Add-In Manager. (The user can also put DLL files in the Microsoft Excel startup directory, in which case they are opened at run time.) By convention, stand-alone DLLs are called XLLs. They should be given a file name with the extension .XLL for Windows.

Note   The easiest way to create a stand-alone XLL is to start with the sample generic code provided in the FRAMEWRK subdirectory or folder.

When using an XLL, the user never sees a macro sheet or add-in sheet. Therefore, an XLL must be able to do everything an XLA (add-in) can do. In particular, XLLs need a way to provide functions that run automatically at open time, close time, and so on.

When developing an XLL, you need to:

- Define the interface to Microsoft Excel. An XLL should export a few functions that are called by Microsoft Excel and the Microsoft Excel Add-In Manager.

- Define the user interface to the XLL. Does the XLL use pull-down menus? Toolbars? Shortcut keys? Or does it only provide additional functions for use on worksheets?

The Interface to Microsoft Excel

To write an XLL, you should provide three functions (described in this section) that are called by Microsoft Excel and three functions that are called by the Add-In Manager. For information about the functions called by the Add-In Manager, see "Supporting the Add-In Manager" on page 188.

The functions in the following table are called by Microsoft Excel.

This function	Is called when
xlAutoOpen()	The XLL is opened.
xlAutoClose()	The XLL is closed.
xlAutoRegister()	Microsoft Excel needs to register a function but doesn't know the argument and return value types.

The only function that is required for Microsoft Excel to open a DLL is xlAutoOpen. For more information on these three functions, see "xlAutoOpen," "xlAutoClose," and "xlAutoRegister" on pages 242, 240, and 243, respectively.

Opening an XLL

You can open an XLL in the same ways in which you open any Microsoft Excel file. You can use the Open command on the File menu, the Microsoft Excel startup directory, the command line, or the OPEN= entries in the registry. You can open an XLL in the macro language by calling the REGISTER function with only one argument (the name of the XLL). Here is what happens:

1. Microsoft Excel tries to register a function in your XLL called xlAutoOpen, which should be declared as type "A" (returns a Boolean, no parameters). For more information, see "xlAutoOpen" on page 242.

2. If that succeeds, Microsoft Excel runs the xlAutoOpen function. This function should:

   - Call xlfRegister to register all the functions that the XLL makes available.

   - Add any menus or menu items that the XLL makes available.

   - Do any other necessary initialization.

   - Return 1.

   There is no guarantee that xlAutoOpen will be called before a function in your XLL is run. For example, the user can simply register and call one of the functions without opening the XLL, bypassing xlAutoOpen.

3. Microsoft Excel unregisters the xlAutoOpen function, since it is no longer needed.

Important Calling xlAutoOpen is the only way the Open command loads an XLL. This function is required in every DLL with the extension XLL.

Unregistering the Entire XLL

A user can call the function UNREGISTER and specify the name of your XLL. For example, if UNREGISTER("GENERIC.XLL") is called from a Microsoft Excel macro or another DLL, this instructs Microsoft Excel to remove that DLL from memory. Here is what happens:

1. Microsoft Excel tries to register a function called xlAutoClose, which should be declared as type A.

2. If xlAutoClose is found, Microsoft Excel runs the xlAutoClose function. This function should:

- Do any necessary global cleanup.

- Remove any menus or menu items that were added in xlAutoOpen.

- Delete any names that were created in xlAutoOpen. Remember that calling xlfRegister with a fourth argument causes a name to be created. You can delete names by calling xlfSetName with the second argument omitted. This is important; otherwise, the names will still appear in the Paste Function dialog box.

3. When xlAutoClose returns, Microsoft Excel unregisters all functions registered in that DLL, no matter who registered them or how often they were registered in that instance of Microsoft Excel.

Note While you are developing XLLs, you may find it convenient to call the UNREGISTER function, with the name of your XLL as its argument, from a macro in Microsoft Excel. This ensures that the XLL is completely unloaded. Thus you can compile a new version of the XLL in another process without conflicts.

Quitting Microsoft Excel

When the user quits Microsoft Excel, all loaded XLLs are unregistered as described in the previous section. The xlAutoClose function is called for every XLL that has one.

Be aware that it is still possible that your XLL will be removed from memory without xlAutoClose being called. For example, the user could unregister every function individually, and xlAutoClose will never be called.

Note There is no menu item that allows a user to close an XLL.

Registering Functions Without a Type String

You may want to allow end users to register functions in your XLL without specifying the *type_text* argument (for more information on the *type_text* argument, see "REGISTER" on page 219). This makes it easier for users to load individual XLL functions. To do this, you need to provide the xlAutoRegister function. Here is what happens:

1. A macro sheet calls REGISTER, specifying the name of the XLL and the name of the function but omitting the *type_text* argument.

2. Microsoft Excel tries to register a function in the XLL called xlAutoRegister, which should be of type RR (which takes a value LPXLOPER and returns a value LPXLOPER). If this fails, the REGISTER function returns #VALUE!

3. If this succeeds, Microsoft Excel calls xlAutoRegister, passing the name of the function (as xltypeStr) as the argument. xlAutoRegister should:

   - Determine whether the function name is recognized. If it is not, your xlAutoRegister function should return #VALUE! as an xltypeErr.

   - If the function is recognized, xlAutoRegister should call xlfRegister as usual, specifying at least the first three arguments (including *type_text*).

   - Return the same value as returned by xlfRegister (an xltypeNum if a success or an xltypeErr if a failure).

Note If xlAutoRegister calls xlfRegister without providing the *type_text* argument, an infinite loop results.

Supporting the Add-In Manager

There are some additional steps you can take to work with the Microsoft Excel Add-In Manager.

This function	Is called when the Add-In Manager
xlAutoAdd()	Adds an XLL
xlAutoRemove()	Removes an XLL
xlAddInManagerInfo()	Needs additional information from the XLL

Adding New XLLs with the Add-In Manager

The following steps describe how to use the Add-In Manager to add new XLLs.

1. The user chooses the Add-Ins... command from the Tools menu and selects the check box next to the name of the add-in or chooses the Browse button if the add-in is in a different directory.

   a. If the user chooses the Browse button, the Add-In Manager displays the Browse dialog box, allowing the user to select XLA files or XLL files.

   b. The user chooses a file. If it is an XLL file, the Add-In Manager attempts to register and run the xlAutoAdd function in the XLL. This function takes no arguments. Your XLL can optionally display a message telling the user that the XLL is now available and how to get it.

2. The Add-In Manager calls REGISTER() on the XLL, which causes the XLL's xlAutoOpen function to run.

3. The Add-In Manager attempts to register and run a function called xlAutoAdd in the XLL. This function takes no arguments. It can do anything you want it to do before your add-in is added by the Add-In Manager.

4. The Add-In Manager also adds an OPEN= line to the "Microsoft Excel" key in the registry. This causes Microsoft Excel to automatically open your XLL whenever Microsoft Excel is started.

5. The Add-In Manager tries to register and call the xlAddInManagerInfo function in your XLL to find out more information about the XLL. For more information, see the section "Supporting the Add-In Manager's Long Names" on page 190.

Removing XLLs with the Add-In Manager

The following steps describe how to use the Add-In Manager to remove installed XLLs.

1. The user runs the Add-Ins... command from the Tools menu and deselects the check box for the XLL.

2. The Add-In Manager attempts to register and run a function called xlAutoRemove in the XLL. This function takes no arguments. It can do anything you want it to do before your add-in is removed with the Add-In Manager.

3. The Add-In Manager calls UNREGISTER on the XLL, which causes the XLL's xlAutoClose function to run and unregisters all the functions in the XLL, removing it from memory.

4. The Add-In Manager also removes the OPEN= line from the "Microsoft Excel" key in the registry.

Supporting the Add-In Manager's Long Names

The Add-In Manager can optionally display a longer, more descriptive name for your XLL, in addition to the file name. When running with MS-DOS, this is preferable to seeing only the eight-character file name. To support this, the Add-In Manager attempts to register and call a function in your XLL named xlAddInManagerInfo. This function is of type "PP", which takes a value LPXLOPER and returns a value LPXLOPER. When the Add-In Manager needs a long file name, it calls this function with 1 as the argument. Your xlAddInManagerInfo function should check this argument. If it is 1, the function should return an xltypeStr containing the long name of the XLL add-in. If the argument is not 1, the function should return #VALUE! as an xlypeErr.

REGISTER.ID

REGISTER.ID is an XLM function that facilitates connecting XLLs to menus, tools, event handlers, and other items that require you to provide the address of a subroutine. The REGISTER.ID function is a direct replacement for any function that requires a macro reference. An example would be a menu that needs to call the function MyFunc in an XLL named MYXLL.XLL.

In the second column of the menu definition table you would place REGISTER.ID("MYXLL.XLL","MyFunc"). When the menu executes the REGISTER.ID, if the XLL has already been registered, it calls the function. If the XLL has not been registered, Microsoft Excel registers it by calling xlAutoRegister and then calls the function.

The Generic Template for XLLs

The sample code in the FRAMEWRK directory contains a template you can use for writing your own Microsoft Excel XLLs. This code demonstrates many of the features of the Microsoft Excel C API. To see the generic add-in code, open GENERIC.C.

When you open the compiled generic add-in (GENERIC.XLL) in Microsoft Excel, it creates a new Generic menu with the four commands listed in the following table.

Command	Action
Dialog	Displays a Microsoft Excel dialog box
Dance	Moves the selection around until you press ESC
Native Dialog	Displays a Windows dialog box that was created using the Windows API
Exit	Closes GENERIC.XLL or Generic and removes the menu

The generic add-in also provides two functions, Func1 and FuncSum, that can be used whenever the generic add-in is open. These functions appear in the Generic Add-In category in the Paste Function dialog box. Also, these functions can be registered without loading all of the generic add-in. To do this, use the following formula:

=REGISTER("GENERIC.XLL","FUNC1")
=REGISTER("GENERIC.XLL","FUNCSUM")

Advanced Flow Control in Macro Sheets

Ordinarily, when Microsoft Excel runs a macro, it does so by evaluating successive cells, one at a time, from top to bottom. However, simple top-to-bottom execution does not allow for any of the flow-control constructs that are essential in a high-level language. Microsoft Excel solves this problem by using the flow-control XLOPER, named xltypeFlow. If a function on the sheet returns a flow-control XLOPER, then instead of going on to the next cell, Microsoft Excel executes the flow-control command contained in that XLOPER.

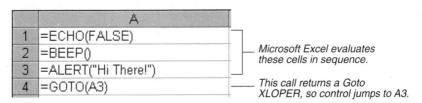

Microsoft Excel evaluates these cells in sequence.

This call returns a Goto XLOPER, so control jumps to A3.

This is how Microsoft Excel controls all flow on macro sheets. It means that functions such as GOTO and RETURN can be implemented as first-class functions. Therefore, you can write your own versions of GOTO and HALT. This capability also explains how statements such as the following work:

=IF(Boolean,GOTO(A3),GOTO(A4))

This capability allows you to write and understand flow-control functions. For example, suppose you want a function that checks the sign of a number and then performs one action if the sign is negative, another action if it is zero, and yet another action if it is positive. The macro could look like the following example.

	A	B
11		
12	Run2(b)	=SWITCH.SIGN(0,B14,B16,B18)
13		=ALERT("Shouldn't be reached")
14		=ALERT("Negative")
15		=RETURN()
16		=ALERT("Zero")
17		=RETURN()
18		=ALERT("Positive")
19		=RETURN()

You can use flow-control XLOPERs to write this function, as shown in the following code example.

```
#include <windows.h>
#include <xlcall.h>

LPXLOPER WINAPI SwitchSign(double d, LPXLOPER pxNeg,
    LPXLOPER pxZero, LPXLOPER pxPos)
{
    // pxNeg, pxZero, and pxPos must be local references.

    static XLOPER xGoto, xError, xSheet;
    LPXLOPER pxChosen;

    if (d < 0)
        pxChosen = pxNeg;
    else if (d == 0)
        pxChosen = pxZero;
    else
        pxChosen = pxPos;

    if (pxChosen->xltype != xltypeSRef)
    {
        xError.xltype = xltypeErr;
        xError.val.err = xlerrValue;
        return &xError;
    }
```

```
// Figure out the Sheet ID of the current sheet, which we need
// to make xGoto

Excel4(xlSheetId, &xSheet, 0);

xGoto.xltype = xltypeFlow;
xGoto.val.flow.xlflow = xlflowGoto;
xGoto.val.flow.valflow.idSheet = xSheet.val.mref.idSheet;
xGoto.val.flow.rw = pxChosen->val.sref.ref.rwFirst;
xGoto.val.flow.col = pxChosen->val.sref.ref.colFirst;

    return &xGoto;
}
```

This sample code is in the SWITCHSN directory or SwitchSn folder.

Note   You can return flow control XLOPERs from your C functions, and you can pass them to Excel4. The only thing you can't do with flow-control XLOPERs is pass them into C functions from Microsoft Excel. In other words, you cannot pass the return value from the GOTO function to one of your own functions. This means you can't write IF in C.

Tips and Special Considerations

This section contains tips for developing DLLs and code resources for Microsoft Excel.

Looking Up Names

In the XLM macro language, you can find out what names refer to simply by invoking them. The only way to do this from a DLL is to call the function xlfEvaluate, which is the equivalent of the XLM macro language function EVALUATE. In the macro language, EVALUATE is not very useful because things are evaluated automatically anyway. However, from C, xlfEvaluate is quite useful.

The xlfEvaluate function takes any string containing a valid Microsoft Excel expression (anything that could be typed into a worksheet cell) and evaluates it using the standard Microsoft Excel evaluator. For example:

```
XLOPER x1, x2;

/* Evaluate the string "15+17" */
x1.xltype = xltypeStr;
x1.val.str = "\005" "15+17";

Excel4(xlfEvaluate, &x2, 1, (LPXLOPER) &x1);

/* x2 now contains 32 */
```

Although you can theoretically evaluate any expression, remember that the string you pass has to be parsed, which is a slow process. So if speed is important, avoid using xlfEvaluate.

Note Calling xlfEvaluate is equivalent to pressing F9 in the formula bar. It cannot evaluate external references to sheets that are not open.

The xlfEvaluate function is most commonly used to look up the values assigned to names in a sheet. For example:

```
XLOPER x1, x2;

/* Look up the defined name "profits" on the active sheet */
x1.xltype = xltypeStr;
x1.val.str = "\010!profits";

Excel4(xlfEvaluate, &x2, 1, (LPXLOPER) &x1);
Excel4(xlFree, 0, 1, (LPXLOPER) &x2);

/* x2 now contains the definition of "profits" */
```

Note that xlfEvaluate cannot evaluate command equivalents, because they cannot be entered into cells on worksheets.

Calling Macro Language Functions from DLLs

The "Calling the Function from Within Microsoft Excel" section, on page 147, discussed using REGISTER and CALL to call DLL functions from the macro language. You can also call macro language functions from DLLs.

You can use xlUDF to call *user-defined functions,* that is, functions defined in a macro sheet or add-in. For the first argument to xlUDF, use a reference to the function you want to execute. Then pass all the arguments to the function you are calling. For example, if you had a user-defined function named FUNC, you could call FUNC(5) as follows:

```
XLOPER xFuncStr, xFuncRef, x5, xResult;

xFuncStr.xltype = xltypeStr;
xFuncStr.val.str = "\004FUNC";

x5.xltype = xltypeNum;
x5.val.num = 5;

/*
** Lookup the name FUNC using EVALUATE
*/

Excel4(xlfEvaluate, &xFuncRef, 1, (LPXLOPER) &xFuncStr);
Excel4(xlUDF, &xResult, 2, (LPXLOPER) &xFuncRef, (LPXLOPER) &x5);

/*
** After using xResult, don't forget to free it:
*/

Excel4(xlFree, &xResult, 2, (LPXLOPER) &xResult, (LPXLOPER) &xFuncRef);
```

Performing Lengthy Operations

Windows 95 and Windows NT use *preemptive multitasking.* This means that the operating system determines when an application must give up the processor so that other applications can run. Even though the operating system can preempt Microsoft Excel it is still a good idea to give up the processor during long tasks. Normally, Microsoft Excel gives up the processor frequently, allowing background tasks to run smoothly.

If you expect your DLL function to take a long time, you will need to:

- Give up the processor as frequently as possible.
- Determine whether the user has canceled the function by pressing ESC. If the user has canceled, you may want to terminate the lengthy operation.

There is a single function called xlAbort that handles both of these tasks at once. First it yields, giving other applications in the system a chance to run. Then it checks whether the user has canceled by pressing ESC. If so, xlAbort returns TRUE; if not, it returns FALSE.

When the user cancels the function by pressing ESC, the DLL should clean up and return as quickly as possible. However, you might want to prompt the user to confirm the cancellation, offering the option of continuing. If the user wants to continue, the pending cancellation can be cleared by calling xlAbort with one argument, an xltypeBool with the value FALSE.

For an example of the xlAbort function, see the fDance function in GENERIC.C in the FRAMEWRK directory.

Dealing with Uncalculated Cells

During the recalculation of a worksheet, Microsoft Excel uses sophisticated heuristics to determine which cells are scheduled to be recalculated and in which order. This means that if you enter a function on a worksheet that calls a DLL and that function tries to look up the value of another cell, you cannot be sure whether the value has been recalculated yet. You need to be concerned about this only if all of the following conditions apply:

- You are writing a DLL function that will be entered on a worksheet.
- That function looks at the value of other cells on the worksheet.
- The DLL is not a macro type (the data type string does not contain "#"). For more information on this see Register (Form 1) "Handling Uncalculated Cells" in Chapter 2.

If your DLL functions are not meant to be entered on worksheets, or if they do not try to find out the values of cells elsewhere on the worksheet (for example, using xlCoerce), you do not need to worry about the possibility of uncalculated cells.

Here is an example scenario: A DLL function called GetB5 returns the value of cell B5. The function would look like this:

```
LPXLOPER WINAPI GetB5(void)
{
    static XLOPER xResult, xReference, xNum;

    xReference.xltype = xltypeSRef;
    xReference.val.sref.count = 1;
    xReference.val.sref.ref.rwFirst =
        xReference.val.sref.ref.rwLast   = 4;
    xReference.val.sref.ref.colFirst =
        xReference.val.sref.ref.colLast = 1;

    xNum.xltype = xltypeInt;
    xNum.val.w = xltypeNum;

    Excel4(xlCoerce, &xResult, 2, (LPXLOPER) &xReference,
        (LPXLOPER) &xNum);

    return &xResult;
}
```

This function can be registered with a *type_text* argument of "R!". The exclamation point means that the function is volatile and needs to be recalculated whenever the sheet changes. To work around this, set recalculation to manual. Next, enter the following formulas on a worksheet.

Formulas

	B
1	15
2	=B1+1
3	=B2+1
4	=B3+1
5	=B4+1
6	

Values

	B
1	15
2	16
3	17
4	18
5	19
6	

Microsoft Excel schedules the cells to be calculated in descending order. That is, first B1 will be calculated, then B2, then B3, and so on. What happens when we insert the GetB5 call on line B6?

Formulas

	B
1	15
2	=B1+1
3	=B2+1
4	=B3+1
5	=B4+1
6	=GetB5()

Values

	B
1	15
2	16
3	17
4	18
5	19
6	19

Initially, the value is correct. But Microsoft Excel has no way of knowing that the function GetB5 depends on the value of Cell B5. So if you change B1 . . .

Formulas

	B
1	25
2	=B1+1
3	=B2+1
4	=B3+1
5	=B4+1
6	=GetB5()

Values

	B
1	25
2	16
3	17
4	18
5	19
6	19

. . . and then recalculate by pressing F9, Microsoft Excel schedules B6 to be calculated first. Now when GetB5 tries to look at the value of B5, it finds that the cell has not been calculated yet. The xlCoerce function call returns xlretUncalced. However, Microsoft Excel remembers that it moved to that uncalculated cell and schedules B5 to be recalculated again later. Because the GetB5 function returns a wrong value, Microsoft Excel recalculates B2 through B5, and finally, calls GetB5 once again. So the final values are correct:

Formulas

	B
1	25
2	=B1+1
3	=B2+1
4	=B3+1
5	=B4+1
6	=GetB5()

Values

	B
1	25
2	26
3	27
4	28
5	29
6	29

Finally, Microsoft Excel now knows that B6 is dependent on B5, and rightly schedules it to be calculated last in the future. GetB5 will not see xlretUncalced again.

Experienced XLM macro language users will recognize that this is not the behavior of the Microsoft Excel macro language. If GetB5 had been written in the XLM macro language, the first recalculation would simply have given the wrong value. Microsoft Excel would still reschedule B6, so the next recalculation would be correct. If, for some reason, you require this macro language behavior, you can specify # in the *type_text* argument to the REGISTER function.

Getting the Instance and Windows Handles

To program in the Windows environment, it is sometimes helpful to find out the Microsoft Excel instance handle (hInst) or top-level window handle (hWnd). Two special functions, xlGetInst and xlGetHwnd, have been provided for this purpose. These functions require special care under Win32. This is because `sizeof(HWND)` on Win32 is a `long` but the field used to receive the `HWND` parameter in the `XLOPER` structure is a `short`. Consequently the high word of the actual Microsoft Excel `HWND` is truncated. To work around this problem call `xlGetHwnd` to get the low word of the actual `hwnd`, then iterate the list of top-level windows and look for a match with the returned low word. This code illustrates the technique:

```
typedef struct _EnumStruct {
    HWND      hwnd;
    unsigned short  wLoword;
} EnumStruct;

#define CLASS_NAME_BUFFER    50

/*
**
** Function: EnumProc
**
** Comments:   Used to find the hWnd in the Win32 version of Excel.
**             This is the callback routine that checks each hwnd.
**
** Arguments: hwnd - The hwnd of the window currently being looked at
**            EnumStruct * - A structure containing loword of hwnd of
**                        interest and space to return full hwnd.
**
** Returns:    BOOL - indicates success or failure
**
```

```
** Date                Developer               Action
** ----------------------------------------------------------
*/
BOOL CALLBACK EnumProc(HWND hwnd, EnumStruct * pEnum)
{
    // first check class of the window.  Must be "XLMAIN"
    char szClass[CLASS_NAME_BUFFER+1];

    GetClassName(hwnd, szClass, CLASS_NAME_BUFFER);

    if(!lstrcmpi(szClass, "XLMAIN"))
    {
        // if that is a match, check the loword of the window handle
        if(LOWORD((DWORD)hwnd) == pEnum->wLoword)
        {
            pEnum->hwnd = hwnd;
            return FALSE;
        }
    }
    // no match continue the enumeration
    return TRUE;
}


/*
**
** Function: GetHwnd
**
** Comments:  Used to find the hWnd in the Win32 version of Excel.
**            This routine sets up the callback and checks the results.
**
** Arguments: pHwnd - This is actually the returned hwnd
**
** Returns:   BOOL - Indicating success or failure.
**
** Date                Developer               Action
** ----------------------------------------------------------
*/
BOOL GetHwnd(HWND *pHwnd)
{
    XLOPER x;
```

```
    // Get the loword of the hwnd
    if(Excel4(xlGetHwnd, &x, 0) == xlretSuccess)
    {
        EnumStruct enm;

        // Set up the structure
        enm.hwnd = NULL;
        enm.wLoword = x.val.w;

        // Start the enumeration
        EnumWindows((WNDENUMPROC)EnumProc, (LPARAM) &enm);

        // Check results
        if(enm.hwnd != NULL)
        {
            *pHwnd = enm.hwnd;
            return TRUE;
        }
    }

    return FALSE;
}
```

While it is possible to obtain the instance handle, under Win32 it is not as useful as it was under Win16. The window handle is useful for creating child windows and custom Windows dialog boxes.

Considerations for the Function Wizard

The Function Wizard allows the user to construct an expression's arguments interactively. As a part of this process, the Function Wizard evaluates functions with the user's proposed arguments and displays the result. Each time an argument is entered the function is recalculated. For simple functions that quickly calculate a value this process does not cause a problem. Unfortunately, functions that access external data as a part of calculations, or functions that require a significant amount of time in order to calculate, don't work well, because the time required to calculate or retrieve external data is annoyingly long.

The Function Wizard cannot automatically determine which functions should not be calculated during expression construction. It is therefore up to each XLL function to refuse to calculate if it is called at an inappropriate time. Use the following code to determine if the function wizard window is showing.

```
#define CLASS_NAME_BUFFER    50

typedef struct _EnumStruct {
    BOOL bFuncWiz;
    short hwndXLMain;
} EnumStruct, FAR * LPEnumStruct;

double WINAPI FuncWiz(double FAR * pdOne, double FAR * pdTwo)
{
    double dResult;

    if(IsCalledByFuncWiz())
        return 0;

    dResult = *pdOne * *pdTwo;
    return dResult;
}

BOOL IsCalledByFuncWiz(void)
{
    XLOPER xHwndMain;
    EnumStruct  enm;

    if (Excel4(xlGetHwnd, &xHwndMain, 0) == xlretSuccess)
    {
        enm.bFuncWiz = FALSE;
        enm.hwndXLMain = xHwndMain.val.w;
        EnumWindows((WNDENUMPROC) EnumProc,
            (LPARAM) ((LPEnumStruct)  &enm));
        return enm.bFuncWiz;
    }
    return FALSE;    //safe case: Return False if not sure
}
```

```
BOOL CALLBACK EnumProc(HWND hwnd, LPEnumStruct pEnum)
{
    // first check the class of the window.  Will be szXLDialogClass
    // if function wizard dialog is up in Excel
    char rgsz[CLASS_NAME_BUFFER];
    GetClassName(hwnd, (LPSTR)rgsz, CLASS_NAME_BUFFER);
    if (2 == CompareString(MAKELCID(MAKELANGID(LANG_ENGLISH,
        SUBLANG_ENGLISH_US),SORT_DEFAULT), NORM_IGNORECASE,
        (LPSTR)rgsz,  (lstrlen((LPSTR)rgsz)>lstrlen("bosa_sdm_XL"))
        ? lstrlen("bosa_sdm_XL"):-1, "bosa_sdm_XL", -1))
    {
        if(LOWORD((DWORD) GetParent(hwnd)) == pEnum->hwndXLMain)
        {
            pEnum->bFuncWiz = TRUE;
            return FALSE;
        }
    }
    // no luck - continue the enumeration
    return TRUE;
}
```

CHAPTER 8

Applications Programming Interface Function Reference

Introduction

This chapter lists alphabetically the Microsoft Excel functions most useful to DLLs that use the C API. You can call almost any function from a DLL, with the exception of some macro control functions. These macro control functions are listed in the following section. For information about functions not included in this chapter, see the online Microsoft Excel Macro Function Reference.

This chapter contains Microsoft Windows code examples. Source code for the examples is in the SAMPLES directory on the CD-ROM. In the text, every example includes the path and file name of the corresponding disk file. If there is a description of the example, it usually appears under the Example heading.

Functions Included in This Chapter

The functions listed in this chapter include the following:

- The Excel4 and Excel4v callback functions.
- Functions you are likely to use to interact with Microsoft Excel DLLs from a macro sheet: CALL, REGISTER, REGISTER.ID, and UNREGISTER.
- Functions that are especially useful in DLLs: CALLER and EVALUATE.
- Microsoft Excel special service functions, which can be called only from DLLs:

xlAbort	xlFree	xlSheetId
xlCoerce	xlGetBinaryName	xlSheetNm
xlDisableXLMsgs	xlGetHwnd	xlStack
xlEnableXLMsgs	xlGetInst	xlUDF
xlDefineBinaryName	xlSet	

- Functions you should provide in your XLL to qualify as a stand-alone DLL (XLL):

xlAddInManagerInfo	xlAutoClose	xlAutoRegister
xlAutoAdd	xlAutoOpen	xlAutoRemove

- Functions in the Framework library, which provide a good starting point for writing Microsoft Excel DLLs and XLLs.

The following are the macro control functions that cannot be called from DLLs:

BREAK	ENDIF	IF	RETURN
ELSE	FOR	NEXT	WHILE
ELSEIF	FOR.CELL		

Functions in the Framework Library

The Framework library was created to help make writing XLLs easier. It includes simple functions for managing XLOPER memory, creating temporary XLOPERs, robustly calling the Excel4 function, and printing debugging strings on an attached terminal.

The functions included in this library help simplify a piece of code that looks like this:

```
XLOPER xMissing, xBool;
xMissing.xltype = xltypeMissing;
xBool.xltype = xltypeBool;
xBool.val.bool = 0;
Excel4(xlcDisplay, 0, 2, (LPXLOPER) &xMissing, (LPXLOPER) &xBool);
```

To look like this:

```
Excel(xlcDisplay, 0, 2, TempMissing(), TempBool(0));
```

The following functions are included in the Framework library:

DebugPrintf	TempActiveRef	TempNum
Excel	TempActiveCell	TempStr
FreeAllTempMemory	TempActiveRow	TempBool
InitFramework	TempActiveColumn	TempInt
QuitFramework	TempMissing	TempErr

Using these functions shortens the amount of time required to write a DLL or XLL. Starting development from the sample application GENERIC also shortens development time. Use GENERIC.C as a template to help set up the framework of an XLL and then replace the existing code with your own.

The temporary XLOPER functions create XLOPER values using memory from a local heap managed by the Framework library. The XLOPER values remain valid until you call the FreeAllTempMemory function or the Excel function (the Excel function frees all temporary memory before it returns).

To use the Framework library functions, you must include the FRAMEWRK.H file in your C code and add the FRAMEWRK.C or FRMWRK32.LIB files to your code project.

CALL (Form 1)

Called from a macro sheet or worksheet. This function calls a registered function in a DLL or a code resource. The function must already have been registered using REGISTER or REGISTER.ID.

Returns the return value from the function that was called.

Syntax

```
CALL(register_id,argument1, ...)
```

register_id (xltypeNum)
   The register ID of the function. You can get this using REGISTER.

argument1, ...
   Zero or more arguments to the function that is being called. These arguments are optional.

Remarks

If the function was originally registered, and a function name was specified in the *function_text* argument, this function can alternately be called as follows:

```
=function_text(argument1, ...)
```

Example

The following example registers the CalcCircum function in CIRCUM.DLL, and then calls the function using the defined name for cell B1.

	A	B
1	fCircum	=REGISTER("CIRCUM","CalcCircum","EE")
2		=CALL(fCircum, 100)
3		=UNREGISTER(fCircum)
4		=RETURN()

Cell B1 has the defined name fCircum.

Related Functions

CALL (Form 2), REGISTER, REGISTER.ID, UNREGISTER

CALL (Form 2)

Called from a macro sheet or worksheet. If the function is not yet registered, it is registered when called, and then the specified procedure in the DLL or code resource is called. If the function is already registered, it is called without reregistering.

Returns the return value from the function that was called.

Syntax

```
CALL(module_text,procedure,type_text,argument1, ...)
```

module_text (xltypeStr)
    The name of the DLL containing the function.

procedure (xltypeStr or xltypeNum)
    If a string, the name of the function to call. If a number, the ordinal export number of the code function to call. For clarity and robustness, always use the string form.

type_text (xltypeStr)
    An optional string specifying the types of all the arguments to the function, and the type of the return value of the function. You can omit this argument for a stand-alone DLL (XLL) that provides the xlAutoRegister function. For more information about data types, see the "Remarks" section under "REGISTER (Form 1)" on page 220.

argument1, ...
    Zero or more arguments to the function. These arguments are optional.

Remarks

This form of call is equivalent to using Call (Form 1), as follows:

=CALL(REGISTER.ID(*module_text*, *procedure*, *type_text*), *argument1*, ...)

Example

The following example registers and calls the CalcCircum function in CIRCUM.DLL.

	B
6	=CALL("CIRCUM","CalcCircum","EE",100)
7	=RETURN()

Related Functions

CALL (Form 1), REGISTER, REGISTER.ID, UNREGISTER

CALLER

Called from a DLL.

Returns information about the cell, range of cells, command on a menu, tool on a toolbar, or object that called the macro that is currently running.

Code called from	Returns
DLL	The Register ID.
A single cell	A cell reference.
Menu	A four-element array, containing the bar ID, the menu position, the submenu position, and the command position.
Toolbar	A two-element array. The first element is the toolbar number for built-in toolbars or a toolbar name for custom toolbars. The second item is the position on the toolbar.
Graphic object	The object identifier (object name).
ON.ENTER	A reference to the cell being entered.
ON.DOUBLECLICK	The cell that was double-clicked (not necessarily the active cell).
Auto_Open, AutoClose, Auto_Activate or Auto_Deactivate macro	The name of the calling sheet.
Other methods not listed	#REF! Error.

The return value is one of the following XLOPER data types: xltypeRef, xltypeSRef, xltypeNum, xltypeStr, xltypeErr, or xltypeMulti. For more information about XLOPERs, see "The XLOPER Data Type" on page 151.

Syntax

```
Excel4(xlfCaller, (LPXLOPER) pxRes,0);
```

Example

\SAMPLES\EXAMPLE\EXAMPLE.C

```
short WINAPI CallerExample(void)
{
    XLOPER xRes;

    Excel4(xlfCaller, (LPXLOPER)&xRes, 0);
    Excel4(xlcSelect, 0, 1, (LPXLOPER)&xRes);
    Excel4(xlFree, 0, 1, (LPXLOPER)&xRes);
    return 1;
}
```

Remarks

This function is the only exception to the rule that worksheet functions can be called only from DLLs that were called from worksheets.

debugPrintf

Framework library function. This function writes a debugging string to an attached terminal. The terminal should be set up for 9600 baud, 8 data bits, no parity, and 1 stop bit.

This function does not return a value.

Syntax

```
void WINAPI debugPrintf(LPSTR lpFormat, arguments);
```

lpFormat (LPSTR)
   The format string, which is identical to what you would use with the `sprintf` function.

arguments
   Zero or more arguments to match the format string.

Example

This function prints a string to show that control was passed to the routine.

\SAMPLES\EXAMPLE\EXAMPLE.C

```
short debugPrintfExample(void)
{
    debugPrintf("Made it!\n");
    return 1;
}
```

EVALUATE

This function uses the Microsoft Excel parser and function evaluator to evaluate any expression that could be entered in a worksheet cell.

Returns the result of evaluating the string.

Syntax

```
Excel4(xlfEvaluate, LPXLOPER pxRes, 1, LPXLOPER pxFormulaText)
```

pxFormulaText (xltypeStr)
   The string to evaluate, optionally beginning with an equal sign (=).

Remarks

Limitations

The string can contain only functions, not command equivalents. It is equivalent to pressing F9 from the formula bar.

Primary Use

The primary use of the EVALUATE function is to allow DLLs to find out the value assigned to a defined name on a sheet.

External References

EVALUATE cannot be used to evaluate references to an external sheet that is not open.

Macro Example

The following example takes a text value, a5, and jumps to the location it represents by using the EVALUATE function.

	A
1	a5
2	=EVALUATE(a1&"()")
3	=RETURN
4	
5	=ALERT("Made it!")
6	=RETURN()

Example

This example uses xlfEvaluate to coerce the text "B38" to the contents of cell B38.

\SAMPLES\EXAMPLE\EXAMPLE.C

```
short int WINAPI EvaluateExample(void)
{
    XLOPER xFormulaText, xRes, xRes2, xInt;

    xFormulaText.xltype = xltypeStr;
    xFormulaText.val.str = "\004!B38";
    Excel4(xlfEvaluate, (LPXLOPER)&xRes, 1, (LPXLOPER)&xFormulaText);

    xInt.xltype = xltypeInt;
    xInt.val.w = 2;
    Excel4(xlcAlert, (LPXLOPER)&xRes2, 2, (LPXLOPER)&xRes,
        (LPXLOPER)&xInt);
    Excel4(xlFree, 0, 1, (LPXLOPER)&xRes);
    Excel4(xlFree, 0, 1, (LPXLOPER)&xRes2);

    return 1;
}
```

Excel

Framework library function. This is a wrapper for the Excel4 function. It checks to see that none of the arguments is zero, which would indicate that a temporary XLOPER failed. If an error occurs, it prints a debug message. When finished, it frees all temporary memory.

Returns one of the following (int).

Value	Return code	Description
0	xlretSuccess	The function was called successfully. This does not mean that the function did not return a Microsoft Excel error value; to find that out, you have to look at the resulting XLOPER.
1	xlretAbort	An abort occurred (internal abort). You might get this if a macro closes its own macro sheet by calling CLOSE, or if Microsoft Excel is out of memory. In this case you must exit immediately. The DLL can call only xlFree before it exits. The user will be able to save any work interactively using the Save command on the File menu.
2	xlretInvXlfn	An invalid function number was supplied. If you are using constants from XLCALL.H, this shouldn't happen.

Value	Return code	Description
4	xlretInvCount	An invalid number of arguments was entered. Remember that no Microsoft Excel function can take more than 30 arguments, and some require a fixed number of arguments.
8	xlretInvXloper	An invalid XLOPER structure or an argument of the wrong type was used.
16	xlretStackOvfl	(Windows only) A stack overflow occurred. Use xlStack to monitor the amount of room left on the stack. If possible, avoid allocating large local (automatic) arrays on the stack ; make them static. (Note that a stack overflow may occur without being detected.)
32	xlretFailed	A command-equivalent function failed. This is equivalent to a macro command displaying the macro error alert dialog box.
64	xlretUncalced	An attempt was made to dereference a cell that has not been calculated yet, because it was scheduled to be recalculated after the current cell. In this case the DLL needs to exit immediately. It can call only xlFree before it exits. For more information, see "Dealing with Uncalculated Cells" on page 196.

Syntax

```
Excel(int iFunction, LPXLOPER pxRes, int iCount,
LPXLOPER argument1, ...)
```

iFunction (int)

A number indicating the command, function, or special function you want to call. For a list of valid *iFunction* values and related information, see the "Remarks" section under "Excel4" on page 215.

pxRes (LPXLOPER)

A pointer to an allocated XLOPER (10 bytes) that will hold the result of the evaluated function.

iCount (int)

The number of arguments that will be passed to the function.

argument1, ... (LPXLOPER)

The optional arguments to the function. All arguments must be pointers to XLOPERs.

Example

This example passes a bad argument to the Excel function, which sends a message to the debugging terminal.

\SAMPLES\EXAMPLE\EXAMPLE.C

```
short WINAPI ExcelExample(void)
{
    Excel(xlcDisplay, 0, 1, 0);
    return 1;
}
```

Related Function

Excel4

Excel4

This function calls an internal Microsoft Excel macro function or special command from a DLL or code resource.

Returns one of the following (int).

Value	Return code	Description
0	xlretSuccess	The function was called successfully. This does not mean that the function did not return a Microsoft Excel error value; to find that out, you have to look at the resulting XLOPER.
1	xlretAbort	An abort occurred (internal abort). You might get this if a macro closes its own macro sheet by calling CLOSE, or if Microsoft Excel is out of memory. In this case you must exit immediately. The DLL can call only xlFree before it exits. The user will be able to save any work interactively using the Save command on the File menu.
2	xlretInvXlfn	An invalid function number was supplied. If you are using constants from XLCALL.H, this shouldn't happen.
4	xlretInvCount	An invalid number of arguments was entered. Remember that no Microsoft Excel function can take more than 30 arguments, and some require a fixed number of arguments.
8	xlretInvXloper	An invalid XLOPER structure or an argument of the wrong type was used.
16	xlretStackOvfl	(Windows only) A stack overflow occurred. Use xlStack to monitor the amount of room left on the stack. Don't allocate large local (automatic) arrays on the stack if possible; make them static. (Note that a stack overflow may occur without being detected.)

Value	Return code	Description
32	xlretFailed	A command-equivalent function failed. This is equivalent to a macro command displaying the macro error alert dialog box.
64	xlretUncalced	An attempt was made to dereference a cell that has not been calculated yet, because it was scheduled to be recalculated after the current cell. In this case the DLL needs to exit immediately. It can call only xlFree before it exits. For more information, see "Dealing with Uncalculated Cells" on page 196.

Syntax

```
Excel4(int iFunction, LPXLOPER pxRes, int iCount,
LPXLOPER argument1, ...)
```

iFunction (int)

A number indicating the command, function, or special function you want to call. For a list of valid *iFunction* values, see the following "Remarks" section.

pxRes (LPXLOPER)

A pointer to an allocated XLOPER (10 bytes) that will hold the result of the evaluated function.

iCount (int)

The number of arguments that will be passed to the function.

argument1, ... (LPXLOPER)

The optional arguments to the function. All arguments must be pointers to XLOPERs.

Remarks

Valid *iFunction* values

Valid *iFunction* values are any of the xlf... or xlc... constants defined in XLCALL.H or any of the following special functions:

xlAbort	xlEnableXLMsgs	xlGetInst	xlSheetNm
xlCoerce	xlFree	xlSet	xlStack
xlDefineBinaryName	xlGetBinaryName	xlSheetId	xlUDF
xlDisableXLMsgs	xlGetHwnd		

Different Types of Functions

Excel4 distinguishes between three classes of functions. The functions are classified according to the three states in which Microsoft Excel may be calling the DLL. Class 1 applies when the DLL is called from a worksheet as a result of recalculation. Class 2 applies when the DLL is called from within a function macro or from a worksheet where it was registered with a number sign (#) in the type text. Class 3 applies when a DLL is called from an object, macro, menu, toolbar, shortcut key, ExecuteExcel4Macro, or the Tools/Macro/Run command. The following table shows what functions are valid in each class.

Class 1	Class 2	Class 3
Any worksheet function	Any worksheet function	Any function, including xlSet and command-equivalent functions
Any xl... function except xlSet	Any xl... function except xlSet	
XlfCaller	Macro sheet functions that return a value but perform no action	

Displaying the Dialog Box for a Command-Equivalent Function

If a command-equivalent function has an associated dialog box, you can set the xlPrompt bit in *iFunction*. This means that Microsoft Excel will display the appropriate dialog box before carrying out the command.

Writing International DLLs

If you set the xlIntl bit in *iFunction,* the function or command will be carried out as if it were being called from an International Macro Sheet. This means that the command will behave as it would on the U.S. version of Microsoft Excel, even if it is running on an international (localized) version.

xlretUncalced or xlretAbort

After receiving one of these return values, your DLL needs to clean up and exit immediately. Callbacks into Microsoft Excel, except xlFree, are disabled after receiving one of these return values.

Example

This example uses the Excel4 function to select the cell from which it was called.

\SAMPLES\EXAMPLE\EXAMPLE.C

```
short WINAPI Excel4Example(void)
{
    XLOPER xRes;

    Excel4(xlfCaller, (LPXLOPER)&xRes, 0);
    Excel4(xlcSelect, 0, 1, (LPXLOPER)&xRes);
    Excel4(xlFree, 0, 1, (LPXLOPER)&xRes);

    return 1;
}
```

Related Functions

Excel4v, Excel

Excel4v

This function calls an internal Microsoft Excel function from a DLL or code resource. This form accepts its arguments as an array.

Returns the same value as Excel4.

Syntax

```
int _cdecl Excel4v(int iFunction, LPXLOPER pxRes, int iCount,
LPXLOPER rgx[])
```

iFunction (int)

A number indicating the command, function, or special function you want to call. For more information, see the "Remarks" section under "Excel4" on page 215.

pxRes (LPXLOPER)

A pointer to an allocated XLOPER (10 bytes) that will hold the result of the evaluated function.

iCount (int)

The number of arguments that will be passed to the function.

rgx (LPXLOPER [])

An array containing the arguments to the function. All arguments in the array must be pointers to XLOPERs.

Remarks

This function is provided so you can write a wrapper function that calls Excel4. Otherwise, it behaves exactly like Excel4.

Example

See the code for the Excel function in FRAMEWRK.C in the FRAMEWRK directory.

Related Functions

Excel4, Excel

InitFramework

Framework library function. This function initializes the Framework library.

This function does not return a value.

Syntax

```
InitFramework(void);
```

This function has no arguments.

Example

This example uses the InitFramework function to free all temporary memory.

\SAMPLES\EXAMPLE\EXAMPLE.C

```
short WINAPI InitFrameworkExample(void)
{
    InitFramework();
    return 1;
}
```

QuitFramework

This function does not return a value.

Syntax

```
QuitFramework(void);
```

This function has no arguments.

REGISTER (Form 1)

Called from a Microsoft Excel XLM macro sheet or DLL. This function makes a function or command in a DLL or command available to Microsoft Excel, and returns the register ID identifying the function for use by CALL and UNREGISTER.

Returns the register ID of the function (xltypeNum), which can be used in subsequent CALL and UNREGISTER calls.

Syntax

From a macro sheet:

```
REGISTER(module_text,procedure,type_text,function_text,
argument_text,macro_type,category,shortcut_text)
```

From a DLL:

```
Excel4(xlfRegister, LPXLOPER pxRes, 8,
    LPXLOPER pxModuleText,    LPXLOPER pxProcedure,
    LPXLOPER pxTypeText,      LPXLOPER pxFunctionText,
    LPXLOPER pxArgumentText,  LPXLOPER pxMacroType,
    LPXLOPER pxCategory,      LPXLOPER pxShortcutText);
```

module_text (xltypeStr)
   The name of the DLL containing the function.

procedure (xltypeStr or xltypeNum)
   If a string, the name of the function to call. If a number, the ordinal export number of the function to call. For clarity and robustness, always use the string form.

type_text (xltypeStr)
   An optional string specifying the types of all the arguments to the function and the type of the return value of the function. For more information, see the following "Remarks" section. This argument can be omitted for a stand-alone DLL (XLL) that includes an xlAutoRegister function.

function_text (xltypeStr)
   The name of the function as it will appear in the Function Wizard. This argument is optional; if omitted, the function will not be available in the Function Wizard, and it can be called only using the CALL function.

argument_text (xltypeStr)
   An optional text string describing the arguments to the function. The user sees this in the Function Wizard. If omitted, it will be constructed based on the *type_text*.

macro_type (xltypeNum)

An optional argument indicating the type of function. Use 0 for none, 1 for a function (default), or 2 for a command. This argument can be used to define hidden functions (use *macro_type* = 0) or to define functions available only from macro sheets (use *macro_type* = 2).

category (xltypeStr or xltypeNum)

An optional argument allowing you to specify which category the new function or command should belong to. The Function Wizard divides functions by type (category). You can specify a category name or a sequential number, where the number is the position in which the category appears in the Function Wizard. For more information, see "Category Names" on page 225. If omitted, the User Defined category is assumed.

shortcut_text (xltypeStr)

A one-character, case-sensitive string specifying the control key that will be assigned to this command. For example, "A" will assign this command to CONTROL+SHIFT+A. This argument is optional and is used for commands only.

Remarks

Data Types

In the CALL, REGISTER, and REGISTER.ID functions, the *type_text* argument specifies the data type of the return value and the data types of all arguments to the DLL function or code resource. The first character of *type_text* specifies the data type of the return value. The remaining characters indicate the data types of all the arguments. For example, a DLL function that returns a floating-point number and takes an integer and a floating-point number as arguments would require "BIB" for the *type_text* argument.

The following table contains a complete list of the data type codes that Microsoft Excel recognizes, a description of each data type, how the argument or return value is passed, and a typical declaration for the data type in the C programming language.

Code	Description	Pass by	C declaration
A	Logical (FALSE = 0, TRUE = 1)	Value	`short int`
B	IEEE 8-byte floating-point number	Value	`double`
C	Null-terminated string (maximum string length = 255 characters)	Reference	`char *`
D	Byte-counted string (first byte contains length of string, maximum string length = 255 characters)	Reference	`unsigned char *`

Code	Description	Pass by	C declaration
E	IEEE 8-byte floating-point number	Reference	`double *`
F	Null-terminated string (maximum string length = 255 characters)	Reference (modify in place)	`char *`
G	Byte-counted string (first byte contains length of string, maximum string length = 255 characters)	Reference (modify in place)	`unsigned char *`
H	Unsigned 2-byte integer	Value	`unsigned short int`
I	Signed 2-byte integer	Value	`short int`
J	Signed 4-byte integer	Value	`long int`
K	Array	Reference	`FP *`
L	Logical (FALSE = 0, TRUE = 1)	Reference	`short int *`
M	Signed 2-byte integer	Reference	`short int *`
N	Signed 4-byte integer	Reference	`long int *`
O	Array	Reference	Three arguments are passed: `unsigned short int *` `unsigned short int *` `double []`
P	Microsoft Excel OPER data structure	Reference	`OPER *`
R	Microsoft Excel XLOPER data structure	Reference	`XLOPER *`

When working with the data types displayed in the preceding table, keep the following in mind:

- The C-language declarations are based on the assumption that your compiler defaults to 8-byte doubles, 2-byte short integers, and 4-byte long integers.

- All functions in DLLs and code resources are called using the __stdcall calling convention. Most C compilers allow you to use the __stdcall calling convention by adding the __stdcall keyword to the function declaration, as shown in the following example:

```
__stdcall void main (rows,columns,a)
```

- If a function uses a pass-by-reference data type for its return value, you can pass a null pointer as the return value. Microsoft Excel will interpret the null pointer as the #NUM! error value.

Additional Data Type Information

This section contains detailed information about the E, F, G, K, O, P, and R data types, and other information about the *type_text* argument.

E Data Type

Microsoft Excel expects a DLL using the E data type to pass pointers to floating-point numbers on the stack. This can cause problems with some languages (for example, Borland C++) that expect the number to be passed on the coprocessor emulator stack. The workaround is to pass a pointer to the number on the coprocessor stack. The following example shows how to return a double from Borland C++:

```
typedef double * lpDbl;
extern "C" lpDbl __stdcall AddDbl(double D1,
    double D2, WORD npDbl)
{
    lpDbl Result;
    Result = (lpDbl)MK_FP(_SS, npDbl);
    *Result = D1 + D2;
    return (Result);
}
```

F and G Data Types

With the F and G data types, a function can modify a string buffer that is allocated by Microsoft Excel. If the return value type code is F or G, then Microsoft Excel ignores the value returned by the function. Instead, Microsoft Excel searches the list of function arguments for the first corresponding data type (F or G) and then takes the current contents of the allocated string buffer as the return value. Microsoft Excel allocates 256 bytes for the argument, so the function may return a larger string than it received.

K Data Type

The K data type uses a pointer to a variable-size FP structure. You should define this structure in the DLL or code resource as follows:

```
typedef struct _FP
{
    unsigned short int rows;
    unsigned short int columns;
    double array[1];    /* Actually, array[rows][columns] */
} FP;
```

The declaration `double array[1]` allocates storage only for a single-element array. The number of elements in the actual array equals the number of rows multiplied by the number of columns.

O Data Type

The O data type can be used only as an argument, not as a return value. It passes three items: a pointer to the number of rows in an array, a pointer to the number of columns in an array, and a pointer to a two-dimensional array of floating-point numbers.

Instead of returning a value, a function can modify an array passed by the O data type. To do this, you could use ">O" as the *type_text* argument. For more information about modifying an array, see the section "Modifying in Place – Functions Declared as Void" on page 225.

The O data type was created for direct compatibility with FORTRAN DLLs, which pass arguments by reference.

P Data Type

The P data type is a pointer to an OPER structure. The OPER structure contains 8 bytes of data, followed by a 2-byte identifier that specifies the type of data. With the P data type, a DLL function or code resource can take and return any Microsoft Excel data type.

The OPER structure is defined as follows:

```
typedef struct _oper
{
    union
    {
        double num;
        unsigned char *str;
        unsigned short int bool;
        unsigned short int err;
        struct
        {
            struct _oper *lparray;
            unsigned short int rows;
            unsigned short int columns;
        } array;
    } val;
    unsigned short int type;
} OPER;
```

The *type* field contains one of the values listed in the following table.

Type	Description	Val field to use
1	Numeric	num
2	String (first byte contains length of string)	str
4	Boolean (logical)	bool

Type	Description	Val field to use
16	Error: the error values are: 0 #NULL! 7 #DIV/0! 15 #VALUE! 23 #REF! 29 #NAME? 36 #NUM! 42 #N/A	err
64	Array	array
128	Missing argument	
256	Empty cell	

The last two values can be used only as arguments, not return values. The missing argument value (128) is passed when the caller omits an argument. The empty cell value (256) is passed when the caller passes a reference to an empty cell.

R Data Type—Calling Microsoft Excel Functions from DLLs

The R data type is a pointer to an XLOPER structure, which is an enhanced version of the OPER structure. In Microsoft Excel versions 5.0 and later, you can use the R data type to write DLLs and code resources that call Microsoft Excel functions. With the XLOPER structure, a DLL function can pass sheet references and implement flow control, in addition to passing data. For more information about flow control, see the section "Advanced Flow Control in Macro Sheets" on page 191.

Volatile Functions and Recalculation

Microsoft Excel usually calculates a DLL function (or a code resource) only when it is entered into a cell, when one of its precedents changes, or when the cell is calculated during a macro. On a worksheet, you can make a DLL function or code resource volatile, which means that it recalculates every time the worksheet recalculates. To make a function volatile, add an exclamation point (!) as the last character in the *type_text* argument.

For example, in Microsoft Excel for Windows, the following worksheet formula recalculates every time the worksheet recalculates:

```
CALL("User","GetTickCount","J!")
```

Modifying in Place—Functions Declared as Void

You can use a single digit *n* for the return type code in *type_text,* where *n* is a number from 1 to 9. This tells Microsoft Excel to take the value of the variable in the location pointed to by the *n*th argument in *type_text* as the return value. This is also known as modifying in place. The *n*th argument must be a pass-by-reference data type (C, D, E, F, G, K, L, M, N, O, P, or R). The DLL function or code resource also must be declared with the void keyword in the C language (or the procedure keyword in the Pascal language).

For example, a DLL function that takes a null-terminated string and two pointers to integers as arguments can modify the string in place. Use "1FMM" as the *type_text* argument, and declare the function as void.

Previous versions of Microsoft Excel used the > character to modify the first argument in place—there was no way to modify any argument other than the first. The > character is equivalent to *n* = 1 in Microsoft Excel versions 5.0 and later.

Handling Uncalculated Cells

Appending a number sign (#) to the end of *type_text* changes the way the DLL handles uncalculated cells when called from a worksheet. If the number sign is present, dereferencing uncalculated cells returns the old values (this is the behavior found in the macro language). If the number sign is not present, evaluating an uncalculated cell will result in an xlretUncalced error, and the current function will be called again once the cell has been calculated. In addition, if the number sign is not present, the DLL may call only Class 1 functions. If the number sign is present, the DLL may call any Class 2 function. For more information about working with uncalculated cells, see the section "Dealing with Uncalculated Cells" on page 196.

Category Names

Here are some guidelines for determining which category you should put your XLL functions in (the *category* argument to REGISTER).

- If the function does something that could be done by the user as a part of your add-in's user interface, you should put the function in the Commands category.

- If the function returns information about the state of the add-in or any other useful information, you should put the function in the Information category.

- An add-in should never add functions or commands to the User Defined category. This category is for the exclusive use of end users.

Example for a Macro

The following example registers the CalcCircum function in CIRCUM.DLL, and then calls the function using the defined name for cell B1.

	A	B
1	fCircum	=REGISTER("CIRCUM","CalcCircum","EE")
2		=CALL(fCircum,100)
3		=UNREGISTER(fCircum)
4		=RETURN()

Cell B1 has the defined name fCircum.

Example

See the code for the xlAutoOpen function in GENERIC.C in the FRAMEWRK directory.

Related Functions

CALL, REGISTER.ID, UNREGISTER

REGISTER (Form 2)

Called from a macro sheet or DLL. This function can only be used on an XLL containing an xlAutoOpen procedure. This function registers the xlAutoOpen function, calls it, and then unregisters it.

Returns the name of the DLL or code resource (xltypeStr).

Syntax

From a macro sheet:

```
REGISTER(module_text)
```

From a DLL:

```
Excel4(xlfRegister, LPXLOPER pxRes, 1, LPXLOPER pxModuleText);
```

module_text (xltypeStr)
   The name of the DLL containing the function.

Remarks

This function is to an XLL what OPEN is to a worksheet. A Macro Record of a File Open operation on an XLL will show that REGISTER(*module_text*) is recorded. If OPEN is performed on an XLL, the open function registers xlAutoOpen but does not run it. If an action similar to Open is needed for an XLL, use this form of REGISTER instead.

REGISTER.ID

Called from a macro sheet or DLL. If a function is already registered, returns the existing register ID for that function without reregistering it. If a function is not yet registered, registers it and returns a register ID.

Returns the register ID of the function (xltypeNum), which can be used in subsequent CALL and UNREGISTER calls.

Syntax

From a macro sheet:

```
REGISTER.ID(module_text,procedure,type_text)
```

From a DLL:

```
Excel4(xlfRegisterId, LPXLOPER pxRes, 3, LPXLOPER pxModuleText,
LPXLOPER pxProcedure, LPXLOPER pxTypeText);
```

module_text (xltypeStr)
  The name of the DLL containing the function.

procedure (xltypeStr or xltypeNum)
  If a string, the name of the function to call. If a number, the ordinal export number of the function to call. For clarity and robustness, always use the string form.

type_text (xltypeStr)
  An optional string specifying the types of all the arguments to the function and the type of the return value of the function. For more information, see the following "Remarks" section. This argument can be omitted for a stand-alone DLL (XLL) defining xlAutoRegister.

Remarks

This function is useful when you don't want to worry about maintaining a register ID, but need one later for unregistering. It is also useful for assigning to menus, tools, and buttons when the function you want to assign is in a DLL.

Related Functions

CALL, REGISTER, UNREGISTER

TempActiveCell

Framework library function. This function creates a temporary XLOPER containing a reference to a single cell on the active sheet.

Returns a reference LPXLOPER (xltypeRef) containing the reference of the cell passed in.

Syntax

```
TempActiveCell(WORD rw, BYTE col);
```

rw (WORD)
    The row of the cell. All arguments are zero-based.

col (BYTE)
    The column of the cell.

Example

This example uses the TempActiveCell function to display the contents of cell B121 on the active sheet.

\SAMPLES\EXAMPLE\EXAMPLE.C

```
short WINAPI TempActiveCellExample(void)
{
    Excel4(xlcAlert, 0, 1, TempActiveCell(120,1));
    return 1;
}
```

TempActiveColumn

Framework library function. This function creates a temporary XLOPER containing a reference to an entire column on the active sheet.

Returns a reference LPXLOPER (xltypeRef) containing a reference to the column passed in.

Syntax

```
TempActiveColumn(BYTE col);
```

col (BYTE)
    The column number of the cell. The argument is zero-based.

Example

The following example uses TempActiveColumn to select an entire column.

\SAMPLES\EXAMPLE\EXAMPLE.C

```
short WINAPI TempActiveColumnExample(void)
{
    Excel4(xlcSelect, 0, 1, TempActiveColumn(1));
    return 1;
}
```

TempActiveRef

Framework library function. This function creates a temporary XLOPER containing a rectangular reference to the active sheet.

Returns a reference LPXLOPER (xltypeRef) containing the reference passed in.

Syntax

```
TempActiveRef(WORD rwFirst, WORD rwLast, BYTE colFirst, BYTE colLast);
```

rwFirst (WORD)
   The starting row of the reference. All arguments are zero-based.

rwLast (WORD)
   The ending row of the reference.

colFirst (BYTE)
   The starting column number of the reference.

colLast (BYTE)
   The ending column number of the reference.

Example

This example uses the TempActiveRef function to select cells A112:C117.

\SAMPLES\EXAMPLE\EXAMPLE.C

```
short WINAPI TempActiveRefExample(void)
{
    Excel4(xlcSelect, 0, 1, TempActiveRef(111, 116, 0, 2));
    return 1;
}
```

TempActiveRow

Framework library function. This function creates a temporary XLOPER containing a reference to an entire row on the active sheet.

Returns a reference LPXLOPER (xltypeRef) containing a reference to the row passed in.

Syntax

```
TempActiveRow(WORD rw);
```

rw (WORD)
   The row of the cell. The argument is zero-based.

Example

The following example uses the TempActiveRow function to select an entire row.

\SAMPLES\EXAMPLE\EXAMPLE.C

```
short int WINAPI TempActiveRowExample(void)
{
    Excel4(xlcSelect, 0, 1, TempActiveRow(120));
    return 1;
}
```

TempBool

Framework library function. This function creates a temporary logical (TRUE/FALSE) XLOPER.

Returns a Boolean LPXLOPER (xltypeBool) containing the logical value passed in.

Syntax

```
TempBool(int b);
```

b (int)
   Use 0 to return a FALSE XLOPER; use any other value to return a TRUE XLOPER. In Visual Basic for Applications, -1 represents a TRUE value; for consistency you may want to use -1 to represent TRUE in your XLOPERs also.

Example

The following example uses the TempBool function to clear the status bar. Temporary memory is freed when the Excel function is called.

\SAMPLES\EXAMPLE\EXAMPLE.C

```
short int WINAPI TempBoolExample(void)
{
    Excel(xlcMessage, 0, 1, TempBool(0));
    return 1;
}
```

TempErr

Framework library function. This function creates a temporary error XLOPER.

Returns an error LPXLO0PER (xltypeErr) containing the error code passed in.

Syntax

```
TempErr(WORD err);
```

err (WORD)

The error code to place in the integer OPER. The error codes, which are defined in XLCALL.H, are shown in the following table.

Error	Error value	Decimal equivalent
#NULL	xlerrNull	0
#DIV/0!	xlerrDiv0	7
#VALUE!	xlerrValue	15
#REF!	xlerrRef	23
#NAME?	xlerrName	29
#NUM!	xlerrNum	36
#N/A	xlerrNA	42

Example

This example uses the TempErr function to return a #VALUE! error to Microsoft Excel.

\SAMPLES\EXAMPLE\EXAMPLE.C

```
LPXLOPER WINAPI TempErrExample(void)
{
    return TempErr(xlerrValue);
}
```

TempInt

Framework library function. This function creates a temporary integer XLOPER.

Returns an integer LPXLOPER (xltypeInt) containing the value passed in.

Syntax

```
TempInt(short int I);
```

i (short int)
    The integer to place in the integer OPER.

Example

This example uses the TempInt function to pass an argument to xlfGetWorkspace.

\SAMPLES\EXAMPLE\EXAMPLE.C

```
short WINAPI TempIntExample(void)
{
    XLOPER xRes;

    Excel(xlfGetWorkspace, (LPXLOPER)&xRes, 1, TempInt(44));
    Excel(xlFree, 0, 1, (LPXLOPER)&xRes);
    return 1;
}
```

TempMissing

Framework library function. This function creates a temporary XLOPER containing a "missing" argument. It is used to simulate a missing argument when calling Microsoft Excel.

Returns a missing LPXLOPER (xltypeMissing).

Syntax

```
TempMissing(void);
```

This function has no arguments.

Example

This example uses the TempMissing function to provide a missing argument to xlcWorkspace, which causes Microsoft Excel to switch to the next sheet.

\SAMPLES\EXAMPLE\EXAMPLE.C

```
short WINAPI TempMissingExample(void)
{
    XLOPER xBool;

    xBool.xltype = xltypeBool;
    xBool.val.bool = 0;
    Excel(xlcWorkspace, 0, 4, TempMissing(),
        TempMissing(),TempMissing(),
        (LPXLOPER)&xBool);
    return 1;
}
```

TempNum

Framework library function. This function creates a temporary numeric (IEEE floating-point) XLOPER.

Returns a numeric LPXLOPER (xltypeNum) containing the value passed in.

Syntax

```
TempNum(double d);
```

d (double)
   The number to place in the numeric OPER.

Example

This example uses the TempNum function to pass an argument to xlfGetWorkspace.

\SAMPLES\EXAMPLE\EXAMPLE.C

```
short WINAPI TempNumExample(void)
{
    XLOPER xRes;

    Excel(xlfGetWorkspace, (LPXLOPER)&xRes, 1, TempNum(44));
    Excel(xlFree, 0, 1, (LPXLOPER)&xRes);
    return 1;
}
```

TempStr

Framework library function. This function creates a temporary string XLOPER. The first character of the string passed in will be overwritten by a byte count.

Returns a string LPXLOPER (xltypeStr) containing the string passed in.

Syntax

```
TempStr(LPSTR str);
```

str (LPSTR)
   A pointer to the string to place in the XLOPER.

Example

This example uses the TempStr function to create a string for a message box.

\SAMPLES\EXAMPLE\EXAMPLE.C

```
short WINAPI TempStrExample(void)
{
    Excel4(xlcAlert, 0, 1, TempStr(" Made it!"));
    return 1;
}
```

UNREGISTER (Form 1)

Called from a macro sheet or DLL. This function reduces by one the use count of a function in a DLL or code resource. Each time REGISTER is called, the use count is increased by one. Each time UNREGISTER is called, the use count is decreased by one. When the use count of all the functions in a DLL reaches zero, the DLL is unloaded from memory.

If successful, returns TRUE (xltypeBool).

Syntax

From a macro sheet:

```
UNREGISTER(register_id)
```

From a DLL:

```
Excel4(xlfUnregister, LPXLOPER pxRes, 1, LPXLOPER pxRegisterId);
```

register_id (xltypeNum)
   The registered ID of the function to unregister, which you get from calling REGISTER or REGISTER.ID.

Remarks

If you specified the *function_text* argument to REGISTER, you need to explicitly delete the name by calling SET.NAME and omitting the second argument, so that the function will no longer appear in the Function Wizard.

Example from a Macro Sheet

The following example registers the CalcCircum function in CIRCUM.DLL, calls the function using the defined name for cell B1, and then unregisters the function.

Example

See the code for the fExit function in GENERIC.C in the FRAMEWRK directory.

Related Functions

CALL, REGISTER, REGISTER.ID, UNREGISTER (Form 2)

UNREGISTER (Form 2)

Called from a macro sheet or DLL. This function forces a DLL or code resource to be unloaded completely. It unregisters all of the functions in a DLL (or all of the code resources in a file), even if they are currently in use by another macro, no matter what the use count. This function registers xlAutoClose, calls xlAutoClose, unregisters xlAutoClose, and then unregisters all other functions in the DLL.

If successful, returns TRUE (xltypeBool). If unsuccessful, returns FALSE.

Syntax

From a macro sheet:

```
UNREGISTER(module_text)
```

From a DLL:

```
Excel4(xlfUnregister, LPXLOPER pxRes, 1, LPXLOPER pxModuleText);
```

module_text (xltypeStr)
    The name of the DLL containing the functions.

Remarks

Proceed Carefully

Beware of this form of the function. Because Microsoft Excel keeps use counts for every DLL function and code resource, it is possible to register a function in two different places. However, if you use this form of UNREGISTER, you will be guaranteed to delete all the registrations that exist.

Deleting all registrations is useful when you are developing DLLs so that you can be sure a DLL is completely unloaded from Microsoft Excel while you compile a new version.

Remember to Delete Names

If you specified the *function_text* argument to REGISTER, you need to explicitly delete the names by calling SET.NAME and omitting the second argument so that the function will no longer appear in the Function Wizard.

Related Functions

CALL, REGISTER, REGISTER.ID, UNREGISTER (Form 1)

xlAbort

This function yields the processor to other tasks in the system and checks whether the user has pressed ESC to cancel a macro.

Returns TRUE (xltypeBool) if the user has pressed ESC.

Syntax

```
Excel4(xlAbort, LPXLOPER pxRes, 1, LPXLOPER pxRetain)
```

pxRetain (xltypeBool)
    If FALSE, this function will also clear any pending abort (if you want to continue despite the user abort). This argument is optional; if omitted, this function will check for a user abort without clearing it.

Remarks

Frequent Calls May Be Needed

Functions that will likely take a long time must call this function frequently to yield the processor to other tasks in the system.

Avoid Sensitive Language

Microsoft recommends against using the term "Abort" in your user interface. Use "Cancel," "Halt," or "Stop."

Example

The following code repetitively moves the active cell on a sheet until one minute has elapsed or until you press ESC. It calls the function xlAbort occasionally. This yields the processor, allowing cooperative multitasking.

\SAMPLES\FRAMEWRK\GENERIC.C

```c
int WINAPI fDance(void)
{
    DWORD dtickStart;
    XLOPER xAbort, xConfirm;
    int boolSheet;
    int col=0;
    char rgch[32];

    // Check what kind of sheet is active. If it is
    // a worksheet or XLM macro sheet, this function will
    // move the selection in a loop to show activity.
    // In any case, it will update the status bar
    // with a countdown.

    // Call xlSheetId; if that fails the current sheet
    // is not a macro sheet or worksheet. Next, get the
    // time at which to start. Then start a while loop
    // that will run for one minute. During the while loop,
    // check if the user has pressed ESC. If true, confirm
    // the abort. If the abort is confirmed, clear the message
    // bar and return; if the abort is not confirmed, clear
    // the abort state and continue. After checking for an
    // abort, move the active cell if on a worksheet or macro.
    // Then update the status bar with the time remaining.

    // This block uses TempActiveCell(), which creates a
    // temporary XLOPER. The XLOPER contains a reference to
    // a single cell on the active sheet.
    // This function is part of the framework library.

    boolSheet = (Excel4(xlSheetId, 0, 0) == xlretSuccess);

    dtickStart = GetTickCount();

    while (GetTickCount() < dtickStart + 60000L)
    {
        Excel(xlAbort, &xAbort, 0);
        if (xAbort.val.bool)
        {
            Excel(xlcAlert, &xConfirm, 2,
                TempStr(" Are you sure you want to cancel?"),
                TempNum(1));
```

```
                       if (xConfirm.val.bool)
                       {
                           Excel(xlcMessage, 0, 1, TempBool(0));
                           return 1;
                       }
                       else
                       {
                           Excel(xlAbort, 0, 1, TempBool(0));
                       }
                   }

               if (boolSheet)
               {
                   Excel(xlcSelect, 0, 1, TempActiveCell(0,(BYTE)col));
                   col = (col + 1) & 3;
               }
               wsprintf(rgch," 0:%lu",
                   (60000 + dtickStart - GetTickCount()) / 1000L);
               Excel(xlcMessage, 0, 2, TempBool(1), TempStr(rgch));
           }
           Excel(xlcMessage, 0, 1, TempBool(0));

           return 1;
       }
```

xlAddInManagerInfo

Provided by stand-alone DLLs that are intended to work with the Add-In
Manager. This function provides information about a stand-alone DLL (XLL)
for the benefit of the Add-In Manager.

Syntax

```
LPXLOPER WINAPI xlAddInManagerInfo(LPXLOPER pxAction);
```

pxAction (xltypeInt or xltypeNum)
   The information that is needed.

   If *pxAction* is 1, returns a string (xltypeStr) containing the long name of
   the DLL.

   If *pxAction* is any other value, returns a #VALUE! error.

Example

\SAMPLES\FRAMEWRK\GENERIC.C

```
LPXLOPER WINAPI xlAddInManagerInfo(LPXLOPER xAction)
{
    static XLOPER xInfo, xIntAction;

    /*
    ** This code coerces the passed in value to an integer.
    ** This is how the code determines what is being requested.
    ** If it receives a 1, it returns a string representing
    ** the long name. If it receives anything else, it
    ** returns a #VALUE! error.
    */
    Excel(xlCoerce, &xIntAction, 2, xAction, TempInt(xltypeInt));

    if(xIntAction.val.w == 1)
    {
        xInfo.xltype = xltypeStr;
        xInfo.val.str = "\026Example Standalone DLL";
    }
    else
    {
        xInfo.xltype = xltypeErr;
        xInfo.val.err = xlerrValue;
    }
    return (LPXLOPER)&xInfo;
}
```

xlAutoAdd

Provided by every stand-alone DLL. This function will be called by the Add-In Manager when a stand-alone DLL (XLL) is added by the user.

Should return 1 (int).

Syntax

```
int WINAPI xlAutoAdd(void);
```

This function has no arguments.

Remarks

Use this function if there is anything your XLL needs to do when it is added by the Add-In Manager.

Example

\SAMPLES\FRAMEWRK\EXAMPLE.C

```
int WINAPI xlAutoAdd(void)
{
    // Display a dialog box indicating that
    // the XLL was successfully added
    Excel(xlcAlert, 0, 2,
        TempStr(" Thank you for adding Example.XLL!"),
        TempInt(2));
    return 1;
}
```

Related Function

xlAutoRemove

xlAutoClose

Provided by every stand-alone DLL. This entry point is called by Microsoft Excel when the user quits. It is also called when a Microsoft Excel macro calls UNREGISTER, giving a string argument that is the name of this XLL. This entry point will be called when the Add-In Manager is used to remove this XLL.

Must return 1 (int).

Syntax

```
int WINAPI xlAutoClose(void);
```

This function has no arguments.

Remarks

This function should:

- Remove any menus or menu items that were added in xlAutoOpen.
- Perform any necessary global cleanup.
- Delete any names that were created, especially names of exported functions. Remember that registering functions may cause some names to be created, if the fourth argument to REGISTER is present.

This function does not have to unregister the functions that were registered in xlAutoOpen. Microsoft Excel automatically does this after xlAutoClose returns.

Example

\SAMPLES\FRAMEWRK\GENERIC.C

```
int WINAPI xlAutoClose(void)
{
    int i;

    /*
    ** This block first deletes all names added by xlAutoOpen or by
    ** xlAutoRegister.
    */

    for (i = 0; i < rgFuncsRows; i++)
        Excel(xlfSetName, 0, 1, TempStr(rgFuncs[i][2]));

    return 1;
}
```

Related Function

xlAutoOpen

xlAutoFree

Provided by some DLLs. This routine is called by Microsoft Excel when DLL-managed memory needs to be freed. Inside the xlAutoFree function, callbacks into Microsoft Excel are disabled, with one exception: xlFree can be called to free Microsoft Excel allocated memory. This function receives a pointer to the XLOPER to be freed as the only argument.

This function does not return a value.

Syntax

```
void WINAPI xlAutoFree(LPXLOPER pxFree);
```

pxFree (LPXLOPER)
   A pointer to the memory to be freed.

Remarks

If the xlAutoFree function you provide looks at the xltype field of *pxFree*, remember that the xlbitDLLFree bit will still be set.

In Windows, xlStack, xlEnableXLMsgs, and xlDisableXLMsgs can also be called.

Example
\SAMPLES\EXAMPLE\EXAMPLE.C

```
void WINAPI xlAutoFree(LPXLOPER pxFree)
{
    GlobalUnlock(hArray);
    GlobalFree(hArray);
    return;
}
```

xlAutoOpen

Provided by every stand-alone DLL. After loading the DLL Microsoft Excel calls the XLL's xlAutoOpen function.

The xlAutoOpen function should:

- Register all the functions you want to make available while this XLL is open.
- Add any menus or menu items that this XLL supports.
- Perform any other initialization that you need.

Must return 1 (int).

Syntax
```
int WINAPI xlAutoOpen(void);
```

This function has no arguments.

Remarks
This function is called by Microsoft Excel whenever the XLL is opened, either by choosing Open from the File menu, or because the XLL is in the Excel startup directory. This function is registered but not called if an XLL is opened with OPEN. It is also called when a macro calls REGISTER with the name of this DLL as the only argument.

Example
For a Windows example of this function, see the code for the xlAutoOpen function in GENERIC.C in the FRAMEWRK directory.

Related Functions
xlAutoClose, xlAutoRegister

xlAutoRegister

Provided by some stand-alone DLLs (XLLs). This entry point is called by Microsoft Excel when a REGISTER or CALL statement tries to register a function without specifying the *type_text* argument. If that happens, Microsoft Excel calls xlAutoRegister, passing the name of the function that the user tried to register. xlAutoRegister should use the normal xlRegister function to register the function; but, this time, it must specify the *type_text* argument. This function is required only if the DLL wants to support registering its individual entry points automatically.

If the function name is unknown, this function returns a #VALUE! error (xltypeErr). Otherwise, it returns whatever REGISTER returned (xltypeNum).

Syntax

```
LPXLOPER WINAPI xlAutoRegister(LPXLOPER pxName);
```

pxName (xltypeStr)
   The name of the function that needs to be registered. Not case-sensitive.

Example

\SAMPLES\FRAMEWRK\GENERIC.C

```
LPXLOPER WINAPI xlAutoRegister(LPXLOPER pxName)
{
    static XLOPER xDLL, xRegId;
    int i;

    // This block first initializes xRegId to a
    // #VALUE! error.   This is done in case a function
    // is not found to register.    Next, the code loops
    // through the functions in rgFuncs[]    and uses
    // lpstricmp to determine if the current row in
    // rgFuncs[] represents the function that needs
    // to be registered.    When it finds the proper row,
    // the function is registered and the    register ID
    // is returned to Microsoft Excel. If no matching
    // function is found, an xRegId is returned
    // containing a #VALUE! error.

    xRegId.xltype = xltypeErr;
    xRegId.val.err = xlerrValue;
```

```
for (i = 0; i < rgFuncsRows; i++)
{
    if (!lpstricmp(rgFuncs[i][0], pxName->val.str))
    {
        Excel(xlGetName, &xDLL, 0);

        Excel(xlfRegister, 0, 8,
            (LPXLOPER)&xDLL,
            (LPXLOPER)TempStr(rgFuncs[i][0]),
            (LPXLOPER)TempStr(rgFuncs[i][1]),
            (LPXLOPER)TempStr(rgFuncs[i][2]),
            (LPXLOPER)TempStr(rgFuncs[i][3]),
            (LPXLOPER)TempStr(rgFuncs[i][4]),
            (LPXLOPER)TempStr(rgFuncs[i][5]),
            (LPXLOPER)TempStr(rgFuncs[i][6]));

        /* Free the XLL filename */
        Excel(xlFree, 0, 1, (LPXLOPER)&xDLL);

        return (LPXLOPER)&xRegId;
    }
}

return (LPXLOPER)&xRegId;
}
```

Related Function

xlAutoOpen

xlAutoRemove

Provided by every stand-alone DLL (XLL). This function is called by the Add-In
Manager when a stand-alone DLL is removed by the user.

Must return 1 (int).

Syntax

```
int WINAPI xlAutoRemove(void);
```

This function has no arguments.

Remarks

Use this function if your XLL needs to complete any task when it is removed by
the Add-In Manager.

Example

\SAMPLES\FRAMEWRK\GENERIC.C

```
int WINAPI xlAutoRemove(void)
{
    /*
     * Display a dialog box indicating that
     * the XLL was successfully removed
     */
    Excel(xlcAlert, 0, 2,
        TempStr(" Thank you for removing Example.XLL!"),
        TempInt(2));
    return 1;
}
```

Related Function

xlAutoAdd

xlCoerce

This function converts one type of XLOPER to another, or looks up cell values on a sheet.

Returns the coerced value.

Syntax

```
Excel4(xlCoerce, LPXLOPER pxRes, 2, LPXLOPER pxSource,
LPXLOPER pxDestType);
```

pxSource

The source XLOPER that needs to be converted. May be a reference if you want to look up cell values.

pxDestType (xltypeInt)

A bit mask of which types you are willing to accept. You should use the bitwise OR operator (|) to specify multiple possible types. If this argument is omitted, it is assumed that you want to convert a reference to any nonreference type (this is handy for looking up cell values). This argument is optional.

Example

\SAMPLES\EXAMPLE\EXAMPLE.C

```c
short WINAPI xlCoerceExample(short iVal)
{
    XLOPER xStr, xInt, xDestType;

    xInt.xltype = xltypeInt;
    xInt.val.w = iVal;

    xDestType.xltype = xltypeInt;
    xDestType.val.w = xltypeStr;

    Excel4(xlCoerce, &xStr, 2, (LPXLOPER)&xInt,
        (LPXLOPER)&xDestType);

    Excel4(xlcAlert, 0, 1, (LPXLOPER)&xStr);
    Excel4(xlFree, 0, 1, (LPXLOPER)&xStr);

    return 1;
}
```

Related Function

xlSet

xlDefineBinaryName

Used to allocate persistent storage for a bigdata XLOPER. Data with a defined binary name is saved with the workbook, and can be accessed by name at any time.

Syntax

```c
Excel4(xlDefineBinaryName, 0, 2, LPXLOPER pxName, LPXLOPER pxData);
```

pxName

String XLOPER specifying the name of the data.

pxData

Bigdata XLOPER specifying the data. When you call this function, the lpbData member of the bigdata structure should point to the data for which the name is being defined, and the cbData member should contain the length of the data in bytes.

If the *pxData* argument is not specified (xltypeMissing), the named allocation specified by *pxName* is deleted.

Example

This example accepts a name, a pointer to data, and the length of the data. It uses the xlDefineBinaryName function to allocate memory for the data, and returns the result of the Excel4 function (success or failure).

```
int WINAPI xlDefineBinaryNameExample(LPSTR lpszName,
    LPBYTE lpbData, long cbData)
{
    char stBuf[255];
    XLOPER xName, xData;

    lstrcpy(stBuf + 1, lpszName);
    stBuf[0] = lstrlen(lpszName);

    xName.xltype = xltypeStr;
    xName.val.str = stBuf;

    xData.xltype = xltypeBigData;
    xData.val.bigdata.h.lpbData = lpbData;
    xData.val.bigdata.cbData = cbData;

    return Excel4(xlDefineBinaryName, 0, 2, (LPXLOPER)&xName,
        (LPXLOPER)&xData);
}
```

Related Function

xlGetBinaryName

xlDisableXLMsgs

This function restores the DLL's context. It should be called after you have called xlEnableXLMsgs, when the portions of code that may yield to Microsoft Excel have been executed.

This function does not return a value.

Syntax

```
Excel4(xlDisableXLMsgs, 0, 0);
```

This function has no arguments.

Remarks

This function is very fast and adds little overhead to the DLL.

Example

See the code for the fShowDialog function in GENERIC.C in the FRAMEWRK directory.

Related Function

xlEnableXLMsgs

xlEnableXLMsgs

This function restores Microsoft Excel's context. It should be called before any operations that may yield control to Microsoft Excel. This puts Microsoft Excel into a state in which it is ready to receive messages and use the math coprocessor.

This function does not return a value.

Syntax

```
Excel4(xlEnableXLMsgs, 0, 0);
```

This function has no arguments.

Remarks

This function is very fast and adds little overhead to the DLL.

Example

See the code for the fShowDialog function in GENERIC.C in the FRAMEWRK directory.

Related Function

xlDisableXLMsgs

xlFree

Allows Microsoft Excel to free auxiliary memory associated with an XLOPER. xlFree frees the auxiliary memory and resets the pointer to NULL but does not destroy other parts of the XLOPER.

This function does not return a value.

Syntax

```
Excel4(xlFree, 0, n, LPXLOPER px, ...)
```

px, ...
    One or more XLOPERs to free.

Remarks

You must free every XLOPER that you get as a return value from Excel4 or Excel4v if that XLOPER uses auxiliary memory (if it contains pointers). It is always safe to free XLOPERs even if they did not use auxiliary memory, as long as you got them from Excel4 or Excel4v.

Example

This example calls GET.WORKSPACE(1) to return (as a string) the platform on which Microsoft Excel is currently running. The code copies this returned string into a buffer for later use. The standard `strcpy` function is not used to copy the string to the buffer because `strcpy` expects a null-terminated string and the returned value is a byte-counted string. The code places the buffer back into the XLOPER for later use with the Excel function. Finally, the code displays the string in an alert box.

\SAMPLES\EXAMPLE\EXAMPLE.C

```
short WINAPI xlFreeExample(void)
{
    XLOPER xRes, xInt;
    char buffer[10];
    int i, len;

    xInt.xltype = xltypeInt;
    xInt.val.w = 1;
    Excel(xlfGetWorkspace, (LPXLOPER)&xRes, 1, (LPXLOPER)&xInt);
    len = (BYTE)xRes.val.str[0];
    for(i = 0; i <= len; i++)
        buffer[i] = xRes.val.str[i];
    Excel(xlFree, 0, 1, (LPXLOPER)&xRes);
    xRes.val.str = buffer;

    Excel(xlcAlert, 0, 1, (LPXLOPER)&xRes);
    return 1;
}
```

xlGetBinaryName

Used to return a handle for data saved by the xlDefineBinaryName function. Data with a defined binary name is saved with the workbook, and can be accessed by name at any time.

Syntax

```
Excel4(xlGetBinaryName, LPXLOPER pxRes, 1, LPXLOPER pxName);
```

pxRes

Bigdata XLOPER. When the function returns, the `hdata` member of the XLOPER contains a handle for the named data.

pxName

String XLOPER specifying the name of the data.

Microsoft Excel owns the memory handle returned in `hdata`. In Microsoft Windows, the handle is a global memory handle (allocated by the GlobalAlloc function).

Example

This example accepts a name and the address of a pointer. It uses the xlGetBinaryName function to retrieve a handle for the named data, and then locks the handle and returns the locked pointer at the passed-in address.

```
int WINAPI xlGetBinaryNameExample(LPSTR lpszName,
    LPBYTE *lpbData)
{
    int iRet;
    char stBuf[255];
    XLOPER xName, xData;

    lstrcpy(stBuf + 1, lpszName);
    stBuf[0] = lstrlen(lpszName);

    xName.xltype = xltypeStr;
    xName.val.str = stBuf;

    if ((iRet = Excel4(xlGetBinaryName, (LPXLOPER)&xData, 1,
            (LPXLOPER)&xName)) != xlretSuccess)
        return iRet;
    *lpbData = GlobalLock(xData.val.bigdata.h.hdata);

    return iRet;
}
```

Related Function

xlDefineBinaryName

xlGetHwnd

This function returns the window handle of the top-level Microsoft Excel window.

Contains the window handle (xltypeInt) in the val.w field.

Syntax

```
Excel4(xlGetHwnd, LPXLOPER pxRes, 0);
```

This function has no arguments.

Remarks

This function is useful for writing Windows API code.

Example

See the code for the fShowDialog function in GENERIC.C in the FRAMEWRK directory.

Related Function

xlGetInst

xlGetInst

This function returns the instance handle of the instance of Microsoft Excel that is currently calling a DLL.

The instance handle (xltypeInt) will be in the val.w field.

Syntax

```
Excel4(xlGetInst, LPXLOPER pxRes, 0);
```

This function has no arguments.

Remarks

This function can be used to distinguish between multiple running instances of Microsoft Excel that are calling the DLL.

Example

The following example compares the instance of the last copy of Microsoft Excel that called it to the current copy of Microsoft Excel that called it. If they are the same, it returns 1; if not, it returns 0.

\SAMPLES\EXAMPLE\EXAMPLE.C

```
short WINAPI xlGetInstExample(void)
{
    XLOPER xRes;
    static HANDLE hOld = 0;
    int iRet;

    Excel4(xlGetInst, (LPXLOPER)&xRes, 0);

    if((unsigned int)xRes.val.w != hOld)
        iRet = 0;
    else
        iRet = 1;

    hOld = xRes.val.w;

    return iRet;
}
```

Related Function

xlGetHwnd

xlGetName

Use this function to find the full path and file name of the DLL in the form of a string.

Returns the path and file name (xltypeStr).

Syntax

```
Excel4(xlGetName, LPXLOPER pxRes, 0);
```

This function has no arguments.

Example
\SAMPLES\EXAMPLE\EXAMPLE.C

```
short WINAPI xlGetNameExample(void)
{
    XLOPER xRes;

    Excel4(xlGetName, (LPXLOPER)&xRes, 0);
    Excel4(xlcAlert, 0, 1, (LPXLOPER)&xRes);
    Excel4(xlFree, 0, 1, (LPXLOPER)&xRes);
    return 1;
}
```

xlSet

This function puts constant values into cells or ranges very quickly.

If successful, returns TRUE (xltypeBool). If unsuccessful, returns FALSE.

Syntax

```
Excel4(xlSet, LPXLOPER pxRes, 2, LPXLOPER pxReference,
LPXLOPER pxValue);
```

pxReference (xltypeRef or xltypeSRef)
   A rectangular reference describing the target cell or cells. The reference must describe adjacent cells.

pxValue
   The value to put in the cell or cells. For more information, see the following "Remarks" section.

Remarks

pxValue Argument

pxValue can either be a value or an array. If it is a value, the entire destination range is filled with that value. If it is an array (xltypeMulti), the elements of the array are put into the corresponding locations in the rectangle.

If you use a horizontal array for the second argument, it is duplicated down to fill the entire rectangle. If you use a vertical array, it is duplicated right to fill the entire rectangle. If you use a rectangular array, and it is too small for the rectangular range you want to put it in, that range is padded with #N/As.

To clear an element of the destination rectangle, use an xltypeNil XLOPER in the source array. To clear the entire destination rectangle, omit the second argument.

Restrictions

xlSet cannot be undone. In addition, it destroys any undo information that may have been available before.

xlSet can put only constants, not formulas, into cells.

xlSet behaves as a Class 3 command-equivalent function; that is, it is available only inside a DLL when the DLL is called from an object, macro, menu, toolbar, shortcut key, or the Run button in the Macro dialog box (accessed from the Tools menu).

Example

The following example fills B205:B206 with the value that was passed in from a macro.

\SAMPLES\EXAMPLE\EXAMPLE.C

```
short WINAPI xlSetExample(short int iVal)
{
    XLOPER xRef, xValue;

    xRef.xltype = xltypeSRef;
    xRef.val.sref.count = 1;
    xRef.val.sref.ref.rwFirst = 204;
    xRef.val.sref.ref.rwLast = 205;
    xRef.val.sref.ref.colFirst = 1;
    xRef.val.sref.ref.colLast = 1;
    xValue.xltype = xltypeInt;
    xValue.val.w = iVal;

    Excel4(xlSet, 0, 2, (LPXLOPER)&xRef, (LPXLOPER)&xValue);
    return 1;
}
```

Related Function

xlCoerce

xlSheetId

This function finds the sheet ID of a named sheet in order to construct external references.

Returns the sheet ID in *pxRes->val.mref.idSheet.*

Syntax

```
Excel4(xlSheetId, LPXLOPER pxRes, 1, LPXLOPER pxSheetName);
```

pxSheetName (xltypeStr)

The name of the book and sheet you want to find out about. This argument is optional; if omitted, xlSheetId returns the sheet ID of the active (front) sheet.

Remarks

The sheet must be open to use this function. There is no way to construct a reference to an unopened sheet from DLLs. For more information about using xlSheetId to construct references, see "Using Reference XLOPERs" on page 159.

Example

\SAMPLES\EXAMPLE\EXAMPLE.C

```
short WINAPI xlSheetIdExample(void)
{
    XLOPER xSheetName, xRes;

    xSheetName.xltype = xltypeStr;
    xSheetName.val.str = "\021[BOOK1.XLS]Sheet1"";
    Excel4(xlSheetId, &xRes, 1, (LPXLOPER)&xSheetName);
    Excel4(xlcAlert, 0, 1, TempNum(xRes.val.mref.idSheet));
    Excel4(xlFree, 0, 1, (LPXLOPER)&xRes);
    return 1;
}
```

Related Function

xlSheetNm

xlSheetNm

Returns the name of the sheet (xltypeStr), given an external reference.

Syntax

```
Excel4(xlSheetNm, LPXLOPER pxRes, 1, LPXLOPER pxExtref);
```

pxExtref (xltypeRef)
   An external reference to the sheet whose name you want.

Remarks

This function returns the name of the sheet in the form "[Book1]Sheet1."

Example

The following example returns the name of the sheet from which the function was called.

\SAMPLES\EXAMPLE\EXAMPLE.C

```
short WINAPI xlSheetNmExample(void)
{
    XLOPER xRes, xSheetName;

    Excel4(xlfCaller, &xRes, 0);
    Excel4(xlSheetNm, &xSheetName, 1, (LPXLOPER)&xRes);
    Excel4(xlcAlert, 0, 1, &xSheetName);
    Excel4(xlFree, 0, 1, &xSheetName);
    return 1;
}
```

Related Function

xlSheetId

xlStack

This function checks the amount of space left on the stack.

Returns the number of bytes (xltypeInt) remaining on the stack.

Syntax

```
Excel4(xlStack, LPXLOPER pxRes, 0);
```

This function has no arguments.

Remarks

Microsoft Excel 97 has quite a bit more stack space than previous versions. This has caused a problem, since the amount of stack space is returned as a signed integer. This means that xlStack can return a value between -32767 and 32768. The stack space in Microsoft Excel 97 typically exceeds 40K, which causes xlStack to report a value like -12076. To obtain the correct value, cast the returned value to an unsigned short.

Microsoft Excel has a limited amount of space on the stack, and you should take care not to overrun this space. First, never put large data structures on the stack. Make as many local variables as possible static. Avoid calling functions recursively, because that will quickly fill up the stack.

If you suspect that you are overrunning the stack, call this function frequently to see how much stack space is left.

If you desperately need more stack space than the 44K or so that you normally get, you can use the Windows functions SwitchStackTo and SwitchStackBack.

Example

The following example displays an alert message containing the amount of stack space left.

\SAMPLES\EXAMPLE\EXAMPLE.C

```
short int WINAPI xlStackExample(void)
{
    XLOPER xRes;
    XLOPER xAlert;

    Excel4(xlStack, (LPXLOPER)&xRes, 0);

    xAlert.xltype = xltypeNum;
    // Cast to an unsigned short first to get rid of the overflow
problem
    xAlert.val.num = (double)(unsigned short) xRes.val.w;
    Excel4(xlcAlert, 0, 1, (LPXLOPER)&xAlert);
    return 1;
}
```

xlUDF

Calls a user-defined function. This function allows you to call macro language functions from DLLs.

Returns the return value from the user-defined function.

Syntax

```
Excel4(xlUDF, LPXLOPER pxRes, int iCount, LPXLOPER pxRef,
LPXLOPER pxArg1, ...);
```

pxRef (xltypeRef or xltypeSRef)
   The reference of the function you want to call. If it is named, you can use xlfEvaluate to look up the name first.

pxArg1, ...
   Zero or more arguments to the user-defined function.

Example

The following example runs TestMacro on sheet Macro1 in BOOK1.XLS. Make sure that the macro is on a sheet named Macro1.

\SAMPLES\EXAMPLE\EXAMPLE.C

```
short WINAPI xlUDFExample(void)
{
    XLOPER xMacroName, xMacroRef, xRes;

    xMacroName.xltype = xltypeStr;
    xMacroName.val.str = "\033[BOOK1.XLS]Macro1!TestMacro";
    Excel4(xlfEvaluate, &xMacroRef, 1,
        (LPXLOPER)&xMacroName);
    Excel4(xlUDF, &xRes, 1, (LPXLOPER)&xMacroRef);
    return 1;
}
```

C H A P T E R   9

Microsoft Excel File Format

The binary interchange file format (BIFF) is the file format in which Microsoft Excel workbooks are saved on disk. Microsoft Excel versions 5.0 and later use compound files; this is the OLE 2 implementation of the Structured Storage Model standard. For more information on this technology, see the *OLE 2 Programmer's Reference, Volume One,* and *Inside OLE 2,* both published by Microsoft Press and available from your local bookstore.

File Format Versions

This article documents the file formats shown in the following table:

BIFF version	Microsoft Excel version
BIFF5	Microsoft Excel version 5
BIFF7	Microsoft Excel 95 (also called Microsoft Excel version 7)
BIFF8	Microsoft Excel 97

You can determine the BIFF version from the BOF record. In BIFF4 and earlier, some records (other than the BOF record) contained version information in the high-order byte of their record numbers. This proved to be redundant, so for BIFF5 and later, Microsoft Excel determines the BIFF version by reading the BOF record.

The record descriptions in this document apply to all three of the BIFF versions in the preceding table. If records are different for different BIFF versions, this is shown in the record descriptions.

The following tables describe the new records and changed records in BIFF8. For more information on the new and changed records, see the appropriate record description.

New Records in BIFF8

Number	Record
1B1h	CF
1BAh	CODENAME
1B0h	CONDFMT
1B5h	DCONBIN
161h	DSF
1BEh	DV
1B2h	DVAL
FFh	EXTSST
1B8h	HLINK
FDh	LABELSST
ECh	MSODRAWING
EBh	MSODRAWINGGROUP
EDh	MSODRAWINGSELECTION
DCh	PARAMQRY
1Afh	PROT4REV
1BCh	PROT4REVPASS
1ADh	QSI
1B7h	REFRESHALL
FCh	SST
1AEh	SUPBOOK
C6h	SXDB
122h	SXDBEX
F1h	SXEX
1BBh	SXFDBTYPE
F2h	SXFILT
F9h	SXFMLA
FBh	SXFORMAT
103h	SXFORMULA
F6h	SXNAME
F8h	SXPAIR

Number	Record
F0h	SXRULE
F7h	SXSELECT
100h	SXVDEX
1B6h	TXO
1A9h	USERBVIEW
1AAh	USERSVIEWBEGIN
1ABh	USERSVIEWEND
160h	USESELFS
162h	XL5MODIFY

Changed Records in BIFF8

Number	Record
09h	BOF
85h	BOUNDSHEET
200h	DIMENSIONS
0Bh	INDEX
1Ch	NOTE
5Dh	OBJ
DCh	SXEXT
1Ah	VERTICALPAGEBREAKS
23Eh	WINDOW2
5Ch	WRITEACCESS
59h	XCT
E0h	XF

The User Names and Revision Log streams support the shared list feature that was added in Microsoft Excel 95. The BIFF record data in shared list records (records that begin with RR), and the binary format of the User Names and Revision Log streams are not documented.

The DocumentSummaryInformation and SummaryInformation streams support the document properties available in Microsoft Excel 95 and 97, which are standardized across the Office family of applications.

The Workbook Compound File

An OLE 2 compound file is essentially "a file system within a file." The compound file contains a hierarchical system of storages and streams. A storage is analogous to a directory, and a stream is analogous to a file in a directory. Each Microsoft Excel workbook is stored in a compound file, an example of which is shown in the following illustration. This file is a workbook that contains three sheets: a worksheet with a PivotTable, a Visual Basic module, and a chart.

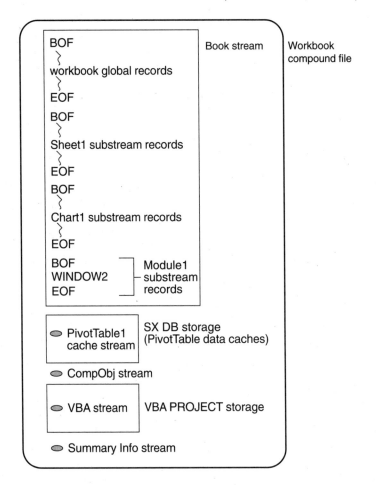

If a workbook contains embedded objects, then the file will also contain storages written by the applications that created the objects. The PivotTable data cache storage and VBA PROJECT storage are not documented. The CompObj stream contains OLE 2 component object data, and the Summary Info stream contains the standardized file summary information such as title, subject, author, and so on.

The Book stream begins with a BOF record, and then contains workbook global records up to the first EOF. The workbook global section contains one BOUNDSHEET record for each sheet in the workbook. You can use the dt field (document type), the lbPlyPos field (stream position of the BOF record for the sheet), and the cch/rgch fields (sheet name as a byte-counted string) to quickly read selected sheets in the workbook.

Each sheet in the workbook is stored after the workbook global section, beginning with BOF and ending with EOF. If you read the file in a continuous stream (instead of using the BOUNDSHEET records), you can test the dt field of each BOF record to determine the sheet type.

Simple Save (New for BIFF7 and Later)

Microsoft Excel 95 and 97 use a new simple save method from OLE 2, which was developed to increase performance. If a workbook contains no Visual Basic modules, no PivotTables, and no embedded objects on worksheets, then Microsoft Excel uses the simple save method.

When Microsoft Excel saves a workbook using simple save, the streams in the file must be at least 4kbytes long. The OLE 2 code adds padding bytes to the streams to ensure that they are at least 4kbytes long. If you use a low-level binary viewer (instead of the BiffView utility) to examine the resulting file, you will see the padding bytes appearing as "garbage" at the end of the streams.

To find the actual end of the Book stream, you can increment a counter every time you read a BOF record and then decrement it every time you read an EOF record. When the counter reaches zero, then you have read the last EOF in the Book stream and you can ignore the rest of the bytes in that stream.

Double Stream File

For improved backward compatibility, Microsoft Excel 97 has a new save file type option: Microsoft Excel 97 & 5.0/95 Workbook. When you save a workbook using this file type, Microsoft Excel writes two complete book streams. The first stream in the file is the Microsoft Excel 5.0/95 format (BIFF5/BIFF7), and the second one is the Microsoft Excel 97 format (BIFF8). The DSF record, which appears only in the BIFF8 stream, indicates that the file is a double stream file.

To distinguish the two streams, the BIFF5/BIFF7 stream is called Book, and the BIFF8 stream is called Workbook.

Unicode Strings in BIFF8

Microsoft Excel 97 uses unicode strings. In BIFF8, strings are stored in a compressed format. Each string contains the following fields:

Offset	Name	Size	Contents
0	cch	2	Count of characters in the string (notice that this is the number of characters, NOT the number of bytes)
2	grbit	1	Option flags
3	rgb	var	Array of string characters and formatting runs

Unicode strings usually require 2 bytes of storage per character. Because most strings in USA/English Microsoft Excel always have the high bytes of unicode characters = 00h, the strings can be saved using a compressed unicode format. The grbit field specifies the compression encoding as shown in the following table.

Bits	Mask	Name	Contents
0	01h	fHighByte	= 0 if all the characters in the string have a high byte of 00h and only the low bytes are saved in the file (compressed)
			= 1 if at least one character in the string has a nonzero high byte and therefore all characters in the string are saved as double-byte characters (not compressed)
1	02h	(Reserved)	Reserved; must be 0 (zero)
2	04h	fExtSt	Extended string follows (Far East versions, see text)
3	08h	fRichSt	Rich string follows
7–4	F0h	(Reserved)	Reserved; must be 0 (zero)

An unformatted string with all high bytes = 00h has grbit = 00h. Also, this implies that there are no formatting runs, which means that the runs count field does not exist.

An unformatted string that has at least one character with a nonzero high byte has grbit = 01h.

A formatted string with all high bytes = 00h has grbit = 08h if the string has several different character formats applied.

The easiest way to understand the contents of BIFF8 strings is to look at an example. Suppose the string **this is red ink** is in a cell, and is formatted so that the word **red** is red. The rgb field of the SST record appears as follows:

```
0f 00 08 02 00 74 68 69 73 20 69 73 20 72 65 64 20 69 6e 6b 08 00      06
00 0b 00 05 00
```

Swapping bytes and reorganizing:

```
000F  08  0002  74 68 69 73 20 69 73 20 72 65 64 20 69 6E 6B
      0008  0006  000B  0005
```

This data parses as shown in the following table:

Data	Description
000F	String contains 15 characters.
08	The grbit is 08h, which indicates a rich string.
0002	Count of formatting runs (runs follow the string and are not included in the character count; if there are no formatting runs, this field does not exist).
74 68 69 73 20 69 73 20 72 65 64 20 69 6E 6B	The string characters; note that in this case, each character is one byte.
0008 0006	Run number 1: index to FONT record 6 (ifnt, 0-based) for characters beginning with character number 8 (0-based).
000B 0005	Run number 2: index to FONT record 5 (ifnt, 0-based) for characters beginning with character number B (0-based).

Extended Strings in Far East Versions

In Far East versions (for example, Japanese Microsoft Excel), extended strings may appear in the SST record (fExtSt is set in the grbit field). These strings store additional fields that contain phonetic, language ID, or keyboard ID information. The first two fields of extended strings (cch and grbit) are identical to the nonextended strings described in the preceding text.

Extended strings contain the fields shown in following tables.

Extended strings (not rich: fRichSt is not set)

Offset	Name	Size	Contents
0	cch	2	Count of characters in the string data (notice that this is the number of characters, NOT the number of bytes)
2	grbit	1	Option flags (see preceding table)
3	cchExtRst	4	Length of ExtRst data
7	rgb	var	String data
var	ExtRst	var	ExtRst data (not documented; length of this field is given by cchExtRst)

Extended strings (rich: fRichSt is set)

Offset	Name	Size	Contents
0	cch	2	Count of characters in the string data (notice that this is the number of characters, NOT the number of bytes)
2	grbit	1	Option flags (see preceding table)
3	crun	2	Count of formatting runs
5	cchExtRst	4	Length of ExtRst data
9	rgb	var	String data
var	rgSTRUN	var	Array of formatting run structures; length is equal to (crun x 8) bytes
var	ExtRst	var	ExtRst data (not documented; length of this field is given by cchExtRst)

Other Microsoft Excel File Formats

Although chart records are written as part of the Book stream, they are documented in another article. Microsoft Excel creates several other files, some of which are documented. The workspace file (.XLW extension in Microsoft Windows) and the toolbar file (.XLB extension in Microsoft Windows) are not documented.

This article contains BIFF documentation for Microsoft Excel version 5.0, Microsoft Excel 95, and Microsoft Excel 97 only. Earlier versions of BIFF documentation are available on the Development Library (published by the Microsoft Developer Network). The library is a CD-based reference source for Windows-based developers. For more information about this service, contact Microsoft Developer Network via e-mail (devnetwk@microsoft.com), via Compuserve (>INTERNET:devnetwk@microsoft.com), or call (800) 759-5474.

BIFF Record Information

Although different BIFF record types contain different information, every record has the same basic format. All BIFF records consist of the following three sections:

Record Number

This 16-bit word identifies the record. The hexadecimal value of the record number is included in parentheses in the heading of the record description. For example, the EOF record's heading appears in this article as "EOF: End of File (0Ah)."

Record Data Length

This 16-bit word equals the length of the following record data, in bytes. The record length depends on the type of data in the record. For example, the EOF record is always the same length, while a FORMULA record varies in length depending on the length of the formula itself.

Record Data

This is the portion of the record containing the actual data that describes the formula, window, object, and so on.

The format for all BIFF records is described in the following table.

Offset	Length (bytes)	Contents
0	2	Record number
2	2	Record data length
4	Variable	Record data

In BIFF8, a BIFF record has a length limit of 8228 bytes, including the record type and record length fields. Therefore, the record data field must be no longer than 8224 bytes.

In BIFF7 and earlier, a BIFF record has a length limit of 2084 bytes, including the record type and record length fields. Therefore, the record data field must be no longer than 2080 bytes.

In all BIFF versions, if the record exceeds the maximum length, then one or more CONTINUE records can follow the parent record. For example, embedded bitmap graphic objects often use a parent IMDATA record and several CONTINUE records.

If a field (or a bit in a field) is marked "Reserved," then your application should treat the field or bit as a "don't-care" when you read or write the BIFF file. If a field (or bit in a field) is marked "Reserved; must be zero," then you must write zeros to the field or bit when you write a BIFF file.

Byte Swapping

Microsoft Excel BIFF files are transportable across the MS-DOS/Windows (Intel 80x86) and Apple Macintosh (Motorola 680x0) operating systems, among others. To support transportability, Microsoft Excel writes BIFF files in the 80x86 format, where the low-order byte of the word appears first in the file, followed by the high-order byte.

Whenever Microsoft Excel for the Macintosh reads or writes a BIFF file, it calls a function that swaps the high- and low-order bytes of every 16-bit word in every record in the file. For 32-bit longs, the bytes in each 16-bit word are swapped first, and then the two 16-bit words are swapped. Be sure to include a byte-swap function in any custom BIFF utility you write for the Macintosh.

Indexing in BIFF Records

In BIFF files, rows and columns are always stored 0-based, rather than with an offset of 1 as they appear in a sheet. For example, cell A1 is stored as row 0 (rw = 00h), column 0 (col = 00h); cell B3 is row 2 (rw = 02h), column 1 (col = 01h), and so on.

In most cases, you can use the variable-naming conventions in this article to determine if a variable is 0-based. Variable names that begin with the letter i are usually indexes, which are 0-based. For example, the variable ixfe occurs in every cell record; it is a 0-based index into the table of XF records. Variable names that begin with the letter c are usually counts, which are 1-based. For example, many records contain a cch, which is a count of characters in the following string.

Undefined Cells in the Sheet

To reduce file size, cells that don't contain values or formulas and aren't referenced by formulas in any other cell are considered to be undefined cells. Such undefined cells don't appear in the BIFF file.

For example, if a worksheet has a value in cell A3, and the formula =A3+A4 in cell B10, then the only defined cells on the worksheet are A3, A4, and B10. No other cells need to exist.

Using this technique, entire rows can be undefined if they have no defined cells in them. In the preceding example, only rows 3, 4, and 10 are defined, so the file contains only three ROW records.

Cell Records

The term "cell records" refers to the BIFF record types that actually contain cell data. Cell records that appear in BIFF5/BIFF7/BIFF8 files are shown in the following table.

Record	Contents
ARRAY	An array-entered formula
BLANK	An empty cell
BOOLERR	A Boolean or error value
FORMULA	A cell formula, stored as parse tokens
LABEL	A string constant
LABELSST	String constant that uses BIFF8 shared string table (new to BIFF8)
NUMBER	An IEEE floating-point number
MULBLANK	Multiple empty cells (new to BIFF5)
MULRK	Multiple RK numbers (new to BIFF5)
RK	An RK number
RSTRING	Cell with character formatting
SHRFMLA	A shared formula (new to BIFF5)
STRING	A string that represents the result of a formula

Microsoft Excel stores cell records in blocks that have at most 32 rows. Each row that contains cell records has a corresponding ROW record in the block, and each block contains a DBCELL record at the end of the block. For more information about row blocks and about optimizing your code when searching for cell records, see "Finding Cell Records in BIFF Files" on page 440.

BIFF Record Order

BIFF record order has changed as the file format has evolved. The simplest way to determine BIFF record order is to create a workbook in Microsoft Excel and then use the BiffView utility to examine the record order.

BIFF Records: Alphabetical Order

Record	Number
1904: 1904 Date System	22h
ADDIN: Workbook Is an Add-in Macro	87h
ADDMENU: Menu Addition	C2h
ARRAY: Array-Entered Formula	221h
AUTOFILTER: AutoFilter Data	9Eh
AUTOFILTERINFO: Drop-Down Arrow Count	9Dh
BACKUP: Save Backup Version of the File	40h
BLANK: Cell Value, Blank Cell	201h
BOF: Beginning of File	809h
BOOKBOOL: Workbook Option Flag	DAh
BOOLERR: Cell Value, Boolean or Error	205h
BOTTOMMARGIN: Bottom Margin Measurement	29h
BOUNDSHEET: Sheet Information	85h
CALCCOUNT: Iteration Count	0Ch
CALCMODE: Calculation Mode	0Dh
CF: Conditional Formatting Conditions	1B1h
CONDFMT: Conditional Formatting Range Information	1B0h
CODENAME: VBE Object Name	42h
CODEPAGE: Default Code Page	42h
COLINFO: Column Formatting Information	7Dh
CONTINUE: Continues Long Records	3Ch
COORDLIST: Polygon Object Vertex Coordinates	A9h
COUNTRY: Default Country and WIN.INI Country	8Ch
CRN: Nonresident Operands	5Ah
DBCELL: Stream Offsets	D7h
DCON: Data Consolidation Information	50h
DCONBIN: Data Consolidation Information	1B5h
DCONNAME: Data Consolidation Named References	52h

Record	Number
DCONREF: Data Consolidation References	51h
DEFAULTROWHEIGHT: Default Row Height	225h
DEFCOLWIDTH: Default Width for Columns	55h
DELMENU: Menu Deletion	C3h
DELTA: Iteration Increment	10h
DIMENSIONS: Cell Table Size	200h
DOCROUTE: Routing Slip Information	B8h
DSF: Double Stream File	161h
DV: Data Validation Criteria	1BEh
DVAL: Data Validation Information	1B2h
EDG: Edition Globals	88h
EOF: End of File	0Ah
EXTERNCOUNT: Number of External References	16h
EXTERNNAME: Externally Referenced Name	223h
EXTERNSHEET: External Reference	17h
EXTSST: Extended Shared String Table	FFh
FILEPASS: File Is Password-Protected	2Fh
FILESHARING: File-Sharing Information	5Bh
FILESHARING2: File-Sharing Information for Shared Lists	1A5h
FILTERMODE: Sheet Contains Filtered List	9Bh
FNGROUPCOUNT: Built-in Function Group Count	9Ch
FNGROUPNAME: Function Group Name	9Ah
FONT: Font Description	231h
FOOTER: Print Footer on Each Page	15h
FORMAT: Number Format	41Eh
FORMULA: Cell Formula	406h
GCW: Global Column-Width Flags	ABh
GRIDSET: State Change of Gridlines Option	82h
GUTS: Size of Row and Column Gutters	80h
HCENTER: Center Between Horizontal Margins	83h
HEADER: Print Header on Each Page	14h
HIDEOBJ: Object Display Options	8Dh
HLINK: Hyperlink	1B8h
HORIZONTALPAGEBREAKS: Explicit Row Page Breaks	1Bh

Record	Number
IMDATA: Image Data	7Fh
INDEX: Index Record	20Bh
INTERFACEEND: End of User Interface Records	E2h
INTERFACEHDR: Beginning of User Interface Records	E1h
ITERATION: Iteration Mode	11h
LABEL: Cell Value, String Constant	204h
LABELSST: Cell Value, String Constant/SST	FDh
LEFTMARGIN: Left Margin Measurement	26h
LHNGRAPH: Named Graph Information	95h
LHRECORD: .WK? File Conversion Information	94h
LPR: Sheet Was Printed Using LINE.PRINT(	98h
MMS: ADDMENU/DELMENU Record Group Count	C1h
MSODRAWING: Microsoft Office Drawing	ECh
MSODRAWINGGROUP: Microsoft Office Drawing Group	EBh
MSODRAWINGSELECTION: Microsoft Office Drawing Selection	EDh
MULBLANK: Multiple Blank Cells	BEh
MULRK: Multiple RK Cells	BDh
NAME: Defined Name	218h
NOTE: Comment Associated with a Cell	1Ch
NUMBER: Cell Value, Floating-Point Number	203h
OBJ: Describes a Graphic Object	5Dh
OBJPROTECT: Objects Are Protected	63h
OBPROJ: Visual Basic Project	D3h
OLESIZE: Size of OLE Object	DEh
PALETTE: Color Palette Definition	92h
PANE: Number of Panes and Their Position	41h
PARAMQRY: Query Parameters	DCh
PASSWORD: Protection Password	13h
PLS: Environment-Specific Print Record	4Dh
PRECISION: Precision	0Eh
PRINTGRIDLINES: Print Gridlines Flag	2Bh
PRINTHEADERS: Print Row/Column Labels	2Ah
PROTECT: Protection Flag	12h
PROT4REV: Shared Workbook Protection Flag	1AFh

Record	Number
QSI: External Data Range	1ADh
RECIPNAME: Recipient Name	B9h
REFMODE: Reference Mode	0Fh
REFRESHALL: Refresh Flag	1B7h
RIGHTMARGIN: Right Margin Measurement	27h
RK: Cell Value, RK Number	7Eh
ROW: Describes a Row	208h
RSTRING: Cell with Character Formatting	D6h
SAVERECALC: Recalculate Before Save	5Fh
SCENARIO: Scenario Data	AFh
SCENMAN: Scenario Output Data	AEh
SCENPROTECT: Scenario Protection	DDh
SCL: Window Zoom Magnification	A0h
SELECTION: Current Selection	1Dh
SETUP: Page Setup	A1h
SHRFMLA: Shared Formula	BCh
SORT: Sorting Options	90h
SOUND: Sound Note	96h
SST: Shared String Table	FCh
STANDARDWIDTH: Standard Column Width	99h
STRING: String Value of a Formula	207h
STYLE: Style Information	293h
SUB: Subscriber	91h
SUPBOOK: Supporting Workbook	1AEh
SXDB: PivotTable Cache Data	C6h
SXDBEX: PivotTable Cache Data	122h
SXDI: Data Item	C5h
SXEX: PivotTable View Extended Information	F1h
SXEXT: External Source Information	DCh
SXFDBTYPE: SQL Datatype Identifier	1BBh
SXFILT: PivotTable Rule Filter	F2h
SXFORMAT: PivotTable Format Record	FBh
SXFORMULA: PivotTable Formula Record	103h
SXFMLA: PivotTable Parsed Expression	F9h

Record	Number
SXIDSTM: Stream ID	D5h
SXIVD: Row/Column Field IDs	B4h
SXLI: Line Item Array	B5h
SXNAME: PivotTable Name	F6h
SXPAIR: PivotTable Name Pair	F8h
SXPI: Page Item	B6h
SXRULE: PivotTable Rule Data	F0h
SXSTRING: String	CDh
SXSELECT: PivotTable Selection Information	F7h
SXTBL: Multiple Consolidation Source Info	D0h
SXTBPG: Page Item Indexes	D2h
SXTBRGIITM: Page Item Name Count	D1h
SXVD: View Fields	B1h
SXVDEX: Extended PivotTable View Fields	100h
SXVI: View Item	B2h
SXVIEW: View Definition	B0h
SXVS: View Source	E3h
TABID: Sheet Tab Index Array	13Dh
TABIDCONF: Sheet Tab ID of Conflict History	EAh
TABLE: Data Table	236h
TEMPLATE: Workbook Is a Template	60h
TOPMARGIN: Top Margin Measurement	28h
TXO: Text Object	1B6h
UDDESC: Description String for Chart Autoformat	DFh
UNCALCED: Recalculation Status	5Eh
USERBVIEW: Workbook Custom View Settings	1A9h
USERSVIEWBEGIN: Custom View Settings	1AAh
USERSVIEWEND: End of Custom View Records	1ABh
USESELFS: Natural Language Formulas Flag	160h
VCENTER: Center Between Vertical Margins	84h
VERTICALPAGEBREAKS: Explicit Column Page Breaks	1Ah
WINDOW1: Window Information	3Dh
WINDOW2: Sheet Window Information	23Eh
WINDOWPROTECT: Windows Are Protected	19h

Record	Number
WRITEACCESS: Write Access User Name	5Ch
WRITEPROT: Workbook Is Write-Protected	86h
WSBOOL: Additional Workspace Information	81h
XCT: CRN Record Count	59h
XF: Extended Format	E0h
XL5MODIFY: Flag for DSF	162h

BIFF Records: Record Number Order

Number	Record
0Ah	EOF: End of File
0Ch	CALCCOUNT: Iteration Count
0Dh	CALCMODE: Calculation Mode
0Eh	PRECISION: Precision
0Fh	REFMODE: Reference Mode
10h	DELTA: Iteration Increment
11h	ITERATION: Iteration Mode
12h	PROTECT: Protection Flag
13h	PASSWORD: Protection Password
14h	HEADER: Print Header on Each Page
15h	FOOTER: Print Footer on Each Page
16h	EXTERNCOUNT: Number of External References
17h	EXTERNSHEET: External Reference
19h	WINDOWPROTECT: Windows Are Protected
1Ah	VERTICALPAGEBREAKS: Explicit Column Page Breaks
1Bh	HORIZONTALPAGEBREAKS: Explicit Row Page Breaks
1Ch	NOTE: Comment Associated with a Cell
1Dh	SELECTION: Current Selection
22h	1904: 1904 Date System
26h	LEFTMARGIN: Left Margin Measurement
27h	RIGHTMARGIN: Right Margin Measurement
28h	TOPMARGIN: Top Margin Measurement
29h	BOTTOMMARGIN: Bottom Margin Measurement
2Ah	PRINTHEADERS: Print Row/Column Labels
2Bh	PRINTGRIDLINES: Print Gridlines Flag

Number	Record
2Fh	FILEPASS: File Is Password-Protected
3Ch	CONTINUE: Continues Long Records
3Dh	WINDOW1: Window Information
40h	BACKUP: Save Backup Version of the File
41h	PANE: Number of Panes and Their Position
42h	CODENAME: VBE Object Name
42h	CODEPAGE: Default Code Page
4Dh	PLS: Environment-Specific Print Record
50h	DCON: Data Consolidation Information
51h	DCONREF: Data Consolidation References
52h	DCONNAME: Data Consolidation Named References
55h	DEFCOLWIDTH: Default Width for Columns
59h	XCT: CRN Record Count
5Ah	CRN: Nonresident Operands
5Bh	FILESHARING: File-Sharing Information
5Ch	WRITEACCESS: Write Access User Name
5Dh	OBJ: Describes a Graphic Object
5Eh	UNCALCED: Recalculation Status
5Fh	SAVERECALC: Recalculate Before Save
60h	TEMPLATE: Workbook Is a Template
63h	OBJPROTECT: Objects Are Protected
7Dh	COLINFO: Column Formatting Information
7Eh	RK: Cell Value, RK Number
7Fh	IMDATA: Image Data
80h	GUTS: Size of Row and Column Gutters
81h	WSBOOL: Additional Workspace Information
82h	GRIDSET: State Change of Gridlines Option
83h	HCENTER: Center Between Horizontal Margins
84h	VCENTER: Center Between Vertical Margins
85h	BOUNDSHEET: Sheet Information
86h	WRITEPROT: Workbook Is Write-Protected
87h	ADDIN: Workbook Is an Add-in Macro
88h	EDG: Edition Globals
89h	PUB: Publisher

Number	Record
8Ch	COUNTRY: Default Country and WIN.INI Country
8Dh	HIDEOBJ: Object Display Options
90h	SORT: Sorting Options
91h	SUB: Subscriber
92h	PALETTE: Color Palette Definition
94h	LHRECORD: .WK? File Conversion Information
95h	LHNGRAPH: Named Graph Information
96h	SOUND: Sound Note
98h	LPR: Sheet Was Printed Using LINE.PRINT(
99h	STANDARDWIDTH: Standard Column Width
9Ah	FNGROUPNAME: Function Group Name
9Bh	FILTERMODE: Sheet Contains Filtered List
9Ch	FNGROUPCOUNT: Built-in Function Group Count
9Dh	AUTOFILTERINFO: Drop-Down Arrow Count
9Eh	AUTOFILTER: AutoFilter Data
A0h	SCL: Window Zoom Magnification
A1h	SETUP: Page Setup
A9h	COORDLIST: Polygon Object Vertex Coordinates
ABh	GCW: Global Column-Width Flags
AEh	SCENMAN: Scenario Output Data
AFh	SCENARIO: Scenario Data
B0h	SXVIEW: View Definition
B1h	SXVD: View Fields
B2h	SXVI: View Item
B4h	SXIVD: Row/Column Field IDs
B5h	SXLI: Line Item Array
B6h	SXPI: Page Item
B8h	DOCROUTE: Routing Slip Information
B9h	RECIPNAME: Recipient Name
BCh	SHRFMLA: Shared Formula
BDh	MULRK: Multiple RK Cells
BEh	MULBLANK: Multiple Blank Cells
C1h	MMS: ADDMENU/DELMENU Record Group Count
C2h	ADDMENU: Menu Addition

Number	Record
C3h	DELMENU: Menu Deletion
C5h	SXDI: Data Item
C6h	SXDB: PivotTable Cache Data
CDh	SXSTRING: String
D0h	SXTBL: Multiple Consolidation Source Info
D1h	SXTBRGIITM: Page Item Name Count
D2h	SXTBPG: Page Item Indexes
D3h	OBPROJ: Visual Basic Project
D5h	SXIDSTM: Stream ID
D6h	RSTRING: Cell with Character Formatting
D7h	DBCELL: Stream Offsets
DAh	BOOKBOOL: Workbook Option Flag
DCh	PARAMQRY: Query Parameters
DCh	SXEXT: External Source Information
DDh	SCENPROTECT: Scenario Protection
DEh	OLESIZE: Size of OLE Object
DFh	UDDESC: Description String for Chart Autoformat
E0h	XF: Extended Format
E1h	INTERFACEHDR: Beginning of User Interface Records
E2h	INTERFACEEND: End of User Interface Records
E3h	SXVS: View Source
EAh	TABIDCONF: Sheet Tab ID of Conflict History
EBh	MSODRAWINGGROUP: Microsoft Office Drawing Group
ECh	MSODRAWING: Microsoft Office Drawing
EDh	MSODRAWINGSELECTION: Microsoft Office Drawing Selection
F0h	SXRULE: PivotTable Rule Data
F1h	SXEX: PivotTable View Extended Information
F2h	SXFILT: PivotTable Rule Filter
F6h	SXNAME: PivotTable Name
F7h	SXSELECT: PivotTable Selection Information
F8h	SXPAIR: PivotTable Name Pair
F9h	SXFMLA: PivotTable Parsed Expression
FBh	SXFORMAT: PivotTable Format Record
FCh	SST: Shared String Table

Number	Record
FDh	LABELSST: Cell Value, String Constant/SST
FFh	EXTSST: Extended Shared String Table
100h	SXVDEX: Extended PivotTable View Fields
103h	SXFORMULA: PivotTable Formula Record
122h	SXDBEX: PivotTable Cache Data
13Dh	TABID: Sheet Tab Index Array
160h	USESELFS: Natural Language Formulas Flag
161h	DSF: Double Stream File
162h	XL5MODIFY: Flag for DSF
1A5h	FILESHARING2: File-Sharing Information for Shared Lists
1A9h	USERBVIEW: Workbook Custom View Settings
1AAh	USERSVIEWBEGIN: Custom View Settings
1ABh	USERSVIEWEND: End of Custom View Records
1ADh	QSI: External Data Range
1AEh	SUPBOOK: Supporting Workbook
1AFh	PROT4REV: Shared Workbook Protection Flag
1B0h	CONDFMT: Conditional Formatting Range Information
1B1h	CF: Conditional Formatting Conditions
1B2h	DVAL: Data Validation Information
1B5h	DCONBIN: Data Consolidation Information
1B6h	TXO: Text Object
1B7h	REFRESHALL: Refresh Flag
1B8h	HLINK: Hyperlink
1BBh	SXFDBTYPE: SQL Datatype Identifier
1BCh	PROT4REVPASS: Shared Workbook Protection Password
1BEh	DV: Data Validation Criteria
200h	DIMENSIONS: Cell Table Size
201h	BLANK: Cell Value, Blank Cell
203h	NUMBER: Cell Value, Floating-Point Number
204h	LABEL: Cell Value, String Constant
205h	BOOLERR: Cell Value, Boolean or Error
207h	STRING: String Value of a Formula
208h	ROW: Describes a Row
20Bh	INDEX: Index Record

Number	Record
218h	NAME: Defined Name
221h	ARRAY: Array-Entered Formula
223h	EXTERNNAME: Externally Referenced Name
225h	DEFAULTROWHEIGHT: Default Row Height
231h	FONT: Font Description
236h	TABLE: Data Table
23Eh	WINDOW2: Sheet Window Information
293h	STYLE: Style Information
406h	FORMULA: Cell Formula
41Eh	FORMAT: Number Format
809h	BOF: Beginning of File

Record Descriptions

The first two fields in every BIFF record are record number and record length. Because these fields have the same offset and size in every BIFF record, they're not documented in the following descriptions. For more information about the record number and record length fields, see "BIFF Record Information" on page 267.

1904: 1904 Date System (22h)

The 1904 record stores the date system used by Microsoft Excel.

Record Data

Offset	Name	Size	Contents
4	f1904	2	= 1 if the 1904 date system is used

ADDIN: Workbook Is an Add-in Macro (87h)

This record has no record data field. If the ADDIN record is present in the BIFF file, it signifies that the macro is an add-in macro. The ADDIN record, if present, must immediately follow the first BOF record in the Book stream.

ADDMENU: Menu Addition (C2h)

The ADDMENU record stores a menu addition. When you add a menu object (a menu bar, a menu, a menu item, or a submenu item) to the user interface, Microsoft Excel writes a group of ADDMENU records for each object. The first record stores the menu bar, the second stores the menu, the third stores the menu item, and the fourth stores the submenu item (note how this is identical to the menu hierarchy in the user interface). The number of records in the group depends on the level of the menu structure at which the addition occurs. For example, adding a menu to a menu bar causes two ADDMENU records to be written. Adding a submenu item to a menu item causes four records to be written.

If fInsert is true (equal to 01h), the menu object is added at this level of the hierarchy. For example, if fInsert is true in the second ADDMENU record of the group, Microsoft Excel adds a new menu to an existing menu bar. If fInsert is false (equal to 00h), the record is a placeholder, and one of the following ADDMENU records in the group will define the menu addition.

For menu items and submenu items, the icetab field stores the index to the added command, if the item is attached to a built-in command. The icetabBefore field stores the index to the command before which the new command is added. If either of these indexes equals FFFFh, the corresponding string from the rgch field is used instead of a built-in command.

The caitm field is equal to the number of following ADDMENU records that are to be inserted at this level of the menu hierarchy.

Record Data

Offset	Name	Size	Contents
4	icetabItem	2	Icetab of the command
6	icetabBefore	2	Icetab of the existing command before which the new command is inserted
8	caitm	1	Number of ADDMENU records at the next level of the menu hierarchy
9	fInsert	1	= 1, insert this menu object = 0, this is a placeholder record
10	rgch	var	stItem, stBefore, stMacro, stStatus, stHelp strings (see text)

The rgch field stores five concatenated strings, as described in the following table. Null strings will appear in the rgch field as a single byte (00h).

String	Contents
stItem	Text of the menu object
stBefore	Text of the item before which this item is added
stMacro	Macro name, encoded using a technique similar to the encoded file names in the EXTERNSHEET record (for more information, see "EXTERNSHEET" on page 310)
stStatus	Status bar text (for add-ins)
stHelp	Help file name and context ID (for add-ins)

ARRAY: Array-Entered Formula (221h)

An ARRAY record describes a formula that was array-entered into a range of cells. The range of cells in which the array is entered is defined by the rwFirst, rwLast, colFirst, and colLast fields.

The ARRAY record occurs directly after the FORMULA record for the cell in the upper-left corner of the array—that is, the cell defined by the rwFirst and colFirst fields.

The parsed expression is the array formula, stored in the Microsoft Excel internal format. For an explanation of the parsed format, see "Microsoft Excel Formulas" on page 444.

Record Data

Offset	Name	Size	Contents
4	rwFirst	2	First row of the array
6	rwLast	2	Last row of the array
8	colFirst	1	First column of the array
9	colLast	1	Last column of the array
10	grbit	2	Option flags
12	chn	4	(See text)
16	cce	2	Length of the parsed expression
18	rgce	var	Parsed expression

You should ignore the chn field when you read the BIFF file. If you write a BIFF file, the chn field must be 00000000h.

The grbit field contains the option flags listed in the following table.

Offset	Bits	Mask	Name	Contents
0	0	01h	fAlwaysCalc	Always calculate the formula.
	1	02h	fCalcOnLoad	Calculate the formula when the file is opened.
	7–2	FCh	(unused)	
1	7–0	FFh	(unused)	

AUTOFILTER: AutoFilter Data (9Eh)

This record stores data for an active AutoFilter.

Record Data—BIFF7 and Later

Offset	Name	Size	Contents
4	iEntry	2	Index of the active AutoFilter
6	grbit	2	Option flags
8	doper1	10	DOPER structure for the first filter condition (see text)
18	doper2	10	DOPER structure for the second filter condition (see text)
28	rgch	var	String storage for vtString DOPER (see text)

The grbit field contains the option flags listed in the following table.

Offset	Bits	Mask	Name	Contents
0	1–0	0003h	wJoin	= 1 if the custom filter conditions are ANDed = 0 if the custom filter conditions are ORed
	2	0004h	fSimple1	= 1 if the first condition is a simple equality (for optimization)
	3	0008h	fSimple2	= 1 if the second condition is a simple equality (for optimization)
	4	0010h	fTop10	= 1 if the condition is a Top 10 AutoFilter
	5	0020h	fTop	= 1 if the Top 10 AutoFilter shows the top items; = 0 if it shows the bottom items

Offset	Bits	Mask	Name	Contents
	6	0040h	fPercent	= 1 if the Top 10 AutoFilter shows percentage; = 0 if it shows items
	15–7	FF80h	wTop10	The number of items to show (from 1 to 500 decimal, expressed as a binary number)

Record Data—BIFF5

Offset	Name	Size	Contents
4	iEntry	2	Index of the active AutoFilter
6	grbit	2	Option flags
8	doper1	10	DOPER structure for first filter condition (see text)
18	doper2	10	DOPER structure for the second filter condition (see text)
28	rgch	var	String storage for vtString DOPER (see text)

The grbit field contains the option flags listed in the following table.

Offset	Bits	Mask	Name	Contents
0	1–0	03h	wJoin	= 1 if the custom filter conditions are ANDed = 0 if the custom filter conditions are ORed
	2	04h	fSimple1	= 1 if the first condition is a simple equality (for optimization)
	3	08h	fSimple2	= 1 if the second condition is a simple equality (for optimization)
	7–4	F0h	(Reserved)	
1	7–0	FFh	(Reserved)	

DOPER Structures

The database oper structures (DOPERs) are 10-byte parsed definitions of the filter conditions that appear in the Custom AutoFilter dialog box. The DOPER structures are defined in the following sections.

DOPER Structure for RK Numbers (vt = 02h)

Offset	Name	Size	Contents
0	vt	1	Data type (see text)
1	grbitSgn	1	Comparison code (see text)
2	rk	4	RK number (see "RK" on page 376)
6	(reserved)	4	

DOPER Structure for IEEE Floating-Point Numbers (vt = 04h)

Offset	Name	Size	Contents
0	vt	1	Data type (see text)
1	grbitSgn	1	Comparison code (see text)
2	num	8	IEEE floating-point number

DOPER Structure for Strings (vt = 06h)

Offset	Name	Size	Contents
0	vt	1	Data type (see text)
1	grbitSgn	1	Comparison code (see text)
2	(reserved)	4	
6	cch	1	Length of the string (the string is stored in rgch field that follows the DOPER structures)
7	(reserved)	3	

DOPER Structure for Boolean and Error Values (vt = 08h)

Offset	Name	Size	Contents
0	vt	1	Data type (see text)
1	grbitSgn	1	Comparison code (see text)
2	fError	1	Boolean/error flag
3	bBoolErr	1	Boolean value or error value
4	(reserved)	6	

The bBoolErr field contains the Boolean or error value, as determined by the fError field. If the fError field contains a 0 (zero), the bBoolErr field contains a Boolean value; if the fError field contains a 1, the bBoolErr field contains an error value.

Boolean values are 1 for true and 0 for false.

Error values are listed in the following table.

Error value	Value (hex)	Value (dec.)
#NULL!	00h	0
#DIV/0!	07h	7
#VALUE!	0Fh	15
#REF!	17h	23
#NAME?	1Dh	29
#NUM!	24h	36
#N/A	2Ah	42

The vt field contains the data type of the DOPER, as shown in the following table. For the DOPER types 00h, 0Ch, and 0Eh, the remaining 9 bytes of the DOPER are ignored.

vt	DOPER type
00h	Filter condition not used
02h	RK number
04h	IEEE number
06h	String
08h	Boolean or error value
0Ch	Match all blanks
0Eh	Match all non-blanks

The grbitSgn field corresponds to comparison operators, as shown in the following table.

grbitSgn	Operator
01	<
02	=
03	<=
04	>
05	<>
06	>=

AUTOFILTERINFO: Drop-Down Arrow Count (9Dh)

This record stores the count of AutoFilter drop-down arrows. Each drop-down arrow has a corresponding OBJ record. If at least one AutoFilter is active (in other words, the range has been filtered at least once), there will be a corresponding FILTERMODE record in the file. There will also be one AUTOFILTER record for each active filter.

Record Data

Offset	Name	Size	Contents
4	cEntries	2	Number of AutoFilter drop-down arrows on the sheet

BACKUP: Save Backup Version of the File (40h)

The BACKUP record specifies whether Microsoft Excel should save backup versions of a file.

Record Data

Offset	Name	Size	Contents
4	fBackupFile	2	= 1 if Microsoft Excel should save a backup version of the file

BLANK: Cell Value, Blank Cell (201h)

A BLANK record describes an empty cell. The rw field contains the 0-based row number. The col field contains the 0-based column number.

Record Data

Offset	Name	Size	Contents
4	rw	2	Row
6	col	2	Column
8	ixfe	2	Index to the XF record

BOF: Beginning of File (809h)

The BOF record marks the beginning of the Book stream in the BIFF file. It also marks the beginning of record groups (or "substreams" of the Book stream) for sheets in the workbook. For BIFF2 through BIFF4, you can determine the BIFF version from the high-order byte of the record number field, as shown in the following table. For BIFF5/BIFF7, and BIFF8 you must use the vers field at offset 4 to determine the BIFF version.

BOF Record Number Field

Offset	Name	Size	Contents
0	vers	1	version: = 00 BIFF2 = 02 BIFF3 = 04 BIFF4 = 08 BIFF5/BIFF7/BIFF8
1	bof	1	09h

Record Data—BIFF8

Offset	Name	Size	Contents
4	vers	2	Version number: = 0600 for BIFF8
6	dt	2	Substream type: 0005h = Workbook globals 0006h = Visual Basic module 0010h = Worksheet or dialog sheet 0020h = Chart 0040h = Microsoft Excel 4.0 macro sheet 0100h = Workspace file
8	rupBuild	2	Build identifier (=0DBBh for Microsoft Excel 97)
10	rupYear	2	Build year (=07CCh for Microsoft Excel 97)
12	bfh	4	File history flags
16	sfo	4	Lowest BIFF version (see text)

The rupBuild and rupYear fields contain numbers that identify the version (build) of Microsoft Excel that wrote the file. If you write a BIFF file, you can use the BiffView utility to determine the current values of these fields by examining a BOF record in a workbook file.

The sfo field contains the earliest version (vers field) of Microsoft Excel that can read all records in this file.

The bfh field contains the following flag bits:

Bits	Mask	Name	Contents
0	00000001h	fWin	= 1 if the file was last edited by Microsoft Excel for Windows
1	00000002h	fRisc	= 1 if the file was last edited by Microsoft Excel on a RISC platform

Bits	Mask	Name	Contents
2	00000004h	fBeta	= 1 if the file was last edited by a beta version of Microsoft Excel
3	00000008h	fWinAny	= 1 if the file has ever been edited by Microsoft Excel for Windows
4	00000010h	fMacAny	= 1 if the file has ever been edited by Microsoft Excel for the Macintosh
5	00000020h	fBetaAny	= 1 if the file has ever been edited by a beta version of Microsoft Excel
7–6	000000C0h	(Reserved)	Reserved; must be 0 (zero)
8	00000100h	fRiscAny	= 1 if the file has ever been edited by Microsoft Excel on a RISC platform
31–9	FFFFFE00	(Reserved)	Reserved; must be 0 (zero)

Record Data—BIFF5 and BIFF7

Offset	Name	Size	Contents
4	vers	2	Version number (0500 for BIFF5 and BIFF7)
6	dt	2	Substream type: 0005h = Workbook globals 0006h = Visual Basic module 0010h = Worksheet or dialog sheet 0020h = Chart 0040h = Microsoft Excel 4.0 macro sheet 0100h = Workspace file
8	rupBuild	2	Build identifier (internal use only)
10	rupYear	2	Build year (internal use only)

BOOKBOOL: Workbook Option Flag (DAh)

This record saves a workbook option flag.

Record Data

Offset	Name	Size	Contents
4	fNoSaveSupp	2	=1 if the Save External Link Values option is turned off (Options dialog box, Calculation tab)

BOOLERR: Cell Value, Boolean or Error (205h)

A BOOLERR record describes a cell that contains a constant Boolean or error value. The rw field contains the 0-based row number. The col field contains the 0-based column number.

Record Data

Offset	Name	Size	Contents
4	rw	2	Row
6	col	2	Column
8	ixfe	2	Index to the XF record
10	bBoolErr	1	Boolean value or error value
11	fError	1	Boolean/error flag

The bBoolErr field contains the Boolean or error value, as determined by the fError field. If the fError field contains a 0 (zero), the bBoolErr field contains a Boolean value; if the fError field contains a 1, the bBoolErr field contains an error value.

Boolean values are 1 for true and 0 for false.

Error values are listed in the following table.

Error value	Value (hex)	Value (dec.)
#NULL!	00h	0
#DIV/0!	07h	7
#VALUE!	0Fh	15
#REF!	17h	23
#NAME?	1Dh	29
#NUM!	24h	36
#N/A	2Ah	42

BOTTOMMARGIN: Bottom Margin Measurement (29h)

The BOTTOMMARGIN record specifies the bottom margin in inches when a sheet is printed. The num field is in 8-byte IEEE floating-point format.

Record Data

Offset	Name	Size	Contents
4	num	8	Bottom margin

BOUNDSHEET: Sheet Information (85h)

This record stores the sheet name, sheet type, and stream position.

BIFF8 Record Data

Offset	Name	Size	Contents
4	lbPlyPos	4	Stream position of the start of the BOF record for the sheet
8	grbit	2	Option flags
10	cch	2	Length of the sheet name
12	rgch	var	Sheet name

BIFF7 Record Data

Offset	Name	Size	Contents
4	lbPlyPos	4	Stream position of the start of the BOF record for the sheet
8	grbit	2	Option flags
10	cch	1	Length of the sheet name
11	rgch	var	Sheet name

The grbit field contains the options listed in the following table.

Offset	Bits	Mask	Name	Contents
0	7–0	0Fh	dt	Sheet type: 00h = worksheet or dialog sheet 01h = Microsoft Excel 4.0 macro sheet 02h = chart 06h = Visual Basic module
1	1–0	03h	hsState	Hidden state: 00h = visible 01h = hidden 02h = very hidden (see text)
	7–2	FCh	(Reserved)	

A Visual Basic procedure can set the **Visible** property of a sheet to create a very hidden sheet. A very hidden sheet can be made visible again by a Visual Basic procedure, but there is no way to make the sheet visible through the user interface of Microsoft Excel.

CALCCOUNT: Iteration Count (0Ch)

The CALCCOUNT record stores the Maximum Iterations option from the Options dialog box, Calculation tab.

Record Data

Offset	Name	Size	Contents
4	cIter	2	Iteration count

CALCMODE: Calculation Mode (0Dh)

The CALCMODE record stores options from the Options dialog box, Calculation tab.

Record Data

Offset	Name	Size	Contents
4	fAutoRecalc	2	Calculation mode: = 0 for manual = 1 for automatic = –1 for automatic, except tables

CF: Conditional Formatting Conditions (1B1h)

This record stores a conditional formatting condition.

Record Data—BIFF8

Offset	Name	Size	Contents
4	ct	1	Conditional Formatting type
5	cp	1	Conditional Formatting operator
6	cce1	2	Count of bytes in rgce1
8	cce2	2	Count of bytes in rgce2
10	rgbdxf	var	Conditional format to apply
var	rgce1	var	First formula for this condition
var	rgce2	var	Second formula for this condition

CODENAME: VBE Object Name (42h)

The CODENAME record stores the name for a worksheet object. It is not necessarily the same name as you see in the workbook sheet tab, but the name you see in the VBE project window for the worksheet.

Record Data—BIFF8

Offset	Name	Size	Contents
4	stCodeName	var	The name as a unicode string; for more information, see "Unicode Strings in BIFF8" on page 264.

CODEPAGE: Default Code Page (42h)

The CODEPAGE record stores the default code page (character set) that was in use when the workbook was saved.

Record Data

Offset	Name	Size	Contents
4	cv	2	Code page the file is saved in: 01B5h (437 dec.) = IBM PC (Multiplan) 8000h (32768 dec.) = Apple Macintosh 04E4h (1252 dec.) = ANSI (Microsoft Windows)

COLINFO: Column Formatting Information (7Dh)

The COLINFO record describes the column formatting for a range of columns.

Record Data

Offset	Name	Size	Contents
4	colFirst	2	First formatted column (0-based)
6	colLast	2	Last formatted column (0-based)
8	coldx	2	Column width, in 1/256s of a character width
10	ixfe	2	Index to XF record that contains the default format for the column (for more information about the XF records, see "XF" on page 426)
12	grbit	2	Options
14	(reserved)	1	Reserved; must be 0 (zero)

The grbit field contains the options listed in the following table.

Offset	Bits	Mask	Name	Contents
0	0	01h	fHidden	= 1 if the column range is hidden
	7–1	FEh	(Unused)	
1	2–0	07h	iOutLevel	Outline level of column range
	3	08h	(Reserved)	Reserved; must be 0 (zero)
	4	10h	fCollapsed	= 1 if the column range is collapsed in outlining
	7–5	E0h	(Reserved)	Reserved; must be 0 (zero)

CONDFMT: Conditional Formatting Range Information (1B0h)

This record stores conditional formatting range information.

Record Data—BIFF8

Offset	Name	Size	Contents
4	ccf	2	Number of conditional formats
6	grbit	2	Option flags
8	rwFirst	2	First row to conditionally format (0-based)
10	rwLast	2	Last row to conditionally format (0-based)
12	colFirst	2	First column to conditionally format (0-based)
14	colLast	2	Last column to conditionally format (0-based)
16	rgbSqref	var	Array of sqref structures

The grbit field contains the options listed in the following table.

Bits	Mask	Name	Contents
0	01h	fToughRecalc	= 1 if the appearance of the cell requires significant processing
15–1	FFFEh	(Reserved)	Reserved; must be 0 (zero)

The sqref structure stores a union of multiple areas on a worksheet. The sqref structure is shown in the following table.

Offset	Name	Size	Contents
0	irefMac	2	Number of areas that follow
2	reref	var	Array of ref structures

The ref structure is shown in the following table.

Offset	Name	Size	Contents
0	rwFirst	2	First row in the reference
2	rwLast	2	Last row in the reference
4	colFirst	2	First column in the reference
6	colLast	2	Last column in the reference

CONTINUE: Continues Long Records (3Ch)

Records that are longer than 8228 bytes (2084 bytes in BIFF7 and earlier) must be split into several records. The first section appears in the base record; subsequent sections appear in CONTINUE records.

In BIFF8, the TXO record is always followed by CONTINUE records that store the string data and formatting runs.

Record Data

Offset	Name	Size	Contents
4		var	Continuation of record data

COORDLIST: Polygon Object Vertex Coordinates (A9h)

This record stores the coordinates of the vertices in a polygon object.

Record Data

Offset	Name	Size	Contents
4	rgVTX	var	Array of vertex coordinates

The VTX structure is defined as follows:

```
typedef struct _vtx
    {
    unsigned short int x;
    unsigned short int y;
    }
        VTX;
```

The upper-left corner of a polygon's bounding rectangle is (x = 0h, y = 0h), and the lower-right corner is (x = 4000h, y = 4000h), as shown in the following illustration.

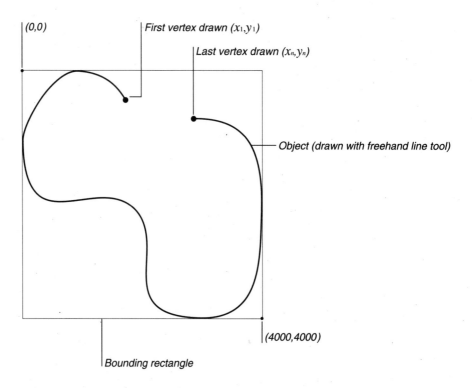

After the polygon is drawn, Microsoft Excel normalizes the coordinates in rgVTX to the bounding rectangle. The actual size of the polygon can be derived from the size of the bounding rectangle in the common object fields section of the OBJ record.

COUNTRY: Default Country and WIN.INI Country (8Ch)

This record contains localization information.

Record Data

Offset	Name	Size	Contents
4	iCountryDef	2	Default country index
6	iCountryWinIni	2	Country index from the Win.ini file

The default country index, iCountryDef, is determined by the localized version of Microsoft Excel that created the BIFF file. For example, all BIFF files created by the U.S. version of Microsoft Excel have iCountryDef = 1. If Microsoft Excel for Windows created the BIFF file, iCountryWinIni is equal to the index that corresponds to the country setting in the Win.ini file. Country indexes are defined in the following table.

Index	Country
1	United States
2	Canada
3	Latin America, except Brazil
31	Netherlands
32	Belgium
33	France
34	Spain
39	Italy
41	Switzerland
43	Austria
44	United Kingdom
45	Denmark
46	Sweden
47	Norway
49	Germany
52	Mexico
55	Brazil
61	Australia
64	New Zealand
81	Japan
82	South Korea
351	Portugal
354	Iceland
358	Finland
785	Saudi Arabia
886	Republic of China
972	Israel

CRN: Nonresident Operands (5Ah)

The CRN record describes nonresident operands in a formula. For example, if you have a worksheet that contains the formula =EXT.XLS!A1*A3, where EXT.XLS is not the active workbook, the nonresident operand EXT.XLS!A1 generates a CRN record that describes cell A1. If the nonresident operand contains more than one row, there is one CRN record for each row. For example, if the formula =EXT.XLS!A1:A4*4 is array-entered on a worksheet, there will be four CRN records.

If a worksheet contains two different formulas and each formula has multiple nonresident operands, Microsoft Excel may create one CRN record or several CRN records, depending on how the nonresident cells are arranged. For example, suppose that a worksheet contains two formulas (in different cells), =EXT.XLS!A1*2 and =EXT.XLS!B1*2. Because the nonresident operands are in a row and are not separated by an empty cell, Microsoft Excel creates only one CRN record containing information about cells A1 and B1.

If, however, the formulas are =EXT.XLS!A1*2 and =EXT.XLS!C1*2, Microsoft Excel creates two CRN records because an empty cell (B1) separates the two operands, A1 and C1.

Record Data

Offset	Name	Size	Contents
4	colLast	1	Last column of the nonresident operand
5	colFirst	1	First column of the nonresident operand
6	rw	2	Row of the nonresident operand
8	OPER	var	OPER structure; see the following description

The OPER structure repeats for each cell in the nonresident operand. For example, the formula =SUM(EXT.XLS!A1:A3) produces one CRN record with three OPER structures.

OPER Structure If the Cell Contains a Number

Offset	Name	Size	Contents
0	grbit	1	= 01h for a cell that contains a number
1	num	8	IEEE floating-point number

OPER Structure If the Cell Contains a String

Offset	Name	Size	Contents
0	grbit	1	= 02h for a cell that contains a string
1	cch	1	Number of characters in the string
2	rgch	var	String

OPER Structure If the Cell Contains a Boolean Value

Offset	Name	Size	Contents
0	grbit	1	= 04h for a cell that contains a Boolean value
1	f	2	= 1 if TRUE = 0 if FALSE
3	(unused)	6	

OPER Structure If the Cell Contains an Error Value

Offset	Name	Size	Contents
0	grbit	1	= 10h for a cell that contains an error value
1	err	2	Error value
3	(unused)	6	

DBCELL: Stream Offsets (D7h)

The DBCELL record stores stream offsets for the BIFF file. There is one DBCELL record for each block of ROW records and associated cell records. Each block can contain data for up to 32 rows. For more information about the DBCELL record, see "Finding Cell Records in BIFF Files" on page 440.

Record Data

Offset	Name	Size	Contents
4	dbRtrw	4	Offset from the start of the DBCELL record to the start of the first ROW record in the block; this is an offset to an earlier position in the stream.
8	rgdb	var	Array of stream offsets (2 bytes each). For more information, see "Finding Cell Records in BIFF Files" on page 440.

DCON: Data Consolidation Information (50h)

The DCON record stores options from the Consolidate dialog box (Data menu).

Record Data

Offset	Name	Size	Contents
4	iiftab	2	Index to the data consolidation function (see the following table)
6	fLeftCat	2	= 1 if the Left Column option is turned on
8	fTopCat	2	= 1 if the Top Row option is turned on
10	fLinkConsol	2	= 1 if the Create Links To Source Data option is turned on

The iiftab field, described in the following table, corresponds to the Function option in the Consolidate dialog box (Data menu).

Function	Iiftab
Average	0
Count Nums	1
Count	2
Max	3
Min	4
Product	5
StdDev	6
StdDevp	7
Sum	8
Var	9
Varp	10

DCONBIN: Data Consolidation Information (1B5h)

The DCONBIN record stores a data consolidation reference. DCONBIN is identical to DCONNAME, except that DCONBIN is used when the data consolidation reference refers to a built-in name (as described by a NAME record). The stFile field contains an encoded workbook name; for information about this field, see "EXTERNSHEET" on page 310.

Record Data—BIFF8

Offset	Name	Size	Contents
4	cchName	1	Length of the named range of the source area
5	stName	var	Named range of the source area for consolidation
var	cchFile	1	Length of the workbook name
var	stFile	var	Workbook name

DCONNAME: Data Consolidation Named References (52h)

The DCONNAME record contains the complete description of a named range of cells for the Consolidate command (Data menu). The stFile field contains an encoded workbook name; for information about this field, see "EXTERNSHEET" on page 310.

Record Data

Offset	Name	Size	Contents
4	cchName	1	Length of the named range of the source area
5	stName	var	Named range of the source area for consolidation
var	cchFile	1	Length of the workbook name
var	stFile	var	Workbook name

DCONREF: Data Consolidation References (51h)

The DCONREF record contains the complete description of a range of cells for the Consolidate command (Data menu). The rgch field contains an encoded workbook name; for information about this field, see "EXTERNSHEET" on page 310.

Record Data

Offset	Name	Size	Contents
4	rwFirst	2	First row of the source area for consolidation
6	rwLast	2	Last row of the source area for consolidation
8	colFirst	1	First column of the source area for consolidation
9	colLast	1	Last column of the source area for consolidation
10	cch	1	Length of the workbook name
11	rgch	1	Workbook name

DEFAULTROWHEIGHT: Default Row Height (225h)

The DEFAULTROWHEIGHT record specifies the height of all undefined rows on the sheet. The miyRw field contains the row height in units of $1/20^{th}$ of a point. This record does not affect the row height of any rows that are explicitly defined.

Record Data

Offset	Name	Size	Contents
4	grbit	2	Option flags (see the following table)
6	miyRw	2	Default row height

The grbit field contains the option flags listed in the following table.

Offset	Bits	Mask	Name	Contents
0	0	01h	fUnsynced	= 1 if all undefined rows have incompatible font height and row height
	1	02h	fDyZero	= 1 if all undefined rows have 0 (zero) height
	2	04h	fExAsc	= 1 if all undefined rows have an extra space above
	3	08h	fExDsc	= 1 if all undefined rows have an extra space below
	7–4	F0h	(Unused)	
1	7–0	FFh	(Unused)	

DEFCOLWIDTH: Default Width for Columns (55h)

The DEFCOLWIDTH record specifies the width, measured in characters, for columns not explicitly sized in the COLWIDTH record.

Record Data

Offset	Name	Size	Contents
4	cchdefColWidth	2	Default width of the columns

DELMENU: Menu Deletion (C3h)

The DELMENU record stores a menu deletion and is very similar to the ADDMENU record. For more information about menu system modification, see "ADDMENU" on page 281.

If fDelete is true (equal to 01h), the menu object is deleted at this level of the hierarchy. For example, if fDelete is true in the second DELMENU record of the group, Microsoft Excel deletes the specified menu from a menu bar. If fDelete is false (equal to 00h), the record is a placeholder, and one of the following DELMENU records in the group will define the menu deletion.

For menu items and submenu items, the icetabItem field stores the index to the deleted command if the item is attached to a built-in command. If icetabItem equals FFFFh, the stItem string from the rgch field is used instead.

Record Data

Offset	Name	Size	Contents
4	icetabItem	2	Icetab of the command
6	cditm	1	Number of DELMENU records at the next level of the menu hierarchy
7	fDelete	1	= 1, delete this menu object = 0, this is a placeholder record
8	fMultiple	1	= 1 if this item has subitems
9	rgch	var	stItem (see text)

The first byte of the stItem string is the byte count, and the last byte is reserved.

DELTA: Iteration Increment (10h)

The DELTA record stores the Maximum Change value from the Options dialog box, Calculation tab. The number is in 8-byte IEEE floating-point format.

Record Data

Offset	Name	Size	Contents
4	numDelta	8	Maximum iteration change

DIMENSIONS: Cell Table Size (200h)

The DIMENSIONS record contains the minimum and maximum bounds of the sheet. It provides a concise indication of the sheet size.

Note that both the rwMac and colMac fields are greater by 1 than the actual last row and column. For example, a worksheet that exists between cells B3 and D6 would have the following dimensions in the dimensions record (note rows and columns are 0-based in BIFF files in which row 1 and column A are both coded as 0):

rwMic   = 2—indicates that 3 is the first row

colMic = 1—indicates that B is the first column

rwMac   = 6—indicates that 6 is the last row

colMac = 4—indicates that D is the last column

Record Data—BIFF8

Offset	Name	Size	Contents
4	rwMic	4	First defined row on the sheet
8	rwMac	4	Last defined row on the sheet, plus 1
12	colMic	2	First defined column on the sheet
14	colMac	2	Last defined column on the sheet, plus 1
16	(Reserved)	2	Reserved; must be 0 (zero)

Record Data—BIFF7 and earlier

Offset	Name	Size	Contents
4	rwMic	2	First defined row on the sheet
6	rwMac	2	Last defined row on the sheet, plus 1
8	colMic	2	First defined column on the sheet
10	colMac	2	Last defined column on the sheet, plus 1
12	(Reserved)	2	Reserved; must be 0 (zero)

DOCROUTE: Routing Slip Information (B8h)

This record stores originator information for a routing slip and other information for document routing. The rgch field contains the concatenation of seven null-terminated strings: Subject, Message, Route ID, Custom Message Type, Book Title, Originator's Friendly Name, and Originator's System-Specific Address. The lengths of the strings are contained in the seven fields, cchSubject through ulEIDSize.

Record Data

Offset	Name	Size	Contents
4	iStage	2	Routing stage
6	cRecip	2	Number of recipients
8	delOption	2	Delivery option: = 0, one at a time = 1, all at once
10	wFlags	2	Option flags
12	cchSubject	2	Length of the Subject string
14	cchMessage	2	Length of the Message string
16	cchRouteID	2	Length of the Route ID string
18	cchCustType	2	Length of the Custom Message Type string

Offset	Name	Size	Contents
20	cchBookTitle	2	Length of the Book Title string
22	cchOrg	2	Length of the Originator's Friendly Name string
24	ulEIDSize	4	Length of the Originator's System-Specific Address string
28	rgch	var	(See text)

The wFlags field contains the option flags listed in the following table.

Offset	Bits	Mask	Name	Contents
0	0	01h	fRouted	= 1 if the document has been routed
	1	02h	fReturnOrig	= 1 if the document should be returned to its originator
	2	04h	fTrackStatus	= 1 if the status message should be sent
	3	08h	fCustomType	= 1 if the status message is a custom message type
	6–4	70h	(Reserved)	
	7	80h	fSaveRouteInfo	= 1 if the routing slip information should be saved
1	7–0	FFh	(Reserved)	

DSF: Double Stream File (161h)

The DSF record stores a flag that indicates if the workbook is a double stream file.

Record Data—BIFF8

Offset	Name	Size	Contents
4	fDSF	2	= 1 if the workbook is a double stream file

DV: Data Validation Criteria (1BEh)

This record stores data validation criteria for a range of cells.

Record Data—BIFF8

Offset	Name	Size	Contents
4	dwDvFlags	4	Option flags; see following table
8	rgb	var	Array of data validation criteria (see text) followed by Title, Prompt, and Error sts, Min and Max rgces, and cref REFs

The dwDvFlags field contains the option flags listed in the following table.

Bits	Mask	Name	Contents
3–0	0000000Fh	ValType	Validation type
6v4	00000070h	ErrStyle	Error alert style
7	00000080h	fStrLookup	= 1 if this is list-type validation with an explicitly expressed list of valid inputs
8	00000100h	fAllowBlank	= 1 suppress an error when any cell referenced by the validation formula is blank
9	00000200h	fSuppressCombo	= 1 if this is list-type validation, with no drop-down to be displayed in the cell when selected
17–10	0003FC00h	mdImeMode	The IME mode to be used for this cell (Far East versions only)
18	00040000h	fShowInputMsg	= 1 show input message box
19	00080000h	fShowErrorMsg	= 1 show error message box
23–20	00F00000h	typOperator	Operator type
31–24	FF000000h	Reserved	Reserved; must be 0 (zero)

DVAL: Data Validation Information (1B2h)

This record stores data validation information.

Record Data—BIFF8

Offset	Name	Size	Contents
4	wDviFlags	2	Option flags; see following table
6	xLeft	4	The x coordinate of the input window
10	yTop	4	The y coordinate of the input window
14	idObj	4	For a list with in-cell drop-down, the object id of drop-down OBJ record
18	idvMac	4	Number of DV records that follow

The wDviFlags field contains the option flags listed in the following table.

Bits	Mask	Name	Contents
0	0001h	fWnClosed	= 1 the input window has been closed
1	0002h	fWnPinned	= 1 the input window is pinned in place
2	0004h	fCached	= 1 if information about a cell's data validation has been cached
15–3	FFF8h	(Reserved)	Reserved; must be 0 (zero)

EDG: Edition Globals (88h)

The EDG record contains information about the publisher/subscriber feature. This record can be created only by Microsoft Excel for the Macintosh. However, if any other platform version of Microsoft Excel encounters the EDG record in a BIFF file, it leaves the record in the file, unchanged, when the file is saved.

Record Data

Offset	Name	Size	Contents
4	lcsec	4	Count of all section records that have ever been created in this document, plus 1 (includes published embedded charts)
8	crtpub	2	Count of all PUB records in the file (includes published embedded charts)
10	(Reserved)	2	Reserved; must be 0 (zero)

EOF: End of File (0Ah)

The EOF record marks the end of the workbook stream or the end of one of the substreams in the workbook stream. It has no record data field and is simply 0A000000h.

EXTERNCOUNT: Number of External References (16h)

The EXTERNCOUNT record specifies the number of externally referenced workbooks, DDE references, and OLE references contained in a Microsoft Excel workbook.

For example, a worksheet contains the following formulas in cells A1:A3:

=SALES.XLS!Profits

=Signal|System!Formats

=Signal|StockInfo!MSFT

This worksheet would have a value of 3 in the cxals field of the EXTERNCOUNT record, corresponding to the three external references SALES.XLS, Signal|System, and Signal|StockInfo.

Record Data

Offset	Name	Size	Contents
4	cxals	2	Number of external references

EXTERNNAME: Externally Referenced Name (223h)

The EXTERNNAME record stores an externally referenced name, DDE link, or OLE link. All EXTERNNAME records associated with a supporting workbook must directly follow the EXTERNSHEET record for the workbook. The order of EXTERNNAME records in a BIFF file should not be changed.

External Name

When the EXTERNNAME record stores an external name, fOle and fOleLink are both equal to zero (FALSE), and the record has the form shown in the following table.

Offset	Name	Size	Contents
4	grbit	2	Option flags
6	(Reserved)	4	Reserved; must be 0 (zero)
10	cch	1	Length of the external name
11	rgch	var	External name
var	cce	2	Length of the name definition
var	rgce	var	Name definition, in parsed expression format; for more information, see "Microsoft Excel Formulas" on page 444.

The grbit field contains the option flags listed in the following table.

Bits	Mask	Name	Contents
0	0001h	fBuiltin	= 1 if the name is a built-in name
1	0002h	fWantAdvise	N/A for External Names (must be 0 (zero))
2	0004h	fWantPict	N/A for External Names (must be 0 (zero))
3	0008h	fOle	N/A for External Names (must be 0 (zero))
4	0010h	fOleLink	N/A for External Names (must be 0 (zero))
15–5	FFE0h	(reserved)	Reserved; must be 0 (zero)

DDE Link

When the EXTERNNAME record stores a DDE link, the record has the form shown in the following table.

Offset	Name	Size	Contents
4	grbit	2	Option flags
6	(Reserved)	4	Reserved; must be 0 (zero)
10	cch	1	Length of the external name

Offset	Name	Size	Contents
11	rgch	var	External name
var	rgoper	var	Array of OPERs that stores the current value of the name

The grbit field contains the option flags listed in the following table.

Bits	Mask	Name	Contents
0	0001h	fBuiltin	N/A for DDE links (must be 0 (zero))
1	0002h	fWantAdvise	= 0 for manual DDE links = 1 for automatic DDE links
2	0004h	fWantPict	= 1 if Microsoft Excel wants a cfPict clipboard format representation of the data; OBJ and IMDATA records store the image
3	0008h	fOle	= 1 if this record stores the OLE StdDocumentName identifier (no rgoper follows rgch)
4	0010h	fOleLink	= 0 for DDE links
14–5	7FE0h	cf	The clipboard format for which the DDE Advise succeeded; this is used to reduce the time required for future Advise cycles
15	8000h	(Reserved)	Reserved; must be 0 (zero)

OLE Link

When the EXTERNNAME record stores an OLE link, fWantAdvise and fOleLink are equal to 1 (TRUE), and the record has the form shown in the following table.

Offset	Name	Size	Contents
4	grbit	2	Option flags
6	lStgName	4	OLE 2 storage identifier
10	cch	1	Length of the link name
11	rgch	var	Link name

The grbit field contains the option flags listed in the following table.

Bits	Mask	Name	Contents
0	0001h	fBuiltin	N/A for OLE links (must be 0 (zero))
1	0002h	fWantAdvise	= 0 for manual OLE links = 1 for automatic OLE links
2	0004h	fWantPict	= 1 if Microsoft Excel wants a cfPict clipboard format representation of the data; OBJ and IMDATA records store the image

Bits	Mask	Name	Contents
3	0008h	fOle	N/A for OLE links (must be 0 (zero))
4	0010h	fOleLink	= 1 for OLE links
15–5	FFE0h	(Reserved)	Reserved; must be 0 (zero)

EXTERNSHEET: External Reference (17h)

The EXTERNSHEET record specifies externally referenced workbooks. In BIFF7 and earlier, multiple EXTERNSHEET records form a table in the file. The cxals field of the EXTERNCOUNT record specifies the number of EXTERNSHEET records. You should not change the order of EXTERNSHEET records.

In BIFF8, the SUPBOOK record stores the encoded pathname and file name. There is one SUPBOOK record for each externally referenced workbook. The EXTERNSHEET record contains a table (rgXTI) that points to the SUPBOOK records. Several ptgs in a BIFF8 formula contain an ixti field; this is the 0-based index to the rgXTI table in the EXTERNSHEET record.

An externally referenced workbook is called a source workbook. The workbook that refers to it is called a dependent workbook.

Record Data—BIFF8

Offset	Name	Size	Contents
4	cXTI	2	Number of XTI structures that follow
6	rgXTI	var	Array of XTI structures

Each 6-byte XTI structure contains the following data.

Offset	Name	Size	Contents
0	iSUPBOOK	2	Index (0-based) to table of SUPBOOK redcords
2	itabFirst	2	Index (0-based) to first sheet tab in the reference
4	itabLast	2	Index (0-based) to last sheet tab in the reference

Record Data—BIFF7 and earlier

Offset	Name	Size	Contents
4	cch	1	Length of the file name
5	rgch	var	File name

The cch field contains the length of the source workbook file name. The rgch field contains the source workbook file name.

File name Encoding

Whenever possible, file names are encoded to make BIFF files transportable across file systems. Encoded file names are identified by the first character of the rgch field. The first character of the rgch field may be any one of the values listed in the following table.

Name	Value	Meaning
chEmpty	00	Reference to an empty workbook name (see text)
chEncode	01	File name has been encoded (see the following table)
chSelf	02	Self-referential external reference (see text)

chEmpty indicates that the file name is an external reference to an empty workbook name, as in the formula =Sheet1!$A$1.

chSelf indicates that the file name is an external reference in which the dependent and source workbooks are the same. An example of this is the workbook SALES.XLS, which contains the formula =SALES.XLS!$A$1.

A chDDE key (03h) can occur in the rgch field; it is not necessarily the first character in the field, as are chEmpty, chEncode, and chSelf. This key indicates that the external reference is a DDE or OLE link. In a DDE link, the chDDE key replaces the | (pipe) character that separates the DDE application and topic. In an OLE link, chDDE separates the classname and file name.

A chEncode at the beginning of rgch indicates that the file name of the source workbook has been encoded to a less system-dependent file name. The special keys listed in the following table are recognized in the rgch field.

Name	Value	PC file systems
chVolume	01	Represents an MS-DOS drive letter. It is followed by the drive letter. For example, the formula ='D:\SALES.XLS'!A1 generates the chVolume key when the dependent workbook is not on the D drive. UNC file names, such as \\server\share\myfile.xls, generate an @ character after the chVolume key; this replaces the initial double backslash (\\).

Name	Value	PC file systems
chSameVolume	02	Indicates that the source workbook is on the same drive as the dependent workbook (the drive letter is omitted). For example, the formula =‘\SALES.XLS’!A1 generates the chSameVolume key when the dependent workbook is not in the root directory.
ChDownDir	03	Indicates that the source workbook is in a subdirectory of the current directory. For example, the formula =‘XL\SALES.XLS’!A1 generates the chDownDir key. The subdirectory name precedes the chDownDir key, and the file name follows it.
chUpDir	04	Indicates that the source workbook is in the parent directory of the current directory. For example, the formula =‘..\SALES.XLS’!A1 generates the chUpDir key.
chLongVolume	05	(Not used)
chStartupDir	06	Indicates that the source workbook is in the startup directory (the Xlstart subdirectory of the directory that contains Excel.exe).
chAltStartupDir	07	Indicates that the source workbook is in the alternate startup directory.
chLibDir	08	Indicates that the source workbook is in the Library directory.

EXTSST: Extended Shared String Table (FFh)

The EXTSST record contains a hash table that optimizes external copy operations.

Record Data—BIFF8

Offset	Name	Size	Contents
4	Dsst	2	Number of strings in each bucket
6	Rgisstinf	var	Array of ISSTINF structures

Each ISSTINF contains the following:

Offset	Name	Size	Contents
0	ib	4	The stream position where the strings begin (stream pointer into the SST record)
4	cb	2	Offset into the SST record that points to where the bucket begins
6	(Reserved)	2	Reserved; must be 0 (zero)

When writing a BIFF file, you cannot write out SST and LABELSST records without including the EXTSST record, because this will cause Microsoft Excel to crash when it performs an external copy.

Although you have to write out an EXTSST record, you do not have to fill out the entire record. Only the fields that have nonempty buckets have to be calculated; the rest of the bytes of the EXTSST can be garbage. If you examine a BIFF8 file, you'll notice that only a few bytes of the EXTSST contain valid data (assuming that the file is a small one with only a few strings).

FILEPASS: File Is Password-Protected (2Fh)

If you type a protection password (File menu, Save As command, Options dialog box), the FILEPASS record appears in the BIFF file. The wProtPass field contains the encrypted password. All records after FILEPASS are encrypted; you cannot read these encrypted records.

Note that this record specifies a file protection password, as opposed to the PASSWORD record (type 13h), which specifies a sheet-level or workbook-level protection password.

Record Data

Offset	Name	Size	Contents
4	wProtPass	4	Encrypted password

FILESHARING: File-Sharing Information (5Bh)

This record stores file-sharing options selected in the Options dialog box, accessed by using the Save As command (File menu). The write reservation password that you type in the dialog box is encrypted to an integer, wResPass. This record also contains the user name of the file's creator, stUNWriteRes.

Changes for BIFF7

There are minor changes to the behavior of this record in BIFF7. For Microsoft Excel version 7.0 workbooks that do not contain shared lists, this record behaves as it does in BIFF5.

For Microsoft Excel version 7.0 workbooks that contain shared lists, there will be both FILESHARING and FILESHARING2 records in the Book stream. In this case, FILESHARING always contains a dummy password. FILESHARING2 contains either a dummy password if the workbook is not write-protected, or a valid password if the workbook is write-protected.

Record Data

Offset	Name	Size	Contents
4	fReadOnlyRec	2	= 1 if the Read Only Recommended option is selected in the Options dialog box
6	wResPass	2	Encrypted password (if this field is 0 (zero), there is no write reservation password)
8	cch	1	Length of the user name
9	stUNWriteRes	var	User name

FILESHARING2: File-Sharing Information for Shared Lists (1A5h)

In Microsoft Excel version 7.0 workbooks that contain shared lists, FILESHARING2 contains either a dummy password if the workbook is not write-protected, or a valid password if the workbook is write-protected. If the workbook does not contain shared lists, this record does not appear in the file.

This record does not appear in BIFF5 files.

Record Data

Offset	Name	Size	Contents
4	fReadOnlyRec	2	= 1 if the Read Only Recommended option is selected in the Options dialog box
6	wResPass	2	Encrypted password (if this field is 0 (zero), there is no write reservation password)
8	cch	1	Length of the user name
9	stUNWriteRes	var	User name

FILTERMODE: Sheet Contains Filtered List (9Bh)

If the sheet contains a filtered list, the file will contain a FILTERMODE record. This record has no record data field.

FNGROUPCOUNT: Built-in Function Group Count (9Ch)

This record stores the number of built-in function groups (Financial, Math & Trig, Date & Time, and so on) in the current version of Microsoft Excel.

Record Data

Offset	Name	Size	Contents
4	cFnGroup	2	Number of built-in function groups

FNGROUPNAME: Function Group Name (9Ah)

This record stores the name of a custom function category.

Record Data

Offset	Name	Size	Contents
4	cch	1	Size of the function category name
5	rgch	var	Function category name

FONT: Font Description (231h)

The workbook font table contains at least five FONT records. FONT records are numbered as follows: ifnt = 00h (the first FONT record in the table), ifnt = 01h, ifnt = 02h, ifnt = 03h, ifnt = 05h (minimum table), and then ifnt = 06h, ifnt = 07h, and so on. Notice that ifnt = 04h never appears in a BIFF file. This is for backward-compatibility with previous versions of Microsoft Excel. If you read FONT records, remember to index the table correctly, skipping ifnt = 04h.

Record Data

Offset	Name	Size	Contents
4	dyHeight	2	Height of the font (in units of $1/20^{\text{th}}$ of a point).
6	grbit	2	Font attributes (see the following table).
8	icv	2	Index to the color palette.
10	bls	2	Bold style; a number from 100dec to 1000dec (64h to 3E8h) that indicates the character weight ("boldness"). The default values are 190h for normal text and 2BCh for bold text.
12	sss	2	Superscript/subscript: 00h = None 01h = Superscript 02h = Subscript
14	uls	1	Underline style: 00h = None 01h = Single 02h = Double 21h = Single Accounting 22h = Double Accounting
15	bFamily	1	Font family, as defined by the Windows API LOGFONT structure.
16	bCharSet	1	Character set, as defined by the Windows API LOGFONT structure.
17	(Reserved)	1	Reserved; must be 0 (zero).
18	cch	1	Length of the font name.
19	rgch	var	Font name.

The grbit field contains the font attributes listed in the following table.

Offset	Bits	Mask	Name	Contents
0	0	01h	(Reserved)	Reserved; must be 0 (zero)
	1	02h	fItalic	= 1 if the font is italic
	2	04h	(Reserved)	Reserved; must be 0 (zero)
0	3	08h	fStrikeout	= 1 if the font is struck out
	4	10h	fOutline	= 1 if the font is outline style (Macintosh only)
	5	20h	fShadow	= 1 if the font is shadow style (Macintosh only)
	7–6	C0h	(Reserved)	Reserved; must be 0 (zero)
1	7–0	FFh	(Unused)	

FOOTER: Print Footer on Each Page (15h)

The FOOTER record stores a print footer string for a sheet. This string appears at the bottom of every page when the sheet is printed.

Record Data

Offset	Name	Size	Contents
4	cch	1	Length of the footer string (bytes)
5	rgch	var	Footer string

FORMAT: Number Format (41Eh)

The FORMAT record describes a number format in the workbook.

All the FORMAT records should appear together in a BIFF file. The order of FORMAT records in an existing BIFF file should not be changed. You can write custom number formats in a file, but they should be added at the end of the existing FORMAT records.

Record Data

Offset	Name	Size	Contents
4	ifmt	2	Format index code (for internal use only)
6	cch	1	Length of the format string
7	rgch	var	Number format string

Microsoft Excel uses the ifmt field to identify built-in formats when it reads a file that was created by a different localized version. For more information about built-in formats, see "XF" on page 426.

FORMULA: Cell Formula (406h)

A FORMULA record describes a cell that contains a formula.

Record Data

Offset	Name	Size	Contents
4	rw	2	Row
6	col	2	Column
8	ixfe	2	Index to XF record
10	num	8	Current value of the formula (see text)

Offset	Name	Size	Contents
18	grbit	2	Option flags
20	chn	4	(See text)
24	cce	2	Length of the parsed expression
26	rgce	var	Parsed expression

The chn field should be ignored when you read the BIFF file. If you write a BIFF file, the chn field must be 00000000h.

The grbit field contains the option flags listed in the following table.

Offset	Bits	Mask	Name	Contents
0	0	01h	fAlwaysCalc	Always calculate the formula.
	1	02h	fCalcOnLoad	Calculate the formula when the file is opened.
	2	04h	(Reserved)	
	3	08h	fShrFmla	= 1 if the formula is part of shared formula group.
	7–4	F0h	(Unused)	
1	7–0	FFh	(Unused)	

For more information about shared formulas, see "SHRFMLA" on page 386.

The rw field contains the 0-based row number. The col field contains the 0-based column number.

If the formula evaluates to a number, the num field contains the current calculated value of the formula in 8-byte IEEE format. If the formula evaluates to a string, a Boolean value, or an error value, the most significant 2 bytes of the num field are FFFFh.

A Boolean value is stored in the num field, as shown in the following table. For more information about Boolean values, see "BOOLERR" on page 290.

Offset	Name	Size	Contents
0	otBool	1	= 1 always
1	(Reserved)	1	Reserved; must be 0 (zero)
2	f	1	Boolean value
3	(Reserved)	3	Reserved; must be 0 (zero)
6	fExprO	2	= FFFFh

An error value is stored in the num field, as shown in the following table. For more information about error values, see "BOOLERR" on page 290.

Offset	Name	Size	Contents
0	otErr	1	= 2 always
1	(Reserved)	1	Reserved; must be 0 (zero)
2	err	1	Error value
3	(Reserved)	3	Reserved; must be 0 (zero)
6	fExprO	2	= FFFFh

If the formula evaluates to a string, the num field has the structure shown in the following table.

Offset	Name	Size	Contents
0	otString	1	= 0 always
1	(Reserved)	5	Reserved; must be 0 (zero)
6	fExprO	2	= FFFFh

The string value is not stored in the num field; instead, it is stored in a STRING record that immediately follows the FORMULA record.

The cce field contains the length of the formula. The rgce field contains the formula in its parsed format. For more information, see "Microsoft Excel Formulas" on page 444.

GCW: Global Column-Width Flags (ABh)

This record contains an array of 256 flag bits, where each bit represents a column on the sheet. If a bit is true, it means that the corresponding column has the Use Standard Width option turned on. If a bit is false, it means that the column has the Use Standard Width option turned off. If the Standard Width measurement has been changed (that is, if it is no longer the default), Microsoft Excel writes a STANDARDWIDTH record.

Record Data

Offset	Name	Size	Contents
4	cb	2	Number of bytes in the global column-width flags
6	grbitGCW	2	Global column-width flags for columns A through P
8	grbitGCW	2	Global column-width flags for columns Q through AF
...	...	...	...
4+cb	grbitGCW	2	Global column-width flags for columns IG through IV

The grbitGCW field contains the option flags listed in the following table.

Bits	Mask	Name	Contents
0 (LSB)	0001h	fGCWcol1	Flag for column 1 (for example, column A)
1	0002h	fGCWcol2	Flag for column 2 (for example, column B)
2	0004h	fGCWcol3	Flag for column 3 (for example, column C)
...	...	...	...
15	8000h	fGCWcol16	Flag for column 16 (for example, column P)

GRIDSET: State Change of Gridlines Option (82h)

This record indicates that the user changed the state of the Gridlines option in the Page Setup dialog box, Sheet tab.

Record Data

Offset	Name	Size	Contents
4	fGridSet	2	= 1 if the user has ever changed the setting of the Gridlines option

GUTS: Size of Row and Column Gutters (80h)

This record contains the size of the row and column gutters, measured in screen units. The row and column gutters are the spaces that contain outline symbols. They are located above column headings and to the left of row headings.

Record Data

Offset	Name	Size	Contents
4	dxRwGut	2	Size of the row gutter that appears to the left of the rows
6	dyColGut	2	Size of the column gutter that appears above the columns
8	iLevelRwMac	2	Maximum outline level (for the row gutter)
10	iLevelColMac	2	Maximum outline level (for the column gutter)

HCENTER: Center Between Horizontal Margins (83h)

If the Horizontally option is selected on the Margins tab in the Page Setup dialog box, fHCenter = 1.

Record Data

Offset	Name	Size	Contents
4	fHCenter	2	= 1 if the sheet is to be centered between horizontal margins when printed

HEADER: Print Header on Each Page (14h)

The HEADER record specifies a print header string for a sheet. This string appears at the top of every page when the sheet is printed.

Record Data

Offset	Name	Size	Contents
4	cch	1	Length of the header string (bytes)
5	rgch	var	Header string

HIDEOBJ: Object Display Options (8Dh)

The HIDEOBJ record stores options selected in the Options dialog box, View tab.

Record Data

Offset	Name	Size	Contents
4	fHideObj	2	= 2 if the Hide All option is turned on = 1 if the Show Placeholders option is turned on = 0 if the Show All option is turned on

HLINK: Hyperlink (1B8h)

The HLINK record stores a hyperlink.

Record Data—BIFF8

Offset	Name	Size	Contents
4	rwFirst	2	First row of the hyperlink
6	rwLast	2	Last row of the hyperlink
8	colFirst	2	First column of the hyperlink
10	colLast	2	Last column of the hyperlink
12	rgbHlink	var	Hyperlink stream (from the Office DLL; this stream is not documented)

HORIZONTALPAGEBREAKS: Explicit Row Page Breaks (1Bh)

The HORIZONTALPAGEBREAKS record contains a list of explicit row page breaks.

Record Data—BIFF8

Offset	Name	Size	Contents
4	cbrk	2	Number of page breaks
6	rgbrk	var	Array of brk structures

The cbrk field contains the number of page breaks. Each element of the rgbrk structure contains three 2-byte integers: the first specifies the row of the break, the second specifies the starting column, and the third specifies the ending column for the break. All row and column numbers are 1-based, and the breaks occur after the row or column. This array is sorted by row, and then by starting/ending column. No two page breaks may overlap.

Record Data—BIFF7 and earlier

Offset	Name	Size	Contents
4	cbrk	2	Number of page breaks
6	rgrw	var	Array of rows

The cbrk field contains the number of page breaks. The rgrw field is an array of 2-byte integers that specifies rows. Microsoft Excel sets a page break before each row contained in the list of rows in the rgrw field. The rows must be sorted in ascending order.

IMDATA: Image Data (7Fh)

The IMDATA record contains the complete description of a bitmapped graphic object, such as a drawing created by a graphics tool.

Record Data

Offset	Name	Size	Contents
4	cf	2	Image format: = 02h, Windows metafile or Macintosh PICT format = 09h, Windows bitmap format = 0Eh, Native format (see text)
6	env	2	Environment from which the file was written: = 1, Microsoft Windows = 2, Apple Macintosh
8	lcb	4	Length of the image data
12	data	var	Image data

For more information about the Microsoft Windows metafile file format, see the documentation for the Microsoft Windows Software Development Kit.

For more information about the Apple Macintosh PICT file format, see *The Programmer's Apple Mac Sourcebook* (published by Microsoft Press, ISBN 1-55615-168-3), section 2.087, "PICT File Format"; or see *Inside Macintosh Volume V* (published by Addison-Wesley Publishing Company, Inc., ISBN 0-201-17719-6).

If the image is in Microsoft Windows bitmap format (cf = 09h), the data field consists of a BITMAPCOREINFO data structure followed by the actual bitmap. The BITMAPCOREINFO data structure consists of a BITMAPCOREHEADER structure, followed by an array of RGBTRIPLE structures that define the color table. For more information about these structures, see the documentation for the Microsoft Windows Software Development Kit.

Native format (cf = 0Eh) stores an embedded object from another application. The image data is in the foreign application's format and cannot be directly processed by Microsoft Excel.

INDEX: Index Record (20Bh)

Microsoft Excel writes an INDEX record immediately after the BOF record for each worksheet substream in a BIFF file. For more information about the INDEX record, see "Finding Cell Records in BIFF Files" on page 440.

Record Data—BIFF8

Offset	Name	Size	Contents
4	(Reserved)	4	Reserved; must be 0 (zero)
8	rwMic	4	First row that exists on the sheet
12	rwMac	4	Last row that exists on the sheet, plus 1
16	(Reserved)	4	Reserved; must be 0 (zero)
20	rgibRw	var	Array of file offsets to the DBCELL records for each block of ROW records. A block contains ROW records for up to 32 rows. For more information, see "Finding Cell Records in BIFF Files" on page 440.

Record Data—BIFF7 and earlier

Offset	Name	Size	Contents
4	(Reserved)	4	Reserved; must be 0 (zero)
8	rwMic	2	First row that exists on the sheet
10	rwMac	2	Last row that exists on the sheet, plus 1
12	(Reserved)	4	Reserved; must be 0 (zero)
16	rgibRw	var	Array of file offsets to the DBCELL records for each block of ROW records. A block contains ROW records for up to 32 rows. For more information, see "Finding Cell Records in BIFF Files" on page 440.

The rwMic field contains the number of the first row in the sheet that contains a value or a formula that is referenced by a cell in some other row. Because rows (and columns) are always stored 0-based rather than 1-based (as they appear on the screen), cell A1 is stored as row 0, cell A2 is row 1, and so on. The rwMac field contains the 0-based number of the last row in the sheet, plus 1.

INTERFACEEND: End of User Interface Records (E2h)

This record marks the end of the user interface section of the Book stream. It has no record data field.

INTERFACEHDR: Beginning of User Interface Records (E1h)

This record marks the beginning of the user interface section of the Book (Workbook) stream. In BIFF7 and earlier, it has no record data field. In BIFF8 and later, the INTERFACEHDR record data field contains a 2-byte word that is the code page. This is exactly the same as the cv field of the the CODEPAGE record.

Record Data—BIFF8

Offset	Name	Size	Contents
4	cv	2	Code page the file is saved in: 01B5h (437 dec.) = IBM PC (Multiplan) 8000h (32768 dec.) = Apple Macintosh 04E4h (1252 dec.) = ANSI (Microsoft Windows)

ITERATION: Iteration Mode (11h)

The ITERATION record stores the Iteration option from the Options dialog box, Calculation tab.

Record Data

Offset	Name	Size	Contents
4	fIter	2	= 1 if the Iteration option is on

LABEL: Cell Value, String Constant (204h)

A LABEL record describes a cell that contains a string constant. The rw field contains the 0-based row number. The col field contains the 0-based column number. The string length is contained in the cch field and must be in the range of 0000h–00FFh (0–255). The string itself is contained in the rgch field.

Record Data

Offset	Name	Size	Contents
4	rw	2	Row
6	col	2	Column
8	ixfe	2	Index to the XF record
10	cch	2	Length of the string
12	rgch	var	The string

LABELSST: Cell Value, String Constant/SST (FDh)

A LABELSST record describes a cell that contains a string constant from the shared string table, which is new to BIFF8. The rw field contains the 0-based row number. The col field contains the 0-based column number. The string itself is contained in an SST (shared string table) record, and the isst field is a 0-based index into the shared string table.

Record Data—BIFF8

Offset	Name	Size	Contents
4	rw	2	Row
6	col	2	Column
8	ixfe	2	Index to the XF record
10	isst	4	Index into the SST record

LEFTMARGIN: Left Margin Measurement (26h)

The LEFTMARGIN record specifies the width of the left margin, in inches. The num field is in 8-byte IEEE floating-point format.

Record Data

Offset	Name	Size	Contents
4	num	8	Left margin

LHNGRAPH: Named Graph Information (95h)

Record Data

This record is similar to the .WKS NGRAPH record, except that the first 13 references are not written. Instead, there are 13 integers that indicate whether the references X, A–F, and Data Label A–F are defined.

LHRECORD: .WK? File Conversion Information (94h)

This record contains information that Microsoft Excel uses when it converts an .XLS file to a .WKS, .WK1, or .WK3 file, or vice versa.

Record Data

LHRECORD contains subrecords that resemble BIFF records. Each subrecord consists of the three fields described in the following table.

Offset (within subrecord)	Length (bytes)	Contents
0	2	Subrecord type (rtlh)
2	2	Length of the subrecord data
4	var	Subrecord data

The following table describes the subrecords.

rtlh	Subrecord name	Contents
01h	(Reserved)	Reserved for future use.
02h	lhrtHpstGrHeader	Header string for the /Graph Save Print help command.
03h	lhrtHpstGrFooter	Footer string for the /Graph Save Print help command.
04h	lhrtNumGrLftMgn	Left margin for the /Graph Save Print help command (IEEE number).

rtlh	Subrecord name	Contents
05h	lhrtNumGrRgtMgn	Right margin for the /Graph Save Print help command (IEEE number).
06h	lhrtNumGrTopMgn	Top margin for the /Graph Save Print help command (IEEE number).
07h	lhrtNumGrBotMgn	Bottom margin for the /Graph Save Print help command (IEEE number).
08h	lhrtGrlh	Current /Graph View data. Structure similar to the .WKS GRAPH record except that the first 13 references are not written. Instead, there are 13 integers that indicate whether the references X, A–F, and Data Label A–F are defined.
09h	lhrtcchGlColWidth	Current global column width (integer).
0Ah	(Reserved)	Reserved for future use.
0Bh	lhrttblType	Current table type: = 0, none (default) = 1, table1 = 2, table2
0Ch	(Reserved)	Reserved for future use.

LPR: Sheet Was Printed Using LINE.PRINT() (98h)

If this record appears in a file, it indicates that the sheet was printed using the LINE.PRINT() macro function. The LPR record stores options associated with this function.

Record Data

Offset	Name	Size	Contents
4	grbit	2	Option flags
6	cchMargLeft	2	Left margin, expressed as a count of characters
8	cchMargRight	2	Right margin, expressed as a count of characters
10	cliMargTop	2	Top margin, expressed as a count of lines
12	cliMargBot	2	Bottom margin, expressed as a count of lines
14	cliPg	2	Number of lines per page
16	cch	1	Length of the printer setup string
17	rgch	var	Printer setup string

The grbit field contains the option flags listed in the following table.

Offset	Bits	Mask	Name	Contents
0	0	01h	fWait	= 1, alert the user after each sheet is printed
	1	02h	fFormatted	= 1, print headers and footers
	2	04h	fAutoLF	= 1, write only the carriage return (CR) character (no line feed) at the end of the line
	7–3	F8h	(Unused)	
1	7–0	FFh	(Unused)	

MMS: ADDMENU/DELMENU Record Group Count (C1h)

This record stores the number of ADDMENU groups and DELMENU groups in the Book stream.

Record Data

Offset	Name	Size	Contents
4	caitm	1	Number of ADDMENU record groups
5	cditm	1	Number of DELMENU record groups

MSODRAWING: Microsoft Office Drawing (ECh)

This record contains a drawing object provided by the Microsoft Office Drawing tool. For more information on this file format, see the article "Microsoft Office Drawing File Format" on the Microsoft Developer Network Online Web site (http://www.microsoft.com/msdn/).

Record Data—BIFF8

Offset	Name	Size	Contents
4	rgMSODrawing	(var)	Microsoft Office Drawing data

MSODRAWINGGROUP: Microsoft Office Drawing Group (EBh)

This record contains a group drawing object provided by the Microsoft Office Drawing tool. For more information on this file format, see the article "Microsoft Office Drawing File Format" on the Microsoft Developer Network Online Web site (http://www.microsoft.com/msdn/).

Record Data—BIFF8

Offset	Name	Size	Contents
4	rgMSODrawiGr	(var)	Microsoft Office Drawing group data

MSODRAWINGSELECTION: Microsoft Office Drawing Selection (EDh)

This record contains a selection of drawing objects. The objects are provided by the Microsoft Office Drawing tool. For more information on this file format, see the article "Microsoft Office Drawing File Format" on the Microsoft Developer Network Online Web site (http://www.microsoft.com/msdn/).

Record Data—BIFF8

Offset	Name	Size	Contents
4	rgMSODrSelr	(var)	Microsoft Office Drawing selection data

MULBLANK: Multiple Blank Cells (BEh)

The MULBLANK record stores up to the equivalent of 256 BLANK records; the MULBLANK record is a file size optimization. The number of ixfe fields can be determined from the ColLast field and is equal to (colLast - colFirst + 1). The maximum length of the MULBLANK record is (256 x 2 + 10) = 522 bytes, because Microsoft Excel has at most 256 columns. Note that storing 256 blank cells in the MULBLANK record takes 522 bytes as compared with 2560 bytes for 256 BLANK records.

Record Data

Offset	Name	Size	Contents
4	rw	2	Row number (0-based)
6	colFirst	2	Column number (0-based) of the first column of the multiple RK record
8	rgixfe	var	Array of indexes to XF records
10	colLast	2	Last column containing the BLANKREC structure

MULRK: Multiple RK Cells (BDh)

The MULRK record stores up to the equivalent of 256 RK records; the MULRK record is a file size optimization. The number of 6-byte RKREC structures can be determined from the ColLast field and is equal to (colLast - colFirst + 1). The maximum length of the MULRK record is (256 x 6 + 10) = 1546 bytes, because Microsoft Excel has at most 256 columns. Note that storing 256 RK numbers in the MULRK record takes 1546 bytes as compared with 3584 bytes for 256 RK records.

Record Data

Offset	Name	Size	Contents
4	rw	2	Row number (0-based)
6	colFirst	2	Column number (0-based) of the first column of the multiple RK record
8	rgrkrec	var	Array of 6-byte RKREC structures
var	colLast	2	Last column containing the RKREC structure

The RKREC structure is defined as follows:

```
typedef struct rkrec
        {
        SHORT ixfe;      /* index to XF record */
        long RK;      /* RK number */
        }
    RKREC;
```

NAME: Defined Name (218h)

The NAME record describes a defined name in the workbook.

Record Data

Offset	Name	Size	Contents
4	grbit	2	Option flags
6	chKey	1	Keyboard shortcut
7	cch	1	Length of the name text
8	cce	2	Length of the name definition
10	ixals	2	Index to the sheet that contains this name, if the name is a local name (see text)
12	itab	2	This field is equal to ixals
14	cchCustMenu	1	Length of the custom menu text

Offset	Name	Size	Contents
15	cchDescription	1	Length of the description text
16	cchHelptopic	1	Length of the help topic text
17	cchStatustext	1	Length of the status bar text
18	rgch	var	Name text
var	rgce	var	Name definition (see text)
var	rgchCustMenu	var	Custom menu text
var	rgchDescr	var	Description text
var	rgchHelptopic	var	Help topic text
var	rgchStatustext	var	Status bar text

The grbit field contains the option flags listed in the following table.

Bits	Mask	Name	Contents
0	0001h	fHidden	= 1 if the name is hidden
1	0002h	fFunc	= 1 if the name is a function
2	0004h	fOB	= 1 if the name is a Visual Basic procedure
3	0008h	fProc	= 1 if the name is a function or command name on a macro sheet
4	0010h	fCalcExp	= 1 if the name contains a complex function
5	0020h	fBuiltin	= 1 if the name is a built-in name
11–6	0FC0h	fgrp	Function group index
12	1000h	fBig	= 1 if the name refers to binary data (see text)
15–13	C000h	(Reserved)	

If the fBig bit in the grbit field is equal to 1, the NAME record contains a name attached to binary data. These names can be created only by calling the xlDefineBinaryName function from the Microsoft Excel C API. The first byte is the length of the name, which is followed by the name string. Following the name string is the data to which the name refers. The data can be up to 2^{32} bytes long and can span multiple CONTINUE records.

The fCalcExp bit is set if the name definition contains a function that returns an array (for example, TREND, MINVERSE), contains a ROW or COLUMN function, or contains a user-defined function.

The chKey byte is significant only when the fProc bit is set in the grbit field. chKey is the keyboard shortcut for a command macro name. If the name is not a command macro name or has no keyboard shortcut, chKey is meaningless.

The cch field contains the length of the name text, and the rgch field contains the text itself. The cce field contains the length of the name definition, and the rgce field contains the definition itself. The location of rgce within the record depends on the length of the name text (rgch) field.

The name definition (rgce) is stored in the Microsoft Excel parsed format. For more information, see "Microsoft Excel Formulas" on page 444.

The NAME record stores two types of names: global names and local names. A global name is defined for an entire workbook, and a local name is defined on a single sheet. For example, MyName is a global name, whereas Sheet1!MyName is a local name. The ixals field in the NAME record will be nonzero for local names and will index the list of EXTERNSHEET records for the sheets in the workbook. The following field, itab, is equal to ixals.

All NAME records should appear together in a BIFF file. The order of NAME records in an existing BIFF file should not be changed. You can add new names to a file, but you should add them at the end of the NAME list (block of NAME records). Microsoft Excel saves the names to the BIFF file in alphabetic order, but this is not a requirement; Microsoft Excel will sort the name list, if necessary, when it loads a BIFF file.

Built-in Names

Microsoft Excel contains several built-in names—such as Criteria, Database, Auto_Open, and so on—for which the NAME records do not contain the actual name. Instead, cch always equals 1, and a single byte is used to identify the name as shown in the following table.

Built-in name	rgch
Consolidate_Area	00
Auto_Open	01
Auto_Close	02
Extract	03
Database	04
Criteria	05
Print_Area	06
Print_Titles	07
Recorder	08
Data_Form	09
Auto_Activate	0A
Auto_Deactivate	0B
Sheet_Title	0C

NOTE: Comment Associated with a Cell (1Ch)

The NOTE record specifies a comment associated with a particular cell. In Microsoft Excel 95 (BIFF7) and earlier versions, this record stores a note (cell note). This feature was significantly enhanced in Microsoft Excel 97, so the name was changed to comment.

Record Data—BIFF8

Offset	Name	Size	Contents
4	rw	2	Row of the comment
6	col	2	Column of the comment
8	grbit	2	Options flag (see table below)
10	idObj	2	Object id for OBJ record that contains the comment
12	stAuthor	var	Name of the original comment author

The grbit field contains the option flags listed in the following table.

Bits	Mask	Name	Contents
0	0001h	(Reserved)	Reserved; must be 0 (zero)
1	0002h	fShow	= 0 if the comment is hidden (default)
15–2	FFFCh	(Reserved)	Reserved; must be 0 (zero)

The rw and col fields specify the cell that contains the comment. The rw field contains the 0-based row number; the col field contains the 0-based column number.

The idObj field denotes the id of the graphic object (OBJ record) that contains the comment. Each comment has a corresponding OBJ record in which the ot field specifies the object type as Comment Shape. The text of the comment (as well as the formatting information) is in the corresponding OBJ record and its supporting records.

The stAuthor field contains the name of the original author of the comment, as a byte-counted string; the count is an unsigned short (2 bytes) that precedes the string. The string itself is padded with NULL bytes until it is word-aligned. The NULLs appear after the count and before the string data.

Record Data—BIFF7 and earlier

Offset	Name	Size	Contents
4	rw	2	Row of the note
6	col	2	Column of the note
8	cch	2	Length of the note (bytes)
10	rgch	var	Text of the note

The cell is denoted by the rw and col fields. The rw field contains the 0-based row number. The col field contains the 0-based column number.

The cch field contains the length of the note in bytes. The rgch field contains the text of the note in ASCII format.

Notes longer than 2048 characters (bytes) must be divided into several NOTE records, with each record containing no more than 2048 characters. In this case, the first NOTE record contains the fields listed in the following table.

Offset	Name	Size	Contents
4	rw	2	Row of the note
6	col	2	Column of the note
8	cch	2	Total length of the note
10	rgch	2048	First 2048 characters of the note

Each successive NOTE record contains the fields listed in the following table.

Offset	Name	Size	Contents
4	rw	2	= –1 always (FFFFh)
6	(Reserved)	2	Reserved; must be 0 (zero)
8	cch	2	Length of this section of the note
10	rgch	var	This section of the note

NUMBER: Cell Value, Floating-Point Number (203h)

A NUMBER record describes a cell containing a constant floating-point number. The rw field contains the 0-based row number. The col field contains the 0-based column number. The number is contained in the num field in 8-byte IEEE floating-point format.

Record Data

Offset	Name	Size	Contents
4	rw	2	Row
6	col	2	Column
8	ixfe	2	Index to the XF record
10	num	8	Floating-point number value

OBJ: Describes a Graphic Object (5Dh)

BIFF files may contain several different variations of the OBJ record. They correspond to the graphic objects and dialog box controls available in Microsoft Excel: line object, rectangle object, check box object, and so on.

Record Data—BIFF8

In BIFF8, the OBJ record contains a partial description of a drawing object, and the MSODRAWING, MSODRAWINGGROUP, and MSODRAWINGSELECTION records contain the remaining drawing object data.

To store an OBJ record in BIFF8, Microsoft Excel writes a collection of subrecords. The structure of a subrecord is identical to the structure of a BIFF record. Each subrecord begins with a 2-byte id number, ft (see the following table). Next a 2-byte length field, cb, specifies the length of the subrecord data field. The subrecord data field follows the length field.

The first subrecord is always ftCmo (common object data), and the last subrecord is always ftEnd.

Subrecord	Number	Description
ftEnd	00h	End of OBJ record
(Reserved)	01h	
(Reserved)	02h	
(Reserved)	03h	
ftMacro	04h	Fmla-style macro
ftButton	05h	Command button
ftGmo	06h	Group marker
ftCf	07h	Clipboard format

Subrecord	Number	Description
ftPioGrbit	08h	Picture option flags
ftPictFmla	09h	Picture fmla-style macro
ftCbls	0Ah	Check box link
ftRbo	0Bh	Radio button
ftSbs	0Ch	Scroll bar
ftNts	0Dh	Note structure
ftSbsFmla	0Eh	Scroll bar fmla-style macro
ftGboData	0Fh	Group box data
ftEdoData	10h	Edit control data
ftRboData	11h	Radio button data
ftCblsData	12h	Check box data
ftLbsData	13h	List box data
ftCblsFmla	14h	Check box link fmla-style macro
ftCmo	15h	Common object data

ftCmo (15h)

Offset	Name	Size	Contents
0	ft	2	= ftCmo (15h)
2	cb	2	Length of ftCmo data
4	ot	2	Object type (see following table)
6	id	2	Object ID number
8	grbit	2	Option flags (see following table)
14	(Reserved)	12	Reserved; must be 0 (zero)

The grbit field at byte 8 contains the flag bits listed in the following table.

Bits	Mask	Name	Contents
0	0001h	fLocked	= 1 if the object is locked when the sheet is protected
3–1	000Eh	(Reserved)	Reserved; must be 0 (zero)
4	0010h	fPrint	= 1 if the object is printable
12–5	1FE0h	(Reserved)	Reserved; must be 0 (zero)
13	2000h	fAutoFill	= 1 if the object uses automatic fill style
14	4000h	fAutoLine	= 1 if the object uses automatic line style
15	8000h	(Reserved)	Reserved; must be 0 (zero)

The ot field contains the object type.

ot	Object type
00	Group
01	Line
02	Rectangle
03	Oval
04	Arc
05	Chart
06	Text
07	Button
08	Picture
09	Polygon
0A	(Reserved)
0B	Check box
0C	Option button
0D	Edit box
0E	Label
0F	Dialog box
10	Spinner
11	Scroll bar
12	List box
13	Group box
14	Combo box
15	(Reserved)
16	(Reserved)
17	(Reserved)
18	(Reserved)
19	Comment
1A	(Reserved)
1B	(Reserved)
1C	(Reserved)
1D	(Reserved)
1E	Microsoft Office drawing

ftEnd (00h)

The ftEnd file type marks the end of an OBJ record.

Offset	Name	Size	Contents
0	ft	2	= ftEnd (00h)
2	cb	2	Length of ftEnd (= 00h)

ftMacro (04h)

Offset	Name	Size	Contents
0	ft	2	= ftMacro (04h)
2	cb	2	Length of ftMacro
4	Reserved	var	

ftButton (05h)

Offset	Name	Size	Contents
0	ft	2	= ftButton (05h)
2	cb	2	Length of ftButton
4	Reserved	var	

ftGmo (06h)

Offset	Name	Size	Contents
0	ft	2	= ftGmo (06h)
2	cb	2	Length of ftGmo
4	Reserved	var	

ftCf (07h)

Offset	Name	Size	Contents
0	ft	2	= ftCf (07h)
2	cb	2	Length of ftCf
4	(Reserved)	var	Reserved

ftPioGrbit (08h)

Offset	Name	Size	Contents
0	ft	2	= ftPioGrbit (08h)
2	cb	2	Length of ftPioGrbit
4	(Reserved)	var	Reserved

ftPictFmla (09h)

Offset	Name	Size	Contents
0	ft	2	= ftPictFmla (09h)
2	cb	2	Length of ftPictFmla
4	(Reserved)	var	Reserved

ftCbls (0Ah)

Offset	Name	Size	Contents
0	ft	2	= ftCbls (0Ah)
2	cb	2	Length of ftCbls
4	(Reserved)	var	Reserved

ftRbo (0Bh)

Offset	Name	Size	Contents
0	ft	2	= ftRbo (0Bh)
2	cb	2	Length of ftRbo
4	(Reserved)	var	Reserved

ftSbs (0Ch)

Offset	Name	Size	Contents
0	ft	2	= ftSbs (0Ch)
2	cb	2	Length of ftSbs
4	(Reserved)	var	Reserved

ftNts (0Dh)

Offset	Name	Size	Contents
0	ft	2	=ftNts (0Dh)
2	cb	2	Length of ftNts
4	(Reserved)	var	Reserved

ftSbsFmla (0Eh)

Offset	Name	Size	Contents
0	ft	2	= ftSbsFmla (0Eh)
2	cb	2	Length of ftSbsFmla
4	(Reserved)	var	Reserved

ftGboData (0Fh)

The ftGboData file type contains group box object data.

Offset	Name	Size	Contents
0	ft	2	=ftGboData (0Fh)
2	cb	2	Length of ftGboData
4	(Reserved)	var	Reserved

ftEdoData (10h)

Offset	Name	Size	Contents
0	ft	2	= ftEdoData (10h)
2	cb	2	Length of ftEdoData
4	(Reserved)	var	Reserved

ftRboData (11h)

Offset	Name	Size	Contents
0	ft	2	= ftRboData (11h)
2	cb	2	Length of ftRboData
4	(Reserved)	var	Reserved

ftCblsData (12h)

Offset	Name	Size	Contents
0	ft	2	= ftCblsData (12h)
2	cb	2	Length of ftCblsData
4	(Reserved)	var	Reserved

ftLbsData (13h)

Offset	Name	Size	Contents
0	ft	2	= ftLbsData (13h)
2	cb	2	Length of ftLbsData
4	(Reserved)	var	Reserved

ftCblsFmla (14h)

Offset	Name	Size	Contents
0	ft	2	= ftCblsFmla (14h)
2	cb	2	Length of ftCblsFmla
4	(Reserved)	var	Reserved

Record Data—BIFF5 and BIFF7

The first 36 bytes of every OBJ record are fields that are common to all object types. The remaining fields are object-specific and are described in separate sections following the common object fields.

Common Object Fields

Offset	Name	Size	Contents
4	cObj	4	Count (1-based) of the objects in the file
8	OT	2	Object type: Group object: OT = 00h Line object: OT = 01h Rectangle object: OT = 02h Oval object: OT = 03h Arc object: OT = 04h Chart object: OT = 05h Text object: OT = 06h Button object: OT = 07h Picture object: OT = 08h Polygon object: OT = 09h Check box object: OT = 0Bh Option button object: OT = 0Ch Edit box object: OT = 0Dh Label object: OT = 0Eh Dialog frame object: OT = 0Fh Spinner object: OT = 10h Scroll bar object: OT = 11h List box object: OT = 12h Group box object: OT = 13h Drop-down object: OT = 14h
10	id	2	Object identification number
12	grbit	2	Option flags (see the following table)
14	colL	2	Column containing the upper-left corner of the object's bounding rectangle
16	dxL	2	X (horizontal) position of the upper-left corner of the object's bounding rectangle, relative to the left side of the underlying cell, expressed as $1/1024^{th}$ of the cell's width
18	rwT	2	Row containing the upper-left corner of the object's bounding rectangle

Offset	Name	Size	Contents
20	dyT	2	Y (vertical) position of the upper-left corner of the object's bounding rectangle, relative to the top of the underlying cell, expressed as $1/1024^{th}$ of the cell's height
22	colR	2	Column containing the lower-right corner of the object's bounding rectangle.
24	dxR	2	X (horizontal) position of the lower-right corner of the object's bounding rectangle, relative to the left side of the underlying cell, expressed as $1/1024^{th}$ of the cell's width.
26	rwB	2	Row containing the lower-right corner of the object's bounding rectangle.
28	dyB	2	Y (vertical) position of the lower-right corner of the object's bounding rectangle, relative to the top of the underlying cell, expressed as $1/1024^{th}$ of the cell's height.
30	cbMacro	2	Length of the FMLA structure that stores the definition of the attached macro; see FMLA Structure. Some objects may store the length of the FMLA structure in a cbFmla that immediately preceded the FMLA; in these objects, cbMacro is ignored.
32	(Reserved)	6	Reserved; must be 0 (zero).

The grbit field at byte 12 contains the flag bits listed in the following table.

Offset	Bits	Mask	Name	Contents
0	0	01h	fSel	= 1 if the object is selected
	1	02h	fAutoSize	= 1 if the object moves and sizes with the cells
	2	04h	fMove	= 1 if the object moves with the cells (Format Object dialog box, Properties tab)
	3	08h	(Reserved)	Reserved; must be 0 (zero)
	4	10h	fLocked	= 1 if the object is locked when the sheet is protected
	5	20h	(Reserved)	Reserved; must be 0 (zero)
	6	40h	(Reserved)	Reserved; must be 0 (zero)
	7	80h	fGrouped	= 1 if the object is part of a group of objects

Offset	Bits	Mask	Name	Contents
1	0	01h	fHidden	= 1 if the object is hidden (this can be done only from a macro)
	1	02h	fVisible	= 1 if the object is visible
	2	04h	fPrint	= 1 if the object is printable
	7–3	F8h	(Reserved)	Reserved; must be 0 (zero)

Line Object Fields

Offset	Name	Size	Contents
38	icv	1	Index to the color palette for line color.
39	lns	1	Line style: Solid: lns = 0 Dash: lns = 1 Dot: lns = 2 Dash-dot: lns = 3 Dash-dot-dot: lns = 4 Null (unused): lns = 5 Dark gray: lns = 6 Medium gray: lns = 7 Light gray: lns = 8
40	lnw	1	Line weight: Hairline: lnw = 0 Single: lnw = 1 Double: lnw = 2 Thick: lnw = 3
41	fAuto	1	Bit 0 = 1 if Automatic Border option is turned on (Format Object dialog box, Patterns tab). All other bits in fAuto are don't-care.
42	es	2	End style structure (see the following table).
44	iqu	1	Quadrant index (direction of line): Starts upper left, ends lower right: iqu = 0 Starts upper right, ends lower left: iqu = 1 Starts lower right, ends upper left: iqu = 2 Starts lower left, ends upper right: iqu = 3
45	(Reserved)	1	Reserved; must be 0 (zero).
46	cchName	1	Length of the name (null if no name).
47	stName	var	Name (null if no name; may contain a padding byte to force word-boundary alignment).
var	fmla	var	FMLA structure (see the following section).

The end style structure (es) describes the arrowheads on the end point of the line. The structure contains four 4-bit fields, as described in the following table.

Offset	Bits	Mask	Name	Contents
0	3–0	0Fh	sest	Arrowhead style: None: sest = 0 Open: sest = 1 Filled: sest = 2 Double-ended open: sest = 3 Double-ended filled: sest = 4
	7–4	F0h	sesw	Arrowhead width: Narrow: sesw = 0 Medium: sesw = 1 Wide: sesw = 2
1	3–0	0Fh	sesl	Arrowhead length: Short: sesl = 0 Medium: sesl = 1 Long: sesl = 2
	7–4	F0h	(Unused)	

FMLA Structure

The FMLA structure stores a parsed expression for the macro that is attached to the object. For more information about parsed expressions, see "Microsoft Excel Formulas" on page 444. The FMLA structure is null if the object does not have a macro attached.

In some object types, the FMLA structure length is given by cbMacro in the common object fields. In other object types, the FMLA structure length is given by a cbFmla that immediately precedes the FMLA. In these object types, ignore cbMacro. There may be an optional padding byte at the end of the FMLA to force it to end on a word boundary. The FMLA structure has the form shown in the following table.

Offset	Name	Size	Contents
0	cce	2	Length of the parsed expression.
2	(Reserved)	4	
6	rgce	var	Parsed expression (may contain a padding byte to force word-boundary alignment).

Rectangle Object Fields

Offset	Name	Size	Contents
38	icvBack	1	Index to the color palette for background color.
39	icvFore	1	Index to the color palette for foreground color.
40	fls	1	Fill pattern.
41	fAuto	1	Bit 0 = 1 if the Automatic Fill option is turned on (Format Object dialog box, Patterns tab). All other bits in fAuto are don't-care.
42	icv	1	Index to the color palette for line color.
43	lns	1	Line style (see "Line Object Fields").
44	lnw	1	Line weight (see "Line Object Fields").
45	fAuto	1	Bit 0 = 1 if the Automatic Border option is turned on (Format Object dialog box, Patterns tab). All other bits in fAuto are don't-care.
46	frs	2	Frame style structure (see the following table).
48	cchName	1	Length of the name (null if no name).
49	stName	var	Name (null if no name; may contain a padding byte to force word-boundary alignment).
var	fmla	var	FMLA structure (see "FMLA Structure").

The frame style structure (frs) contains 16 bits. Because dxyCorner overlaps the byte boundary, the structure is defined as a single 16-bit field instead of two 8-bit fields.

Offset	Bits	Mask	Name	Contents
0	0	0001h	frt	= 1 if the rectangle has rounded corners (Format Object dialog box, Patterns tab)
	1	0002h	fShadow	= 1 if the rectangle has a shadow border (Format Object dialog box, Patterns tab)
	9–2	03FCh	dxyCorner	Diameter of the oval (actually a circle) that defines the rounded corners (if frt = 1)
	15–10	FC00h	(Unused)	

Oval Object Fields

Offset	Name	Size	Contents
38	icvBack	1	Index to the color palette for background color.
39	icvFore	1	Index to the color palette for foreground color.
40	fls	1	Fill pattern.
41	fAuto	1	Bit 0 = 1 if the Automatic Fill option is turned on (Format Object dialog box, Patterns tab). All other bits in fAuto are don't-care.
42	icv	1	Index to the color palette for line color.
43	lns	1	Line style (see "Line Object Fields").
44	lnw	1	Line weight (see "Line Object Fields").
45	fAuto	1	Bit 0 = 1 if the Automatic Border option is turned on (Format Object dialog box, Patterns tab). All other bits in fAuto are don't-care.
46	frs	2	Frame style structure (see the following table).
48	cchName	1	Length of the name (null if no name).
49	stName	var	Name (null if no name; may contain a padding byte to force word-boundary alignment).
var	fmla	var	FMLA structure (see "FMLA Structure").

The frame style structure (frs) contains 16 bits. dxyCorner is not used for oval objects.

Offset	Bits	Mask	Name	Contents
0	0	0001h	frt	(Not used for oval objects)
	1	0002h	fShadow	= 1 if the oval has a shadow border (Format Object dialog box, Patterns tab)
	2–9	03FCh	dxyCorner	(Not used for oval objects)
	10–15	FC00h	(Unused)	

Arc Object Fields

Offset	Name	Size	Contents
38	icvBack	1	Index to the color palette for background color.
39	icvFore	1	Index to the color palette for foreground color.
40	fls	1	Fill pattern.
41	fAuto	1	Bit 0 = 1 if the Automatic Fill option is turned on (Format Object dialog box, Patterns tab). All other bits in fAuto are don't-care.

Offset	Name	Size	Contents
42	icv	1	Index to the color palette for line color.
43	lns	1	Line style (see "Line Object Fields").
44	lnw	1	Line weight (see "Line Object Fields").
45	fAuto	1	Bit 0 = 1 if the Automatic Border option is turned on (Format Object dialog box, Patterns tab). All other bits in fAuto are don't-care.
46	iqu	1	Quadrant index (the section of an oval that describes the arc): Upper-right quadrant of the oval: iqu = 0 Upper-left quadrant of the oval: iqu = 1 Lower-left quadrant of the oval: iqu = 2 Lower-right quadrant of the oval: iqu = 3
47	(Reserved)	1	Reserved; must be 0 (zero).
48	cchName	1	Length of the name (null if no name).
49	stName	var	Name (null if no name; may contain a padding byte to force word-boundary alignment).
var	fmla	var	FMLA structure (see "FMLA Structure").

Chart Object Fields

Offset	Name	Size	Contents
38	icvBack	1	Index to the color palette for background color.
39	icvFore	1	Index to the color palette for foreground color.
40	fls	1	Fill pattern.
41	fAuto	1	Bit 0 = 1 if the Automatic Fill option is turned on (Format Object dialog box, Patterns tab). All other bits in fAuto are don't-care.
42	icv	1	Index to the color palette for line color.
43	lns	1	Line style (see "Line Object Fields").
44	lnw	1	Line weight (see "Line Object Fields").
45	fAuto	1	Bit 0 = 1 if the Automatic Border option is turned on (Format Object dialog box, Patterns tab). All other bits in fAuto are don't-care.
46	frs	2	Frame style structure (see "Rectangle Object Fields").
48	grbit	2	Option flags (shown LSB to MSB): fLinked:1 = 1 if linked to a chart sheet Reserved:15 Reserved; must be 0 (zero)

Offset	Name	Size	Contents
50	(Reserved)	16	Reserved; must be 0 (zero).
66	cchName	1	Length of the name (null if no name).
67	stName	var	Name (null if no name; may contain a padding byte to force word-boundary alignment).
var	fmla	var	FMLA structure (see "FMLA Structure").

An embedded chart BIFF substream immediately follows the chart object record. This embedded chart file begins with a BOF record and ends with an EOF record. For more information, see Chapter 10 "Microsoft Excel Chart Records" on page 477.

Text Object Fields

Offset	Name	Size	Contents
38	icvBack	1	Index to the color palette for background color.
39	icvFore	1	Index to the color palette for foreground color.
40	fls	1	Fill pattern.
41	fAuto	1	Bit 0 = 1 if the Automatic Fill option is turned on (Format Object dialog box, Patterns tab). All other bits in fAuto are don't-care.
42	icv	1	Index to the color palette for line color.
43	lns	1	Line style (see "Line Object Fields").
44	lnw	1	Line weight (see "Line Object Fields").
45	fAuto	1	Bit 0 = 1 if the Automatic Border option is turned on (Format Object dialog box, Patterns tab). All other bits in fAuto are don't-care.
46	frs	2	Frame style structure (see the preceding section "Rectangle Object Fields").
48	cbText	2	Length of the object text.
50	(Reserved)	2	Reserved; must be 0 (zero).
52	cbRuns	2	Total length of all TXORUNS structures in the record.
54	ifntEmpty	2	If cbRuns = 0, the text object is empty, and these 2 bytes contain the index to the FONT record for the object.
			If the object contains text, cbRuns > 0, and these 2 bytes are reserved.
56	(Reserved)	2	Reserved; must be 0 (zero).
58	grbit	2	Option flags (see the following table).

Offset	Name	Size	Contents
60	rot	2	Orientation of text within the object boundary (Format Object dialog box, Alignment tab): = 0, no rotation (text appears left to right) = 1, text appears top to bottom; letters are upright = 2, text is rotated 90 degrees counterclockwise = 3, text is rotated 90 degrees clockwise
62	(Reserved)	12	Reserved; must be 0 (zero).
74	cchName	1	Length of the name (null if no name).
75	stName	var	Name (null if no name; may contain a padding byte to force word-boundary alignment).
var	fmla	var	FMLA structure (see "FMLA Structure").
var	rgch	var	Object text; may contain a single padding byte at the end of the text for word-boundary alignment (cbText does not count this padding byte).
var	TXORUNS	8	TXORUNS structure (see "TXORUNS").
var	TXORUNS	8	TXORUNS structure (see "TXORUNS").

The grbit field at byte 58 contains the option flags listed in the following table.

Offset	Bits	Mask	Name	Contents
0	0	01h	(Reserved)	Reserved; must be 0 (zero)
	3–1	0Eh	alcH	Horizontal text alignment: 1 = left-aligned 2 = centered 3 = right-aligned 4 = justified
	6–4	70h	alcV	Vertical text alignment: 1 = left-aligned 2 = centered 3 = right-aligned 4 = justified
	7	80h	fAutoTextSize	= 1 if the Automatic Size option is turned on (Format Object dialog box, Alignment tab)
1	0	01h	(Unused)	
	1	02h	fLockText	= 1 if the Lock Text option is turned on (Format Object dialog box, Protection tab)
	2	04h	fFuzzy	= 1 if the object is selected (the broken border is displayed)
	7–3	F8h	(Reserved)	Reserved; must be 0 (zero)

TXORUNS

The TXORUNS structure contains formatting information about the object text string. A TXORUNS structure occurs every time the text formatting changes. The TXORUNS structure is described in the following table.

Offset	Name	Size	Contents
0	ichFirst	2	Index to the first character to which the formatting applies
2	ifnt	2	Index to the FONT record
4	(Reserved)	4	

There are always at least two TXORUNS structures in the text object record, even if the entire text string is normal font (ifnt = 0). The last TXORUNS structure, which ends the formatting information for the string, always has ichFirst = cbText, and ifnt = 0.

Button Object Fields

Offset	Name	Size	Contents
38	icvBack	1	Index to the color palette for background color (fixed for buttons).
39	icvFore	1	Index to the color palette for foreground color (fixed for buttons).
40	fls	1	Fill pattern (fixed for buttons).
41	grbit	1	Option flags (fixed for buttons).
42	icv	1	Index to the color palette for line color (fixed for buttons).
43	lns	1	Line style (fixed for buttons).
44	lnw	1	Line weight (fixed for buttons).
45	fAuto	1	Bit 0 = 1 (fixed for buttons).
46	frs	2	Frame style structure (ignored for buttons).
48	cbText	2	Length of the object text.
50	(Reserved)	2	Reserved; must be 0 (zero).
52	cbRuns	2	Total length of all TXORUNS structures in record.
54	ifntEmpty	2	If cbRuns = 0, the button object is empty, and these 2 bytes contain the index to the FONT record for the object. If the object contains text, cbRuns > 0, and these 2 bytes are reserved.

Offset	Name	Size	Contents
56	(Reserved)	2	Reserved; must be 0 (zero).
58	grbit	2	Option flags (see the following table).
60	rot	2	Orientation of text within the object boundary (Format Object dialog box, Alignment tab): = 0, no rotation (text appears left to right) = 1, text appears top to bottom; letters are upright = 2, text is rotated 90 degrees counterclockwise = 3, text is rotated 90 degrees clockwise
62	(Reserved)	6	Reserved; must be 0 (zero).
68	grbit	2	Option flags (shown LSB to MSB): fDefault:1 = 1 if this is the default button fHelp:1 = 1 if this is the Help button fCancel:1 = 1 if this is the cancel button fDismiss:1 = 1 if this is the dismiss button Reserved:12 Reserved; must be 0 (zero)
70	accel	2	Accelerator key character.
72	accel2	2	Accelerator key character (Far East versions only).
74	cchName	1	Length of the name (null if no name).
75	stName	var	Name (null if no name; may contain a padding byte to force word-boundary alignment).
var	fmla	var	FMLA structure (see "FMLA Structure").
var	rgch	var	Object text; may contain a single padding byte at the end of the text for word-boundary alignment (cbText does not count this padding byte).
var	TXORUNS	8	TXORUNS structure (see "TXORUNS").
var	TXORUNS	8	TXORUNS structure (see "TXORUNS").

The grbit field at byte 58 contains the option flags listed in the following table.

Offset	Bits	Mask	Name	Contents
0	0	01h	(Reserved)	Reserved; must be 0 (zero)
	3–1	0Eh	alcH	Horizontal text alignment: 1 = left-aligned 2 = centered 3 = right-aligned 4 = justified
	6–4	70h	alcV	Vertical text alignment: 1 = left-aligned 2 = centered 3 = right-aligned 4 = justified

Offset	Bits	Mask	Name	Contents
	7	80h	fAutoTextSize	= 1 if the Automatic Size option is turned on (Format Object dialog box, Alignment tab)
1	0	01h	(Unused)	
	1	02h	fLockText	= 1 if the Lock Text option is turned on (Format Object dialog box, Protection tab)
	2	04h	fFuzzy	= 1 if the object is selected (the broken border is displayed)
	7–3	F8h	(Reserved)	Reserved; must be 0 (zero)

Picture Object Fields

Offset	Name	Size	Contents
38	icvBack	1	Index to the color palette for background color.
39	icvFore	1	Index to the color palette for foreground color.
40	fls	1	Fill pattern.
41	fAuto	1	Bit 0 = 1 if the Automatic Fill option is turned on (Format Object dialog box, Patterns tab). All other bits in fAuto are don't-care.
42	icv	1	Index to the color palette for line color.
43	lns	1	Line style (see "Line Object Fields").
44	lnw	1	Line weight (see "Line Object Fields").
45	fAuto	1	Bit 0 = 1 if the Automatic Border option is turned on (Format Object dialog box, Patterns tab). All other bits in fAuto are don't-care.
46	frs	2	Frame style structure (see the preceding section "Rectangle Object Fields").
48	cf	2	Image format: = 00h Text format = 01h Null format (no image data) = 02h Windows metafile or Macintosh PICT format = 09h Windows bitmap format
50	(Reserved)	4	Reserved; must be 0 (zero).
54	cbPictFmla	2	Length of the picture FMLA structure (the FMLA that contains the link to the picture).
56	(Reserved)	2	Reserved; must be 0 (zero).

Offset	Name	Size	Contents
58	grbit	2	Option flags (see the following table).
60	(Reserved)	4	Reserved; must be 0 (zero).
64	cchName	1	Length of the name (null if no name).
65	stName	var	Name (null if no name; may contain a padding byte to force word-boundary alignment).
var	fmla	var	Attached macro FMLA structure (see "FMLA Structure").
var	PictFmla	var	Picture FMLA structure (see "FMLA Structure").
var	(Reserved)	4	Reserved; must be 0 (zero).

The grbit field at byte 58 contains the option flags listed in the following table.

Offset	Bits	Mask	Name	Contents
0	0	01h	fAutoPict	= 0 if the user manually sizes picture by dragging a handle
	1	02h	fDde	= 1 if the reference in the FMLA structure is a DDE reference
	2	04h	fIcon	= 1 if the picture is from a DDE link, and the only available representation of the picture is an icon
	7–3	F8h	(Unused)	
1	7–0	FFh	(Unused)	

Sheet Background in Microsoft Excel for Windows 95

The sheet background bitmap for worksheets and charts is stored as a hidden picture object that has the name__BkgndObj (the stName field at byte 65). An IMDATA record will also appear in the file to store the image description.

Group Object Fields

Offset	Name	Size	Contents
34	(Reserved)	4	Reserved; must be 0 (zero).
38	idNext	2	Object ID number (id) of the object that follows the last object in this group. If there are no objects following the group, idNext = 0.
40	(Reserved)	16	Reserved; must be 0 (zero).

A Group OBJ record precedes the OBJ records for the group members.

Polygon Object Fields

Offset	Name	Size	Contents
38	icvBack	1	Index to the color palette for background color.
39	icvFore	1	Index to the color palette for foreground color.
40	fls	1	Fill pattern.
41	fAuto	1	Bit 0 = 1 if the Automatic Fill option is turned on (Format Object dialog box, Patterns tab). All other bits in fAuto are don't-care.
42	icv	1	Index to the color palette for line color.
43	lns	1	Line style (see the preceding section "Line Object Fields").
44	lnw	1	Line weight (see preceding section "Line Object Fields").
45	fAuto	1	Bit 0 = 1 if the Automatic Border option is turned on (Format Object dialog box, Patterns tab). All other bits in fAuto are don't-care.
46	frs	2	Frame style structure (see the preceding section "Rectangle Object Fields").
48	wstate	2	If bit 0 = 1, the polygon is closed. All other bits are don't-care.
50	(Reserved)	10	
60	iMacSav	2	Number of vertices in the polygon (1-based).
62	(Reserved)	8	
70	cchName	1	Length of the name (null if no name).
71	stName	var	Name (null if no name; may contain a padding byte to force word-boundary alignment).
var	fmla	var	FMLA structure (see "FMLA Structure").

For polygon objects, a COORDLIST record follows the OBJ record.

Check Box Object Fields

Offset	Name	Size	Contents
38	icvBack	1	Index to the color palette for background color (fixed for check box objects).
39	icvFore	1	Index to the color palette for foreground color (fixed for check box objects).
40	fls	1	Fill pattern (ignored for check box objects).
41	fAuto	1	(Ignored for check box objects).

Offset	Name	Size	Contents
42	icv	1	Index to the color palette for line color (fixed for check box objects).
43	lns	1	Line style (ignored for check box objects).
44	lnw	1	Line weight (ignored for check box objects).
45	fAuto	1	(Ignored for check box objects).
46	frs	2	Frame style structure (ignored for check box objects).
48	(Reserved)	10	Reserved; must be 0 (zero).
58	grbit	2	Option flags (see the following table).
60	(Reserved)	20	Reserved; must be 0 (zero).
80	cchName	1	Length of the name (null if no name).
81	stName	var	Name (null if no name; may contain a padding byte to force word-boundary alignment).
var	cbFmla1	2	Length of the FMLA structure for the attached macro (never null).
var	fmla1	var	FMLA structure for the attached macro (see "FMLA Structure").
var	cbFmla2	2	Length of the FMLA structure for the cell link (never null).
var	fmla2	var	FMLA structure for the cell link (see "FMLA Structure").
var	cbText	2	Length of the object text (never null).
var	rgch	var	Object text; may contain a single padding byte at the end of the text for word-boundary alignment (cbText does not count this padding byte).
var	fChecked	2	= 0 if the check box is not checked = 1 if the check box is checked = 2 if the check box is gray (mixed)
var	accel	2	Accelerator key character.
var	accel2	2	Accelerator key character (Far East versions only).
var	grbit	2	Option flags (shown LSB to MSB): fNo3d:1 = 1 if 3-D shading is turned off fBoxOnly:1 = 1 if only the box is drawn Reserved:14 Reserved; must be 0 (zero)

The grbit field at byte 58 contains the option flags listed in the following table.

Offset	Bits	Mask	Name	Contents
0	7–0	FFh	(Reserved)	Reserved; must be 0 (zero)
1	0	01h	(Unused)	
	1	02h	fLockText	= 1 if the Lock Text option is turned on (Format Object dialog box, Protection tab)
	2	04h	fFuzzy	= 1 if the object is selected (the broken border is displayed)
	7–3	F8h	(Reserved)	Reserved; must be 0 (zero)

Dialog Frame Object Fields

Offset	Name	Size	Contents
38	icvBack	1	Index to the color palette for background color (fixed for dialog frame objects).
39	icvFore	1	Index to the color palette for foreground color (fixed for dialog frame objects).
40	fls	1	Fill pattern (ignored for dialog frame objects).
41	grbit	1	Option flags (ignored for dialog frame objects).
42	icv	1	Index to the color palette for line color (fixed for dialog frame objects).
43	lns	1	Line style (ignored for dialog frame objects).
44	lnw	1	Line weight (ignored for dialog frame objects).
45	fAuto	1	Bit 0 = 1 for dialog frame objects.
46	frs	2	Frame style structure (ignored for dialog frame objects).
48	cbText	2	Length of the object text.
50	(Reserved)	8	Reserved; must be 0 (zero).
58	grbit	2	Option flags (see the following table).
60	(Reserved)	14	Reserved; must be 0 (zero).
74	cchName	1	Length of the name (null if no name).
75	stName	var	Name (null if no name; may contain a padding byte to force word-boundary alignment).
var	fmla	var	FMLA structure (see "FMLA Structure").
var	rgch	var	Object text; may contain a single padding byte at the end of the text for word-boundary alignment (cbText does not count this padding byte).
var	TXORUNS	8	TXORUNS structure (see text).
var	TXORUNS	8	TXORUNS structure (see text).

The grbit field at byte 58 contains the option flags listed in the following table.

Offset	Bits	Mask	Name	Contents
0	7–0	FFh	(Reserved)	Reserved; must be 0 (zero)
1	0	01h	(Unused)	
	1	02h	fLockText	= 1 if the Lock Text option is turned on (Format Object dialog box, Protection tab)
	2	04h	fFuzzy	= 1 if an object is selected (the broken border is displayed)
	7–3	F8h	(Reserved)	Reserved; must be 0 (zero)

The TXORUNS structure contains formatting information about the object text string, which is the dialog box caption. There are two TXORUNS structures in the dialog frame object record. The first has ichFirst = 00h, and it has ifnt pointing to the FONT record for the text. The second has ichFirst = cbText, and it contains no other useful information. The TXORUNS structure is shown in the following table.

Offset	Name	Size	Contents
0	ichFirst	2	Index to the first character to which the formatting applies
2	ifnt	2	Index to the FONT record
4	(Reserved)	4	

Drop-Down Object Fields

Offset	Name	Size	Contents
38	icvBack	1	Index to the color palette for background color (fixed for drop-down objects).
39	icvFore	1	Index to the color palette for foreground color (fixed for drop-down objects).
40	fls	1	Fill pattern (ignored for drop-down objects).
41	grbit	1	Option flags (ignored for drop-down objects).
42	icv	1	Index to the color palette for line color (fixed for drop-down objects).
43	lns	1	Line style (ignored for drop-down objects).
44	lnw	1	Line weight (ignored for drop-down objects).
45	fAuto	1	Bit 0 = 1 for drop-down objects.
46	frs	2	Frame style structure (ignored for drop-down objects).

Offset	Name	Size	Contents
48	(Reserved)	4	Reserved; must be 0 (zero).
52	iVal	2	Scroll bar position.
54	iMin	2	Scroll bar minimum value.
56	iMax	2	Scroll bar maximum value.
58	dInc	2	Amount to scroll when an arrow is clicked.
60	dPage	2	Amount to scroll when the scroll bar is clicked.
62	fHoriz	2	= 1 if the scroll bar is horizontal.
64	dxScroll	2	Width of the scroll bar.
66	grbit	2	Option flags (shown LSB to MSB): (Reserved):3 Reserved; must be 0 (zero) fNo3d:1 = 1 if 3-D shading is turned off (Reserved):12 Reserved; must be 0 (zero)
68	(Reserved)	18	Reserved; must be 0 (zero).
86	ifnt	2	Index to the FONT record for list box.
88	(Reserved)	14	Reserved; must be 0 (zero).
102	xLeft	2	X (horizontal) position of the upper-left corner of the drop-down object's bounding rectangle.
104	yTop	2	Y (vertical) position of the upper-left corner of the drop-down object's bounding rectangle.
106	xRight	2	X (horizontal) position of the lower-right corner of the drop-down object's bounding rectangle.
108	yBot	2	Y (vertical) position of the lower-right corner of the drop-down object's bounding rectangle.
110	(Reserved)	4	Reserved; must be 0 (zero).
114	cchName	1	Length of the name (null if no name).
115	stName	var	Name (null if no name; may contain a padding byte to force word-boundary alignment).
var	cbFmla1	2	Length of the FMLA structure for the attached macro (never null).
var	fmla1	var	FMLA structure for the attached macro (see "FMLA Structure").
var	cbFmla2	2	Length of the FMLA structure for the cell link (never null).
var	fmla2	var	FMLA structure for the cell link (see "FMLA Structure").
var	cbFmla3	2	Length of the FMLA structure for the input range (never null).

Offset	Name	Size	Contents
var	fmla3	var	FMLA structure for the input range (see "FMLA Structure").
var	cLines	2	Number of elements in the list box (1-based).
var	iSel	2	Index of the selected item (1-based).
var	grbit	2	Option flags (shown LSB to MSB): f(reserved):2 Reserved; must be 0 (zero) fValidIds:1 – 1 if idEdit is valid fNo3d:1 = 1 if 3-D shading is turned off (Reserved):12 Reserved; must be 0 (zero)
var	(Reserved)	2	Reserved; must be 0 (zero).

var	grbit	2	Option flags (shown LSB to MSB):
			wStyle:2 Drop-down style:
			        0 = combo,
			        1 = combo edit,
			        2 = simple
			        3 = max
			(Reserved):14 Reserved; must be 0 (zero)

var	cLine	2	Maximum number of lines that the drop-down list box contains before a scroll bar is added.
var	dxMin	2	Minimum allowable width of the drop-down list box.
var	(Reserved)	2	Reserved; must be 0 (zero).

Edit Box Object Fields

Offset	Name	Size	Contents
38	icvBack	1	Index to the color palette for background color (fixed for edit box objects).
39	icvFore	1	Index to the color palette for foreground color (fixed for edit box objects).
40	fls	1	Fill pattern (ignored for edit box objects).
41	grbit	1	Option flags (ignored for edit box objects).
42	icv	1	Index to the color palette for line color (fixed for edit box objects).
43	lns	1	Line style (ignored for edit box objects).
44	lnw	1	Line weight (ignored for edit box objects).
45	fAuto	1	Bit 0 = 1 for edit box objects.
46	frs	2	Frame style structure (ignored for edit box objects).

Offset	Name	Size	Contents
48	(Reserved)	10	Reserved; must be 0 (zero).
58	grbit	2	Option flags (see the following table).
60	(Reserved)	14	Reserved; must be 0 (zero).
74	cchName	1	Length of the name (null if no name).
75	stName	var	Name (null if no name; may contain a padding byte to force word-boundary alignment).
var	cbFmla	2	Length of the FMLA structure for the attached macro (never null).
var	fmla	var	FMLA structure for the attached macro (see "FMLA Structure").
var	cbText	2	Length of the object text (never null).
var	rgch	var	Object text; may contain a single padding byte at the end of the text for word-boundary alignment (cbText does not count this padding byte).
var	ivtEdit	2	Edit validation: = 000, Text = 001, Integer = 010, Number = 011, Reference = 100, Formula
var	fMultiLine	2	= 1 if the edit is a multiline edit.
var	fVScroll	2	= 1 if the edit box has a vertical scroll bar.
var	idList	2	Object ID of the linked list box or linked drop-down, if the edit box is part of a combination list-edit box or combination drop-down edit box. If idList = 0, this is a simple edit box.

The grbit field at byte 58 contains the option flags listed in the following table.

Offset	Bits	Mask	Name	Contents
0	7–0	FFh	(Reserved)	Reserved; must be 0 (zero)
1	0	01h	(Unused)	
	1	02h	fLockText	= 1 if the Lock Text option is turned on (Format Object dialog box, Protection tab)
	2	04h	fFuzzy	= 1 if the object is selected (the broken border is displayed)
	7–3	F8h	(Reserved)	Reserved; must be 0 (zero)

Group Box Object Fields

Offset	Name	Size	Contents
38	icvBack	1	Index to the color palette for background color (fixed for group box objects).
39	icvFore	1	Index to the color palette for foreground color (fixed for group box objects).
40	fls	1	Fill pattern (ignored for group box objects).
41	grbit	1	Option flags (ignored for group box objects).
42	icv	1	Index to the color palette for line color (fixed for group box objects).
43	lns	1	Line style (ignored for group box objects).
44	lnw	1	Line weight (ignored for group box objects).
45	fAuto	1	Bit 0 = 1 for group box objects.
46	frs	2	Frame style structure (ignored for group box objects).
48	(Reserved)	10	Reserved; must be 0 (zero).
58	grbit	2	Option flags (see the following table).
60	(Reserved)	26	Reserved; must be 0 (zero).
86	cchName	1	Length of the name (null if no name).
87	stName	var	Name (null if no name; may contain a padding byte to force word-boundary alignment).
var	cbFmla	2	Length of the FMLA structure (never null).
var	fmla	var	FMLA structure (see "FMLA Structure").
var	cbText	2	Length of object text (never null).
var	rgch	var	Object text; may contain a single padding byte at the end of the text for word-boundary alignment (cbText does not count this padding byte).
var	accel	2	Accelerator key character.
var	accel2	2	Accelerator key character (Far East versions only).
var	grbit	2	Option flags (shown LSB to MSB): fNo3d:1 = 1 if 3-D shading is off (Reserved):15 Reserved; must be 0 (zero)

The grbit field at byte 58 contains the option flags listed in the following table.

Offset	Bits	Mask	Name	Contents
0	7–0	FFh	(Reserved)	Reserved; must be 0 (zero)
1	0	01h	(Unused)	
	1	02h	fLockText	= 1 if the Lock Text option is on (Format Object dialog box, Protection tab)
	2	04h	fFuzzy	= 1 if the object is selected (the broken border is displayed)
	7–3	F8h	(Reserved)	Reserved; must be 0 (zero)

Label Object Fields

Offset	Name	Size	Contents
38	icvBack	1	Index to the color palette for background color (fixed for label objects).
39	icvFore	1	Index to the color palette for foreground color (fixed for label objects).
40	fls	1	Fill pattern (ignored for label objects).
41	grbit	1	Option flags (ignored for label objects).
42	icv	1	Index to the color palette for line color (fixed for label objects).
43	lns	1	Line style (ignored for label objects).
44	lnw	1	Line weight (ignored for label objects).
45	fAuto	1	Bit 0 = 1 for label objects.
46	frs	2	Frame style structure (ignored for label objects).
48	cbText	2	Length of object text.
50	(Reserved)	8	Reserved; must be 0 (zero).
58	grbit	2	Option flags (see the following table).
60	(Reserved)	14	Reserved; must be 0 (zero).
74	cchName	1	Length of the name (null if no name).
75	stName	var	Name (null if no name; may contain a padding byte to force word-boundary alignment).
var	fmla	var	FMLA structure (see "FMLA Structure").
var	rgch	var	Object text; may contain a single padding byte at the end of the text for word-boundary alignment (cbText does not count this padding byte).
var	TXORUNS	8	TXORUNS structure (see text).
var	TXORUNS	8	TXORUNS structure (see text).

The grbit field at byte 58 contains the option flags listed in the following table.

Offset	Bits	Mask	Name	Contents
0	7–0	FFh	(Reserved)	Reserved; must be 0 (zero)
1	0	01h	(Unused)	
	1	02h	fLockText	= 1 if the Lock Text option is on (Format Object dialog box, Protection tab)
	2	04h	fFuzzy	– 1 if object is selected (the broken border is displayed)
	7–3	F8h	(Reserved)	Reserved; must be 0 (zero)

The TXORUNS structure contains formatting information about the object text string, which is the label string. There are two TXORUNS structures in the label object record. The first has ichFirst = 00h and has ifnt pointing to the FONT record for the label. The second has ichFirst = cbText and contains no other useful information. The TXORUNS structure is shown in the following table.

Offset	Name	Size	Contents
0	ichFirst	2	Index to the first character to which the formatting applies
2	ifnt	2	Index to the FONT record
4	(Reserved)	4	

List Box Object Fields

Offset	Name	Size	Contents
38	icvBack	1	Index to the color palette for background color (fixed for list box objects).
39	icvFore	1	Index to the color palette for foreground color (fixed for list box objects).
40	fls	1	Fill pattern (ignored for list box objects).
41	grbit	1	Option flags (ignored for list box objects).
42	icv	1	Index to the color palette for line color (fixed for list box objects).
43	lns	1	Line style (ignored for list box objects).
44	lnw	1	Line weight (ignored for list box objects).
45	fAuto	1	Bit 0 = 1 for list box objects.
46	frs	2	Frame style structure (ignored for list box objects).
48	(Reserved)	4	Reserved; must be 0 (zero).

Offset	Name	Size	Contents
52	iVal	2	Scroll bar position.
54	iMin	2	Scroll bar minimum value.
56	iMax	2	Scroll bar maximum value.
58	dInc	2	Amount to scroll when the arrow is clicked.
60	dPage	2	Amount to scroll when the scroll bar is clicked.
62	fHoriz	2	= 1 if the scroll bar is horizontal.
64	dxScroll	2	Width of the scroll bar.
66	grbit	2	Option flags (shown LSB to MSB): (Reserved):3 Reserved; must be 0 (zero). fNo3d:1 = 1 if 3-D shading is off. (Reserved):12 Reserved; must be 0 (zero).
68	(Reserved)	18	Reserved; must be 0 (zero).
86	ifnt	2	Index to the FONT record for the list box.
88	(Reserved)	4	Reserved; must be 0 (zero).
92	cchName	1	Length of the name (null if no name).
93	stName	var	Name (null if no name; may contain a padding byte to force word-boundary alignment).
var	cbFmla1	2	Length of the FMLA structure for the attached macro (never null).
var	fmla1	var	FMLA structure for the attached macro (see "FMLA Structure").
var	cbFmla2	2	Length of the FMLA structure for the cell link (never null).
var	fmla2	var	FMLA structure for the cell link (see "FMLA Structure").
var	cbFmla3	2	Length of the FMLA structure for input range (never null).
var	fmla3	var	FMLA structure for input range (see "FMLA Structure").
var	cLines	2	Number of elements in the list box (1-based).
var	iSel	2	Index of the selected item (1-based).
var	grbit	2	Option flags (shown LSB to MSB): f(reserved):2 Reserved; must be 0 (zero). fValidIds:1 = 1 if idEdit is valid. fNo3d:1 = 1 if 3-D shading is off. wListSelType:2 List box selection type: 0 = standard. 1 = multiselect. 2 = extended-select (Reserved):10 Reserved; must be 0 (zero).

Offset	Name	Size	Contents
var	idEdit	2	Object ID of the linked edit box, if the list box is part of a combination list-edit box. If idList = 0, this is a simple list box.
var	rgbSel	var	Array of bytes, indicating which items are selected in a multiselect or extended-select list box. The number of elements in the array is equal to cLines. If an item is selected in the list box, the corresponding element in the array = 1.

Option Button Object Fields

Offset	Name	Size	Contents
38	icvBack	1	Index to the color palette for background color (fixed for option button objects).
39	icvFore	1	Index to the color palette for foreground color (fixed for option button objects).
40	fls	1	Fill pattern (ignored for option button objects).
41	fAuto	1	(Ignored for option button objects).
42	icv	1	Index to the color palette for line color (fixed for option button objects).
43	lns	1	Line style (ignored for option button objects).
44	lnw	1	Line weight (ignored for option button objects).
45	fAuto	1	(Ignored for option button objects).
46	frs	2	Frame style structure (ignored for option button objects).
48	(Reserved)	10	Reserved; must be 0 (zero).
58	grbit	2	Option flags (see the following table).
60	(Reserved)	32	Reserved; must be 0 (zero).
92	cchName	1	Length of the name (null if no name).
93	stName	var	Name (null if no name; may contain a padding byte to force word-boundary alignment).
var	cbFmla1	2	Length of the FMLA structure for the attached macro (never null).
var	fmla1	var	FMLA structure for the attached macro (see "FMLA Structure").
var	cbFmla2	2	Length of FMLA structure for the cell link (never null).
var	fmla2	var	FMLA structure for the cell link (see "FMLA Structure").

Offset	Name	Size	Contents
var	cbText	2	Length of the object text (never null).
var	rgch	var	Object text; may contain a single padding byte at the end of the text for word-boundary alignment (cbText does not count this padding byte).
var	fChecked	2	= 0 if the option button is not checked. = 1 if the option button is checked.
var	accel	2	Accelerator key character.
var	accel2	2	Accelerator key character (Far East versions only).
var	grbit	2	Option flags (shown LSB to MSB): fNo3d:1 = 1 if 3-D shading is off. fBoxOnly:1 = 1 if only the box is drawn. Reserved:14 Reserved; must be 0 (zero).
var	idRadNext	2	Object ID of the next option button in the group.
var	fFirstBtn	2	= 1 if this option button is the first in the group.

The grbit field at byte 58 contains the option flags listed in the following table.

Offset	Bits	Mask	Name	Contents
0	7–0	FFh	(Reserved)	Reserved; must be 0 (zero)
1	0	01h	(Unused)	
	1	02h	fLockText	= 1 if the Lock Text option is on (Format Object dialog box, Protection tab)
	2	04h	fFuzzy	= 1 if the object is selected (the broken border is displayed)
	7–3	F8h	(Reserved)	Reserved; must be 0 (zero)

Scroll Bar Object Fields

Offset	Name	Size	Contents
38	icvBack	1	Index to the color palette for background color (fixed for scroll bar objects).
39	icvFore	1	Index to the color palette for foreground color (fixed for scroll bar objects).
40	fls	1	Fill pattern (ignored for scroll bar objects).
41	grbit	1	Option flags (ignored for scroll bar objects).
42	icv	1	Index to the color palette for line color (fixed for scroll bar objects).
43	lns	1	Line style (ignored for scroll bar objects).

Offset	Name	Size	Contents
44	lnw	1	Line weight (ignored for scroll bar objects).
45	fAuto	1	Bit 0 = 1 for scroll bar objects.
46	frs	2	Frame style structure (ignored for scroll bar objects).
48	(Reserved)	4	Reserved; must be 0 (zero).
52	iVal	2	Scroll bar position.
54	iMin	2	Scroll bar minimum value.
56	iMax	2	Scroll bar maximum value.
58	dInc	2	Amount to scroll when the arrow is clicked.
60	dPage	2	Amount to scroll when the scroll bar is clicked.
62	fHoriz	2	= 1 if the scroll bar is horizontal.
64	dxScroll	2	Width of the scroll bar.
66	grbit	2	Option flags (shown LSB to MSB): (Reserved):3 Reserved; must be 0 (zero). fNo3d:1 = 1 if 3-D shading is off. (Reserved):12 Reserved; must be 0 (zero).
68	cchName	1	Length of the name (null if no name).
69	stName	var	Name (null if no name; may contain a padding byte to force word-boundary alignment).
var	cbFmla1	2	Length of the FMLA structure for the attached macro (never null).
var	fmla1	var	FMLA structure for the attached macro (see "FMLA Structure").
var	cbFmla2	2	Length of the FMLA structure for the cell link (never null).
var	fmla2	var	FMLA structure for the cell link (see "FMLA Structure").

Spinner Object Fields

Offset	Name	Size	Contents
38	icvBack	1	Index to the color palette for background color (fixed for spinner objects).
39	icvFore	1	Index to the color palette for foreground color (fixed for spinner objects).
40	fls	1	Fill pattern (ignored for spinner objects).
41	grbit	1	Option flags (ignored for spinner objects).

Offset	Name	Size	Contents
42	icv	1	Index to the color palette for line color (fixed for spinner objects).
43	lns	1	Line style (ignored for spinner objects).
44	lnw	1	Line weight (ignored for spinner objects).
45	fAuto	1	Bit 0 = 1 for spinner objects.
46	frs	2	Frame style structure (ignored for spinner objects).
48	(Reserved)	4	Reserved; must be 0 (zero).
52	iVal	2	Spinner position.
54	iMin	2	Spinner minimum value.
56	iMax	2	Spinner maximum value.
58	dInc	2	Amount to scroll when the spinner is clicked.
60	(Reserved)	2	Reserved; must be 0 (zero).
62	fHoriz	2	= 1 if the spinner is horizontal.
64	dxScroll	2	Width of the spinner.
66	grbit	2	Option flags (shown LSB to MSB): (Reserved):3 Reserved; must be 0 (zero). fNo3d:1 = 1 if 3-D shading is off. (Reserved):12 Reserved; must be 0 (zero).
68	cchName	1	Length of the name (null if no name).
69	stName	var	Name (null if no name; may contain a padding byte to force word-boundary alignment).
var	cbFmla1	2	Length of the FMLA structure for the attached macro (never null).
var	fmla1	var	FMLA structure for the attached macro (see "FMLA Structure").
var	cbFmla2	2	Length of the FMLA structure for the cell link (never null).
var	fmla2	var	FMLA structure for the cell link (see "FMLA Structure").

OBJPROTECT: Objects Are Protected (63h)

The OBJPROTECT record stores an option from the Protection command.

Record Data

Offset	Name	Size	Contents
4	fLockObj	2	= 1 if objects are protected

OBPROJ: Visual Basic Project (D3h)

The contents of this record are reserved.

Record Data

Offset	Name	Size	Contents
4	(Reserved)	var	

OLESIZE: Size of OLE Object (DEh)

This record stores the size of an embedded OLE object (when Microsoft Excel is a server).

Record Data

Offset	Name	Size	Contents
4	(Reserved)	2	
6	rwFirst	2	First row
8	rwLast	2	Last row
10	colFirst	1	First column
11	colLast	1	Last column

PALETTE: Color Palette Definition (92h)

The PALETTE record describes the colors selected in the Options dialog box, Color tab. Each rgch field contains 4 bytes: rgbRed, rgbGreen, rgbBlue, and an unused byte. The 3 color bytes correspond to the Red, Green, and Blue values in the Color Picker dialog box, and the unused byte is don't-care. The Color Picker dialog box appears when you click the Modify button on the Color tab. If the worksheet uses the default palette, the BIFF file does not contain the PALETTE record.

Record Data

Offset	Name	Size	Contents
4	ccv	2	Count of color values that follow
6	rgch	4	Color value of the first color in the palette
10	rgch	4	Color value of the second color in the palette
14	rgch	4	Color value of the third color in the palette
...	...	...	...
var	rgch	4	Color value of the last color (= ccv) in the palette

PANE: Number of Panes and Their Position (41h)

The PANE record describes the number and position of unfrozen panes in a window.

Record Data

Offset	Name	Size	Contents
4	x	2	Horizontal position of the split; 0 (zero) if none
6	y	2	Vertical position of the split; 0 (zero) if none
8	rwTop	2	Top row visible in the bottom pane
10	colLeft	2	Leftmost column visible in the right pane
12	pnnAct	2	Pane number of the active pane

The x and y fields contain the position of the vertical and horizontal splits, respectively, in units of 1/20th of a point. Either of these fields can be 0 (zero), indicating that the window is not split in the corresponding direction.

For a window with a horizontal split, the rwTop field is the topmost row visible in the bottom pane or panes. For a window with a vertical split, the colLeft field contains the leftmost column visible in the right pane or panes.

The pnnAct field indicates which pane is the active pane. The pnnAct field contains one of the following values:

    0 = lower right
    1 = upper right
    2 = lower left
    3 = upper left

If the window has frozen panes, as specified in the WINDOW2 record, x and y have special meaning. If there is a vertical split, x contains the number of columns visible in the top pane. If there is a horizontal split, y contains the number of rows visible in the left pane. Both types of splits can be present in a window, as in unfrozen panes.

PARAMQRY: Query Parameters (DCh)

This record contains query data.

Note PARAMQRY has the same record number as SXEXT. This has no adverse ramifications in a BIFF file because PARAMQRY always occurs in conjunction with an SXEXT record.

Record Data—BIFF8

Offset	Name	Size	Contents
4	wTypeSql	2	Used for ODBC queries; the parameter SQL type
6	grbit	2	Option flags; see following table
8	fVal	2	A true/false value if pbt = 2 and the parameter is a Boolean
10	rgb	var	(See text)

The grbit field contains the option flags listed in the following table.

Bits	Mask	Name	Contents
1–0	0003h	pbt	Parameter binding type: = 0 Prompt type (for example, "Please enter a date") = 1 Fixed value type (for example, 10, "MSFT", 01/06/97, and so on) = 2 Reference type (for example, "=Sheet2!$A$5")
2	0004h	fAuto	= 1 for automatic parameters
3	0008h	fNonDefaultName	= 0 then program prompts for the name
15–4	FFF0h	Reserved	Reserved; must be 0 (zero)

The rgb field can contain several different data types. If pbt = 0, then rgb contains the prompt string as a unicode string; for more information see "Unicode Strings in BIFF8" on page 264.

If pbt = 1 (a value field), then rgb contains one of the following:

An 8-byte IEEE number for dates and decimal numbers
A 4-byte long integer
A variable-length unicode string for bound string values
No data if the value is Boolean; the value is then stored in fVal

If pbt = 2, then the rgb contains a parsed expression for the reference.

PASSWORD: Protection Password (13h)

The PASSWORD record contains the encrypted password for a protected sheet or workbook. Note that this record specifies a sheet-level or workbook-level protection password, as opposed to the FILEPASS record, which specifies a file password.

Record Data

Offset	Name	Size	Contents
4	wPassword	2	Encrypted password

PLS: Environment-Specific Print Record (4Dh)

The PLS record saves printer settings and printer driver information.

Record Data, Macintosh

Offset	Name	Size	Contents
4	wEnv	2	Operating environment: 0 = Microsoft Windows 1 = Apple Macintosh
6	rgb	var	TPrint structure (for more information about this structure, see *Inside Macintosh, Volume II,* page 149).

Record Data, Windows

Offset	Name	Size	Contents
4	wEnv	2	Operating environment: 0 = Microsoft Windows 1 = Apple Macintosh
6	rgb	var	DEVMODE structure (for more information about this structure, see the documentation for the Microsoft Windows Software Development Kit).

PRECISION: Precision (0Eh)

The PRECISION record stores the Precision As Displayed option from the Options dialog box, Calculation tab.

Record Data

Offset	Name	Size	Contents
4	fFullPrec	2	= 0 if Precision As Displayed option is selected

PRINTGRIDLINES: Print Gridlines Flag (2Bh)

This record stores the Gridlines option from the Page Setup dialog box, Sheet tab.

Record Data

Offset	Name	Size	Contents
4	fPrintGrid	2	= 1 to print gridlines

PRINTHEADERS: Print Row/Column Labels (2Ah)

The PRINT HEADERS record stores the Row And Column Headings option from the Page Setup dialog box, Sheet tab.

Record Data

Offset	Name	Size	Contents
4	fPrintRwCol	2	= 1 to print row and column headings

PROTECT: Protection Flag (12h)

The PROTECT record stores the protection state for a sheet or workbook.

Record Data

Offset	Name	Size	Contents
4	fLock	2	= 1 if the sheet or workbook is protected

PROT4REV: Shared Workbook Protection Flag (1AFh)

The PROT4REV record stores a shared-workbook protection flag.

Record Data—BIFF8

Offset	Name	Size	Contents
4	fRevLock	2	= 1 if the Sharing with Track Changes option is on (Protect Shared Workbook dialog box)

PROT4REVPASS: Shared Workbook Protection Password (1BCh)

The PROT4REV record stores an encrypted password for shared-workbook protection.

Record Data—BIFF8

Offset	Name	Size	Contents
4	wRevPass	2	Encrypted password (if this field is 0 (zero), there is no Shared Workbook Protection Password; the password is entered in the Protect Shared Workbook dialog box)

PUB: Publisher (89h)

The PUB record contains information about the publisher/subscriber feature. This record can be created only by Microsoft Excel for the Macintosh. However, if Microsoft Excel for any other operating environment encounters the PUB record in a BIFF file, it leaves the record in the file, unchanged, when the file is saved.

Record Data

Offset	Name	Size	Contents
4	grbit	2	Option flags
6	ref	6	Reference structure describing the published area on the worksheet
12	sec	36	Section record associated with the published area
48	rgbAlias	var	Contents of the alias pointed to by the section record

The grbit field contains the option flags listed in the following table.

Offset	Bits	Mask	Name	Contents
0	0	01h	fAprPrinted	= 1 if the published appearance is shown when printed
	1	02h	fSizPrinted	= 1 if the published size is shown when printed
	7–2	FCh	(Unused)	
1	7–0	FFh	(Unused)	

QSI: External Data Range (1ADh)

This record stores an external data range.

Record Data—BIFF8

Offset	Name	Size	Contents
4	grbit	2	Option flags; see following table.
6	itblAutoFmt	2	Index to autoformat table.
8	grbitAtrAutoFmt	2	Low-order 6 bits contain autoformat attribute flag bits; the high-order 10 bits are reserved.
10	Reserved	4	Reserved; must be 0 (zero).
14	cchName	1	Length of name.
15	rgchName	var	Name string.

The grbit field contains the option flags listed in the following table.

Bits	Mask	Name	Contents
0	0001h	fTitles	= 1 if the range contains titles
1	0002h	fRowNums	= 1 if the range uses row numbers
2	0004h	fDisableRefresh	= 1 if refresh is disabled
6–3	0078h	Reserved	Reserved; must be 0 (zero)
7	0080h	fFill	= 1 if the range has a fill applied
8	0100h	fAutoFormat	= 1 if the range has an autoformat applied
9	0200h	Reserved	Reserved; must be 0 (zero)
10	0400h	fDisableEdit	= 1 if the cells are locked for editing
15–11	F800h	Reserved	Reserved; must be 0 (zero)

RECIPNAME: Recipient Name (B9h)

This record stores recipient information about a routing slip. The rgch field contains the concatenation of two null-terminated strings: Recipient's Friendly Name, and Recipient's System-Specific Address.

Record Data

Offset	Name	Size	Contents
4	cchRecip	2	Length of the recipient's friendly name string
6	ulEIDSize	4	Length of the recipient's system-specific address string
10	rgchRecip	var	(See text)

REFMODE: Reference Mode (0Fh)

The REFMODE record stores the Reference Style option from the Options dialog box, General tab.

Record Data

Offset	Name	Size	Contents
4	fRefA1	2	Reference mode: = 1 for A1 mode = 0 for R1C1 mode

REFRESHALL: Refresh Flag (1B7h)

This record stores an option flag.

Record Data—BIFF8

Offset	Name	Size	Contents
4	fRefreshAll	2	= 1 then Refresh All should be done on all external data ranges and PivotTables when loading the workbook (the default is = 0)

RIGHTMARGIN: Right Margin Measurement (27h)

The RIGHTMARGIN record specifies the right margin in inches. The num field is in 8-byte IEEE floating-point format.

Record Data

Offset	Name	Size	Contents
4	num	8	Right margin

RK: Cell Value, RK Number (7Eh)

Microsoft Excel uses an internal number type, called an RK number, to save memory and disk space.

Record Data

Offset	Name	Size	Contents
4	rw	2	Row number
6	col	2	Column number
8	ixfe	2	Index to the XF record that contains the cell format
10	rk	4	RK number (see the following description)

An RK number is either a 30-bit integer or the most significant 30 bits of an IEEE number. The two LSBs of the 32-bit rk field are always reserved for RK type encoding; this is why the RK numbers are 30 bits, not the full 32. See the following diagram.

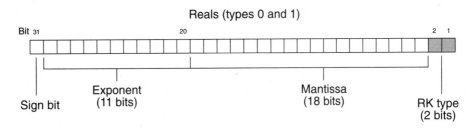

Reals (types 0 and 1)

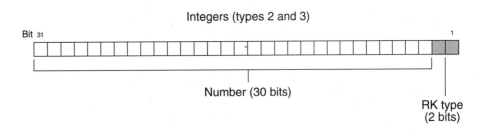

Integers (types 2 and 3)

There are four different RK number types, as described in the following table.

RK type	Encode priority	Number (decimal)	RK number (hex)	Description of 30-bit encoding
0	1	1	3F F0 00 00	IEEE number
1	3	1.23	40 5E C0 01	IEEE number x 100
2	2	12345678	02 F1 85 3A	Integer
3	4	123456.78	02 F1 85 3B	Integer x 100

Microsoft Excel always attempts to store a number as an RK number instead of an IEEE number. There is also a specific priority of RK number encoding that the program uses. The following flowchart is a simplified version of the encoding algorithm. The algorithm always begins with an IEEE (full 64-bit) number.

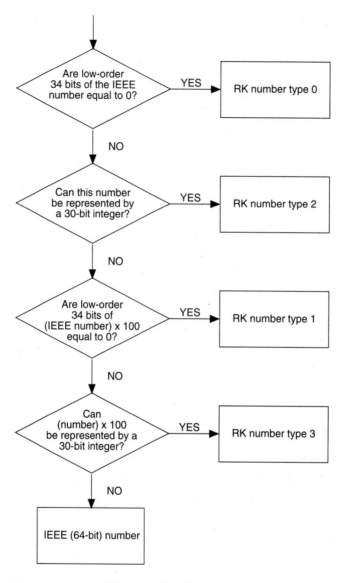

You can use the following C code to demonstrate how to decode RK numbers:

```
double NumFromRk(long rk)
    {
    double num;
    if(rk & 0x02)
        {
        // int
        num = (double) (rk >> 2);
        }
```

```
    else
        {
        // hi words of IEEE num
        *((long *)&num+1) = rk & 0xfffffffc;
        *((long *)&num) = 0;
        }
    if(rk & 0x01)
        // divide by 100
        num /= 100;
    return num;
    }
main()
    {
    printf("%f\n", NumFromRk (0x02f1853b));
    }
```

If you write a NUMBER record to a BIFF file, Microsoft Excel may convert the number to an RK number when it reads the file.

ROW: Describes a Row (208h)

A ROW record describes a single row on a Microsoft Excel sheet. ROW records and their associated cell records occur in blocks of up to 32 rows. Each block ends with a DBCELL record. For more information about row blocks and about optimizing your code when searching for cell records, see "Finding Cell Records in BIFF Files" on page 440.

Record Data

Offset	Name	Size	Contents
4	rw	2	Row number.
6	colMic	2	First defined column in the row.
8	colMac	2	Last defined column in the row, plus 1.
10	miyRw	2	Row height.
12	irwMac	2	Used by Microsoft Excel to optimize loading the file; if you are creating a BIFF file, set irwMac to 0.
14	(Reserved)	2	

Offset	Name	Size	Contents
16	grbit	2	Option flags.
18	ixfe	2	If fGhostDirty = 1 (see grbit field), this is the index to the XF record for the row. Otherwise, this field is undefined.
			Note: ixfe uses only the low-order 12 bits of the field (bits 11–0). Bit 12 is fExAsc, bit 13 is fExDsc, and bits 14 and 15 are reserved. fExAsc and fExDsc are set to true if the row has a thick border on top or on bottom, respectively.

The grbit field contains the option flags listed in the following table.

Offset	Bits	Mask	Name	Contents
0	2–0	07h	iOutLevel	Outline level of the row
	3	08h	(Reserved)	
	4	10h	fCollapsed	= 1 if the row is collapsed in outlining
	5	20h	fDyZero	= 1 if the row height is set to 0 (zero)
0	6	40h	fUnsynced	= 1 if the font height and row height are not compatible
	7	80h	fGhostDirty	= 1 if the row has been formatted, even if it contains all blank cells
1	7–0	FFh	(Reserved)	

The rw field contains the 0-based row number. The colMic and colMac fields give the range of defined columns in the row.

The miyRw field contains the row height, in units of 1/20th of a point. The miyRw field may have the 8000h (2^{15}) bit set, indicating that the row is standard height. The low-order 15 bits must still contain the row height. If you hide the row—either by setting row height to 0 (zero) or by using the Hide command—miyRw still contains the original row height. This allows Microsoft Excel to restore the original row height when you click the Unhide button.

Each row can have default cell attributes that control the format of all undefined cells in the row. By specifying default cell attributes for a particular row, you are effectively formatting all the undefined cells in the row without using memory for those cells. Default cell attributes do not affect the formats of cells that are explicitly defined.

For example, if you want all of row 3 to be left-aligned, you could define all 256 cells in the row and specify that each individual cell be left-aligned. This would require storage for each of the 256 cells. An easy alternative would be to set the default cell for row 3 to be left-aligned and not define any individual cells in row 3.

RSTRING: Cell with Character Formatting (D6h)

When part of a string in a cell has character formatting, an RSTRING record is written instead of the LABEL record. The RSTRING record is obsolete in BIFF8, replaced by the LABELSST and SST records.

Record Data

Offset	Name	Size	Contents
4	rw	2	Row
6	col	2	Column
8	ixfe	2	Index to the XF record
10	cch	2	Length of the string
12	rgch	var	String
var	cruns	1	Count of STRUN structures
var	rgstrun	var	Array of STRUN structures

The STRUN structure contains formatting information about the string. A STRUN structure occurs every time the text formatting changes. The STRUN structure is described in the following table.

Offset	Name	Size	Contents
0	ich	1	Index to the first character to which the formatting applies
1	ifnt	1	Index to the FONT record

SAVERECALC: Recalculate Before Save (5Fh)

If the Recalculate Before Save option is selected in the Options dialog box, Calculation tab, then fSaveRecalc = 1.

Record Data

Offset	Name	Size	Contents
4	fSaveRecalc	2	= 1 to recalculate before saving

SCENARIO: Scenario Data (AFh)

This record stores information about an individual scenario.

Record Data

Offset	Name	Size	Contents
4	cref	2	Number of changing cells
6	fLocked	1	= 1 if the scenario is locked for changes
7	fHidden	1	= 1 if the scenario is hidden
8	cchName	1	Length of the name
9	cchComment	1	Length of the comment
10	cchNameUser	1	Length of the user name
11	rgch	var	Concatenation of the scenario name string, the user name string (preceded by a duplicate of cchNameUser), and the comment string (preceded by a duplicate of cchComment)
var	rgRef	var	Array of cell references that contains changing cells (see text)
var	rgst	var	Array of byte-counted strings that contains changing cell values (see text)
var	rgIfmt	var	Array of ifmt integers (see text)

The changing cells for the scenario are stored in the three arrays at the end of the record. The rgRef array contains the cell addresses, as shown in the following table.

Offset	Name	Size	Contents
0	rw	2	Row number (0-based)
2	col	2	Column number (0-based)

In BIFF8, the cell values are always stored as an array of unicode strings; for more information see "Unicode Strings in BIFF8" on page 264.

In BIFF7, the cell values are always stored as an array of byte-counted strings, as shown in the following table.

Offset	Name	Size	Contents
0	cch	1	Length of the string
1	rgch	var	String

Finally, the cell number format indexes (ifmt) are stored as an array of 2-byte integers, following the array of cell value strings. These are stored only when the scenario contains cells with date/time number formats. If the cells contain any other number format, the rgIfmt will contain 0's (zeros).

SCENMAN: Scenario Output Data (AEh)

This records stores the general information about the set of scenarios on a worksheet.

Record Data

Offset	Name	Size	Contents
4	csct	2	Number of scenarios
6	isctCur	2	Index of the current scenario
8	isctShown	2	Index of the last displayed scenario
10	irefRslt	2	Number of reference areas in the following scenario result array
12	rgref	var	Scenario result array (see the following table)

Each reference area in the scenario result array contains the fields listed in the following table.

Offset	Name	Size	Contents
0	rwFirst	2	First row
2	rwLast	2	Last row
4	colFirst	1	First column
5	colLast	1	Last column

SCENPROTECT: Scenario Protection (DDh)

This record stores the scenario protection flag.

Record Data

Offset	Name	Size	Contents
4	fScenProtect	2	= 1 if scenarios are protected

SCL: Window Zoom Magnification (A0h)

This record stores the window zoom magnification.

Record Data

Offset	Name	Size	Contents
4	nscl	2	Numerator of a reduced fraction
6	dscl	2	Denominator of a reduced fraction

The magnification is stored as a reduced fraction. For example, if the magnification is 75 percent, nscl = 03h and dscl = 04h ($3/4 = 0.75 = 75\%$). If the magnification is 11 percent, nscl = 0Bh (11 decimal) and dscl = 64h (100 decimal). If the BIFF file does not contain the SCL record, the magnification is 100 percent.

SELECTION: Current Selection (1Dh)

The SELECTION record stores the selection.

Record Data

Offset	Name	Size	Contents
4	pnn	1	Number of the pane described
5	rwAct	2	Row number of the active cell
7	colAct	2	Column number of the active cell
9	irefAct	2	Ref number of the active cell
11	cref	2	Number of refs in the selection
13	rgref	var	Array of refs

The pnn field indicates which pane is described. It contains one of the following values:

0 = lower right
1 = upper right
2 = lower left
3 = upper left

For a window that has no splits, the pnn field = 3.

The rwAct and colAct fields specify the active cell.

The irefAct field is a 0-based index into the array of ref structures (refs), specifying which ref contains the active cell. The rgref is an array because it is possible to create a multiple selection. In the case of a multiple selection, each selection is described by a ref, including the active cell (even if it is included in one of the other selections).

The selection (of cells) is described by the rgref array. The number of refs in the rgref field is equal to cref. Each ref in the array is 6 bytes long and contains the fields listed in the following table.

Offset	Name	Size	Contents
0	rwFirst	2	First row in the reference
2	rwLast	2	Last row in the reference
4	colFirst	1	First column in the reference
5	colLast	1	Last column in the reference

If a selection is so large that it exceeds the maximum BIFF record size, it is broken down into multiple consecutive SELECTION records. Each record contains a portion of the larger selection. Only the cref and rgref fields vary in the multiple records; the pnn, rwAct, colAct, and irefAct fields are the same across all records in the group.

SETUP: Page Setup (A1h)

The SETUP record stores options and measurements from the Page Setup dialog box.

Record Data

Offset	Name	Size	Contents
4	iPaperSize	2	Paper size (see fNoPls in the following table)
6	iScale	2	Scaling factor (see fNoPls in the following table)
8	iPageStart	2	Starting page number
10	iFitWidth	2	Fit to width; number of pages
12	iFitHeight	2	Fit to height; number of pages
14	grbit	2	Option flags (see the following table)
16	iRes	2	Print resolution (see fNoPls in the following table)
18	iVRes	2	Vertical print resolution (see fNoPls in the following table)
20	numHdr	8	Header margin (IEEE number)
28	numFtr	8	Footer margin (IEEE number)
36	iCopies	2	Number of copies (see fNoPls in the following table)

The grbit field contains the option flags listed in the following table.

Offset	Bits	Mask	Name	Contents
0	0	01h	fLeftToRight	Print over, and then down.
	1	02h	fLandscape	= 0, Landscape mode = 1, Portrait mode (see fNoPls below).
	2	04h	fNoPls	= 1, then the iPaperSize, iScale, iRes, iVRes, iCopies, and fLandscape data have not been obtained from the printer, so they are not valid.
	3	08h	fNoColor	= 1, print black and white.
	4	10h	fDraft	= 1, print draft quality.
	5	20h	fNotes	= 1, print notes.
	6	40h	fNoOrient	= 1, orientation not set.
	7	80h	fUsePage	= 1, use custom starting page number instead of Auto.
1	7–0	FFh	(Unused)	

SHRFMLA: Shared Formula (BCh)

The SHRFMLA record is a file size optimization. It is used with the FORMULA record to compress the amount of storage required for the parsed expression (rgce). In earlier versions of Microsoft Excel, if you read a FORMULA record in which the rgce field contained a ptgExp parse token, the FORMULA record contained an array formula. In Microsoft Excel version 5.0 and later, this could indicate either an array formula or a shared formula.

If the record following the FORMULA is an ARRAY record, the FORMULA record contains an array formula. If the record following the FORMULA is a SHRFMLA record, the FORMULA record contains a shared formula. You can also test the fShrFmla bit in the FORMULA record's grbit field to determine this.

When reading a file, you must convert the FORMULA and SHRFMLA records to an equivalent FORMULA record if you plan to use the parsed expression. To do this, take all of the FORMULA record up to (but not including) the cce field, and then append to that the SHRFMLA record from its cce field to the end. You must then convert some ptgs; this is explained later in this article.

Following the SHRFMLA record will be one or more FORMULA records containing ptgExp tokens that have the same rwFirst and colFirst fields as those in the ptgExp in the first FORMULA. There is only one SHRFMLA record for each shared-formula record group.

To convert the ptgs, search the rgce field from the SHRFMLA record for any ptgRefN, ptgRefNV, ptgRefNA, ptgAreaN, ptgAreaNV, or ptgAreaNA tokens. Add the corresponding FORMULA record's rw and col fields to the rwFirst and colFirst fields in the ptgs from the SHRFMLA. Finally, convert the ptgs as shown in the following table.

Convert this ptg	To this ptg
ptgRefN	ptgRef
ptgRefNV	ptgRefV
ptgRefNA	ptgRefA
ptgAreaN	ptgArea
ptgAreaNV	ptgAreaV
ptgAreaNA	ptgAreaA

For more information about ptgs and parsed expressions, see "Microsoft Excel Formulas" on page 444.

Remember that STRING records can appear after FORMULA records if the formula evaluates to a string.

If your code writes a BIFF file, always write standard FORMULA records; do not attempt to use the SHRFMLA optimization.

Record Data

Offset	Name	Size	Contents
4	rwFirst	2	First row
6	rwLast	2	Last row
8	colFirst	1	First column
9	colLast	1	Last column
10	(Reserved)	2	
12	cce	2	Length of the parsed expression
14	rgce	var	Parsed expression

SORT: Sorting Options (90h)

This record stores options from the Sort and Sort Options dialog boxes.

Record Data

Offset	Name	Size	Contents
4	grbit	2	Option flags
6	cchKey1	1	Length of the string for sort key 1
7	cchKey2	1	Length of the string for sort key 2
8	cchKey3	1	Length of the string for sort key 3
9	rgchKey1	var	String for sort key 1
var	rgchKey2	var	String for sort key 2
var	rgchKey3	var	String for sort key 3

The grbit field contains the option flags listed in the following table.

Offset	Bits	Mask	Name	Contents
0	0	0001h	fCol	= 1 if the Sort Left To Right option is on.
	1	0002h	fKey1Dsc	= 1 if key 1 sorts in descending order.
	2	0004h	fKey2Dsc	= 1 if key 2 sorts in descending order.
	3	0008h	fKey3Dsc	= 1 if key 3 sorts in descending order.
	4	0010h	fCaseSensitive	= 1 if the sort is case-sensitive.
	9–5	03E0h	iOrder	Index to the table in the First Key Sort Order option. The Normal sort order corresponds to iOrder = 0.
	10	0400h	fAltMethod	Used only in Far East versions of Microsoft Excel.
	15–11	F800h	(Reserved)	

SOUND: Sound Note (96h)

The SOUND record contains the complete description of a sound note.

Record Data

Offset	Name	Size	Contents
4	cf	2	Clipboard format; 4257h (16983 decimal) for sound notes
6	env	2	Environment from which the file was written: = 1, Microsoft Windows = 2, Apple Macintosh

Offset	Name	Size	Contents
8	lcb	4	Length of the sound data
12	data	var	Sound data

SST: Shared String Table (FCh)

The SST record contains string constants.

Record Data—BIFF8

Offset	Name	Size	Contents
4	cstTotal	4	Total number of strings in the shared string table and extended string table (EXTSST record)
8	cstUnique	4	Number of unique strings in the shared string table
12	rgb	var	Array of unique strings (see text)

The rgb field contains an array of unicode strings. For more information, see "Unicode Strings in BIFF8" on page 264.

STANDARDWIDTH: Standard Column Width (99h)

The STANDARDWIDTH record records the measurement from the Standard Width dialog box.

Record Data

Offset	Name	Size	Contents
4	DxGCol	2	Standard column width, in increments of 1/256th of a character width

STRING: String Value of a Formula (207h)

When a formula evaluates to a string, a STRING record occurs after the FORMULA record. If the formula is part of an array, the STRING record occurs after the ARRAY record.

Record Data

Offset	Name	Size	Contents
4	cch	2	Length of the string
6	rgch	var	String

STYLE: Style Information (293h)

Each style in a Microsoft Excel workbook, whether built-in or user-defined, requires a style record in the BIFF file. When Microsoft Excel saves the workbook, it writes the STYLE records in alphabetical order, which is the order in which the styles appear in the drop-down list box.

Record Data—Built-in Styles

Offset	Name	Size	Contents
4	ixfe	2	Index to the style XF record.
			Note: ixfe uses only the low-order 12 bits of the field (bits 11–0). Bits 12, 13, and 14 are unused, and bit 15 (fBuiltIn) is 1 for built-in styles.
6	istyBuiltIn	1	Built-in style numbers: = 00h Normal = 01h RowLevel_n = 02h ColLevel_n = 03h Comma = 04h Currency = 05h Percent = 06h Comma[0] = 07h Currency[0]
7	iLevel	1	Level of the outline style RowLevel_n or ColLevel_n (see text).

Record Data—User-Defined Styles

Offset	Name	Size	Contents
4	ixfe	2	Index to the style XF record.
			Note: ixfe uses only the low-order 12 bits of the field (bits 11–0). Bits 12, 13, and 14 are unused, and bit 15 (fBuiltIn) is 0 for user-defined styles.
6	cch	1	Length of the style name.
7	rgch	(var)	Style name.

The automatic outline styles—RowLevel_1 through RowLevel_7, and ColLevel_1 through ColLevel_7—are stored by setting istyBuiltIn to 01h or 02h and then setting iLevel to the style level minus 1. If the style is not an automatic outline style, ignore this field.

SUB: Subscriber (91h)

The SUB record contains information about the publisher/subscriber feature. This record can be created only by Microsoft Excel for the Macintosh. However, if Microsoft Excel for any other platform encounters the SUB record in a BIFF file, it leaves the record in the file, unchanged, when the file is saved.

Record Data

Offset	Name	Size	Contents
4	ref	6	Reference structure describing the subscribed area on the worksheet.
10	drwReal	2	Actual number of rows in the subscribed area.
12	dcolReal	2	Actual number of columns in the subscribed area.
14	grbit	2	Option flags.
16	cbAlias	2	Size of rgbAlias.
18	sec	36	Section record associated with the subscribed area.
54	rgbAlias	var	Contents of the alias pointed to by the section record.
var	stz	var	Null-terminated string containing the path of publisher. The first byte is a length byte, which does not count the terminating null byte.

The grbit field contains the option flags listed in the following table.

Offset	Bits	Mask	Name	Contents
0	0	01h	(Reserved)	
	1	02h	fObj	= 1 if subscribed in the object layer
	7–2	FCh	(Reserved)	
1	7–0	FFh	(Reserved)	

SUPBOOK: Supporting Workbook (1AEh)

This record stores data about a supporting external workbook.

Record Data—BIFF8

Offset	Name	Size	Contents
4	Ctab	2	Number of tabs in the workbook
6	StVirtPath	var	Encoded file name of the workbook, as a unicode string (see text)
var	Rgst	var	An array of strings, the sheet tab names, as unicode strings

For more information about Unicode strings, see "Unicode Strings in BIFF8" on page 264.

File name Encoding

Whenever possible, file names are encoded to make BIFF files transportable across file systems. Encoded file names are identified by the first character of the rgch field. The first character of the rgch field may be any one of the values listed in the following table.

Name	Value	Meaning
chEmpty	00	Reference to an empty workbook name (see text)
chEncode	01	File name has been encoded (see the following table)
chSelf	02	Self-referential external reference (see text)

chEmpty indicates that the file name is an external reference to an empty workbook name, as in the formula =Sheet1!$A$1.

chSelf indicates that the file name is an external reference in which the dependent and source workbooks are the same. An example of this is the workbook SALES.XLS, which contains the formula =SALES.XLS!$A$1.

A chDDE key (03h) can occur in the rgch field; it is not necessarily the first character in the field, as are chEmpty, chEncode, and chSelf. This key indicates that the external reference is a DDE or OLE link. In a DDE link, the chDDE key replaces the | (pipe) character that separates the DDE application and topic. In an OLE link, chDDE separates the classname and file name.

A chEncode at the beginning of rgch indicates that the file name of the source workbook has been encoded to a less system-dependent file name. The special keys listed in the following table are recognized in the rgch field.

Name	Value	PC file systems	Macintosh file system
chVolume	01	Represents an MS-DOS drive letter. It is followed by the drive letter. For example, the formula ='D:\SALES.XLS'!A1 generates the chVolume key when the dependent workbook is not on the D drive. UNC file names, such as \\server\share\myfile.xls, generate an @ character after the chVolume key; this replaces the initial double backslash (\\).	Represents a single-character volume name. Because single-character volume names are uncommon on the Macintosh, the chLongVolume key is used to represent volume names that are longer than a single character.
chSameVolume	02	Indicates that the source workbook is on the same drive as the dependent workbook (the drive letter is omitted). For example, the formula ='\SALES.XLS'!A1 generates the chSameVolume key when the dependent workbook is not in the root directory.	Indicates that the source workbook is in the same volume as the dependent workbook (the volume name is omitted).
ChDownDir	03	Indicates that the source workbook is in a subdirectory of the current directory. For example, the formula ='XL\SALES.XLS'!A1 generates the chDownDir key. The subdirectory name precedes the chDownDir key, and the file name follows it.	Indicates that the source workbook is in a folder in the current folder. For example, the formula =':XL:Sales1992'!A1 generates the chDownDir key. The folder name precedes the chDownDir key, and the file name follows it.

Name	Value	PC file systems	Macintosh file system
chUpDir	04	Indicates that the source workbook is in the parent directory of the current directory. For example, the formula ='..\SALES.XLS'!A1 generates the chUpDir key.	Indicates that the source workbook is in the parent folder of the current folder. For example, the formula ='::Sales1992'!A1 generates the chUpDir key.
chLongVolume	05	(Not used)	The chLongVolume key is followed by the length of the name (1 byte) and then by the volume name string.
chStartupDir	06	Indicates that the source workbook is in the startup directory (the Xlstart subdirectory of the directory that contains Excel.exe).	Indicates that the source workbook is in the Excel Startup Folder (5), which is in the System Folder.
chAltStartupDir	07	Indicates that the source workbook is in the alternate startup directory.	Indicates that the source workbook is in the alternate startup folder.
chLibDir	08	Indicates that the source workbook is in the Library directory.	Indicates that the source workbook is in the Macro Library folder.

SXDB: PivotTable Cache Data (C6h)

The SXDB is stored on a separate stream that maintains information about each PivotTable cache. The SXDB record is followed by a single SXDBEX record and several FDB records, one for each field in the PivotTable, given by cfdbTot.

Record Data—BIFF8

Offset	Name	Size	Contents
4	crdbdb	4	Number of records in database
8	idstm	2	Identifies the stream

Offset	Name	Size	Contents
10	grbit	2	= 01h, fSaveData—data is being saved with table layout.
			= 02h, fInvalid—the PivotTable must be refreshed before the next update.
			= 04h, fRefreshOnLoad—the PivotTable will be refreshed on load.
			= 08h, fOptimizeCache—the cache is optimized to use the least amount of memory.
			= 10h, fBackgroundQuery—results of the query are obtained in the background.
			= 20h, fEnableRefresh—refresh is enabled.
12	crdbDbb	2	Number of records for each database block.
14	cfdbdb	2	Number of base fields in databases.
16	cfdbTot	2	Number of base fields, grouped fields, and calculated fields.
18	crdbUsed	2	This value is not used and can be set to zero.
20	vsType	2	Data source is one of: 1, Excel worksheet 2, External Data 4, Consolidation 8, Scenario PivotTable
22	cchWho	2	Number of characters in the string containing the name of the user who last refreshed the PivotTable.
24	rgb	(var)	String which is of length given by cchWho and represents the number of the user who last refreshed the PivotTable.

SXDBEX: PivotTable Cache Data (122h)

The SXDBEX record is an extension of the SXDB record. Both records contain PivotTable cache data.

Record Data—BIFF8

Offset	Name	Size	Contents
4	numDate	8	The date that the PivotTable cache was created or was last refreshed. The date is stored as an 8-byte IEEE floating-point number.
12	cSxFormula	4	Count of SXFORMULA records for this cache.

SXDI: Data Item (C5h)

This record contains information about the PivotTable data item.

Record Data

Offset	Name	Size	Contents
4	isxvdData	2	Field that this data item is based on.
6	iiftab	2	Index to the aggregation function: = 00h, Sum = 01h, Count = 02h, Average = 03h, Max = 04h, Min = 05h, Product = 06h, Count Nums = 07h, StdDev = 08h, StdDevp = 09h, Var = 0Ah, Varp
8	df	2	Data display format: = 00h, Normal = 01h, Difference from = 02h, Percentage of = 03h, Percentage difference from = 04h, Running total in = 05h, Percentage of row = 06h, Percentage of column = 07h, Percentage of total = 08h, Index
10	isxvd	2	Index to the SXVD record used by the data display format.
12	isxvi	2	Index to the SXVI record used by the data display format.
14	ifmt	2	Index to the format table for this item.
16	cchName	2	Length of the name; if the name = FFFFh, rgch is null and the name in the PivotTable cache storage is used.
18	rgch	var	Name.

SXEX: PivotTable View Extended Information (F1h)

This record follows the SXVIEW record and contains information about additional features added to PivotTables in Microsoft Excel 97.

Record Data—BIFF8

Offset	Name	Size	Contents
4	csxformat	2	Number of SXFORMAT records to follow
6	cchErrorString	2	Number of characters for DisplayErrorString string
8	cchNullString	2	Number of characters for DisplayNullString string
10	cchTag	2	Number of characters in Tag string
12	csxselect	2	Number of RTSXSELECT records to follow
14	crwPage	2	Number of page field per row
16	ccolPage	2	Number of page field per column
18	grbit1	2	= 01h, fAcrossPageLay = 1eh, cWrapPage = 20h, fPreserveFormattingNow = 40h, fManualUpdate
20	grbit2	2	= 01h, fEnableWizard = 02h, fEnableDrilldown = 04h, fEnableFieldDialog = 08h, fPreserveFormatting = 10h, fMergeLabels = 20h, fDisplayErrorString = 40h, fDisplayNullString = 80h, fSubtotalHiddenPageItems
22	cchPageFieldStyle	2	Number of characters for page field style string
24	cchTableStyle	2	Number of characters for table style string
26	cchVacateStyle	2	Number of characters for vacate style string
28	rgb	(var)	Array of characters for ErrorString, NullString, Tag, PageFieldStyle, TableStyle, VacateStyle

SXEXT: External Source Information (DCh)

This record stores information about the SQL query string that retrieves external data for a PivotTable. The record is followed by SXSTRING records that contain the SQL strings and then by a SXSTRING record that contains the SQL server connection string.

Note PARAMQRY has the same record number as SXEXT. This has no adverse ramifications in a BIFF file because PARAMQRY always occurs in conjunction with an SXEXT record.

Record Data—BIFF8

Offset	Name	Size	Contents
4	grbit	2	Options flags; see following table
6	cparams	2	Number of parameter strings
8	cstQuery	2	Number of strings for SQL statement or URL
10	cstWebPost	2	Number of strings for post method of Web query
12	cstSQLSav	2	Number of strings for SQL statement for server-based page fields
14	cstOdbcConn	2	Number of strings for ODBC connection string

The grbit field contains the following flags.

Bits	Mask	Name	Contents
2–0	0007h	dbt	= 1 ODBC data source = 2 DAO recordset (no actual information about the recordset is saved) = 3 reserved = 4 Web (WWW) query
3	0008h	fOdbcConn	= 1 for ODBC connection
4	0010h	fSql	= 1 for ODBC connection
5	0020h	fSqlSav	= 1 for server-based page fields
6	0040h	fWeb	= 1 for a Web (WWW) query
7	0080h	fSavePwd	= 1 if the Save Password option is on
8	0100h	fTablesOnlyHTML	= 1 if the Save Tables in HTML Only option is on
15–9	FE00h	Reserved	Reserved. Should be set to zero.

The following records occur after a SXEXT record:

Record name	Contents
SXSTRING SXSTRING . . .	Collection of cstQuery SXTSRING records that should be concatenated to give the URL (Web query), SQL string (ODBC query) or parameterized SQL string (for server-based page field)
SXSTRING SXSTRING . . .	Collection of cstOdbcConn SXTSRING records that should be concatenated to give the ODBC connection string (ODBC queries only)
SXSTRING SXSTRING . . .	Collection of cstWebPost SXTSRING records that should be concatenated to give the post method data (Web query only, optional)
PARAMQRY PARAMQRY . . .	Collection of cparams PARAMQRY parameter definition records
SXSTRING SXSTRING . . .	Collection of cstSQLSav SXTSRING records that should be concatenated to give the original SQL string for an ODBC query with server-based page fields

Record Data—BIFF7 and earlier

Offset	Name	Size	Contents
4	id	2	Connection ID of the SQL server
6	fError	2	= 1 if an error occurred during the last attempt to communicate with the server
8	cstSQL	2	Number of SXSTRING records that follow

SXFDBTYPE: SQL Datatype Identifier (1BBh)

This record contains a SQL datatype identifier.

Record Data—BIFF8

Offset	Name	Size	Contents
4	wTypeSql	2	The SQL datatype of the field described in the immediately preceding SXFDB record. These are the same values as found in the ODBC SDK. See the SQL datatypes in SQL.H

SXFILT: PivotTable Rule Filter (F2h)

This record stores PivotTable Rule Filter options.

Record Data—BIFF8

Offset	Name	Size	Contents
4	grbit1	2	= 0001h, fRwField, field is in row area. = 0002h, fColumnField, field is in column area. = 0004h, fPageField, field is in page area. = 0008h, fDataField, field is in data area. = ffc0h, iDim.
8	grbit2	2	= 03ffh, isxvd. = fc00h, reserved—should always be zero.
10	grbitSbt	2	= 01h, Data = 02h, Default = 04h, SUM = 08h, COUNTA = 10h, COUNT = 20h, AVERAGE = 40h, MAX = 80h, MIN = 100h, PRODUCT = 200h, STDEV = 400h, STDEVP = 800h, VAR = 1000h, VARP
12	cisxvi	2	Number of SXVI records.

SXFMLA: PivotTable Parsed Expression (F9h)

This record stores a PivotTable parsed expression.

Record Data—BIFF8

Offset	Name	Size	Contents
4	cce	2	Size of rgce
6	csxname	2	Number of RTSXNAME records to follow this record
8	rgce		Parsed expressed whose size is given by cce

SXFORMAT: PivotTable Format Record (FBh)

This record stores formatting data.

Record Data—BIFF8

Offset	Name	Size	Contents
4	rlType	2	= 0h, clear
			= 1h, format applied
6	cbData	2	Length of data

SXFORMULA: PivotTable Formula Record (103h)

This record stores a PivotTable formula.

Record Data—BIFF8

Offset	Name	Size	Contents
4	unused	2	Reserved. Should be set to zero.
6	ifdb	2	−1 if the calculated item formula applies to all fields, or, if positive, the field that this calculated item formulas applies to.

SXIDSTM: Stream ID (D5h)

This record is a header record for a group of SXVS, SXEXT, and SXSTRING records that describe the PivotTable streams in the SX DB storage (the PivotTable cache storage). The idstm field identifies the stream.

Record Data

Offset	Name	Size	Contents
4	idstm	2	Stream ID

SXIVD: Row/Column Field IDs (B4h)

This record stores an array of field ID numbers (2-byte integers) for the row fields and column fields in a PivotTable. Two SXIVD records appear in the file: the first contains the array of row field IDs, and the second contains the array of column field IDs.

Record Data

Offset	Name	Size	Contents
4	rgisxvd	var	Array of 2-byte integers; contains either row field IDs or column field IDs

SXLI: Line Item Array (B5h)

The SXLI record stores an array of variable-length SXLI structures, which describe the row and column items in a PivotTable. There are two SXLI records for each PivotTable: the first stores row items, and the second stores column items.

Record Data

Offset	Name	Size	Contents
4	rgsxli	var	Array of SXLI structures

The SXLI structure has variable length but will always be at least 10 bytes long, with one element in the rgisxvi array (the index to the SXVI record for the item). The SXLI structure is shown in the following table.

Offset	Name	Size	Contents
0	cSic	2	Count of items that are identical to the previous element in rgsxvi; for $0 <= i < cSic$, rgisxvi[i] is the same as the previous line.
2	itmtype	2	Item type: = 00h, Data = 01h, Default = 02h, SUM = 03h, COUNTA = 04h, COUNT = 05h, AVERAGE = 06h, MAX = 07h, MIN = 08h, PRODUCT = 09h, STDEV = 0Ah, STDEVP = 0Bh, VAR = 0Ch, VARP = 0Dh, Grand total
4	isxviMac	2	Maximum index to the rgisxvi[i] array.
6	grbit	2	Option flags; see the following table.
8	rgisxvi	2	Array of indexes to SXVI records; the number of elements in the array is (isxviMac + 1).

The grbit field contains the flags listed in the following table.

Offset	Bits	Mask	Name	Contents
0	0	0001h	fMultiDataName	= 1, use the data field name for the subtotal (instead of using "Total").
	8–1	01F7h	iData	For a multidata subtotal, iData is the index to the data field.
	9	0200h	fSbt	= 1, this item is a subtotal.
	10	0400h	fBlock	= 1, this item is a block total.
	11	0800h	fGrand	= 1, this item is a grand total.
	12	1000h	fMultiDataOnAxis	= 1, this axis contains multi-data.
	15–13	E000h	(Reserved)	Reserved; must be 0 (zero).

SXNAME: PivotTable Name (F6h)

This records stores a PivotTable name.

Record Data—BIFF8

Offset	Name	Size	Contents
4	grbit	2	= 02h, fErrName, the name is invalid and should be displayed and evaluated as #NAME.
6	ifdb	2	Field to aggregate in calculated field formulas.
8	ifn	2	Function to use for aggregation in calculated field formulas.
			= 01h, SUM
			= 02h, COUNTA
			= 03h, COUNT
			= 04h, AVERAGE
			= 05h, MAX
			= 06h, MIN
			= 07h, PRODUCT
			= 08h, STDEV
			= 09h, STDEVP
			= 0Ah, VAR
			= 0Bh, VARP
10	csxpair	2	Number of SXPAIR records to follow this record.

SXPAIR: PivotTable Name Pair (F8h)

This record stores a PivotTable name pair.

Record Data—BIFF8

Offset	Name	Size	Contents
4	isxvd	2	Field.
6	iCache	2	Index of item in field.
8	unused	2	Reserved, should be set to zero.
10	grbit	2	= 01h, fCalculatedItem. = 06h, reserved. = 08h, fPhysical, item is referred to by position (physical) rather than by name (logical) = 10h, fRelative, if fPhysical is true, then item is referred to using relative references rather than absolute references.

SXPI: Page Item (B6h)

This record contains information about the PivotTable page item.

Record Data

Offset	Name	Size	Contents
4	isxvi	2	Index to the SXVI record for the page item
6	isxvd	2	Index to the SXVD record for the page item
8	idObj	2	Object ID for the page item drop-down arrow

SXRULE: PivotTable Rule Data (F0h)

This record stores PivotTable rule data.

Record Data—BIFF8

Offset	Name	Size	Contents
4	iDim	1	Position of current field in axis.
5	isxvd	1	Current field.

Offset	Name	Size	Contents
6	grbit	2	= 0001h, current field is in row area.
			= 0002h, current field is in column area.
			= 0004h, current field is in page area.
			= 0008h, current field is in data area.
			= 00f0h, sxrtype:
			= 0100h, reserved.
			= 0200h, fNoHeader—header is not selected.
			= 0400h, fNoData—data is not selected.
			= 0800h, fGrandRw—row grandtotal is selected.
			= 1000h, fGrandCol—column grandtotal is selected.
			= 2000h, fGrandRwSav.
			= 4000h, fCacheBased.
			= 8000h, fGrandColSav.
8	unused	2	
10	csxfilt	2	Number of SXFILT records following this record.

SXSELECT: PivotTable Selection Information (F7h)

This record stores PivotTable selection information.

Record Data—BIFF8

Offset	Name	Size	Contents
4	iwnx	2	0-based index of the window of the sheet
6	pnn	2	0-based index of the pane of the window
8	Reserved	2	Should be zero
10	Reserved	2	Should be zero
12	Reserved	2	Should be zero
14	Reserved	2	Should be zero
16	Reserved	2	Should be zero
18	Reserved	2	Should be zero
20	Reserved	2	Should be zero
22	Reserved	2	Should be zero
24	Reserved	2	Should be zero
26	Reserved	2	Should be zero
28	Reserved	2	Should be zero

SXSTRING: String (CDh)

This record contains an SQL query string, an SQL server connection string, or a page item name from a multiple-consolidation PivotTable.

Record Data

Offset	Name	Size	Contents
4	cch	2	Length of the string
6	rgch	var	String

SXTBL: Multiple Consolidation Source Info (D0h)

This record stores information about multiple-consolidation PivotTable source data.

Record Data

Offset	Name	Size	Contents
4	cdref	2	Count (1-based) of DCONREF or DCONNAME records that follow the SXTBL record
6	csxtbpg	2	Count (1-based) of SXTBPG records that follow the DCONREF or DCONNAME records
8	grbitPages	2	(See the following table)

The grbitPages field contains an encoded count of page fields, as shown in the following table.

Offset	Bits	Mask	Name	Contents
0	14–0	7FFFh	cPages	Count (1-based) of page fields
	15	8000h	fAutoPage	= 1 if the user selected the Create A Single Page Field For Me option in the PivotTable Wizard dialog box

SXTBPG: Page Item Indexes (D2h)

This record stores an array of page item indexes that represent the table references for a multiple-consolidation PivotTable.

Record Data

Offset	Name	Size	Contents
4	rgiitem	var	Array of 2-byte indexes to page items (iitem)

SXTBRGIITM: Page Item Name Count (D1h)

This record stores the number of page item names in a multiple-consolidation PivotTable. The names are stored in SXSTRING records that follow the SXTBRGIITM.

Record Data

Offset	Name	Size	Contents
4	cItems	2	Number of page item names (number of SXTBRGIITM records that follow)

SXVD: View Fields (B1h)

This record contains PivotTable view fields and other information.

Record Data

Offset	Name	Size	Contents
4	sxaxis	2	Axis: = 0, no axis = 1, row = 2, column = 4, page = 8, data
6	cSub	2	Number of subtotals attached.
8	grbitSub	2	Item subtotal type (see the following table).
10	cItm	2	Number of items.
12	cchName	2	Length of the name; if the name = FFFFh, rgch is null and the name in the cache is used.
14	rgch	var	Name.

The subtotal type (grbitSub) bits are defined as shown in the following table.

Name	Contents
bitFNone	0000h
bitFDefault	0001h
bitFSum	0002h
bitFCounta	0004h
bitFAverage	0008h
bitFMax	0010h
bitFMin	0020h

Name	Contents
bitFProduct	0040h
bitFCount	0080h
bitFStdev	0100h
bitFStdevp	0200h
bitFVar	0400h
bitFVarp	0800h

SXVDEX: Extended PivotTable View Fields (100h)

This record contains extended PivotTable view fields information.

Record Data—BIFF8

Offset	Name	Size	Contents
4	grbit1	4	= 0001h, fShowAllItems—show all items for this field. = 0002h, fDragToRow—user can drag field to row area. = 0004h, fDragToColumn—user can drag field to column area. = 0008h, fDragToPage—user can drag field to page area. = 0010h, fDragToHide—user can remove field from view. = 0060h, reserved. = 0080h, fServerBased—this field is a server-based field in the page area. = 0100h, reserved. = 0200h, fAutoSort—autosort is enabled. = 0400h, fAscendSort—autosort ascending. = 0800h, fAutoShow—autoshow is enabled. = 1000h, fAscendShow—show top values. = 2000h, fCalculatedField—calculated field. = c000h, reserved.
8	Reserved	1	
9	citmShow	1	Number of items to show for AutoShow, default is 10.
10	isxdiSort	2	0-based index of data field that AutoSort is based on or −1 for current field.
12	isxdiShow	2	0-based index of data field that AutoShow is based on.
14	ifmt	2	Number format of field or 0 if none.

SXVI: View Item (B2h)

This record contains information about a PivotTable item.

Record Data

Offset	Name	Size	Contents
4	itmtype	2	Item type: = FEh, Page = FFh, Null = 00h, Data = 01h, Default = 02h, SUM = 03h, COUNTA = 04h, COUNT = 05h, AVERAGE = 06h, MAX = 07h, MIN = 08h, PRODUCT = 09h, STDEV = 0Ah, STDEVP = 0Bh, VAR = 0Ch, VARP = 0Dh, Grand total
6	grbit	2	Option flags.
8	iCache	2	Index to the PivotTable cache.
10	cchName	2	Length of the name; if the name = FFFFh, rgch is null and the name in the cache is used.
12	rgch	var	Name.

The grbit field contains the option flags listed in the following table.

Offset	Bits	Mask	Name	Contents
0	0	01h	fHidden	= 1 if the item is hidden.
	1	02h	fHideDetail	= 1 if detail is hidden.
	2	04h	fFormula	= 1 if item is a calculated item.
	3	08h	fMissing	= 2 if item is an item that does not exist in any records.
	7–4	F0h	(Reserved)	Reserved, must be 0 (zero).
1	7–0	FFh	(Reserved)	Reserved, must be 0 (zero).

SXVIEW: View Definition (B0h)

This record contains top-level PivotTable information.

Record Data

Offset	Name	Size	Contents
4	rwFirst	2	First row of the PivotTable
6	rwLast	2	Last row of the PivotTable
8	colFirst	2	First column of the PivotTable
10	colLast	2	Last column of the PivotTable
12	rwFirstHead	2	First row containing PivotTable headings
14	rwFirstData	2	First row containing PivotTable data
16	colFirstData	2	First column containing PivotTable data
18	iCache	2	Index to the cache
20	(Reserved)	2	Reserved; must be 0 (zero)
22	sxaxis4Data	2	Default axis for a data field
24	ipos4Data	2	Default position for a data field
26	cDim	2	Number of fields
28	cDimRw	2	Number of row fields
30	cDimCol	2	Number of column fields
32	cDimPg	2	Number of page fields
34	cDimData	2	Number of data fields
36	cRw	2	Number of data rows
38	cCol	2	Number of data columns
40	grbit	2	Option flags
42	itblAutoFmt	2	Index to the PivotTable autoformat
44	cchName	2	Length of the PivotTable name
46	cchData	2	Length of the data field name
48	rgch	var	PivotTable name, followed by the name of a data field

The grbit field contains the option flags listed in the following table.

Offset	Bits	Mask	Name	Contents
0	0	0001h	fRwGrand	= 1 if the PivotTable contains grand totals for rows
	1	0002h	fColGrand	= 1 if the PivotTable contains grand totals for columns
	2	0004h	(Reserved)	Reserved; must be 0 (zero)
	3	0008h	fAutoFormat	= 1 if the PivotTable has an autoformat applied
	4	0010h	fWH	= 1 if the width/height autoformat is applied
	5	0020h	fFont	= 1 if the font autoformat is applied
	6	0040h	fAlign	= 1 if the alignment autoformat is applied
	7	0080h	fBorder	= 1 if the border autoformat is applied
	8	0100h	fPattern	= 1 if the pattern autoformat is applied
	9	0200h	fNumber	= 1 if the number autoformat is applied
	15–10	FC00h	(Reserved)	Reserved; must be 0 (zero)

SXVS: View Source (E3h)

This record contains an integer that defines the data source for a PivotTable.

Record Data

Offset	Name	Size	Contents
4	vs	2	Data source: = 01h, Microsoft Excel list or database = 02h, External data source (Microsoft Query) = 04h, Multiple consolidation ranges = 08h, Another PivotTable = 10h, A Scenario Manager summary report

TABID: Sheet Tab Index Array (13Dh)

This record contains an array of sheet tab index numbers. The record is used by the Shared Lists feature.

The sheet tab indexes have type short int (2 bytes each). The index numbers are 0-based and are assigned when a sheet is created; the sheets retain their index numbers throughout their lifetime in a workbook. If you rearrange the sheets in a workbook, the rgiTab array will change to reflect the new sheet arrangement.

This record does not appear in BIFF5 files.

Record Data

Offset	Name	Size	Contents
4	rgiTab	var	Array of tab indexes

TABIDCONF: Sheet Tab ID of Conflict History (EAh)

This record contains the sheet tab index for the Conflict History worksheet. The record is used by the Shared Lists feature.

This record does not appear in BIFF5 files.

Record Data

Offset	Name	Size	Contents
4	itabConf	2	Sheet tab index for the Conflict History worksheet. If =FFFFh, the user has stopped sharing the workbook.

TABLE: Data Table (236h)

A TABLE record describes a data table created with the Table command (Data menu).

Record Data

Offset	Name	Size	Contents
4	rwFirst	2	First row of the table
6	rwLast	2	Last row of the table
8	colFirst	1	First column of the table
9	colLast	1	Last column of the table
10	grbit	2	Option flags

Offset	Name	Size	Contents
12	rwInpRw	2	Row of the row input cell
14	colInpRw	2	Column of the row input cell
16	rwInpCol	2	Row of the column input cell
18	colInpCol	2	Column of the column input cell

The grbit field contains the option flags listed in the following table.

Offset	Bits	Mask	Name	Contents
0	0	01h	fAlwaysCalc	Always calculate the formula.
	1	02h	fCalcOnLoad	Calculate the formula when the file is opened.
	2	04h	fRw	= 1 input cell is a row input cell. = 0 input cell is a column input cell.
	3	08h	fTbl2	= 1 if two-input data table. = 0 if one-input data table.
	7–4	F0h	(Unused)	
1	7–0	FFh	(Unused)	

The area (range of cells) in which the table is entered is defined by the rwFirst, rwLast, colFirst, and colLast fields. This area is the interior of the table and does not include the outer row or column (these contain the table formulas and/or input values).

In cases where the input cell is a deleted reference (the cell displays #REF!), the rwInp field is –1. The colInp field is not used in this case.

TEMPLATE: Workbook Is a Template (60h)

This record has no record data field. If the TEMPLATE record is present in the Book stream, it signifies that the workbook is a template. The TEMPLATE record, if present, must immediately follow the BOF record.

TOPMARGIN: Top Margin Measurement (28h)

The TOPMARGIN record specifies the top margin in inches when a sheet is printed. The num field is in 8-byte IEEE floating-point format.

Record Data

Offset	Name	Size	Contents
4	num	8	Top margin

TXO: Text Object (1B6h)

This record stores a text object. The TXO record is followed by two CONTINUE records. The first CONTINUE contains the text data, and the second CONTINUE contains the formatting runs. If the text box contains no text, then these CONTINUE records are not written to the file.

Record Data—BIFF8

Offset	Name	Size	Contents
4	grbit	2	Option flags; see following table
6	rot	2	Orientation of text within the object boundary: = 0, no rotation (text appears left to right) = 1, text appears top to bottom; letters are upright = 2, text is rotated 90 degrees counterclockwise = 3, text is rotated 90 degrees clockwise
8	Reserved	6	Reserved; must be 0 (zero)
14	cchText	2	Length of text (in first CONTINUE record)
16	cbRuns	2	Length of formatting runs (in second CONTINUE record)
14	Reserved	4	Reserved; must be 0 (zero)

The grbit field contains the following option flags.

Bits	Mask	Name	Contents
0	0001h	Reserved	
3–1	000Eh	alcH	Horizontal text alignment: 1 = left-aligned 2 = centered 3 = right-aligned 4 = justified
6–4	0070h	alcV	Vertical text alignment: 1 = top 2 = center 3 = bottom 4 = justify
8–7	0180h	Reserved	
9	0200h	fLockText	= 1 if the Lock Text option is on (Format Text Box dialog box, Protection tab)
15–10	FC00h	Reserved	

The first CONTINUE record contains the text characters, the length of which is given by cchText. The first byte of this CONTINUE record's data field specifies if the text is compressed unicode or unicode. If the byte = 0h, then all the characters in the string have a high byte of 00h and only the low bytes are saved in the file (compressed). If the byte = 1h, then at least one character in the string has a nonzero high byte and therefore all characters in the string are saved as double-byte unicode characters (not compressed).

The second CONTINUE record contains an array of formatting runs structures (TXORUNS). A TXORUNS structure contains formatting information about the object text string. A TXORUNS structure occurs every time the text formatting changes. The TXORUNS structure is described in the following table.

Offset	Name	Size	Contents
0	ichFirst	2	Index to the first character to which the formatting applies
2	ifnt	2	Index to the FONT record
4	(Reserved)	4	

There are always at least two TXORUNS structures in the second CONTINUE record, even if the entire text string is normal font (ifnt = 0). The last TXORUNS structure, which ends the formatting information for the string, always has ichFirst = cchText, and ifnt = 0.

UDDESC: Description String for Chart Autoformat (DFh)

This record stores the description string for a custom chart autoformat. The record is written only in the chart autoformat file (XL8GALRY.XLS in Microsoft Excel for Windows).

Record Data

Offset	Name	Size	Contents
4	cch	1	Length of the description string
5	rgch	var	Description string

UNCALCED: Recalculation Status (5Eh)

If the UNCALCED record is present in the Book stream, it indicates that the Calculate message was in the status bar when Microsoft Excel saved the file. This occurs if the sheet changed, the Manual calculation option was on, and the Recalculate Before Save option was off (Options dialog box, Calculation tab).

Record Data

Offset	Name	Size	Contents
4	(Reserved)	2	Reserved; must be 0 (zero)

USERBVIEW: Workbook Custom View Settings (1A9h)

The USERBVIEW record stores settings for a custom view in the workbook.

Record Data—BIFF8

Offset	Name	Size	Contents
4	iViewId	4	ID for the custom view.
8	iTabid	4	Tab index for the active sheet (1-based).
12	guid	16	Globally unique identifier for the custom view.
28	x	4	Horizontal position of window.
32	y	4	Vertical position of window.
36	dx	4	Width of window.
40	dy	4	Height of window.
44	wTabRatio	2	Ratio of the width of the workbook tabs to the width of the horizontal scroll bar; to obtain the ratio, convert to decimal and then divide by 1000.
46	grbit1	2	Option flags.
48	grbit2	2	Option flags.
50	wMergeInterval	2	Time interval between automatic merges of shared workbook.
52	(Reserved)	2	
54	st	var	Name of custom view as a unicode string; for more information see "Unicode Strings in BIFF8" on page 264.

The grbit1 field contains the option flags listed in the following table.

Bits	Mask	Name	Contents
0	0001h	fDspFmlaBar	= 1 if the formula bar is displayed
1	0002h	fDspStatus	= 1 if the status bar is displayed

Bits	Mask	Name	Contents
2	0004h	fNoteOff	= 1 if the comment indicator is off
3	0008h	fDspHScroll	= 1 if the horizontal scroll bar is displayed
4	0010h	fDspVScroll	= 1 if the vertical scroll bar is displayed
5	0020h	fBotAdornment	= 1 if the workbook tabs are displayed
6	0040h	fZoom	= 1 if the workbook window is maximized
8–7	0180h	fHideObj	= 10 if the Hide All option is turned on = 01 if the Show Placeholders option is turned on = 00 if the Show All option is turned on
15–9	FE00h	(Reserved)	

The grbit2 field contains the option flags listed in the following table.

Bits	Mask	Name	Contents
15–0	FFFFh	(Reserved)	Reserved; must be 0 (zero)

USERSVIEWBEGIN: Custom View Settings (1AAh)

The USERSVIEWBEGIN record specifies settings for a custom view associated with the sheet. This record also marks the start of custom view records, which save custom view settings. Records between USERSVIEWBEGIN and USERSVIEWEND contain settings for the custom view, not settings for the sheet itself.

Record Data—BIFF8

Offset	Name	Size	Contents
4	guid	16	Globally unique identifier for the custom view
20	iTabid	4	Tab index for the sheet (1-based)
24	wScale	4	Window zoom magnification
28	icv	4	Index to color value
32	pnnSel	4	Pane number of the active pane
36	grbit	4	Option flags
40	refTopLeft	8	Reference structure describing the visible area of the top-left pane (see text)
48	operNum	16	Array of 2 IEEE floating-point numbers that specify the vertical and horizontal positions of the pane split

Offset	Name	Size	Contents
64	colRPane	2	The first visible column of the right pane (=−1 implies no vertical split)
66	rwBPane	2	The first visible of the bottom pane (=−1 implies no horizontal split)

The grbit field contains the option flags listed in the following table.

Bits	Mask	Name	Contents
0	00000001h	fShowBrks	= 1 if page breaks are displayed
1	00000002h	fDspFmlaSv	= 1 if the window should display formulas = 0 if the window should display value
2	00000004h	fDspGridSv	= 1 if the window should display gridlines
3	00000008h	fDspRwColSv	= 1 if the window should display row and column headings
4	00000010h	fDspGutsSv	= 1 if outline symbols are displayed
5	00000020h	fDspZerosSv	= 1 if the window should display 0 (zero) values = 0 if the window should suppress display of 0 (zero) values
6	00000040h	fHorizontal	= 1 if the sheet is to be centered between the horizontal margins when printed
7	00000080h	fVertical	= 1 if the sheet is to be centered between the vertical margins when printed
8	00000100h	fPrintRwCol	= 1 to print row and column headings
9	00000200h	fPrintGrid	= 1 to print gridlines
10	00000400h	fFitToPage	= 1 if the Fit To option is on (Page Setup dialog box, Page tab)
11	00000800h	fPrintArea	= 1 if there is at least one print area on the sheet
12	00001000h	fOnePrintArea	= 1 if there is only one print area on the sheet
13	00002000h	fFilterMode	= 1 if the list is filtered

Bits	Mask	Name	Contents
14	00004000h	fEzFilter	= 1 if AutoFilter is active (the drop-down arrows are displayed)
16–15	00018000h	(Reserved)	
17	00020000h	fSplitV	= 1 if the window is split vertically
18	00040000h	fSplitH	= 1 if the window is split horizontally
20–19	00180000h	fHiddenRw	2 bits true => hidden rws are defined as name
21	00200000h	fHiddenCol	= 1 if there is at least one hidden column on the sheet
23–22	00C00000h	(Reserved)	
24	01000000h	fSizeWithWn	= 1 if the chart is sized with window (chart sheet only)
25	02000000h	fFilterUnique	= 1 if the view contains a filtered list
26	04000000h	fSheetLayoutView	= 1 if the sheet is in page break preview
31–27	F8000000h	(Reserved)	

The sheet view settings are saved using standard BIFF records that occur between the USERSVIEWBEGIN record and the USERSVIEWEND record.

The guid is a unique identifier for a particular custom view for the entire workbook. The same guid can be found on USERSVIEWBEGIN records for other sheets and also in the USERBVIEW record for the workbook.

USERSVIEWEND: End of Custom View Records (1ABh)

The USERSVIEWEND record marks the end of the settings for a custom view associated with the sheet.

Record Data—BIFF8

Offset	Name	Size	Contents
4	fValid	2	= 1 if the view settings saved are valid

The fValid field is 1 if all records from USERSVIEWBEGIN to USERSVIEWEND record are valid. Otherwise it is 0.

USESELFS: Natural Language Formulas Flag (160h)

This record stores a flag bit.

Record Data—BIFF8

Offset	Name	Size	Contents
4	fUsesElfs	2	= 1 if this file was written by a version of Microsoft Excel that can use natural-language formula input

VCENTER: Center Between Vertical Margins (84h)

If the Center On Page Vertically option is on in the Page Setup dialog box, Margins tab, then fVCenter = 1.

Record Data

Offset	Name	Size	Contents
4	fVCenter	2	= 1 if the sheet is to be centered between the vertical margins when printed

VERTICALPAGEBREAKS: Explicit Column Page Breaks (1Ah)

The VERTICALPAGEBREAKS record contains a list of explicit column page breaks.

Record Data—BIFF8

Offset	Name	Size	Contents
4	cbrk	2	Number of page breaks
6	rgbrk	var	Array of brk structures

The cbrk field contains the number of page breaks. Each element of the rgbrk structure contains three 2-byte integers: the first specifies the column of the break, the second specifies the starting row, and the third specifies the ending row for the break. All row and column numbers are 1-based, and the breaks occur after the row or column. This array is sorted by column, and then by starting/ending row. No two page breaks may overlap.

Record Data—BIFF7 and earlier

Offset	Name	Size	Contents
4	cbrk	2	Number of page breaks
6	rgcol	var	Array of columns

The cbrk field contains the number of page breaks. The rgcol field is an array of 2-byte integers that specifies columns. Microsoft Excel sets a page break before each column contained in the list of columns in the rgcol field. The columns must be sorted in ascending order.

WINDOW1: Window Information (3Dh)

The WINDOW1 record contains workbook-level window attributes. The xWn and yWn fields contain the location of the window in units of 1/20th of a point, relative to the upper-left corner of the Microsoft Excel window client area. The dxWn and dyWn fields contain the window size, also in units of 1/20th of a point.

Record Data

Offset	Name	Size	Contents
4	xWn	2	Horizontal position of the window.
6	yWn	2	Vertical position of the window.
8	dxWn	2	Width of the window.
10	dyWn	2	Height of the window.
12	grbit	2	Option flags.
14	itabCur	2	Index of the selected workbook tab (0-based).
16	itabFirst	2	Index of the first displayed workbook tab (0-based).
18	ctabSel	2	Number of workbook tabs that are selected.
20	wTabRatio	2	Ratio of the width of the workbook tabs to the width of the horizontal scroll bar; to obtain the ratio, convert to decimal and then divide by 1000.

The grbit field contains the option flags listed in the following table.

Offset	Bits	Mask	Name	Contents
0	0	01h	fHidden	= 1 if the window is hidden
	1	02h	fIconic	= 1 if the window is currently displayed as an icon
	2	04h	(Reserved)	
	3	08h	fDspHScroll	= 1 if the horizontal scroll bar is displayed
	4	10h	fDspVScroll	= 1 if the vertical scroll bar is displayed
	5	20h	fBotAdornment	= 1 if the workbook tabs are displayed
	7–6	C0h	(Reserved)	
1	7–0	FFh	(Reserved)	

WINDOW2: Sheet Window Information (23Eh)

The WINDOW2 record contains window attributes for a sheet in a workbook.

Record Data—BIFF8

Offset	Name	Size	Contents
4	grbit	2	Option flags
6	rwTop	2	Top row visible in the window
8	colLeft	2	Leftmost column visible in the window
10	icvHdr	4	Index to color value for row/column headings and gridlines
14	wScaleSLV	2	Zoom magnification in page break preview
16	wScaleNormal	2	Zoom magnification in normal view
18	(Reserved)	4	

The grbit field contains the option flags shown in the following table.

Offset	Bits	Mask	Name	Contents
0	0	01h	fDspFmla	= 1 if the window should display formulas = 0 if the window should display value
	1	02h	fDspGrid	= 1 if the window should display gridlines
	2	04h	fDspRwCol	= 1 if the window should display row and column headings
	3	08h	fFrozen	= 1 if the panes in the window should be frozen
	4	10h	fDspZeros	= 1 if the window should display 0 (zero) values = 0 if the window should suppress display of 0 (zero) values
	5	20h	fDefaultHdr	= 1 (see the following explanation) = 0 use rgbHdr color
	6	40h	fArabic	= 1 for the Arabic version of Microsoft Excel
	7	80h	fDspGuts	= 1 if outline symbols are displayed

Offset	Bits	Mask	Name	Contents
1	0	01h	fFrozenNoSplit	= 1 if the panes in the window are frozen but there is no split
	1	02h	fSelected	= 1 if the sheet tab is selected
	2	04h	fPaged	= 1 if the sheet is currently being displayed in the workbook window
	3	08h	fSLV	= 1 if the sheet was saved while in page break preview
	7–4	F0h	(Reserved)	

fDefaultHdr is 1 if the window's row and column headings and gridlines should be drawn in the window's default foreground color. If this field is 0, the color index in the icvHdr field is used instead.

Record Data—BIFF7 and earlier

Offset	Name	Size	Contents
4	grbit	2	Option flags
6	rwTop	2	Top row visible in the window
8	colLeft	2	Leftmost column visible in the window
10	rgbHdr	4	Row/column heading and gridline color

The grbit field contains the option flags shown in the following table.

Offset	Bits	Mask	Name	Contents
0	0	01h	fDspFmla	= 1 if the window should display formulas = 0 if the window should display value
	1	02h	fDspGrid	= 1 if the window should display gridlines
	2	04h	fDspRwCol	= 1 if the window should display row and column headings
	3	08h	fFrozen	= 1 if the panes in the window should be frozen
	4	10h	fDspZeros	= 1 if the window should display 0 (zero) values = 0 if the window should suppress display of 0 (zero) values
	5	20h	fDefaultHdr	= 1 (see the following explanation) = 0 use rgbHdr color
	6	40h	fArabic	= 1 for the Arabic version of Microsoft Excel
	7	80h	fDspGuts	= 1 if outline symbols are displayed

Offset	Bits	Mask	Name	Contents
1	0	01h	fFrozenNoSplit	= 1 if the panes in the window are frozen but there is no split
	1	02h	fSelected	= 1 if the sheet tab is selected
	2	04h	fPaged	= 1 if the sheet is currently being displayed in the workbook window
	7–3	F8h	(Reserved)	

fDefaultHdr is 1 if the window's row and column headings and gridlines should be drawn in the window's default foreground color. If this field is 0, the RGB color in the rgbHdr field is used instead.

WINDOWPROTECT: Windows Are Protected (19h)

The WINDOWPROTECT record stores an option from the Protect Workbook dialog box.

Record Data

Offset	Name	Size	Contents
4	fLockWn	2	= 1 if the workbook windows are protected

WRITEACCESS: Write Access User Name (5Ch)

This record contains the user name, which is the name you type when you install Microsoft Excel.

Record Data—BIFF8

Offset	Name	Size	Contents
4	stName	112	User name as an unformatted unicode string; for more information see "Unicode Strings in BIFF8" on page 264. The name is always padded with spaces so that the size of the stName field is exactly 112 bytes.

Record Data—BIFF7 and earlier

Offset	Name	Size	Contents
4	cch	1	Length of the user name
5	stName	31	User name, padded with spaces (20h) so that the size of the stName field is exactly 31 bytes

WRITEPROT: Workbook Is Write-Protected (86h)

This record is 4 bytes long, and it has no record data field. If the WRITEPROT record is present in the Book stream, it signifies that the worksheet has a Write Reservation password (File menu, Save As command, Options dialog box). For information about the password (wResPass), see "FILESHARING" on page 314.

WSBOOL: Additional Workspace Information (81h)

This record stores information about workspace settings.

Record Data

Offset	Name	Size	Contents
4	grbit	2	Option flags

The grbit field contains the option flags listed in the following table.

Offset	Bits	Mask	Name	Contents
0	0	01h	fShowAutoBreaks	= 1 if automatic page breaks are visible
	3–1	E0h	(Unused)	
	4	10h	fDialog	= 1 if the sheet is a dialog sheet
	5	20h	fApplyStyles	= 0 if automatic styles are applied to an outline
	6	40h	fRwSumsBelow	= 1 if summary rows appear below detail in an outline
	7	80h	fColSumsRight	= 1 if summary columns appear to the right of detail in an outline
1	0	01h	fFitToPage	= 1 if the Fit option is on (Page Setup dialog box, Page tab)
	1	02h	(Reserved)	
	3–2	06h	fDspGuts	= 1 if outline symbols are displayed
	5–4		(Reserved)	
	6		fAee	= 1 if the Alternate Expression Evaluation option is on (Options dialog box, Calculation tab)
	7		fAfe	= 1 if the Alternate Formula Entry option is on (Options dialog box, Calculation tab)

XCT: CRN Record Count (59h)

For BIFF8, an XCT record precedes a CRN record. The XCT and CRN records are grouped with their associated SUPBOOK record.

For BIFF7 and earlier, the XCT record stores the number of CRN records (type 5Ah) in the file. The CRN records immediately follow the XCT record.

Record Data—BIFF8

Offset	Name	Size	Contents
4	ccrn	2	Count of CRN records that follow
6	itab	2	Index (0-based) to sheet tab associated with the CRN record(s)

Record Data—BIFF7 and earlier

Offset	Name	Size	Contents
4	ccrn	2	Count of CRN records that follow

XF: Extended Format (E0h)

The XF record stores formatting properties. There are two different XF records, one for cell records and another for style records. The fStyle bit is true if the XF is a style XF. The ixfe of a cell record (BLANK, LABEL, NUMBER, RK, and so on) points to a *cell* XF record, and the ixfe of a STYLE record points to a *style* XF record. Note that in previous BIFF versions, the record number for the XF record was 43h.

Prior to BIFF5, all number format information was included in FORMAT records in the BIFF file. Beginning with BIFF5, many of the built-in number formats were moved to an internal table and are no longer saved with the file as FORMAT records. You still use the ifmt to associate the built-in number formats with an XF record. However, the internal number formats are no longer visible in the BIFF file.

The following table lists all the number formats that are now maintained internally. Note that 17h through 24h are reserved for international versions and are undocumented at this time.

Index to internal format (ifmt)	Format string
00h	General
01h	0
02h	0.00
03h	#,##0

Index to internal format (ifmt)	Format string
04h	#,##0.00
05h	($#,##0_);($#,##0)
06h	($#,##0_);[Red]($#,##0)
07h	($#,##0.00_);($#,##0.00)
08h	($#,##0.00_);[Red]($#,##0.00)
09h	0%
0ah	0.00%
0bh	0.00E+00
0ch	# ?/?
0dh	# ??/??
0eh	m/d/yy
0fh	d-mmm-yy
10h	d-mmm
11h	mmm-yy
12h	h:mm AM/PM
13h	h:mm:ss AM/PM
14h	h:mm
15h	h:mm:ss
16h	m/d/yy h:mm
25h	(#,##0_);(#,##0)
26h	(#,##0_);[Red](#,##0)
27h	(#,##0.00_);(#,##0.00)
28h	(#,##0.00_);[Red](#,##0.00)
29h	_(* #,##0_);_(* (#,##0);_(* "-"_);_(@_)
2ah	_($* #,##0_);_($* (#,##0);_($* "-"_);_(@_)
2bh	_(* #,##0.00_);_(* (#,##0.00);_(* "-"??_);_(@_)
2ch	_($* #,##0.00_);_($* (#,##0.00);_($* "-"??_);_(@_)
2dh	mm:ss
2eh	[h]:mm:ss
2fh	mm:ss.0
30h	##0.0E+0
31h	@

A BIFF file can contain as many XF records as are necessary to describe the different cell formats and styles in a workbook. The XF records are written in a table in the workbook stream, and the index to the XF record table is a 0-based number called ixfe.

The workbook stream must contain a minimum XF table consisting of 15 style XF records and one cell XF record (ixfe=0 through ixfe=15). The first XF record (ixfe=0) is the XF record for the Normal style. The next 14 records (ixfe=1 through ixfe=14) are XF records that correspond to outline styles RowLevel_1, ColLevel_1, RowLevel_2, ColLevel_2, and so on. The last record (ixfe=15) is the default cell XF for the workbook.

Following these XF records are five additional style XF records (not strictly required) that correspond to the Comma, Comma [0], Currency, Currency [0], and Percent styles.

Cell XF Record—BIFF8

Record Data

Offset	Bits	Mask	Name	Contents
4	15–0	FFFFh	ifnt	Index to the FONT record.
6	15–0	FFFFh	ifmt	Index to the FORMAT record.
8	0	0001h	fLocked	= 1 if the cell is locked.
	1	0002h	fHidden	= 1 if the cell is hidden.
	2	0004h	fStyle	= 0 for cell XF. = 1 for style XF.
	3	0008h	f123Prefix	If the Transition Navigation Keys option is off (Options dialog box, Transition tab), f123Prefix = 1 indicates that a leading apostrophe (single quotation mark) is being used to coerce the cell's contents to a simple string. If the Transition Navigation Keys option is on, f123Prefix = 1 indicates that the cell formula begins with one of the four Lotus 1-2-3 alignment prefix characters: ' left " right ^ centered \ fill

Offset	Bits	Mask	Name	Contents
	15–4	FFF0h	ixfParent	Index to the XF record of the parent style. Every cell XF must have a parent style XF, which is usually ixfeNormal = 0.
10	2–0	0007h	alc	Alignment: 0 = general 1 = left 2 = center 3 = right 4 = fill 5 = justify 6 = center across selection
	3	0008h	fWrap	= 1 wrap text in cell.
	6–4	0070h	alcV	Vertical alignment: 0 = top 1 = center 2 = bottom 3 = justify
	7	0080h	fJustLast	(Used only in Far East versions of Microsoft Excel).
	15–8	FF00h	trot	Rotation, in degrees; 0–90dec is up 0–90 deg., 91–180dec is down 1–90 deg, and 255dec is vertical.
12	3–0	000Fh	cIndent	Indent value (Format Cells dialog box, Alignment tab).
	4	0010h	fShrinkToFit	= 1 if Shrink To Fit option is on (Format Cells dialog box, Alignment tab).
	5	0020h	fMergeCell	= 1 if Merge Cells option is on (Format Cells dialog box, Alignment tab).
	7–6	00C0h	iReadingOrder	Reading direction (Far East versions only): 0 = Context 1 = Left-to-right 2 = Right-to-left
	9–8	0300h	(Reserved)	

Offset	Bits	Mask	Name	Contents
	10	0400h	fAtrNum	= 1 if the ifmt is not equal to the ifmt of the parent style XF.
	11	0800h	fAtrFnt	= 1 if the ifnt is not equal to the ifnt of the parent style XF.
	12	1000h	fAtrAlc	= 1 if either the alc or the fWrap field is not equal to the corresponding field of the parent style XF.
	13	2000h	fAtrBdr	= 1 if any border line field (dgTop, and so on) is not equal to the corresponding field of the parent style XF.
	14	4000h	fAtrPat	= 1 if any pattern field (fls, icvFore, icvBack) is not equal to the corresponding field of the parent style XF.
	15	8000h	fAtrProt	= 1 if either the fLocked field or the fHidden field is not equal to the corresponding field of the parent style XF.
14	3–0	000Fh	dgLeft	Border line style (see the following table).
	7–4	00F0h	dgRight	Border line style (see the following table).
	11–8	0F00h	dgTop	Border line style (see the following table).
	15–12	F000h	dgBottom	Border line style (see the following table).
16	6–0	007Fh	icvLeft	Index to the color palette for the left border color.
	13–7	3F80h	icvRight	Index to the color palette for the right border color.
	15–14	C000h	grbitDiag	1=diag down, 2=diag up, 3=both.
18	6–0	0000007Fh	icvTop	Index to the color palette for the top border color.
	13–7	00003F80h	icvBottom	Index to the color palette for the bottom border color.

Offset	Bits	Mask	Name	Contents
	20–14	001FC000h	icvDiag	for diagonal borders.
	24–21	01E00000h	dgDiag	Border line style (see the following table).
	25	03800000h	(Reserved)	
	31–26	FC000000h	fls	Fill pattern.
22	6–0	007Fh	icvFore	Index to the color palette for the foreground color of thc fill pattern.
	13–7	3F80h	icvBack	Index to the color palette for the background color of the fill pattern.
	14	4000h	fSxButton	= 1 if the XF record is attached to a PivotTable button.
	15	8000h	(Reserved)	

Border Line Styles (BIFF8)

The border line style fields—dgTop, dgLeft, and so on—correspond to the options in the Format Cells dialog box, Border tab, as shown in the following table.

dg* value	Border line style
0h	None
1h	Thin
2h	Medium
3h	Dashed
4h	Dotted
5h	Thick
6h	Double
7h	Hair
8h	Medium dashed
9h	Dash-dot
Ah	Medium dash-dot
Bh	Dash-dot-dot
Ch	Medium dash-dot-dot
Dh	Slanted dash-dot

Style XF Record—BIFF8

The style XF record is identical to the cell XF record, except that some of the fields have slightly different meanings.

Offset	Bits	Mask	Name	Contents
4	15–0	FFFFh	ifnt	Index to the FONT record.
6	15–0	FFFFh	ifmt	Index to the FORMAT record.
8	0	0001h	fLocked	= 1 if the cell is locked.
	1	0002h	fHidden	= 1 if the cell is hidden.
	2	0004h	fStyle	= 0 for cell XF. = 1 for style XF.
	3	0008h	f123Prefix	This bit is always = 0 for style XF.
	15–4	FFF0h	ixfParent	For style XF records, this field equals FFFh (ixfNULL).
10	2–0	0007h	alc	Alignment: 0 = general 1 = left 2 = center 3 = right 4 = fill 5 = justify 6 = center across selection
	3	0008h	fWrap	= 1 wrap text in cell.
	6–4	0070h	alcV	Vertical alignment: 0 = top 1 = center 2 = bottom 3 = justify
	7	0080h	fJustLast	(Used only in Far East versions of Microsoft Excel.)
	15–8	FF00h	trot	Rotation, in degrees; 0–90dec is up 0–90 deg., 91–180dec is down 1–90 deg, and 255dec is vertical.
12	3–0	000Fh	cIndent	Indent value (Format Cells dialog box, Alignment tab).
	4	0010h	fShrinkToFit	= 1 if Shrink To Fit option is on (Format Cells dialog box, Alignment tab).
	5	0020h	fMergeCell	= 1 if Merge Cells option is on (Format Cells dialog box, Alignment tab).

Offset	Bits	Mask	Name	Contents
	7–6	00C0h	iReadingOrder	Reading direction (Far East versions only).
	9–8	0300h	(Reserved)	
	10	0400h	fAtrNum	= 1 if the ifmt is not equal to the ifmt of the parent style XF.
	11	0800h	fAtrFnt	= 1 if the ifnt is not equal to the ifnt of the parent style XF.
	12	1000h	fAtrAlc	= 1 if either the alc or the fWrap field is not equal to the corresponding field of the parent style XF.
	13	2000h	fAtrBdr	= 1 if any border line field (dgTop, and so on) is not equal to the corresponding field of the parent style XF.
	14	4000h	fAtrPat	= 1 if any pattern field (fls, icvFore, icvBack) is not equal to the corresponding field of the parent style XF.
	15	8000h	fAtrProt	= 1 if either the fLocked field or the fHidden field is not equal to the corresponding field of the parent style XF.
14	3–0	000Fh	dgLeft	Border line style (see the following table).
	7–4	00F0h	dgRight	Border line style (see the following table).
	11–8	0F00h	dgTop	Border line style (see the following table).
	15–12	F000h	dgBottom	Border line style (see the following table).
16	6–0	007Fh	icvLeft	Index to the color palette for the left border color.
	13–7	3F80h	icvRight	Index to the color palette for the right border color.
	15–14	C000h	grbitDiag	1=diag down, 2=diag up, 3=both.
18	6–0	0000007Fh	icvTop	Index to the color palette for the top border color.
	13–7	00003F80h	icvBottom	Index to the color palette for the bottom border color.

Offset	Bits	Mask	Name	Contents
	20–14	001FC000h	icvDiag	for diagonal borders.
	24–21	01E00000h	dgDiag	Border line style (see the following table).
	25	03800000h	(Reserved)	
	31–26	FC000000h	fls	Fill pattern.
22	6–0	007Fh	icvFore	Index to the color palette for the foreground color of the fill pattern.
	13–7	3F80h	icvBack	Index to the color palette for the background color of the fill pattern.
	14	4000h	fSxButton	This bit always = 0 for style XF.
	15	8000h	(Reserved)	

Border Line Styles (BIFF8)

The border line style fields—dgTop, dgLeft, and so on—correspond to the options in the Format Cells dialog box, Border tab, as shown in the following table.

dg* value	Border line style
0h	None
1h	Thin
2h	Medium
3h	Dashed
4h	Dotted
5h	Thick
6h	Double
7h	Hair
8h	Medium dashed
9h	Dash-dot
Ah	Medium dash-dot
Bh	Dash-dot-dot
Ch	Medium dash-dot-dot
Dh	Slanted dash-dot

Cell XF Record—BIFF7 and earlier

Record Data

Offset	Bits	Mask	Name	Contents
4	15–0	FFFFh	ifnt	Index to the FONT record.
6	15–0	FFFFh	ifmt	Index to the FORMAT record.
8	0	0001h	fLocked	= 1 if the cell is locked.
	1	0002h	fHidden	= 1 if the cell is hidden.
	2	0004h	fStyle	= 0 for cell XF. = 1 for style XF.
	3	0008h	f123Prefix	If the Transition Navigation Keys option is off (Options dialog box, Transition tab), f123Prefix = 1 indicates that a leading apostrophe (single quotation mark) is being used to coerce the cell's contents to a simple string. If the Transition Navigation Keys option is on, f123Prefix = 1 indicates that the cell formula begins with one of the four Lotus 1-2-3 alignment prefix characters: ' left " right ^ centered \ fill
	15–4	FFF0h	ixfParent	Index to the XF record of the parent style. Every cell XF must have a parent style XF, which is usually ixfeNormal = 0.
10	2–0	0007h	alc	Alignment: 0 = general 1 = left 2 = center 3 = right 4 = fill 5 = justify 6 = center across selection
	3	0008h	fWrap	= 1 wrap text in cell.

Offset	Bits	Mask	Name	Contents
10	6–4	0070h	alcV	Vertical alignment: 0 = top 1 = center 2 = bottom 3 = justify
	7	0080h	fJustLast	(Used only in Far East versions of Microsoft Excel.)
	9–8	0300h	ori	Orientation of text in cell: = 0 no rotation. = 1 text appears top-to-bottom; letters are upright. = 2 text is rotated 90 degrees counterclockwise. = 3 text is rotated 90 degrees clockwise.
	10	0400h	fAtrNum	= 1 if the ifmt is not equal to the ifmt of the parent style XF.
	11	0800h	fAtrFnt	= 1 if the ifnt is not equal to the ifnt of the parent style XF.
	12	1000h	fAtrAlc	= 1 if either the alc or the fWrap field is not equal to the corresponding field of the parent style XF.
	13	2000h	fAtrBdr	= 1 if any border line field (dgTop, and so on) is not equal to the corresponding field of the parent style XF.
	14	4000h	fAtrPat	= 1 if any pattern field (fls, icvFore, icvBack) is not equal to the corresponding field of the parent style XF.
	15	8000h	fAtrProt	= 1 if either the fLocked field or the fHidden field is not equal to the corresponding field of the parent style XF.
12	6–0	007Fh	icvFore	Index to the color palette for the foreground color of the fill pattern.
	12–7	1F80h	icvBack	Index to the color palette for the background color of the fill pattern.
	13	2000h	fSxButton	= 1 if the XF record is attached to a PivotTable button.
	15–14	C000h	(Reserved)	

Offset	Bits	Mask	Name	Contents
14	5–0	003Fh	fls	Fill pattern.
	8–6	01C0h	dgBottom	Border line style (see the following table).
	15–9	FE00h	icvBottom	Index to the color palette for the bottom border color.
16	2–0	0007h	dgTop	Border line style (see the following table).
	5–3	0038h	dgLeft	Border line style (see the following table).
	8–6	01C0h	dgRight	Border line style (see the following table).
	15–9	FE00h	icvTop	Index to the color palette for the top border color.
18	6–0	007Fh	icvLeft	Index to the color palette for the left border color.
	13–7	3F80h	icvRight	Index to the color palette for the right border color.
	15–14	C000h	(Reserved)	

Border Line Styles (BIFF7)

The border line style fields—dgTop, dgLeft, and so on—correspond to the options in the Format Cells dialog box, Border tab, as shown in the following table.

dg* value	Border line style
0h	None
1h	Thin
2h	Medium
3h	Dashed
4h	Dotted
5h	Thick
6h	Double
7h	Hair

Style XF Record—BIFF7 and earlier

The style XF record is identical to the cell XF record, except that some of the fields have slightly different meanings.

Record Data

Offset	Bits	Mask	Name	Contents
4	15–0	FFFFh	ifnt	Index to the FONT record.
6	15–0	FFFFh	ifmt	Index to the FORMAT record.
8	0	0001h	fLocked	= 1 if the cell is locked.
	1	0002h	fHidden	= 1 if the cell is hidden.
	2	0004h	fStyle	= 0 for cell XF. = 1 for style XF.
	3	0008h	f123Prefix	This bit is always = 0 for style XF.
	15–4	FFF0h	ixfParent	For style XF records, this field equals FFFh (ixfNULL).
10	2–0	0007h	alc	Alignment: 0 = general 1 = left 2 = center 3 = right 4 = fill 5 = justify 6 = center across selection
	3	0008h	fWrap	= 1 wrap text in cell.
	6–4	0070h	alcV	Vertical alignment: 0 = top 1 = center 2 = bottom 3 = justify
	7	0080h	fJustLast	(Used only in Far East versions of Microsoft Excel.)
	9–8	0300h	ori	Orientation of text in cell: = 0 no rotation. = 1 text appears top-to-bottom; letters are upright. = 2 text is rotated 90 degrees counterclockwise. = 3 text is rotated 90 degrees clockwise.

Offset	Bits	Mask	Name	Contents
	10	0400h	fAtrNum	= 0 if the style includes Number (Style dialog box).
	11	0800h	fAtrFnt	= 0 if the style includes Font (Style dialog box).
	12	1000h	fAtrAlc	= 0 if the style includes Alignment (Style dialog box).
	13	2000h	fAtrBdr	= 0 if the style includes Border (Style dialog box).
	14	4000h	fAtrPat	= 0 if the style includes Patterns (shading) (Style dialog box).
	15	8000h	fAtrProt	= 0 if the style includes Protection (cell protection) (Style dialog box).
12	6–0	007Fh	icvFore	Index to the color palette for the foreground color of the fill pattern.
	12–7	1F80h	icvBack	Index to the color palette for the background color of the fill pattern.
	13	2000h	fSxButton	This bit always = 0 for style XF.
	15–14	C000h	(Reserved)	
14	5–0	003Fh	fls	Fill pattern.
	8–6	01C0h	dgBottom	Border line style (see the following table).
	15–9	FE00h	icvBottom	Index to the color palette for the bottom border color.
16	2–0	0007h	dgTop	Border line style (see the following table).
	5–3	0038h	dgLeft	Border line style (see the following table).
	8–6	01C0h	dgRight	Border line style (see the following table).
	15–9	FE00h	icvTop	Index to the color palette for the top border color.
18	6–0	007Fh	icvLeft	Index to the color palette for the left border color.
	13–7	3F80h	icvRight	Index to the color palette for the right border color.
	15–14	C000h	(reserved)	

Border Line Styles (BIFF7)

The border line style fields—dgTop, dgLeft, and so on—correspond to the options in the Format Cells dialog box, Border tab, as shown in the following table.

dg* value	Border line style
0h	None
1h	Thin
2h	Medium
3h	Dashed
4h	Dotted
5h	Thick
6h	Double
7h	Hair

XL5MODIFY: Flag for DSF (162h)

This is a new record in BIFF8. In a double stream file, the XL5MODIFY record appears in the BIFF5/BIFF7 stream (the stream named Book). This record is used internally and contains no record data field.

Finding Cell Records in BIFF Files

Microsoft Excel uses the INDEX and DBCELL records to optimize the lookup of cell records (RK, FORMULA, and so on). You can use these records to optimize your code when reading a BIFF file, or you can just read the entire workbook stream to find the cell values you want. The unoptimized method may be slower, depending on the size, structure, and complexity of the file.

If your code writes a BIFF file, you must include the INDEX and DBCELL records with correct values in the record fields. If you do not do this, Microsoft Excel will not be able to optimize lookup, and the program's performance will suffer, especially when the user tries to copy data out of the file that your application has written.

Microsoft Excel stores cell records in blocks that have at most 32 rows. Each row that contains cell records has a corresponding ROW record in the block, and each block contains a DBCELL record at the end of the block.

The following illustration shows how to use the INDEX record to locate the DBCELL records at the end of the record blocks. Notice that the stream position at the start of the first BOF record in the workbook stream is 6F1h. To find the start of each DBCELL record, add this number to each member of the rgibRw array in the INDEX record.

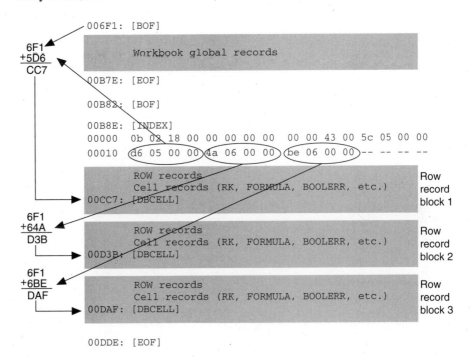

After your code has computed the location of the DBCELL records, you can use the dbRtrw field to find the location of the start of the first ROW record for each block. This field is stored as a positive long integer, although the offset is really a "negative" offset to an earlier position in the file. See the following illustration for details.

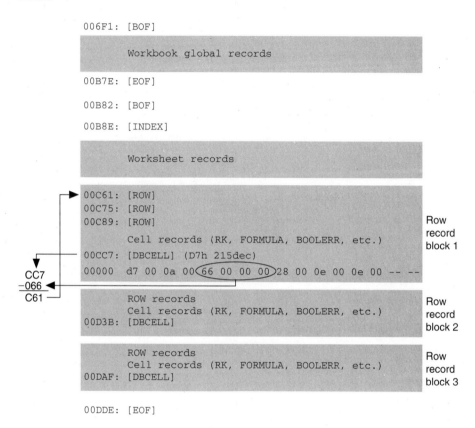

```
006F1: [BOF]

          Workbook global records

00B7E: [EOF]

00B82: [BOF]

00B8E: [INDEX]

          Worksheet records

00C61: [ROW]
00C75: [ROW]                                        Row
00C89: [ROW]                                        record
          Cell records (RK, FORMULA, BOOLERR, etc.)  block 1
00CC7: [DBCELL] (D7h 215dec)
00000  d7 00 0a 00 66 00 00 00 28 00 0e 00 0e 00 -- --

          ROW records
          Cell records (RK, FORMULA, BOOLERR, etc.)  Row
00D3B: [DBCELL]                                      record
                                                     block 2

          ROW records
          Cell records (RK, FORMULA, BOOLERR, etc.)  Row
00DAF: [DBCELL]                                      record
                                                     block 3

00DDE: [EOF]
```

```
 CC7
-066
 C61
```

Finally, your code can compute the start of each cell record in the block by using the members in the rgdb array in the DBCELL record. The offsets in this array use the start of the second ROW record in the block as the initial offset. This is because the code has to read the first ROW record to know what the row number is (and then to make a decision based on the row number), and the stream pointer is at the start of the second ROW record after this. See the following illustration for details.

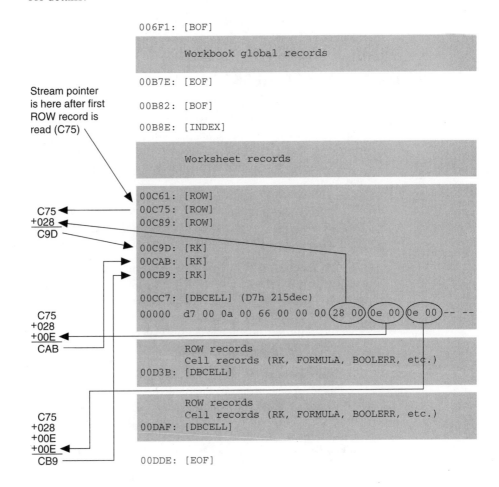

Microsoft Excel Formulas

This section describes how Microsoft Excel stores formulas. Formulas most commonly appear in rgce fields in FORMULA, ARRAY, and NAME records. In this section, *formula* is a synonym for *parsed expression,* which is the internal tokenized representation of a Microsoft Excel formula.

There are no changes to the tokenized representation of a Microsoft Excel formula from BIFF5 to BIFF7; therefore this information applies to both versions.

Parsed Expressions and Tokens

Microsoft Excel uses a modified reverse-Polish technique to store parsed expressions. A parsed expression contains a sequence of parse tokens, each of which is either an operand, an operator token, or a control token. Operand tokens push operands onto the stack. Operator tokens perform arithmetic operations on operands. Control tokens assist in formula evaluation by describing properties of the formula.

A token consists of two parts: a token type and a token value. A token type is called a *ptg* (parse thing) in Microsoft Excel. A ptg is 1 byte long and has a value from 01h to 7Fh. The ptgs above 7Fh are reserved.

The ptg specifies only what kind of information a token contains. The information itself is stored in the token value, which immediately follows the ptg. Some tokens consist of only a ptg, without an accompanying token value. For example, to specify an addition operation, only the token type ptgAdd is required. But to specify an integer operand, you must specify both ptgInt and the token value, which is an integer.

For example, assume that the formula =5+6 is in cell A1. The parsed expression for this formula consists of three tokens: two integer operand tokens (<token 1> and <token 2>) and an operator token (<token 3>), as shown in the following table.

<token 1>	<token 2>	<token 3>
ptgInt 0005h	ptgInt 0006h	ptgAdd

Notice that each ptgInt is immediately followed by the integer token value.

If you type this formula in cell A1 and then examine the FORMULA record (using the BiffView utility), you'll see the following:

```
00000   06 00 1d 00 00 00 00 00 0f 00 00 00 00 00 00 00
00010   26 40 00 00 00 00 e0 fc 07 00 1e 05 00 1e 06 00
00020   03 -- -- -- -- -- -- -- -- -- -- -- -- -- -- --
```

The first 26 bytes of the hex dump contain the record number, record length, rw, col, ixfe, num, grbit, chn, and ccc fields. The remaining 7 bytes contain the two ptgInt (1Eh) tokens—which contain the token values that represent the integers 5 and 6 (0005h and 0006h)—and the ptgAdd (03h) token. If the formula were changed to =5*6, the third token would be ptgMul (05h). For more information about the FORMULA record, see "FORMULA" on page 317.

In many cases, the token value consists of a structure of two or more fields. In these cases, offset-0 (zero) is assumed to be the first byte of the token value—that is, the first byte immediately following the token type.

Microsoft Excel ptgs

The following table contains all ptgs that appear in BIFF files. All other ptgs are reserved.

The ptgSheet and ptgEndSheet tokens are no longer used. The external sheet references are contained in the ptgNameX, ptgRef3d, and ptgArea3d tokens.

Name	Ptg	Type
ptgExp	01h	control
ptgTbl	02h	control
ptgAdd	03h	operator
ptgSub	04h	operator
ptgMul	05h	operator
ptgDiv	06h	operator
ptgPower	07h	operator
ptgConcat	08h	operator
ptgLT	09h	operator
ptgLE	0Ah	operator
ptgEQ	0Bh	operator
ptgGE	0Ch	operator
ptgGT	0Dh	operator
ptgNE	0Eh	operator

Name	Ptg	Type
ptgIsect	0Fh	operator
ptgUnion	10h	operator
ptgRange	11h	operator
ptgUplus	12h	operator
ptgUminus	13h	operator
ptgPercent	14h	operator
ptgParen	15h	control
ptgMissArg	16h	operand
ptgStr	17h	operand
ptgAttr	19h	control
ptgSheet	1Ah	(ptg DELETED)
ptgEndSheet	1Bh	(ptg DELETED)
ptgErr	1Ch	operand
ptgBool	1Dh	operand
ptgInt	1Eh	operand
ptgNum	1Fh	operand
ptgArray	20h	operand, reference class
ptgFunc	21h	operator
ptgFuncVar	22h	operator
ptgName	23h	operand, reference class
ptgRef	24h	operand, reference class
ptgArea	25h	operand, reference class
ptgMemArea	26h	operand, reference class
ptgMemErr	27h	operand, reference class
ptgMemNoMem	28h	control
ptgMemFunc	29h	control
ptgRefErr	2Ah	operand, reference class
ptgAreaErr	2Bh	operand, reference class
ptgRefN	2Ch	operand, reference class
ptgAreaN	2Dh	operand, reference class
ptgMemAreaN	2Eh	control
ptgMemNoMemN	2Fh	control
ptgNameX	39h	operand, reference class
ptgRef3d	3Ah	operand, reference class

Name	Ptg	Type
ptgArea3d	3Bh	operand, reference class
ptgRefErr3d	3Ch	operand, reference class
ptgAreaErr3d	3Dh	operand, reference class
ptgArrayV	40h	operand, value class
ptgFuncV	41h	operator
ptgFuncVarV	42h	operator
ptgNameV	43h	operand, value class
ptgRefV	44h	operand, value class
ptgAreaV	45h	operand, value class
ptgMemAreaV	46h	operand, value class
ptgMemErrV	47h	operand, value class
ptgMemNoMemV	48h	control
ptgMemFuncV	49h	control
ptgRefErrV	4Ah	operand, value class
ptgAreaErrV	4Bh	operand, value class
ptgRefNV	4Ch	operand, value class
ptgAreaNV	4Dh	operand, value class
ptgMemAreaNV	4Eh	control
ptgMemNoMemNV	4Fh	control
ptgFuncCEV	58h	operator
ptgNameXV	59h	operand, value class
ptgRef3dV	5Ah	operand, value class
ptgArea3dV	5Bh	operand, value class
ptgRefErr3dV	5Ch	operand, value class
ptgAreaErr3dV	5Dh	operand, value class
ptgArrayA	60h	operand, array class
ptgFuncA	61h	operator
ptgFuncVarA	62h	operator
ptgNameA	63h	operand, array class
ptgRefA	64h	operand, array class
ptgAreaA	65h	operand, array class
ptgMemAreaA	66h	operand, array class
ptgMemErrA	67h	operand, array class

Name	Ptg	Type
ptgMemNoMemA	68h	control
ptgMemFuncA	69h	control
ptgRefErrA	6Ah	operand, array class
ptgAreaErrA	6Bh	operand, array class
ptgRefNA	6Ch	operand, array class
ptgAreaNA	6Dh	operand, array class
ptgMemAreaNA	6Eh	control
ptgMemNoMemNA	6Fh	control
ptgFuncCEA	78h	operator
ptgNameXA	79h	operand, array class (NEW ptg)
ptgRef3dA	7Ah	operand, array class (NEW ptg)
ptgArea3dA	7Bh	operand, array class (NEW ptg)
ptgRefErr3dA	7Ch	operand, array class (NEW ptg)
ptgAreaErr3dA	7Dh	operand, array class (NEW ptg)

Extended ptgs in BIFF8

In BIFF8, expended ptgs are used to store natural-language formulas. These ptgs contain a ptgExtend (ptg = 18h), followed by a 1-byte extended ptg type, called an eptg, and then followed by extended data if applicable. Extended ptgs are listed in the following table.

Eptg	Eptg Type	Size	Extended info?	Operand Type
0h	Reserved			
1h	eptgElfLel	4	No	Error
2h	eptgElfRw	4	No	Reference
3h	eptgElfCol	4	No	Reference
4h–5h	Reserved			
6h	eptgElfRwV	4	No	Value
7h	eptgElfColV	4	No	Value
8h–9h	Reserved			
Ah	eptgElfRadical	13	No	Reference
Bh	eptgElfRadicalS	13	Yes	Reference
Ch	eptgElfRwS	4	Yes	Reference
Dh	eptgElfColS	4	Yes	Reference
Eh	eptgElfRwSV	4	Yes	Value

Eptg	Eptg Type	Size	Extended info?	Operand Type
Fh	eptgElfColSV	4	Yes	Value
10h	eptgElfRadicalLel	4	No	Error
11h–18h	Reserved			
19h–1Ah	Invalid values			
1Bh	Reserved			
1Ch	Reserved			
1Dh	eptgSxName	4	No	Value
1Eh	Reserved			

The data contained in eptgs is not documented.

For eptgs that have extended info, the extra information is appended to the saved parsed expression, immediately following the last token. The format of the extra information is as follows:

1. First 4 bytes: the lowest 30 bits of these bytes is the count (cLoc) of 4-byte structures following these 4 bytes.

2. The next 4*cLoc bytes are reserved.

As with array constants, if a formula contains more than one eptg with extended information, the token values for the eptgs are appended to the saved parsed expression in order: first the values for the first eptg, then the values for the second eptg, and so on.

Likewise, an expression containing both eptgs and array constants will append the eptg and array constant data in the order that they occur in the parsed expression.

Expression Evaluation

Calculation of Microsoft Excel formulas is a straightforward process. A last-in, first-out (LIFO) stack, the operand stack, is maintained during calculation. When an operand is encountered, it's pushed onto the stack. When an operator is encountered, it operates on the topmost operand or operands. Operator precedence is irrelevant at evaluation time; operators are handled as soon as they're encountered.

There are three kinds of operators: unary, binary, and function. Unary operators, such as the minus sign that negates a number, operate only on the top operand. Binary operators, such as the addition operator, operate on the top two operands. Function operators, which implement Microsoft Excel functions, operate on a variable number of operands, depending on how many arguments the function accepts.

All operators work by popping the required operands from the stack, performing calculations, and then pushing the result back onto the operand stack.

Scanning a Parsed Expression

One fairly common operation you can perform on parsed expressions is to scan them, taking appropriate actions at each ptg. You can do this with a loop by using a pointer variable that points to the next ptg to scan. However, you must increment this pointer carefully, because different ptgs may have token values of different lengths.

One approach is to maintain an array with one element per ptg. Each element contains the size of the token value. To increment the pointer, add the array element corresponding to the current ptg to the pointer. One way of reducing the array size is to limit the array indexes to the range 0–3Fh and then index it using the reference-class ptg (the base ptg) instead of the value-class or array-class ptg. This is possible because the token value is the same for all classes of a particular ptg. For more information about operand classes, see "ptg Values for Operand Tokens" on page 454.

There are two tokens, ptgStr and ptgAttr (when bitFAttrChoose is true), that have variable length and are therefore exceptions to the preceding description. The first token, ptgStr, is followed by a variable-length string. The token value specifies the length of the string, so the pointer can be incremented by reading the string length (cch) and then adding the string length to the pointer.

The other token is ptgAttr when bitFAttrChoose is true. In this case, the token value contains an optimized CHOOSE function, which contains a variable-length sequence of word offsets in the cases (value1, value2, ... arguments) for the CHOOSE function. For these, you can use the wCases field to calculate the pointer increment.

Unary Operator Tokens

The unary operator tokens for Microsoft Excel are described in the following paragraphs. These operators pop the top argument from the operand stack, perform a calculation, and then push the result back onto the operand stack.

ptgUplus: Unary Plus (ptg = 12h)

Has no effect on the operand.

ptgUminus: Unary Minus (ptg = 13h)

Negates the operand on the top of the stack.

ptgPercent: Percent Sign (ptg = 14h)

Divides the top operand by 100.

Binary Operator Tokens

There are several binary operator ptgs. All binary operator ptgs pop the top two arguments from the operand stack, perform the associated calculation, and then push the result back onto the operand stack.

ptgAdd: Addition (ptg = 03h)

Adds the top two operands.

ptgSub: Subtraction (ptg = 04h)

Subtracts the top operand from the second-to-top operand.

ptgMul: Multiplication (ptg = 05h)

Multiplies the top two operands.

ptgDiv: Division (ptg = 06h)

Divides the top operand by the second-to-top operand.

ptgPower: Exponentiation (ptg = 07h)

Raises the second-to-top operand to the power of the top operand.

ptgConcat: Concatenation (ptg = 08h)

Appends the top operand to the second-to-top operand.

ptgLT: Less Than (ptg = 09h)

Evaluates to TRUE if the second-to-top operand is less than the top operand; evaluates to FALSE otherwise.

ptgLE: Less Than or Equal (ptg = 0Ah)

Evaluates to TRUE if the second-to-top operand is less than or equal to the top operand; evaluates to FALSE otherwise.

ptgEQ: Equal (ptg = 0Bh)

Evaluates to TRUE if the top two operands are equal; evaluates to FALSE otherwise.

ptgGE: Greater Than or Equal (ptg = 0Ch)

Evaluates to TRUE if the second-to-top operand is greater than or equal to the top operand; evaluates to FALSE otherwise.

ptgGT: Greater Than (ptg = 0Dh)

Evaluates to TRUE if the second-to-top operand is greater than the top operand; evaluates to FALSE otherwise.

ptgNE: Not Equal (ptg = 0Eh)

Evaluates to TRUE if the top two operands are not equal; evaluates to FALSE otherwise.

ptgIsect: Intersection (ptg = 0Fh)

Computes the intersection of the top two operands. This is the Microsoft Excel space operator.

ptgUnion: Union (ptg = 10h)

Computes the union of the top two operands. This is the Microsoft Excel comma operator.

ptgRange: Range (ptg = 11h)

Computes the minimal bounding rectangle of the top two operands. This is the Microsoft Excel colon operator.

Operand Tokens: Constant

These operand tokens push a single constant operand onto the operand stack.

ptgMissArg: Missing Argument (Operand, ptg = 16h)

Indicates a missing argument to a Microsoft Excel function. For example, the second (missing) argument to the function DCOUNT(Database,,Criteria) would be stored as a ptgMissArg.

ptgStr: String Constant (Operand, ptg = 17h)

Indicates a string constant ptg followed by a string length field (00 to FFh) and the actual string.

Offset	Name	Size	Contents
0	cch	1	The length of the string
1	rgch	var	The string

ptgStr requires special handling when parsed expressions are scanned. For more information, see "Scanning a Parsed Expression" on page 450.

In BIFF8, the rgch contains a unicode string. For more information, see "Unicode Strings in BIFF8" on page 264.

ptgErr: Error Value (Operand, ptg = 1Ch)

This ptg is followed by the 1-byte error value (err). For a list of error values, see "BOOLERR" on page 290.

Offset	Name	Size	Contents
0	err	1	An error value

ptgBool: Boolean (Operand, ptg = 1Dh)

This ptg is followed by a byte that represents TRUE or FALSE.

Offset	Name	Size	Contents
0	f	1	= 1 for TRUE = 0 for FALSE

ptgInt: Integer (Operand, ptg = 1Eh)

This ptg is followed by a word that contains an unsigned integer.

Offset	Name	Size	Contents
0	w	2	An unsigned integer value

ptgNum: Number (Operand, ptg = 1Fh)

This ptg is followed by an 8-byte IEEE floating-point number.

Offset	Name	Size	Contents
0	num	8	An IEEE floating-point number

Operand Tokens

Operand tokens push operand values onto the operand stack. These values fall into one of three classes—reference class, value class, or array class—depending on what type of value the formula expects from the operand. The type of value is determined by the context of the operand when the formula is parsed by Microsoft Excel.

Reference Class

Some operands are required by context to evaluate to references. In this case, the term *reference* is a general term meaning one or more areas on a Microsoft Excel worksheet.

When the Microsoft Excel expression evaluator encounters a reference class operand, it pushes only the reference itself onto the operand stack; it doesn't de-reference it to return the underlying value or values. For example, the function CELL("width",B5) pushes the reference class operand ptgRef (24h) for the second argument. This function returns the column width of cell B5; therefore, only the reference to B5 is required, and there's no need to de-reference to the value stored in cell B5.

Value Class

This is the most common type of operand. Value class operands push a single de-referenced value onto the operand stack. For example, the formula =A1+1 pushes a value class operand ptgRefV (44h) for the cell reference A1.

Array Class

This operand pushes an array of values onto the operand stack. You can specify the values in an array constant or in a reference to cells. For example, the formula =SUM({1,2,3;4,5,6}) pushes an array class ptgArrayA (60h) to represent the arguments to the function.

ptg Values for Operand Tokens

The three classes of operand tokens are divided numerically, as shown in the following table.

Operand class	Ptg values
Reference	20h–3Fh
Value	40h–5Fh
Array	60h–7Fh

The arithmetic difference between ptg classes is 20h. This is the basis for forming the class variants of ptgs. Class variants of ptgs are formed from the reference class ptg, also known as the base ptg. To form the value class ptg from the base ptg, add 20h to the ptg and append V (for "value") to the ptg name. To form the array class ptg from the base ptg, add 40h to the ptg and append A (for "array") to the ptg name. These rules are summarized in the following table for a sample base ptg, ptgRef.

Class	Name	Ptg
Reference	ptgRef	24h
Value	ptgRefV	44h
Array	ptgRefA	64h

The following example is a suggested method for calculating the base ptg from any class variant.

```
if (ptg & 40h)
    {
    /* Value class ptg. Set the 20h bit to
       make it Reference class, then strip
       off the high-order bits. */
    ptgBase = (ptg | 20h) & 3Fh;
    }
else
    {
    /* Reference or Array class ptg. The 20h bit
       is already set, so just have to strip off
       the high-order bits. */
    ptgBase = ptg & 3Fh;
    }
```

A more efficient implementation would define a macro that computes the base ptg, as in the following example.

```
#define PtgBase(ptg) (((ptg & 0x40) ? (ptg | 0x20): ptg) & 0x3F)
```

Operand Tokens: Base

This section describes the operand tokens in their base form (also known as reference class operand tokens).

ptgArray: Array Constant (Operand, ptg = 20h)

Array constant followed by 7 reserved bytes.

The token value for ptgArray consists of the array dimensions and the array values. ptgArray differs from most other operand tokens in that the token value doesn't follow the token type. Instead, the token value is appended to the saved parsed expression, immediately following the last token. The format of the token value is shown in the following table.

Offset	Name	Size	Contents
0	ccol	1	The number of columns in the array constant
1	crw	2	The number of rows in the array constant
3	rgval	var	The array values

An array with 256 columns is stored with a ccol = 0, because a single byte cannot store the integer 256. This is unambiguous, because a 0-column array constant is meaningless.

The number of values in the array constant is equal to the product of the array dimensions, crw*ccol. Each value is either an 8-byte IEEE floating-point number or a string. The two formats for these values are shown in the following tables.

IEEE Floating-Point Number

Offset	Name	Size	Contents
0	grbit	1	= 01h
1	num	8	IEEE floating-point number

String

Offset	Name	Size	Contents
0	grbit	1	= 02h
1	cch	1	The length of the string
2	rgch	var	The string

If a formula contains more than one array constant, the token values for the array constants are appended to the saved parsed expression in order: first the values for the first array constant, then the values for the second array constant, and so on.

If a formula contains very long array constants, the FORMULA, ARRAY, or NAME record containing the parsed expression may overflow into CONTINUE records (to accommodate all of the array values). In such cases, an individual array value is never split between records, but record boundaries are established between adjacent array values.

The reference class ptgArray never appears in a Microsoft Excel formula; only the ptgArrayV and ptgArrayA classes are used.

ptgName: Name (Operand, ptg = 23h)—BIFF8

This ptg stores the index to a name. The ilbl field is a 1-based index to the table of NAME records in the workbook.

Offset	Name	Size	Contents
0	ixti	2	
2	ilbl	2	Index to the NAME table
4	(reserved)	2	Reserved; must be 0 (zero)

ptgName: Name (Operand, ptg = 23h)—BIFF7 and earlier

This ptg stores the index to a name. The ilbl field is a 1-based index to the table of NAME records in the workbook.

Offset	Name	Size	Contents
0	ilbl	2	Index to the NAME table
2	(reserved)	12	Reserved; must be 0 (zero)

ptgRef: Cell Reference (Operand, ptg = 24h)—BIFF8

This ptg specifies a reference to a single cell. It's followed by references for the row and column that contain the cell. The column number is encoded.

Offset	Name	Size	Contents
0	rw	2	The column of the reference
2	grbitCol	2	(See the following table)

Only the low-order 14 bits of the grbitCol field store the column number of the reference. The 2 MSBs specify whether the row and column references are relative or absolute. The following table shows the bit structure of the grbitCol field.

Bits	Mask	Name	Contents
15	8000h	fRwRel	= 1 if the row offset is relative = 0 otherwise
14	4000h	fColRel	= 1 if the column offset is relative = 0 otherwise
13–0	3FFFh	col	The column number or column offset (0-based)

For example, cell C5 is row number 4, column number 2 (Microsoft Excel stores 0-based cell references). Therefore, the absolute reference $C$5 is stored in a ptgRef, as shown in the following file fragment.

```
24 04 00 02 00
```

In this case, rw = 0004h and grbitCol = 0002h. Notice that bits 14 and 15 of grbitCol are both 0 (zero).

The relative reference C5 is stored in a ptgRef, as shown in the following file fragment.

```
24 04 00 02 C0
```

In this case, where grbitCol = C004h and col = 02h, bits 14 and 15 of grbitCol are both 1.

Mixed references are stored in the same way, with appropriate coding in grbitCol.

ptgRef: Cell Reference (Operand, ptg = 24h)—BIFF7 and earlier

This ptg specifies a reference to a single cell. It's followed by references for the row and column that contain the cell. The row number is encoded.

Offset	Name	Size	Contents
0	grbitRw	2	(See the following table)
2	col	1	The column of the reference

Only the low-order 14 bits of the grbitRw field store the row number of the reference. The 2 MSBs specify whether the row and column references are relative or absolute. The following table shows the bit structure of the grbitRw field.

Bits	Mask	Name	Contents
15	8000h	fRwRel	= 1 if the row offset is relative = 0 otherwise
14	4000h	fColRel	= 1 if the column offset is relative = 0 otherwise
13–0	3FFFh	rw	The row number or row offset (0-based)

For example, cell C5 is row number 4, column number 2 (Microsoft Excel stores 0-based cell references). Therefore, the absolute reference $C$5 is stored in a ptgRef, as shown in the following file fragment.

```
24 04 00 02
```

In this case, grbitRw = 0004h and col = 02h. Notice that bits 14 and 15 of grbitRw are both 0 (zero).

The relative reference C5 is stored in a ptgRef, as shown in the following file fragment.

```
24 04 C0 02
```

In this case, where grbitRw = C004h and col = 02h, bits 14 and 15 of grbitRw are both 1.

Mixed references are stored in the same way, with appropriate coding in grbitRw.

ptgArea: Area Reference (Operand, ptg = 25h)—BIFF8

This ptg specifies a reference to a rectangle (range) of cells. ptgArea is followed by 8 bytes that define the first row, last row, first column, and last column of the rectangle. The numbers of the first and last columns are encoded.

Offset	Name	Size	Contents
0	rwFirst	2	The first row of the reference
2	rwLast	2	The last row of the reference
4	grbitColFirst	2	(See the following table)
6	grbitColLast	2	(See the following table)

Only the low-order 14 bits of the grbitColFirst and grbitColLast fields store the column offsets of the reference. The 2 MSBs of each field specify whether the row and column offset are relative or absolute. The following table shows the bit structure of the grbitColFirst and grbitColLast fields.

Bits	Mask	Name	Contents
15	8000h	fRwRel	= 1 if the row offset is relative = 0 otherwise
14	4000h	fColRel	= 1 if the column offset is relative = 0 otherwise
13–0	3FFFh	col	The column number or column offset (0-based)

ptgArea: Area Reference (Operand, ptg = 25h)—BIFF7 and earlier

This ptg specifies a reference to a rectangle (range) of cells. ptgArea is followed by 6 bytes that define the first row, last row, first column, and last column of the rectangle. The numbers of the first and last rows are encoded.

Offset	Name	Size	Contents
0	grbitRwFirst	2	(See the following table)
2	grbitRwLast	2	(See the following table)
4	colFirst	1	The first column of the reference
5	colLast	1	The last column of the reference

Only the low-order 14 bits of the grbitRwFirst and grbitRwLast fields store the row offsets of the reference. The 2 MSBs of each field specify whether the row and column offset are relative or absolute. The following table shows the bit structure of the grbitRwFirst and grbitRwLast fields.

Bits	Mask	Name	Contents
15	8000h	fRwRel	= 1 if the row offset is relative = 0 otherwise
14	4000h	fColRel	= 1 if the column offset is relative = 0 otherwise
13–0	3FFFh	rw	The row number or row offset (0-based)

ptgMemArea: Constant Reference Subexpression (Operand, ptg = 26h)

This ptg is used to optimize reference expressions. A reference expression consists of operands—usually references to cells or areas—joined by reference operators (intersection, union, and range). Three examples of reference expressions are given in the following table.

Reference expression	Evaluates to
(A1,C3,D3:D5)	Two single cells and a 3x1 area
(A1:C3) (B2:D4)	A 2x2 area (the space character is the intersection operator)
(Name C3)	The smallest area that contains both C3 and all the cells referenced in Name (the space character is the intersection operator)

Many reference expressions evaluate to constant references. In the preceding examples, the first two expressions always evaluate to the same reference. The third example doesn't evaluate to a constant reference because the name's definition may change, which might cause the reference expression to evaluate differently.

When a reference expression evaluates to a constant reference, Microsoft Excel stores the constant reference in the parsed formula through a ptgMemArea token. This saves time during expression evaluation, because the constant part of the expression is pre-evaluated. This part of the expression is known as a reference subexpression.

The token value for ptgMemArea consists of two parts: the length of the reference subexpression, and the value of the reference subexpression. The length is stored immediately following the ptgMemArea, whereas the value is appended to the saved parsed expression, immediately following the last token.

The format of the length is shown in the following table.

Offset	Name	Size	Contents
0	(reserved)	4	
4	cce	2	The length of the reference subexpression

Immediately following this part of the token value is the reference subexpression itself.

The rest of the token value (that is, the value of the reference subexpression) is appended to the parsed expression in the format shown in the following table.

Offset	Name	Size	Contents
0	cref	2	The number of rectangles to follow
2	rgref	var	An array of rectangles

Each rgref rectangle is 6 bytes long and contains the fields listed in the following table.

Offset	Name	Size	Contents
0	rwFirst	2	The first row
2	rwLast	2	The last row
4	colFirst	1	The first column
5	colLast	1	The last column

If a formula contains more than one ptgMemArea, the token values are appended to the saved parsed expression in order: first the values for the first ptgMemArea, then the values for the second ptgMemArea, and so on.

If a formula contains very long reference expressions, the BIFF record containing the parsed expression may be too long to fit in a single record. Microsoft Excel will use CONTINUE records to store long formulas. However, an individual rgref rectangle is never split between records; record boundaries occur between successive rectangles. For more information about the CONTINUE records, see "CONTINUE" on page 295.

ptgMemErr: Erroneous Constant Reference Subexpression (Operand, ptg = 27h)

This ptg is closely related to ptgMemArea. It's used for pre-evaluating reference subexpressions that don't evaluate to references.

For example, consider the formula =SUM(C:C 3:3), which is the sum of the intersection of column C and row 3 (the space between C:C and 3:3 is the intersection operator). The argument to the SUM function is a valid reference subexpression that generates a ptgMemArea for pre-evaluation. However, if you delete column C, the formula adjusts to =SUM(#REF! 3:3). In this case, the argument to SUM is still a constant reference subexpression, but it doesn't evaluate to a reference. Therefore, a ptgMemErr is used for pre-evaluation.

The token value consists of the error value and the length of the reference subexpression. Its format is shown in the following table.

Offset	Name	Size	Contents
0	(reserved)	4	
4	cce	2	The length of the reference subexpression

The reference subexpression will contain a ptgRefErr or ptgAreaErr.

ptgRefErr: Deleted Cell Reference (Operand, ptg = 2Ah)—BIFF8

This ptg specifies a cell reference that was adjusted to #REF! as a result of worksheet editing (such as cutting, pasting, and deleting). The ptgRefErr is followed by4 unused bytes.

Offset	Name	Size	Contents
0	(reserved)	4	

The original base type of the adjusted ptg is ptgRef or ptgRefN.

ptgRefErr: Deleted Cell Reference (Operand, ptg = 2Ah)—BIFF7 and earlier

This ptg specifies a cell reference that was adjusted to #REF! as a result of worksheet editing (such as cutting, pasting, and deleting). The ptgRefErr is followed by 3 unused bytes.

Offset	Name	Size	Contents
0	(reserved)	3	

The original base type of the adjusted ptg is ptgRef or ptgRefN.

ptgAreaErr: Deleted Area Reference (Operand, ptg = 2Bh)—BIFF8

This ptg specifies an area reference that was adjusted to #REF! as a result of worksheet editing (such as cutting, pasting, and deleting). The ptgAreaErr is followed by 8 unused bytes.

Offset	Name	Size	Contents
0	(reserved)	8	

The original base type of the adjusted ptg is ptgArea or ptgAreaN.

ptgAreaErr: Deleted Area Reference (Operand, ptg = 2Bh)—BIFF7 and earlier

This ptg specifies an area reference that was adjusted to #REF! as a result of worksheet editing (such as cutting, pasting, and deleting). The ptgAreaErr is followed by 6 unused bytes.

Offset	Name	Size	Contents
0	(reserved)	6	

The original base type of the adjusted ptg is ptgArea or ptgAreaN.

ptgRefN: Cell Reference Within a Shared Formula (Operand, ptg = 2Ch)—BIFF8

Similar to its ptgRef counterpart, the ptgRefN specifies a reference to a single cell. It's followed by references for the row and column that contain the cell; the row number of the cell is encoded as bit fields.

In BIFF5 and later, ptgRefN is used only in shared formulas. In earlier versions of Microsoft Excel, ptgRefN was used in names.

Offset	Name	Size	Contents
0	rw	2	The row (or row offset) of the reference
2	grbitCol	2	(See the following table)

Only the low-order 14 bits of the grbitCol field store the column number of the reference. The 2 MSBs specify whether the row and column references are relative or absolute. The following table shows the bit structure of the grbitCol field.

Bits	Mask	Name	Contents
15	8000h	fRwRel	= 1 if the row offset is relative = 0 otherwise
14	4000h	fColRel	= 1 if the column offset is relative = 0 otherwise
13–0	3FFFh	col	The column number or column offset (0-based)

The only difference between ptgRefN and ptgRef is in the way relative references are stored. Relative references in shared formulas are stored as offsets, not as row and column numbers (as in ptgRef). For more information, see "SHRFMLA" on page 386.

ptgRefN: Cell Reference Within a Shared Formula (Operand, ptg = 2Ch)—BIFF7 and earlier

Similar to its ptgRef counterpart, the ptgRefN specifies a reference to a single cell. It's followed by references for the row and column that contain the cell; the row number of the cell is encoded as bit fields.

In BIFF5 and later, ptgRefN is used only in shared formulas. In earlier versions of Microsoft Excel, ptgRefN was used in names.

Offset	Name	Size	Contents
0	grbitRw	2	(See the following table)
2	col	1	The column (or column offset) of the reference

Only the low-order 14 bits of the grbitRw field store the row number of the reference. The 2 MSBs specify whether the row and column references are relative or absolute. The following table shows the bit structure of the grbitRw field.

Bits	Mask	Name	Contents
15	8000h	fRwRel	= 1 if the row offset is relative = 0 otherwise
14	4000h	fColRel	= 1 if the column offset is relative = 0 otherwise
13–0	3FFFh	rw	The row number or row offset (0-based)

The only difference between ptgRefN and ptgRef is in the way relative references are stored. Relative references in shared formulas are stored as offsets, not as row and column numbers (as in ptgRef). For more information, see "SHRFMLA" on page 386.

ptgAreaN: Area Reference Within a Shared Formula (Operand, ptg = 2Dh)—BIFF8

The ptgAreaN token specifies a reference to a rectangle of cells. Both the first column and last column are encoded.

In BIFF5 and later, ptgAreaN is used only in shared formulas. In earlier versions, it was used in names.

Offset	Name	Size	Contents
0	rwFirst	2	The first row of the absolute reference or relative reference
2	rwLast	2	The last row of the absolute reference or relative reference

Offset	Name	Size	Contents
4	grbitColFirst	2	(See the following table)
6	grbitColLast	2	(See the following table)

Only the low-order 14 bits of the grbitColFirst and grbitColLast fields store the column offsets of the reference. The 2 MSBs of each field specify whether the row and column offset are relative or absolute. The following table shows the bit structure of the grbitColFirst and grbitColLast fields.

Bits	Mask	Name	Contents
15	8000h	fRwRel	= 1 if the row offset is relative = 0 otherwise
14	4000h	fColRel	= 1 if the column offset is relative = 0 otherwise
13–0	3FFFh	col	The column number or column offset (0-based)

The only difference between ptgAreaN and ptgArea is in the way relative references are stored.

ptgAreaN: Area Reference Within a Shared Formula (Operand, ptg = 2Dh) —BIFF7 and earlier

The ptgAreaN token specifies a reference to a rectangle of cells. Both the first row and last row are stored as bit fields.

In BIFF5 and later, ptgAreaN is used only in shared formulas. In earlier versions, it was used in names.

Offset	Name	Size	Contents
0	grbitRwFirst	2	The first row of the absolute reference or relative reference offset bit fields
2	grbitRwLast	2	The last row of the absolute reference or relative reference offset bit fields
4	colFirst	1	The first column of the reference or column offset
5	colLast	1	The last column of the reference or column offset

Only the low-order 14 bits of the grbitRwFirst and grbitRwLast fields store the row offsets of the reference. The 2 MSBs of each field specify whether the row and column offset are relative or absolute. The following table shows the bit structure of the grbitRwFirst and grbitRwLast fields.

Bits	Mask	Name	Contents
15	8000h	fRwRel	= 1 if the row offset is relative = 0 otherwise
14	4000h	fColRel	= 1 if the column offset is relative = 0 otherwise
13–0	3FFFh	rw	The row number or row offset (0-based)

The only difference between ptgAreaN and ptgArea is in the way relative references are stored.

ptgNameX: Name or External Name (Operand, ptg = 39h)—BIFF8

This ptg stores the index to a name.

Offset	Name	Size	Contents
0	ixti	2	Index into the EXTERNSHEET record
2	ilbl	2	The index to the NAME or EXTERNNAME table (1-based)
4	(reserved)	2	Reserved; must be 0 (zero)

ptgNameX: Name or External Name (Operand, ptg = 39h)—BIFF7 and earlier

This ptg stores the index to a name. If the name is in the current workbook (in which case ixals is negative), the ilbl field is a 1-based index to the table of NAME records. If the name is in another workbook (that is, if it's an external name), the ilbl field is a 1-based index to the table of EXTERNNAME records.

Offset	Name	Size	Contents
0	ixals	2	The index to the EXTERNSHEET records. If ixals is negative (for example, FFFFh), the name is in the current workbook.
2	(reserved)	8	
10	ilbl	2	The index to the NAME or EXTERNNAME table (1-based).
12	(reserved)	12	

ptgRef3d: 3-D Cell Reference (Operand, ptg = 3Ah)—BIFF8

This ptg stores a 3-D cell reference (for example, Sheet1:Sheet3!$A$1).

Offset	Name	Size	Contents
0	ixti	2	Index into the EXTERNSHEET record.
2	rw	2	The row of the reference, or the row offset.
4	grbitCol	2	(See the following table.)

Only the low-order 8 bits of the grbitCol field store the column number of the reference. The 2 MSBs specify whether the row and column references are relative or absolute. The following table shows the bit structure of the grbitCol field.

Bits	Mask	Name	Contents
15	8000h	fRwRel	= 1 if the row offset is relative = 0 otherwise
14	4000h	fColRel	= 1 if the column offset is relative = 0 otherwise
13–8	3F00h	(reserved)	
7–0	00FFh	col	The column number or column offset (0-based)

ptgRef3d: 3-D Cell Reference (Operand, ptg = 3Ah)—BIFF7 and earlier

This ptg stores a 3-D cell reference (for example, Sheet1:Sheet3!$A$1). If the reference is to another workbook (in which case ixals is positive), itabFirst isn't used (it will be 0000h), and itabLast is the ixals for the last sheet in the 3-D reference. If either itabFirst or itabLast is equal to FFFFh, that sheet is a deleted sheet.

Offset	Name	Size	Contents
0	ixals	2	The index to the EXTERNSHEET records. If ixals is negative (for example, FFFFh), the reference is in the current workbook.
2	(reserved)	8	
10	itabFirst	2	The index to the first sheet in the 3-D reference (0-based); see the text.
12	itabLast	2	The index to the last sheet in the 3-D reference (0-based); see the text.
14	grbitRw	2	(See the following table.)
16	col	1	The column of the reference, or the column offset.

Only the low-order 14 bits of the grbitRw field store the row number of the reference. The 2 MSBs specify whether the row and column references are relative or absolute. The following table shows the bit structure of the grbitRw field.

Bits	Mask	Name	Contents
15	8000h	fRwRel	= 1 if the row offset is relative = 0 otherwise
14	4000h	fColRel	= 1 if the column offset is relative = 0 otherwise
13–0	3FFFh	rw	The row number or row offset (0-based)

ptgArea3d: 3-D Area Reference (Operand, ptg = 3Bh)—BIFF8

This ptg stores a 3-D area reference (for example, Sheet1:Sheet3!A1:E9).

Offset	Name	Size	Contents
0	ixti	2	Index into the EXTERNSHEET record.
2	rwFirst	2	The first row in the area.
4	rwLast	2	The last row in the area.
6	grbitColFirst	2	The first column of the reference, or the column offset; see following table.
8	grbitColLast	2	The last column of the reference, or the column offset; see following table.

Only the low-order 8 bits of the grbitColFirst and grbitColLast fields store the column number of the reference. The 2 MSBs specify whether the row and column references are relative or absolute. The following table shows the bit structure of the grbitCol field.

Bits	Mask	Name	Contents
15	8000h	fRwRel	= 1 if the row offset is relative = 0 otherwise
14	4000h	fColRel	= 1 if the column offset is relative = 0 otherwise
13–8	3F00h	(reserved)	
7–0	00FFh	col	The column number or column offset (0-based)

ptgArea3d: 3-D Area Reference (Operand, ptg = 3Bh)—BIFF7 and earlier

This ptg stores a 3-D area reference (for example, Sheet1:Sheet3!A1:E9).

Offset	Name	Size	Contents
0	ixals	2	The index to the EXTERNSHEET records. If ixals is negative (for example, FFFFh), the reference is on another sheet in the same workbook.
2	(reserved)	8	
10	itabFirst	2	The index to the first sheet in the 3-D reference (0-based).
12	itabLast	2	The index to the last sheet in the 3-D reference (0-based).

Offset	Name	Size	Contents
14	grbitRwFirst	2	The first row in the area; see the following table.
16	grbitRwLast	2	The last row in the area; see the following table.
18	colFirst	1	The first column of the reference, or the column offset.
19	colLast	1	The last column of the reference, or the column offset.

Only the low-order 14 bits of the grbitRwFirst and grbitRwLast fields store the row offsets of the reference. The 2 MSBs of each field specify whether the row and column offset are relative or absolute. The following table shows the bit structure of the grbitRwFirst and grbitRwLast fields.

Bits	Mask	Name	Contents
15	8000h	fRwRel	= 1 if the row offset is relative = 0 otherwise
14	4000h	fColRel	= 1 if the column offset is relative = 0 otherwise
13–0	3FFFh	rw	The row number or row offset (0-based)

ptgRefErr3d: Deleted 3-D Cell Reference (Operand, ptg = 3Ch)

This ptg stores a 3-D cell reference that was adjusted to #REF! as a result of worksheet editing (such as cutting, pasting, and deleting). The ptgRefErr3d is identical to ptgRef3d.

ptgAreaErr3d: Deleted 3-D Area Reference (Operand, ptg = 3Dh)

This ptg stores a 3-D area reference that was adjusted to #REF! as a result of worksheet editing (such as cutting, pasting, and deleting). The ptgAreaErr3d is identical to ptgArea3d.

Control Tokens

ptgExp: Array Formula or Shared Formula (ptg = 01h)

This ptg indicates an array formula or a shared formula. When ptgExp occurs in a formula, it's the only token in the formula. This indicates that the cell containing the formula is part of an array or part of a shared formula. The actual formula is found in an ARRAY record.

The token value for ptgExp consists of the row and column of the upper-left corner of the array formula.

Offset	Name	Size	Contents
0	rwFirst	2	The row number of the upper-left corner
2	colFirst	2	The column number of the upper-left corner

ptgTbl: Data Table (ptg = 02h)

This ptg indicates a data table. When ptgTbl occurs in a formula, it's the only token in the formula. This indicates that the cell containing the formula is an interior cell in a data table; the table description is found in a TABLE record. Rows and columns that contain input values to be substituted in the table don't contain ptgTbl.

The token value for ptgTbl consists of the row and column of the upper-left corner of the table's interior.

Offset	Name	Size	Contents
0	rwFirst	2	The row number of the upper-left corner
2	colFirst	2	The column number of the upper-left corner

ptgParen: Parenthesis (ptg = 15h)

This ptg is used only when Microsoft Excel unparses a parsed expression (for example, to display it in the formula bar). This ptg isn't used to evaluate parsed expressions. It indicates that the previous token in the parsed expression should be in parentheses. If the previous token is an operand, only that operand is in parentheses. If the previous token is an operator, the operator and all of its operands are in parentheses.

For example, the formula =1+(2) is stored as follows:

```
ptgInt    0001h
ptgInt    0002h
ptgParen
ptgAdd
```

In this case, only the integer operand 2 is in parentheses.

The formula =(1+2) is stored as follows:

```
ptgInt    0001h
ptgInt    0002h
ptgAdd
ptgParen
```

In this example, the parenthesized quantity consists of the ptgAdd operator and both of its operands.

ptgAttr: Special Attribute (ptg = 19h)

This ptg is used for several different purposes. In all cases, the token value consists of a group of flag bits and a data word.

BIFF3 and BIFF4

Offset	Name	Size	Contents
0	grbit	1	Option flags
1	w	2	Data word

BIFF4 when bifFAttrSpace = 1

Offset	Name	Size	Contents
0	grbit	1	Option flags
1	bAttrSpace	1	Spacing attribute
2	bSpace	1	Number of spaces

The grbit field contains the option flags listed in the following table.

Bits	Mask	Name	Contents
0	01h	bitFAttrSemi	= 1 if the formula contains a volatile function
1	02h	bitFAttrIf	= 1 to implement an optimized IF function
2	04h	bitFAttrChoose	= 1 to implement an optimized CHOOSE function
3	08h	bitFAttrGoto	= 1 to jump to another location within the parsed expression
4	10h	bitFAttrSum	= 1 to implement an optimized SUM function
5	20h	bitFAttrBaxcel	= 1 if the formula is a BASIC-style assignment statement
6	40h	bifFAttrSpace	= 1 if the macro formula contains spaces after the equal sign (BIFF3 and BIFF4 only)
7	80	(Unused)	

ptgAttr requires special handling when parsed expressions are scanned. For more information, see "Scanning a Parsed Expression" on page 350.

bitFAttrSemi Set to 1 if the formula contains a volatile function—that is, a function that's calculated in every recalculation. If ptgAttr is used to indicate a volatile function, it must be the first token in the parsed expression. If grbit = bitFAttrSemi, then the b (or w) field is don't-care.

bitFAttrIf   Indicates an optimized IF function. An IF function contains three parts: a condition, a TRUE subexpression, and a FALSE subexpression. The syntax of an associated Microsoft Excel formula would be IF(condition, TRUE subexpression, FALSE subexpression).

bitFAttrIf immediately follows the condition portion of the parsed expression. The b (or w) field specifies the offset to the FALSE subexpression; the TRUE subexpression is found immediately following the ptgAttr token. At the end of the TRUE subexpression, there's a bitFAttrGoto token that causes a jump to beyond the FALSE subexpression. In this way, Microsoft Excel evaluates only the correct subexpression instead of evaluating both of them and discarding the wrong one.

The FALSE subexpression is optional in Microsoft Excel. If it's missing, the b (or w) field specifies an offset to beyond the TRUE subexpression.

bitFAttrChoose   Indicates an optimized CHOOSE function. The cCases (or wCases) field specifies the number of cases in the CHOOSE function. It's followed by an array of word offsets to those cases. The format of this complex token value is shown in the following table.

Offset	Name	Size	Contents
0	grbit	1	bitFAttrChoose (04h).
1	wCases	2	The number of cases in the CHOOSE function.
3	rgw	var	A sequence of word offsets to the CHOOSE cases. The number of words in this field is equal to wCases + 1.

bitFAttrGoto   Instructs the expression evaluator to skip part of the parsed expression during evaluation. The b (or w) field specifies the number of bytes (or words) to skip, minus 1.

bitFAttrSum   Indicates an optimized SUM function (a SUM that has a single argument). For example, the sum of the cells in a 3-D reference—which has the formula =SUM(Sheet1:Sheet3!C11)—generates a ptgAttr with bitFAttrSum TRUE. The b (or w) field is don't-care.

bifFAttrSpace   Indicates that a formula (macro sheet or worksheet) contains spaces or carriage returns. Microsoft Excel retains spaces and returns in macro sheet and worksheet formulas (in version 3.0 and earlier, spaces and returns would have been eliminated when the formula was parsed). The bAttrSpace field contains an attribute code, and the bSpace field contains the number of spaces or returns. The attribute codes are listed in the following table.

Attribute	Value
bitFSpace	00h
bitFEnter	01h
bitFPreSpace	02h
bitFPreEnter	03h
bitFPostSpace	04h
bitFPostEnter	05h
bitFPreFmlaSpace	06h

The bitFSpace and bitFEnter attributes indicate that bSpace contains the number of spaces or returns before the next ptg in the formula.

The bitFPreSpace, bitFPreEnter, bitFPostSpace, and bitFPostEnter attributes occur with a ptgParen. Because one ptgParen represents two matched parentheses, the ptgAttr must encode the position of the space or return if it occurs before either parenthesis. For example, the ptgs that express the worksheet formula = ("spaces"), which contains four spaces before the opening and closing parentheses, would appear in a formula record as shown in the following table.

Hex dump	Ptg type	Decodes to
17 06 73 70 61 63 65 73	ptgStr	The string "spaces" (operand)
19 40 02 04	ptgAttr	Four spaces before the opening parenthesis
19 40 04 04	ptgAttr	Four spaces after the closing parenthesis
15	ptgParen	The enclose operand (ptgStr) in parentheses

The bitFPreFmlaSpace attribute provides compatibility with BIFF3, where spaces can occur only after the equal sign (before the formula) in macro formulas. If the spaces in a BIFF5/BIFF7 formula are also acceptable in a BIFF3 formula, Microsoft Excel writes a bitFPreFmlaSpace attribute to indicate as much.

ptgMemNoMem: Incomplete Constant Reference Subexpression (ptg = 28h)

This ptg is closely related to ptgMemArea. It's used to indicate a constant reference subexpression that couldn't be pre-evaluated because of insufficient memory.

The token value consists of the length of the reference subexpression, as shown in the following table.

Offset	Name	Size	Contents
0	(reserved)	4	
4	cce	2	The length of the reference subexpression

ptgMemFunc: Variable Reference Subexpression (ptg = 29h)

This ptg indicates a reference subexpression that doesn't evaluate to a constant reference. Any reference subexpression that contains one or more of the following items will generate a ptgMemFunc.

Subexpression contains	Example
A function	OFFSET(ACTIVE.CELL(),1,1):$C$2
A name	INDEX(first_cell:$D$2,1,1)
An external reference	SALES.XLS!$A$1:SALES.XLS!$C$3

The token value consists of the length of the reference subexpression.

Offset	Name	Size	Contents
0	cce	2	The length of the reference subexpression

ptgMemAreaN: Reference Subexpression Within a Name (ptg = 2Eh)

This ptg contains a constant reference subexpression within a name definition. Unlike ptgMemArea, ptgMemAreaN isn't used to pre-evaluate the reference subexpression.

The token value consists of the length of the reference subexpression.

Offset	Name	Size	Contents
0	cce	2	The length of the reference subexpression

ptgMemNoMemN: Incomplete Reference Subexpression Within a Name (ptg = 2Fh)

This ptg is closely related to ptgMemAreaN. It's used to indicate a constant reference subexpression within a name that couldn't be evaluated because of insufficient memory.

The token value consists of the length of the reference subexpression, as shown in the following table.

Offset	Name	Size	Contents
0	cce	2	The length of the reference subexpression

Function Operators

The following paragraphs describe the function operator ptgs. All of these operators pop arguments from the operand stack, compute a function, and then push the result back onto the operand stack. The number of operands popped from the stack is equal to the number of arguments passed to the Microsoft Excel function. Some Microsoft Excel functions always require a fixed number of arguments, whereas others accept a variable number of arguments. The SUM function, for example, accepts a variable number of arguments.

Although they're operators, function tokens also behave like operands in that they can occur in any of the three ptg classes: reference, value, or array.

ptgFunc: Function, Fixed Number of Arguments (Operator, ptg = 21h)

This ptg indicates a Microsoft Excel function with a fixed number of arguments. The ptgFunc is followed by the index to the function table.

Offset	Name	Size	Contents
0	iftab	2	The index to the function table; the iftab reference is contained in the file xlcall.h, which is contained on the CD that accompanied this book.

ptgFuncVar: Function, Variable Number of Arguments (Operator, ptg = 22h)

This ptg indicates a Microsoft Excel function with a variable number of arguments. The ptgFuncVar is followed by the number of arguments (1 byte) and then the index to the function table (2 bytes).

Offset	Bits	Mask	Name	Contents
0	6–0	7Fh	cargs	The number of arguments to the function.
	7	80h	fPrompt	= 1, function prompts the user (macro functions that end with a question mark).
1	14–0	7FFFh	iftab	The index to the function table; the iftab reference is contained in the file xlcall.h, which is contained on the CD that accompanied this book.
	15	8000h	fCE	The function is a command-equivalent.

C H A P T E R 1 0

Microsoft Excel Chart Records

This chapter describes the Microsoft Excel chart BIFF file format. The chart BIFF is combined with other sheet BIFF records into the Book stream of a Microsoft Excel workbook file. This article documents only those records unique to charts; these records have record numbers greater than 1000h. Chart BIFF also uses a few records below this range; for information on those records, see "Microsoft Excel File Format."

The chart BIFF usually does not contain a complete description of a Microsoft Excel chart but rather a description of how the chart differs from an internal default chart (the simple column chart). Therefore, many of the records in the chart BIFF modify the default chart description. The internal default chart is *not* the same as the default chart that you set in the Options dialog box.

Although the information contained in BIFF records varies, every record has the same basic format. For more information about the BIFF record format, see BIFF Record Information.

New and Changed Chart Records

The following tables describe the new records and changed chart records in BIFF8. For more information on the new and changed records, see the appropriate record description.

New Chart Records in BIFF8

Number	Record
1060h	FBI
1061h	BOPPOP
1062h	AXCEXT
1063h	DAT
1064h	PLOTGROWTH
1065h	SIINDEX

Changed Chart Records in BIFF8

Number	Record
1066h	GELFRAME
1067h	BOPPOPCUSTOM
1003h	SERIES
1007h	LINEFORMAT
1009h	MARKERFORMAT
100Ah	AREAFORMAT
100Ch	ATTACHEDLABEL
1015h	LEGEND
1017h	BAR
1018h	LINE
1019h	PIE
101Ah	AREA
101Bh	SCATTER
101Eh	TICK
1025h	TEXT
103Ch	PICF
103Eh	RADAR
103Fh	SURF
1044h	SHTPROPS
105Dh	SERFMT

Chart BIFF Hierarchy

The chart BIFF contains a hierarchical series of records that defines the chart format. Much of the chart data is defined as objects; an object starts with a BEGIN record and ends with a matching END record. For example, a series object definition starts with a SERIES record immediately followed by a BEGIN record. All subsequent records up to the matching END record apply to the specified series.

Objects can be nested within objects; nested BEGIN and END records are used as required to describe objects that are part of other objects. The outer object is called the "parent"; the nested object is called a "child."

The BIFF structure is flexible; it varies depending on the chart type and the elements included in the chart. You can examine the record structure of an existing BIFF file with the BiffView utility.

Series and Categories

All charts, whether in column, bar, line, pie, area, or scatter format, contain series data, category data, and value data. The following column chart explains the difference between series and categories.

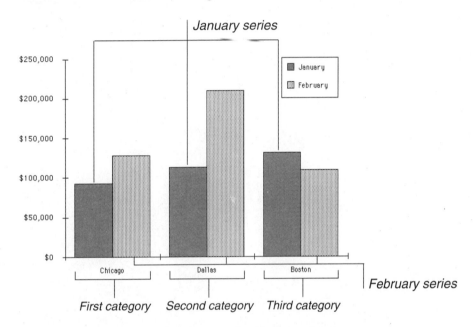

When Microsoft Excel creates a chart from a worksheet, it assigns either the worksheet rows as the series data (and the columns as the category data), or the worksheet columns as the series data (and the rows as categories). If there are fewer rows than columns, then the rows become the series. However, if there are fewer columns than rows, then the columns become the series. If there are an equal number of rows and columns in the range of cells, then the rows become the series.

This algorithm minimizes the number of series on the chart. For example, the following column chart . . .

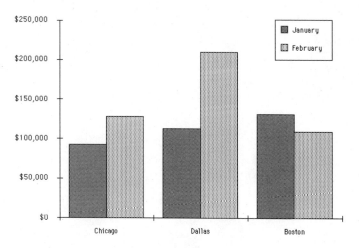

. . . can be created from either of the two following worksheets.

	A	B	C	D
1				
2				
3				
4		January	February	
5	Chicago	$93,000	$128,000	
6	Dallas	$113,000	$210,000	
7	Boston	$132,000	$110,000	
8				

	A	B	C	D	E
1					
2					
3					
4		Chicago	Dallas	Boston	
5	January	$93,000	$113,000	$132,000	
6	February	$128,000	$210,000	$110,000	
7					
8					

In the second worksheet shown here, January and February are the series (because there are fewer rows than columns), and Chicago, Dallas, and Boston are the categories. In these two worksheets, values for each series appear at three locations on the chart.

If you add sales data for March and April, the series are now Chicago, Dallas, and Boston, and the categories are January, February, March, and April. Microsoft Excel automatically exchanges the series and categories to minimize the number of series.

Chart BIFF Records: Alphabetical Order

Number	Record
103A	3D: Chart Group Is a 3-D Chart Group
1051	AI: Linked Data
1050	ALRUNS: Text Formatting
101A	AREA: Chart Group Is an Area Chart Group
100A	AREAFORMAT: Colors and Patterns for an Area
100C	ATTACHEDLABEL: Series Data/Value Labels
1062	AXCEXT: Axis Options
1046	AXESUSED: Number of Axes Sets
101D	AXIS: Axis Type
1021	AXISLINEFORMAT: Defines a Line That Spans an Axis
1041	AXISPARENT: Axis Size and Location
1017	BAR: Chart Group Is a Bar or Column Chart Group
1033	BEGIN: Defines the Beginning of an Object
1061	BOPPOP: Bar of Pie/Pie of Pie Chart Options
1067	BOPPOPCUSTOM: Custom Bar of Pie/Pie of Pie Chart Options
1020	CATSERRANGE: Defines a Category or Series Axis
1002	CHART: Location and Overall Chart Dimensions
1014	CHARTFORMAT: Parent Record for Chart Group
1022	CHARTFORMATLINK: Not Used
101C	CHARTLINE: Drop/Hi-Lo/Series Lines on a Line Chart
1063	DAT: Data Table Options
1006	DATAFORMAT: Series and Data Point Numbers
1024	DEFAULTTEXT: Default Data Label Text Properties
103D	DROPBAR: Defines Drop Bars
1034	END: Defines the End of an Object
1060	FBI: Font Basis
1026	FONTX: Font Index
1032	FRAME: Defines Border Shape Around Displayed Text
1066	GELFRAME: Fill Data
104E	IFMT: Number-Format Index
1015	LEGEND: Legend Type and Position
1043	LEGENDXN: Legend Exception
1018	LINE: Chart Group Is a Line Chart Group

Number	Record
1007	LINEFORMAT: Style of a Line or Border
1009	MARKERFORMAT: Style of a Line Marker
1027	OBJECTLINK: Attaches Text to Chart or to Chart Item
103C	PICF: Picture Format
1019	PIE: Chart Group Is a Pie Chart Group
100B	PIEFORMAT: Position of the Pie Slice
1035	PLOTAREA: Frame Belongs to Plot Area
1064	PLOTGROWTH: Font Scale Factors
104F	POS: Position Information
103E	RADAR: Chart Group Is a Radar Chart Group
1040	RADARAREA: Chart Group Is a Radar Area Chart Group
1048	SBASEREF: PivotTable Reference
101B	SCATTER: Chart Group Is a Scatter Chart Group
105B	SERAUXERRBAR: Series ErrorBar
104B	SERAUXTREND: Series Trendline
105D	SERFMT: Series Format
1003	SERIES: Series Definition
1016	SERIESLIST: Specifies the Series in an Overlay Chart
100D	SERIESTEXT: Legend/Category/Value Text
104A	SERPARENT: Trendline or ErrorBar Series Index
1045	SERTOCRT: Series Chart-Group Index
1044	SHTPROPS: Sheet Properties
1065	SIINDEX: Series Index
103F	SURFACE: Chart Group Is a Surface Chart Group
1025	TEXT: Defines Display of Text Fields
101E	TICK: Tick Marks and Labels Format
1001	UNITS: Chart Units
101F	VALUERANGE: Defines Value Axis Scale

Chart BIFF Records: Record Number Order

Number	Record
1001	UNITS: Chart Units
1002	CHART: Location and Overall Chart Dimensions
1003	SERIES: Series Definition
1006	DATAFORMAT: Series and Data Point Numbers

Number	Record
1007	LINEFORMAT: Style of a Line or Border
1009	MARKERFORMAT: Style of a Line Marker
100A	AREAFORMAT: Colors and Patterns for an Area
100B	PIEFORMAT: Position of the Pie Slice
100C	ATTACHEDLABEL: Series Data/Value Labels
100D	SERIESTEXT: Legend/Category/Value Text
1014	CHARTFORMAT: Parent Record for Chart Group
1015	LEGEND: Legend Type and Position
1016	SERIESLIST: Specifies the Series in an Overlay Chart
1017	BAR: Chart Group Is a Bar or Column Chart Group
1018	LINE: Chart Group Is a Line Chart Group
1019	PIE: Chart Group Is a Pie Chart Group
101A	AREA: Chart Group Is an Area Chart Group
101B	SCATTER: Chart Group Is a Scatter Chart Group
101C	CHARTLINE: Drop/Hi-Lo/Series Lines on a Line Chart
101D	AXIS: Axis Type
101E	TICK: Tick Marks and Labels Format
101F	VALUERANGE: Defines Value Axis Scale
1020	CATSERRANGE: Defines a Category or Series Axis
1021	AXISLINEFORMAT: Defines a Line That Spans an Axis
1022	CHARTFORMATLINK: Not Used
1024	DEFAULTTEXT: Default Data Label Text Properties
1025	TEXT: Defines Display of Text Fields
1026	FONTX: Font Index
1027	OBJECTLINK: Attaches Text to Chart or to Chart Item
1032	FRAME: Defines Border Shape Around Displayed Text
1033	BEGIN: Defines the Beginning of an Object
1034	END: Defines the End of an Object
1035	PLOTAREA: Frame Belongs to Plot Area
103A	3D: Chart Group Is a 3-D Chart Group
103C	PICF: Picture Format
103D	DROPBAR: Defines Drop Bars
103E	RADAR: Chart Group Is a Radar Chart Group
103F	SURFACE: Chart Group Is a Surface Chart Group

Number	Record
1040	RADARAREA: Chart Group Is a Radar Area Chart Group
1041	AXISPARENT: Axis Size and Location
1043	LEGENDXN: Legend Exception
1044	SHTPROPS: Sheet Properties
1045	SERTOCRT: Series Chart-Group Index
1046	AXESUSED: Number of Axes Sets
1048	SBASEREF: PivotTable Reference
104A	SERPARENT: Trendline or ErrorBar Series Index
104B	SERAUXTREND: Series Trendline
104E	IFMT: Number-Format Index
104F	POS: Position Information
1050	ALRUNS: Text Formatting
1051	AI: Linked Data
105B	SERAUXERRBAR: Series ErrorBar
105D	SERFMT: Series Format
1060	FBI: Font Basis
1061	BOPPOP: Bar of Pie/Pie of Pie Chart Options
1062	AXCEXT: Axis Options
1063	DAT: Data Table Options
1064	PLOTGROWTH: Font Scale Factors
1065	SIINDEX: Series Index
1066	GELFRAME: Fill Data
1067	BOPPOPCUSTOM: Custom Bar of Pie/Pie of Pie Chart Options

Record Descriptions

The first two fields in every BIFF record are record number and record length. Because these fields have the same offset and size in every BIFF record, they are not documented in the following descriptions. For more information about the record number and record length fields, see "BIFF Record Information."

3D: Chart Group Is a 3-D Chart Group (103Ah)

This record defines a 3-D chart group and also contains generic formatting information.

Record Data

Offset	Name	Size	Contents
4	anRot	2	Rotation angle (0 to 360 degrees)
6	anElev	2	Elevation angle (–90 to +90 degrees)
8	pcDist	2	Distance from eye to chart (0 to 100)
10	pcHeight	2	Height of plot volume relative to width and depth
12	pcDepth	2	Depth of points relative to width
14	pcGap	2	Space between series
16	grbit	2	Option flags

The grbit field contains the following option flags.

Offset	Bits	Mask	Name	Contents
0	0	01h	fPerspective	1 = use perspective transform
0	1	02h	fCluster	1 = 3-D columns are clustered or stacked
0	2	04h	f3DScaling	1 = use auto scaling
0	3	08h	(reserved)	Reserved; must be zero
0	4	10h	(reserved)	Reserved; must be one
0	5	20h	f2DWalls	use 2D walls and gridlines
0	7–2	FAh	(reserved)	Reserved; must be zero
1	7–0	FFh	(reserved)	Reserved; must be zero

AI: Linked Data (1051h)

This record specifies linked series data or text.

Record Data

Offset	Name	Size	Contents
4	id	1	Link index identifier 0 = linking a series title or text 1 = linking series values 2 = linking series categories
5	rt	1	Reference type 0 = use default categories 1 = text or value entered directly into the formula bar 2 = linked to worksheet 3 = not used 4 = error reported
6	grbit	2	Flags
8	ifmt	2	Index to number format record
10	cce	2	Size of rgce (in bytes)
12	rgce	var	Parsed formula of link

The grbit field contains the following option flags.

Offset	Bits	Mask	Name	Contents
0	0	01h	fCustomIfmt	TRUE if this object has a custom number format; FALSE if number format is linked to data source
0	1	02h	(reserved)	Reserved; must be zero
0	5–2	3Ch	st	Source type (always zero)
0	7–6	C0h	(reserved)	Reserved; must be zero
1	7–0	FFh	(reserved)	Reserved; must be zero

ALRUNS: Text Formatting (1050h)

This record specifies rich-text formatting (bold, italic, font changes, etc.) within chart titles and data labels.

Record Data

Offset	Name	Size	Contents
4	cRuns	2	Number of rich-text runs
6	rgwRuns	var	Array of cRuns four-byte groups. The first two bytes in each group specify the first character in the rich-text run. The second two bytes specify the font index for the text run (see the FONT record for more information about this index).

AREA: Chart Group Is an Area Chart Group (101Ah)

This record defines an area chart group.

Record Data—BIFF8

Offset	Name	Size	Contents
4	grbit	2	format flags

The grbit field contains the following option flags.

Offset	Bits	Mask	Name	Contents
0	0	01h	fStacked	Series in this group are stacked
	1	02h	f100	Each category is broken down as a percentage
	2	04h	fHasShadow	1 = this area has a shadow
	7–3	F8h	(reserved)	Reserved; must be zero
1	7–0	FFh	(reserved)	Reserved; must be zero

When fStacked is true, the value indicators (filled areas) are stacked one on top of the next. The f100 bit can be set only when the fStacked bit is set and indicates that each category is broken down into percentages.

Record Data—BIFF7 and earlier

Offset	Name	Size	Contents
4	grbit	2	format flags

The grbit field contains the following option flags.

Offset	Bits	Mask	Name	Contents
0	0	01h	fStacked	Series in this group are stacked
0	1	02h	f100	Each category is broken down as a percentage
0	7–2	FCh	(reserved)	Reserved; must be zero
1	7–0	FFh	(reserved)	Reserved; must be zero

When fStacked is true, the value indicators (filled areas) are stacked one on top of the next. The f100 bit can be set only when the fStacked bit is set and indicates that each category is broken down into percentages.

AREAFORMAT: Colors and Patterns for an Area (100Ah)

This record describes the patterns and colors used in a filled area.

Record Data—BIFF8

Offset	Name	Size	Contents
4	rgbFore	4	Foreground color: RGB value (high byte = 0)
8	rgbBack	4	Background color: RGB value (high byte = 0)
12	fls	2	Pattern
14	grbit	2	Format flags
16	icvFore	2	Index to foreground color
18	icvBack	2	Index to background color

The grbit field contains the following option flags.

Offset	Bits	Mask	Name	Contents
0	0	01h	fAuto	Automatic format
0	1	02h	fInvertNeg	Foreground and background are swapped when the data value is negative
0	7–2	FCh	(reserved)	Reserved; must be zero
1	7–0	FFh	(reserved)	Reserved; must be zero

Record Data—BIFF7 and earlier

Offset	Name	Size	Contents
4	rgbFore	4	Foreground color: RGB value (high byte = 0)
8	rgbBack	4	Background color: RGB value (high byte = 0)
12	fls	2	Pattern
14	grbit	2	Format flags

The grbit field contains the following option flags.

Offset	Bits	Mask	Name	Contents
0	0	01h	fAuto	Automatic format
0	1	02h	fInvertNeg	Foreground and background are swapped when the data value is negative
0	7–2	FCh	(reserved)	Reserved; must be zero
1	7–0	FFh	(reserved)	Reserved; must be zero

ATTACHEDLABEL: Series Data/Value Labels (100Ch)

The ATTACHEDLABEL record defines the data label type. The ATTACHEDLABEL record applies to the label data identified in the associated DATAFORMAT record.

Record Data—BIFF8

Offset	Name	Size	Contents
4	grbit	2	Value label flags

The grbit field contains the following option flags.

Offset	Bits	Mask	Name	Contents
0	0	01h	fShowValue	1 = show the actual value of the data point
	1	02h	fShowPercent	1 = show value as a percent of the total. This bit applies only to pie charts.
	2	04h	fShowLabPct	1 = show category label and value as a percentage (pie charts only). Should be 1 if fShowLabel and fShowPercent are both 1.
	3	08h	fSmoothedLine	1 = show smoothed line
	4	10h	fShowLabel	1 = show category label
	5	20h	fShowBubbleSizes	1 = show bubble sizes
	7–6	C0h	(reserved)	Reserved; must be zero
1	7–0	FFh	(reserved)	Reserved; must be zero

Record Data—BIFF7 and earlier

Offset	Name	Size	Contents
4	grbit	2	Value label flags

The grbit field contains the following option flags.

Offset	Bits	Mask	Name	Contents
0	0	01h	fShowValue	1 = show the actual value of the data point
0	1	02h	fShowPercent	1 = show value as a percent of the total. This bit applies only to pie charts.
0	2	04h	fShowLabPct	1 = show category label and value as a percentage (pie charts only). Should be 1 if fShowLabel and fShowPercent are both 1.
0	3	08h	(reserved)	Reserved; must be zero
0	4	10h	fShowLabel	1 = show category label
0	7–5	E0h	(reserved)	Reserved; must be zero
1	7–0	FFh	(reserved)	Reserved; must be zero

AXESUSED: Number of Axes Sets (1046h)

This record specifies the number of axes sets (1 = primary only, 2 = primary and secondary) used on the chart (3-D charts can have only primary axes).

Record Data

Offset	Name	Size	Contents
4	cAxes	2	Number of axes sets

AXIS: Axis Type (101Dh)

This record defines the axis type.

Record Data

Offset	Name	Size	Contents
4	wType	2	Axis type 0 = category axis or x axis on a scatter chart 1 = value axis 2 = series axis
6	(reserved)	16	Reserved; must be zero

AXCEXT: Axis Options (1062h)

This record defines axis options.

Record Data—BIFF8

Offset	Name	Size	Contents
4	catMin	2	minimum category on axis
6	catMax	2	maximum category on axis
8	catMajor	2	value of major unit
10	duMajor	2	units of major unit
12	catMinor	2	value of minor unit
14	duMinor	2	units of minor unit
16	duBase	2	base unit of axis
18	catCrossDate	2	crossing point of value axis (date)
20	grbit	2	Option flags (see following table)

The grbit field contains the following option flags.

Offset	Bits	Mask	Name	Contents
0	0	01h	fAutoMin	1 = use default minimum
	1	02h	fautoMax	1 = use default maximum
	2	04h	fautoMajor	1 = use default major unit
	3	08h	fAutoMinor	1 = use default minor unit
	4	10h	fdateAxis	1 = this is a date axis
	5	20h	fAutoBase	1 = use default base
	6	40h	fAutoCross	1 = use default crossing point
	7	80h	fAutoDate	1 = use default date settings for axis
1	7–0	FFh	(reserved)	Reserved; must be zero

AXISLINEFORMAT: Defines a Line That Spans an Axis (1021h)

This record usually follows an AXIS record to define the axis line as it appears on the chart.

Record Data

Offset	Name	Size	Contents
4	id	2	Axis line identifier: 0 = the axis line itself 1 = major grid line along the axis 2 = minor grid line along the axis 3 = walls or floor—walls if parent axis is type 0 or 2; floor if parent axis is type 1

AXISPARENT: Axis Size and Location (1041h)

This record specifies the location and size of the chart axes, in units of 1/4000 of the chart area.

Record Data

Offset	Name	Size	Contents
4	iax	2	Axis index (0 = main, 1 = secondary)
6	x	4	x coordinate of top left corner
10	y	4	y coordinate of top left corner
14	dx	4	length of x axis
18	dy	4	length of y axis

BAR: Chart Group Is a Bar or Column Chart Group (1017h)

This record defines a bar or column chart group.

Record Data—BIFF8

Offset	Name	Size	Contents
4	pcOverlap	2	Space between bars (percent of bar width), default = 0
6	pcGap	2	Space between categories (percent of bar width), default = 50
8	grbit	2	Format flags

The grbit field contains the bar chart display attributes as follows.

Offset	Bits	Mask	Name	Contents
0	0	01h	fTranspose	1 = horizontal bars (bar chart) 0 = vertical bars (column chart)
	1	02h	fStacked	Stack the displayed values
	2	04h	f100	Each category is displayed as a percentage
	3	08h	fHasShadow	1 = this bar has a shadow
	7–4	F0h	(reserved)	Reserved; must be zero
1	7–0	FFh	(reserved)	Reserved; must be zero

When fStacked is true, the bars or columns within a category are stacked one on top of the next. The f100 bit can be set only when the fStacked bit is set, and indicates that each category is broken down into percentages.

Record Data—BIFF7 and earlier

Offset	Name	Size	Contents
4	pcOverlap	2	Space between bars (percent of bar width), default = 0
6	pcGap	2	Space between categories (percent of bar width), default = 50
8	grbit	2	Format flags

The grbit field contains the bar chart display attributes as follows.

Offset	Bits	Mask	Name	Contents
0	0	01h	fTranspose	1 = horizontal bars (bar chart) 0 = vertical bars (column chart)
0	1	02h	fStacked	Stack the displayed values
0	2	04h	f100	Each category is displayed as a percentage
0	7–3	FCh	(reserved)	Reserved; must be zero
1	7–0	FFh	(reserved)	Reserved; must be zero

When fStacked is true, the bars or columns within a category are stacked one on top of the next. The f100 bit can be set only when the fStacked bit is set, and indicates that each category is broken down into percentages.

BEGIN: Defines the Beginning of an Object (1033h)

The BEGIN record is a fixed-length 4-byte record that indicates the beginning of a block of records that forms a data object. Every BEGIN record must have a corresponding END record. The BEGIN record consists of 10330000h.

BOPPOP: Bar of Pie/Pie of Pie Chart Options (1061h)

This record stores options for a bar of pie or pie of pie chart; these are two of the pie chart subtypes.

Record Data—BIFF8

Offset	Name	Size	Contents
4	pst	1	0 = normal pie chart 1 = pie of pie chart 2 = bar of pie chart
5	fAutoSplit	1	1 = use default split value
6	spit	2	Split type: 0 = Position 1 = Value 2 = Percent 3 = Custom
8	iSplitPos	2	For spit = 0, which positions should go to the other pie/bar
10	pcSplitPercent	2	For spit = 2, what percentage should go to the other bar/pie
12	pcPie2Size	2	Size of the second pie as a percentage of the first
14	pcGap	2	Space between the first pie and the second
16	numSplitValue	4	For spit = 1, what values should go to the other bar/pie
20	fHasShadow	2	1 = the second bar/pie has a shadow

BOPPOPCUSTOM: Custom Bar of Pie/Pie of Pie Chart Options (1067h)

This record stores options for a custom bar of pie or pie of pie chart; these are two of the pie chart subtypes.

Record Data—BIFF8

Offset	Name	Size	Contents
4	cxi	2	Count of pie slices in the bar of pie or pie of pie chart
6	rggrbit	var	Array of bytes; each byte contains a bit field that describes the individual point positioning in the series. If a slice is on the secondary pie or bar chart, the corresponding bit is set to 1 (one); otherwise the bit is 0 (zero).

CATSERRANGE: Defines a Category or Series Axis (1020h)

This record defines the scaling options for a category or series axis.

Record Data

Offset	Name	Size	Contents
4	catCross	2	Value axis/category crossing point (2-D charts only)
6	catLabel	2	Frequency of labels
8	catMark	2	Frequency of tick marks
10	grbit	2	Format flags

The catCross field defines the point on the category axis where the value axis crosses. A value of 01 indicates that the value axis crosses to the left, or in the center, of the first category (depending on the value of bit 0 of the grbit field); a value of 02 indicates that the value axis crosses to the left or center of the second category, and so on. Bit 2 of the grbit field overrides the value of catCross when set to 1.

The catLabel field defines how often labels appear along the category or series axis. A value of 01 indicates that a category label will appear with each category, a value of 02 means a label appears every other category, and so on.

The catMark field defines how often tick marks appear along the category or series axis. A value of 01 indicates that a tick mark will appear between each category or series; a value of 02 means a label appears between every other category or series, etc.

The grbit field contains the following option flags.

Offset	Bits	Mask	Name	Contents
0	0	01h	fBetween	Value axis crossing 0 = axis crosses midcategory 1 = axis crosses between categories
0	1	02h	fMaxCross	Value axis crosses at the far right category (in a line, bar, column, scatter, or area chart; 2-D charts only)
0	2	04h	fReverse	Display categories in reverse order
0	7–3	F8h	(reserved)	Reserved; must be zero
1	7–0	FFh	(reserved)	Reserved; must be zero

CHART: Location and Overall Chart Dimensions (1002h)

The CHART record marks the start of the chart data substream in the workbook BIFF stream. This record defines the location of the chart on the display and its overall size. The x and y fields define the position of the upper-left corner of the bounding rectangle that encompasses the chart. The position of the chart is referenced to the page.

The dx and dy fields define the overall size (the bounding rectangle) of the chart, including title, pointing arrows, axis labels, etc.

The position and size are specified in points (1/72 inch), using a fixed-point format (two bytes integer, two bytes fraction).

Record Data

Offset	Name	Size	Contents
4	x	4	x-position of upper-left corner
8	y	4	y-position of upper-left corner
12	dx	4	x-size
16	dy	4	y-size

CHARTFORMAT: Parent Record for Chart Group (1014h)

This record is the parent record for the chart-group format description. Each chart group will have a separate CHARTFORMAT record; followed by a BEGIN record, the chart-group description, and an END record.

Record Data

Offset	Name	Size	Contents
4	(reserved)	16	Reserved; must be zero
20	grbit	2	Format flags
22	icrt	2	Drawing order (0 = bottom of the z-order)

The grbit field contains the following option flags.

Offset	Bits	Mask	Name	Contents
0	0	01h	fVaried	Vary color for each data point
0	7–1	FEh	(reserved)	Reserved; must be zero
1	7–0	FFh	(reserved)	Reserved; must be zero

CHARTFORMATLINK: Not Used (1022h)

This record is written by Microsoft Excel, but it is ignored. Applications writing chart BIFF do not need to write this record, and applications reading chart BIFF can ignore it.

CHARTLINE: Specifies Drop/Hi-Lo/Series Lines on a Line Chart (101Ch)

This record specifies drop lines, hi-lo lines, or series lines on a line chart. If the chart has both drop lines and hi-lo lines, two CHARTLINE records will be present.

Record Data

Offset	Name	Size	Contents
4	id	2	Drop lines/hi-lo lines 0 = drop lines 1 = hi-lo lines 2 = series lines (the lines that connect the columns in a stacked column chart)

DAT: Data Table Options (1063h)

This record stores options for the chart data table.

Record Data—BIFF8

Offset	Name	Size	Contents
4	grbit	2	Option flags (see following table)

The grbit field contains the following flags.

Offset	Bits	Mask	Name	Contents
0	0	01h	fHasBordHorz	1 = data table has horizontal borders
	1	02h	fHasBordVert	1 = data table has vertical borders
	2	04h	fhasBordOutline	1 = data table has a border
	3	08h	fShowSeriesKey	1 = data table shows series keys
	7–4	F0h	reserved	Reserved; must be zero
1	7–0	FFh	reserved	Reserved; must be zero

DATAFORMAT: Series and Data Point Numbers (1006h)

The DATAFORMAT record contains the zero-based numbers of the data point and series. The subordinate records determine the format of the series or point defined by the DATAFORMAT record.

Record Data

Offset	Name	Size	Contents
4	xi	2	Point number (FFFFh means entire series)
6	yi	2	Series index (file relative)
8	iss	2	Series number (as shown in name box—S1, S2, etc.). This can be different from yi if the series order has been changed.
10	grbit	2	format flags

The grbit field contains the following flags.

Offset	Bits	Mask	Name	Contents
0	0	01h	fXL4iss	1 = use Microsoft Excel 4.0 colors for automatic formatting
0	7–1	FEh	(reserved)	Reserved; must be zero
1	7–0	FFh	(reserved)	Reserved; must be zero

DEFAULTTEXT: Default Data Label Text Properties (1024h)

The DEFAULTTEXT record precedes a TEXT record to identify the text defined in the TEXT record as the default properties for certain chart items.

Record Data

Offset	Name	Size	Contents
4	id	2	Object identifier for the text 0 = default text characteristics for "show labels" data labels 1 = default text characteristics for value and percentage data labels 2 = default text characteristics for all text in the chart

DROPBAR: Defines Drop Bars (103Dh)

This record defines drop bars on a line chart. If the chart contains drop bars, the chart BIFF will contain two DROPBAR records. The first DROPBAR record corresponds to the up bar, and the second DROPBAR record corresponds to the down bar.

Record Data

Offset	Name	Size	Contents
4	pcGap	2	Drop bar gap width (0 to 100%)

END: Defines the End of an Object (1034h)

This record is a fixed-length 4-byte record that indicates the end of a data object. Every END record has a corresponding BEGIN record. The END record consists of 10340000h.

FBI: Font Basis (1060h)

The FBI record stores font metrics.

Record Data—BIFF8

Offset	Name	Size	Contents
4	dmixBasis	2	Width of basis when font was applied
6	dmiyBasis	2	Height of basis when font was applied
8	twpHeightBasis	2	Font height applied
10	scab	2	Scale basis
12	ifnt	2	Index number into the font table

FONTX: Font Index (1026h)

This record is the child of a TEXT record and defines a text font by indexing the appropriate font in the font table. The font table is built from FONT records.

Record Data

Offset	Name	Size	Contents
4	ifont	2	Index number into the font table

FRAME: Defines Border Shape Around Displayed Text (1032h)

The FRAME record defines the border that is present around a displayed label as a rectangle. A displayed label can include the chart title, the legend (if not a regular rectangle), a category name, or a value amount.

Record Data

Offset	Name	Size	Contents
4	frt	2	0 = regular rectangle/no border 1–3 (reserved) 4 = rectangle with shadow
6	grbit	2	Flags

The frt field defines the format of the frame border, that is, a rectangle or a rectangle with a shadow along two sides. (The format of the rectangle line and the pattern of the background within the rectangle are defined by the subordinate LINEFORMAT and AREAFORMAT records.)

The grbit field contains the following option flags.

Offset	Bits	Mask	Name	Contents
0	0	01h	fAutoSize	Microsoft Excel calculates size
0	1	02h	fAutoPosition	Microsoft Excel calculates position
0	7–2	FCh	(reserved)	Reserved; must be zero
1	7–0	FFh	(reserved)	Reserved; must be zero

The fAutoSize field indicates that the size of the frame is to be calculated by Microsoft Excel. The dx and dy fields in the parent record are ignored.

The fAutoPosition field indicates that the position of the frame is to be calculated by Microsoft Excel. The dx and dy fields in the parent record are ignored.

GELFRAME: Fill Data (1066h)

This record stores fill effects such as gradient fills, patterns, textures, and so on. The record data is obtained from the Microsoft Office Drawing DLL.

Record Data

Offset	Name	Size	Contents
4	rgb	var	Reserved

IFMT: Number-Format Index (104Eh)

This record specifies the number-format index for an axis.

Record Data

Offset	Name	Size	Contents
4	ifmt	2	Number-format index (number of the FORMAT record in the BIFF, begins at zero)

LEGEND: Legend Type and Position (1015h)

The LEGEND record defines the location of the legend on the display and its overall size. The displayed legend contains all series on the chart.

Record Data—BIFF8

Offset	Name	Size	Contents
4	x	4	x-position of upper-left corner
8	y	4	y-position of upper-left corner
12	dx	4	x-size
16	dy	4	y-size
20	wType	1	Type 0 = bottom 1 = corner 2 = top 3 = right 4 = left 7 = not docked or inside the plot area
21	wSpacing	1	Spacing 0 = close 1 = medium 2 = open
22	grbit	2	Option flags

The x, y, dx, and dy fields are in units of 1/4000 of the chart area.

The x and y fields define the position of the upper-left corner of the bounding rectangle that encompasses the legend. The position of the legend is referenced to the document window. The dx and dy fields define the overall size (the bounding rectangle) of the legend.

The wType field defines the location of the legend relative to the plot rectangle of the chart. The wSpacing field is always 1 for Microsoft Excel.

The grbit field contains the following option flags.

Offset	Bits	Mask	Name	Contents
0	0	01h	fAutoPosition	Automatic positioning (1 = legend is docked)
	1	02h	fAutoSeries	Automatic series distribution (TRUE in Microsoft Excel 5.0)
	2	04h	fAutoPosX	X positioning is automatic
	3	08h	fAutoPosY	Y positioning is automatic
	4	10h	fVert	1 = vertical legend (a single column of entries) 0 = horizontal legend (multiple columns of entries) Manually sized legends always have this bit set to zero
	5	20h	fWasDataTable	1 = chart contains data table
	7–6	C0h	(reserved)	Reserved; must be zero
1	7–0	FFh	(reserved)	Reserved; must be zero

Record Data—BIFF7 and earlier

Offset	Name	Size	Contents
4	x	4	x-position of upper-left corner
8	y	4	y-position of upper-left corner
12	dx	4	x-size
16	dy	4	y-size
20	wType	1	Type 0 = bottom 1 = corner 2 = top 3 = right 4 = left 7 = not docked or inside the plot area

Offset	Name	Size	Contents
21	wSpacing	1	Spacing 0 = close 1 = medium 2 = open
22	grbit	2	Option flags

The x, y, dx, and dy fields are in units of 1/4000 of the chart area.

The x and y fields define the position of the upper-left corner of the bounding rectangle that encompasses the legend. The position of the legend is referenced to the document window. The dx and dy fields define the overall size (the bounding rectangle) of the legend.

The wType field defines the location of the legend relative to the plot rectangle of the chart. The wSpacing field is always 1 for Microsoft Excel.

The grbit field contains the following option flags.

Offset	Bits	Mask	Name	Contents
0	0	01h	fAutoPosition	Automatic positioning (1 = legend is docked)
0	1	02h	fAutoSeries	Automatic series distribution (TRUE in Microsoft Excel 5.0)
0	2	04h	fAutoPosX	X positioning is automatic
0	3	08h	fAutoPosY	Y positioning is automatic
0	4	10h	fVert	1 = vertical legend (a single column of entries) 0 = horizontal legend (multiple columns of entries) Manually sized legends always have this bit set to zero
0	7–5	E0h	(reserved)	Reserved; must be zero
1	7–0	FFh	(reserved)	Reserved; must be zero

LEGENDXN: Legend Exception (1043h)

This record specifies information about a legend entry that has been changed from the default legend-entry settings.

Record Data

Offset	Name	Size	Contents
4	iss	2	Legend-entry index
6	grbit	2	Flags

The grbit field contains the following option flags.

Offset	Bits	Mask	Name	Contents
0	0	01h	fDeleted	TRUE if the legend entry has been deleted
0	1	02h	fLabel	TRUE if the legend entry has been formatted
0	7–2	FCh	(reserved)	Reserved; must be zero
1	7–0	FFh	(reserved)	Reserved; must be zero

Microsoft Excel uses three legend types. On a chart where the legend lists the series names, the iss field will contain FFFF. On a single-series chart formatted to vary by category (a pie chart or column autoformat number two, for example), the legend lists the categories, and the iss field contains the category number. On a surface chart, the legend lists data ranges, and the iss field contains the legend-entry number, starting at zero for the bottom range.

LINE: Chart Group Is a Line Chart Group (1018h)

This record defines a line chart group.

Record Data—BIFF8

Offset	Name	Size	Contents
4	grbit	2	format flags

The grbit field contains the following option flags.

Offset	Bits	Mask	Name	Contents
0	0	01h	fStacked	Stack the displayed values
	1	02h	f100	Each category is broken down as a percentage
	2	04h	fHasShadow	1 = this line has a shadow
	7–3	F8h	(reserved)	Reserved; must be zero
1	7–0	FFh	(reserved)	Reserved; must be zero

When fStacked is true, the value indicators within a category are stacked one on top of the next. The f100 bit can be set only when the fStacked bit is set, and indicates that each category is broken down into percentages.

Record Data—BIFF7 and earlier

Offset	Name	Size	Contents
4	grbit	2	format flags

The grbit field contains the following option flags.

Offset	Bits	Mask	Name	Contents
0	0	01h	fStacked	Stack the displayed values
0	1	02h	f100	Each category is broken down as a percentage
0	7–2	FCh	(reserved)	Reserved; must be zero
1	7–0	FFh	(reserved)	Reserved; must be zero

When fStacked is true, the value indicators within a category are stacked one on top of the next. The f100 bit can be set only when the fStacked bit is set, and indicates that each category is broken down into percentages.

LINEFORMAT: Style of a Line or Border (1007h)

This record defines the appearance of a line, such as an axis line or border.

Record Data—BIFF8

Offset	Name	Size	Contents
4	rgb	4	Color of line; RGB value high byte must be set to zero
8	lns	2	Pattern of line 0 = solid 1 = dash 2 = dot 3 = dash-dot 4 = dash dot-dot 5 = none 6 = dark gray pattern 7 = medium gray pattern 8 = light gray pattern
10	we	2	Weight of line −1 = hairline 0 = narrow (single) 1 = medium (double) 2 = wide (triple)
12	grbit	2	Format flags
14	icv		Index to color of line

The grbit field contains the following option flags.

Offset	Bits	Mask	Name	Contents
0	0	01h	fAuto	Automatic format
0	1	02h	(reserved)	Reserved; must be zero
0	2	04h	fDrawTick	1 = draw tick labels on this axis
0	7–3	F8h	(reserved)	Reserved; must be zero
1	7–0	FFh	(reserved)	Reserved; must be zero

Record Data—BIFF7 and earlier

Offset	Name	Size	Contents
4	rgb	4	Color of line; RGB value high byte must be set to zero
8	lns	2	Pattern of line 0 = solid 1 = dash 2 = dot 3 = dash-dot 4 = dash dot-dot 5 = none 6 = dark gray pattern 7 = medium gray pattern 8 = light gray pattern
10	we	2	Weight of line −1 = hairline 0 = narrow (single) 1 = medium (double) 2 = wide (triple)
12	grbit	2	Format flags

The grbit field contains the following option flags.

Offset	Bits	Mask	Name	Contents
0	0	01h	fAuto	Automatic format
0	1	02h	(reserved)	Reserved; must be zero
0	2	04h	fDrawTick	1 = draw tick labels on this axis
0	7–3	F8h	(reserved)	Reserved; must be zero
1	7–0	FFh	(reserved)	Reserved; must be zero

MARKERFORMAT: Style of a Line Marker (1009h)

This record defines the color and shape of the line markers that appear on scatter and line charts.

Record Data—BIFF8

Offset	Name	Size	Contents
4	rgbFore	4	Foreground color: RGB value (high byte = 0)
8	rgbBack	4	Background color: RGB value (high byte = 0)
12	imk	2	Type of marker 0 = no marker 1 = square 2 = diamond 3 = triangle 4 = X 5 = star 6 = Dow-Jones 7 = standard deviation 8 = circle 9 = plus sign
14	grbit	2	Format flags
16	icvFore	2	Index to color of marker border
18	icvBack	2	Index to color of marker fill
20	miSize	4	Size of line markers

The icvBack field describes the color of the marker's background, such as the center of the square, while the icvFore field describes the color of the border or the marker itself. The imk field defines the type of marker.

The grbit field contains the following option flags.

Offset	Bits	Mask	Name	Contents
0	0	01h	fAuto	Automatic color
0	3–1	0Eh	(reserved)	Reserved; must be zero
0	4	10h	fNotShowInt	1 = "background = none"
0	5	20h	fNotShowBrd	1 = "foreground = none"
0	7–6	C0h	(reserved)	Reserved; must be zero
1	7–0	FFh	(reserved)	Reserved; must be zero

Record Data—BIFF7 and earlier

Offset	Name	Size	Contents
4	rgbFore	4	Foreground color: RGB value (high byte = 0)
8	rgbBack	4	Background color: RGB value (high byte = 0)
12	imk	2	Type of marker 0 = no marker 1 = square 2 = diamond 3 = triangle 4 = X 5 = star 6 = Dow-Jones 7 = standard deviation 8 = circle 9 = plus sign
14	grbit	2	Format flags

The rgbBack field describes the color of the marker's background, such as the center of the square, while the rgbFore field describes the color of the border or the marker itself. The imk field defines the type of marker.

The grbit field contains the following option flags.

Offset	Bits	Mask	Name	Contents
0	0	01h	fAuto	Automatic color
0	3–1	0Eh	(reserved)	Reserved; must be zero
0	4	10h	fNotShowInt	1 = "background = none"
0	5	20h	fNotShowBrd	1 = "foreground = none"
0	7–6	C0h	(reserved)	Reserved; must be zero
1	7–0	FFh	(reserved)	Reserved; must be zero

OBJECTLINK: Attaches Text to Chart or to Chart Item (1027h)

This record links a TEXT record to an object on the chart or to the entire chart.

Record Data

Offset	Name	Size	Contents
4	wLinkObj	2	Object text is linked to 1 = entire chart (chart title) 2 = y axis (y axis title) 3 = x axis (x axis title) 4 = data series or data point (data label) 5 not used 6 not used 7 = z axis (z axis title)
6	wLinkVar1	2	Link index 1, series number
8	wLinkVar2	2	Link index 2, data point number

The wLinkObj field specifies which object the text is linked to. The wLinkVar1 and wLinkVar2 fields define the linked object as a specific series number and data point in the series. The wLinkVar1 and wLinkVar2 fields have meaning only if the wLinkObj field equals 4.

PICF: Picture Format (103Ch)

This record defines the format for a picture attached to a data series or point.

Record Data—BIFF8

Offset	Name	Size	Contents
4	ptyp	2	Picture type: = 1, stretched = 2, stacked = 3, stacked and scaled
6	cf	2	Image format: = 2, Windows metafile or Macintosh PICT format = 9, Windows bitmap format
8	grbit	2	Option flags
10	numScale	8	Scaling value for pictures, units/picture (IEEE floating-point number)

The grbit field contains the following option flags.

Offset	Bits	Mask	Name	Contents
0	7–0	FFh	env	Environment from which the file was written: = 1, Microsoft Windows = 2, Apple Macintosh
1	0	01h	fFmtOnly	Formatting only; no picture attached
1	1	02h	fTopBottom	Picture is attached to top and bottom of column
	2	04h	fBackFront	Picture is attached to back and front of column
	3	08h	fSide	Picture is attached to sides of column
	7–4	F0h	(reserved)	Reserved; must be zero

If fFmtOnly is false, then an IMDATA record, which contains the picture itself, follows the PICF record. If fFmtOnly is true, which occurs only if the parent DATAFORMAT record refers to a single data point, then there is no IMDATA record following the PICF record. In this case, the picture specified for the entire series is used, with formatting specified by the PICF record. For more information about the IMDATA record, see "IMDATA."

Record Data—BIFF7 and earlier

Offset	Name	Size	Contents
4	ptyp	2	Picture type: = 1, stretched = 2, stacked = 3, stacked and scaled
6	cf	2	Image format: = 2, Windows metafile or Macintosh PICT format = 9, Windows bitmap format
8	grbit	2	Option flags
10	numScale	8	Scaling value for pictures, units/picture (IEEE floating-point number)

The grbit field contains the following option flags.

Offset	Bits	Mask	Name	Contents
0	7–0	FFh	env	Environment from which the file was written: = 1, Microsoft Windows = 2, Apple Macintosh
1	0	01h	fFmtOnly	Formatting only; no picture attached
1	7–1	FEh	(reserved)	Reserved; must be zero

If fFmtOnly is false, then an IMDATA record, which contains the picture itself, follows the PICF record. If fFmtOnly is true, which occurs only if the parent DATAFORMAT record refers to a single data point, then there is no IMDATA record following the PICF record. In this case, the picture specified for the entire series is used, with formatting specified by the PICF record. For more information about the IMDATA record, see "IMDATA."

PIE: Chart Group Is a Pie Chart Group (1019h)

This record defines a pie chart group and specifies pie chart options.

Record Data—BIFF8

Offset	Name	Size	Contents
4	anStart	2	Angle of the first pie slice expressed in degrees
6	pcDonut	2	0 = true pie chart non-zero = size of center hole in a donut chart (as a percentage)
8	grbit	2	Option flags (see following table)

The grbit field contains the following option flags.

Bits	Mask	Name	Contents
0	0001h	fHasShadow	1 = this pie has a shadow
1	0002h	fShowLdrLines	1 = show leader lines to data labels
15–2	FFFCh	(reserved)	Reserved; must be zero

The angle of the pie slice has a default value of zero and can be any value in the range of 0 to 359 (0000h to 0167h).

Record Data—BIFF7 and earlier

Offset	Name	Size	Contents
4	anStart	2	Angle of the first pie slice expressed in degrees
6	pcDonut	2	0 = true pie chart non-zero = size of center hole in a donut chart (as a percentage)

The angle of the pie slice has a default value of zero and can be any value in the range of 0 to 359 (0000h to 0167h).

PIEFORMAT: Position of the Pie Slice (100Bh)

The distance of an open pie slice from the center of the pie chart is expressed as a percentage of the pie diameter. For example, if the percent = 33 (21h), the pie slice is one-third of the pie diameter away from the pie center.

Record Data

Offset	Name	Size	Contents
4	percent	2	Distance of pie slice from center of pie

PLOTAREA: Frame Belongs to Plot Area (1035h)

This record immediately precedes a FRAME record. It indicates that the frame record that follows belongs to the plot area.

PLOTGROWTH: Font Scale Factors (1064h)

This record stores scale factors for font scaling.

Record Data—BIFF8

Offset	Name	Size	Contents
4	dxPlotGrowth	4	Horizontal growth of plot area for font scaling
8	dyPlotGrowth	4	Vertical growth of plot area for font scaling

POS: Position Information (104Fh)

This record defines manual position information for the main-axis plot area, legend, and attached text (data labels, axis labels, and chart title). The record data depends on the record's use, as shown in the following sections.

This record is used very rarely and is usually not required; for most applications, the default size and position settings are sufficient. If your application writes chart BIFF, use the default settings whenever possible. To use the default plot area, set the fManPlotArea bit in the SHTPROPS record. To use a default legend position and size, set the fAutoPosition bit in the LEGEND record, and set the fAutoSize bit in the legend FRAME record. No other settings are required to use the default position for text (data labels, axis labels, and chart title).

Plot Area

The POS record is used only for the main axis. The record describes the plot-area bounding box (the plot-area bounding box includes the plot area, tick marks, and a small border around the tick marks). The fManPlotArea bit in the SHTPROPS record must be 1, or the POS record is ignored.

The top left position, width, and height fields use units of 1/4000 of the chart area.

Record Data

Offset	Name	Size	Contents
4	mdTopLt	2	Must be 2
6	mdBotRt	2	Must be 2
8	x1	4	x coordinate of bounding box top left corner
12	y1	4	y coordinate of bounding box top left corner
16	x2	4	width of the bounding box
20	y2	4	height of the bounding box

Legend

The POS record describes the legend position and size.

Record Data

Offset	Name	Size	Contents
4	mdTopLt	2	Must be 5
6	mdBotRt	2	1 = use x2 and y2 for legend size 2 = autosize legend (ignore x2, y2). The fAutoSize bit of the legend FRAME record should be 1 if this field is 2.
8	x1	4	x coordinate of legend top left corner, in units of 1/4000 of the chart area
12	y1	4	y coordinate of legend top left corner, in units of 1/4000 of the chart area
16	x2	4	width of the legend, in points (1/72 inch)
20	y2	4	height of the legend, in points

Text (Chart Title)

The POS record sets the chart title position as an offset from the default position, in units of 1/4000 of the chart area.

Record Data

Offset	Name	Size	Contents
4	mdTopLt	2	Must be 2
6	mdTopRt	2	Must be 2
8	x1	4	offset from default horizontal position
12	y1	4	offset from default vertical position
16	x2	4	ignored (you cannot size the chart title)
20	y2	4	ignored

Text (Axis Title)

The POS record sets the axis title position as an offset from the default position.

Record Data

Offset	Name	Size	Contents
4	mdTopLt	2	Must be 2
6	mdTopRt	2	Must be 2
8	x1	4	offset perpendicular to the axis, in units of 1/1000 of the plot-area bounding box
12	y1	4	offset parallel to the axis, in units of 1/1000 of the axis length
16	x2	4	ignored (you cannot size the axis title)
20	y2	4	ignored

Text (Data Labels)

The POS record sets the label position as an offset from the default position.

Record Data

Offset	Name	Size	Contents
4	mdTopLt	2	Must be 2
6	mdTopRt	2	Must be 2
8	x1	4	**Pie charts**: offset angle from the default, in radians **Bar and Column charts**: offset perpendicular to the bar or column, in units of 1/1000 of the plot area **All other chart types**: horizontal offset from the default position, in units of 1/1000 of the plot area
12	y1	4	**Pie charts**: radial offset, in units of 1/1000 of the pie radius **Bar and Column charts**: offset parallel to the bar or column, in units of 1/1000 of the plot area **All other chart types**: vertical offset from the default position, in units of 1/1000 of the plot area
16	x2	4	ignored (you cannot size the data label)
20	y2	4	ignored

RADAR: Chart Group Is a Radar Chart Group (103Eh)

This record defines a radar chart group.

Record Data—BIFF8

Offset	Name	Size	Contents
4	grbit	2	Option flags

The grbit field contains the following option flags.

Offset	Bits	Mask	Name	Contents
0	0	01h	fRdrAxLab	1 = chart contains radar axis labels
	1	02h	fHasShadow	1 = this radar series has a shadow
	7–2	FCh	(reserved)	Reserved; must be zero
1	7–0	FFh	(reserved)	Reserved; must be zero

Record Data—BIFF7 and earlier

Offset	Name	Size	Contents
4	grbit	2	Option flags

The grbit field contains the following option flags.

Offset	Bits	Mask	Name	Contents
0	0	01h	fRdrAxLab	= 1, chart contains radar axis labels
0	7–1	FEh	(reserved)	Reserved; must be zero
1	7–0	FFh	(reserved)	Reserved; must be zero

RADARAREA: Chart Group Is a Radar Area Chart Group (1040h)

This record defines a radar area chart group.

Record Data

Offset	Name	Size	Contents
4	grbit	2	Option flags

The grbit field contains the following option flags.

Offset	Bits	Mask	Name	Contents
0	0	01h	fRdrAxLab	1 if chart contains radar axis labels
0	7–1	FEh	(reserved)	Reserved; must be zero
1	7–0	FFh	(reserved)	Reserved; must be zero

SBASEREF: PivotTable Reference (1048h)

This record specifies the PivotTable reference used for the chart.

Record Data

Offset	Name	Size	Contents
4	rwFirst	2	First PivotTable row
6	rwLast	2	Last PivotTable row
8	colFirst	2	First PivotTable column
10	colLast	2	Last PivotTable column

SCATTER: Chart Group Is a Scatter Chart Group (101Bh)

This record stores scatter chart properties.

Record Data—BIFF8

Offset	Name	Size	Contents
4	pcBubbleSizeRatio	2	Percent of largest bubble compared to chart in general
6	wBubbleSize	2	Bubble size: 1 = bubble size is area 2 = bubble size is width
8	grbit	2	Option flags (see following table)

The grbit field contains the following option flags.

Offset	Bits	Mask	Name	Contents
0	0	01h	fBubbles	1 = this a bubble series
	1	02h	fShowNegBubbles	1 = show negative bubbles
	2	04h	fHasShadow	1 = bubble series has a shadow
	7–3	F8h	(reserved)	Reserved; must be zero
1	7–0	FFh	(reserved)	Reserved; must be zero

Record Data—BIFF7 and earlier

In BIFF7 and earlier, this record has no record data field. If the SCATTER record is present in the Chart BIFF, it signifies that the chart group is an XY (scatter) chart group.

SERAUXERRBAR: Series ErrorBar (105Bh)

This record defines series error bars.

Record Data

Offset	Name	Size	Contents
4	sertm	1	Error-bar type: 1 = x-direction plus 2 = x-direction minus 3 = y-direction plus 4 = y-direction minus
5	ebsrc	1	Error-bar value source: 1 = percentage 2 = fixed value 3 = standard deviation 4 = custom 5 = standard error
6	fTeeTop	1	TRUE if the error bars are T-shaped (have a line on the top and bottom)
7	(reserved)	1	Reserved; must be 1
8	numValue	8	IEEE number; specifies the fixed value, percentage, or number of standard deviations for the error bars
16	cnum	2	Number of values or cell references used for custom error bars

SERAUXTREND: Series Trendline (104Bh)

This record defines a series trendline.

Record Data

Offset	Name	Size	Contents
4	regt	1	Regression type: 0 = polynomial 1 = exponential 2 = Logarithmic 3 = Power 4 = moving average (a linear trendline has type 0 with order 1)
5	ordUser	1	Polynomial order or moving average period
6	numIntercept	8	IEEE number; specifies forced intercept (#NA if no intercept is specified)

Offset	Name	Size	Contents
14	fEquation	1	TRUE if the equation is displayed
15	fRSquared	1	TRUE if the R-squared value is displayed
16	numForecast	8	IEEE number; specifies number of periods to forecast forward
24	numBackcast	8	IEEE number; specifies number of periods to forecast backward

SERFMT: Series Format (105Dh)

This record specifies series formatting information.

Record Data—BIFF8

Offset	Name	Size	Contents
0	grbit	2	flags

The grbit field contains the following option flags.

Offset	Bits	Mask	Name	Contents
0	0	01h	fSmoothedLine	1 = the line series has a smoothed line
	1	02h	f3DBubbles	1 = draw bubbles with 3-D effects
	2	04h	fArShadow	1 = this series has a shadow
	7–3	F8h	(reserved)	Reserved; must be zero
1	7–0	FFh	(reserved)	Reserved; must be zero

Record Data—BIFF7 and earlier

Offset	Name	Size	Contents
0	grbit	2	flags

The grbit field contains the following option flags.

Offset	Bits	Mask	Name	Contents
0	0	01h	fSmoothedLine	TRUE if the line series has a smoothed line
0	7–1	FEh	(reserved)	Reserved; must be zero
1	7–0	FFh	(reserved)	Reserved; must be zero

SERIES: Series Definition (1003h)

This record describes the series of the chart, and contains the type of data and number of data fields that make up the series. Series can contain 4000 points in Microsoft Excel version 5.

The sdtX and sdtY fields define the type of data that is contained in this series. At present, the two types of data used in Microsoft Excel chart series are numeric and text (date and sequence information is not used). The cValx and cValy fields contain the number of cell records in the series.

Record Data—BIFF8

Offset	Name	Size	Contents
4	sdtX	2	Type of data in categories 0 = categories contain date information (not used) 1 = categories contain numeric information 2 = categories contain sequence information (not used) 3 = categories contain text information
8	sdtY	2	Type of data in values 0 = values contain date information (not used) 1 = values contain numeric information 2 = values contain sequence information (not used) 3 = values contain text information
10	cValx	2	Count of categories
12	cValy	2	Count of values
14	sdtBSize	2	Type of data in Bubble size series: 0 = dates 1 = numeric 2 = sequence 3 = text
16	cValBSize	2	Count of Bubble series values

Record Data—BIFF7 and earlier

Offset	Name	Size	Contents
4	sdtX	2	Type of data in categories 0 = categories contain date information (not used) 1 = categories contain numeric information 2 = categories contain sequence information (not used) 3 − categories contain text information
8	sdtY	2	Type of data in values 0 = values contain date information (not used) 1 = values contain numeric information 2 = values contain sequence information (not used) 3 = values contain text information
10	cValx	2	Count of categories
12	cValy	2	Count of values

SERIESLIST: Specifies the Series in an Overlay Chart (1016h)

This record is subordinate to the second CHARTFORMAT (overlay) record in a file and defines the series that are displayed as the overlay to the main chart. The first CHARTFORMAT (main chart) record in a file does not require a SERIESLIST record because all series, except those specified for the overlay, are included in the main chart.

Record Data

Offset	Name	Size	Contents
4	cser	2	Count of series (size of rgiser)
6	rgiser	var	List of series numbers (words)

SERIESTEXT: Legend/Category/Value Text (100Dh)

The value of the id field determines the assignment of the text field.

Record Data

Offset	Name	Size	Contents
4	id	2	Text identifier: 0 = series name or text
6	cch	1	Length of text field
7	rgch	var	The series text string

Values greater than zero in the id field do not apply to Microsoft Excel.

SERPARENT: Trendline or ErrorBar Series Index (104Ah)

This record indicates the series index for the series that the trendline or error bar is attached to. The series index is the number of the series in the BIFF (starting with series one).

Record Data

Offset	Name	Size	Contents
4	series	2	Series index for the series that the trendline or error bar is attached to

SERTOCRT: Series Chart-Group Index (1045h)

This record is part of the series specifications and indicates the chart-group index for the series. The chart-group index specifies the number of the chart group (specified by a CHARTFORMAT record) in the BIFF, starting with chart group zero.

Record Data

Offset	Name	Size	Contents
0	chartgroup	2	Chart-group index

SHTPROPS: Sheet Properties (1044h)

This record specifies chart sheet properties.

Record Data—BIFF8

Offset	Name	Size	Contents
4	grbit	2	Property flags
6	mdBlank	1	Empty cells plotted as: 0 = not plotted 1 = zero 2 = interpolated

The grbit field contains the following option flags.

Offset	Bits	Mask	Name	Contents
0	0	01h	fManSerAlloc	1 = chart type has been manually formatted (changed from the default)
	1	02h	fPlotVisOnly	1 = plot visible cells only
	2	04h	fNotSizeWith	1 = do not size chart with window
	3	08h	fManPlotArea	0 = use default plot area dimensions 1 = POS record describes plot area dimensions
	4	10h	fAlwaysAutoPlotArea	1 = user has modified chart enough that fManPlotArea should be set to 0
	7–5	E0h	(reserved)	Reserved; must be zero
1	7–0	FFh	(reserved)	Reserved; must be zero

Record Data—BIFF7 and earlier

Offset	Name	Size	Contents
4	grbit	2	Property flags
6	mdBlank	1	Empty cells plotted as: 0 = not plotted 1 = zero 2 = interpolated

The grbit field contains the following option flags.

Offset	Bits	Mask	Name	Contents
0	0	01h	fManSerAlloc	1 = chart type has been manually formatted (changed from the default)
0	1	02h	fPlotVisOnly	1 = plot visible cells only
0	2	04h	fNotSizeWith	1 = do not size chart with window
0	3	08h	fManPlotArea	0 = use default plot area dimensions 1 = POS record describes plot area dimensions
0	7–4	F0h	(reserved)	Reserved; must be zero
1	7–0	FFh	(reserved)	Reserved; must be zero

SIINDEX: Series Index (1065h)

This record defines where a series appears in the list of series.

Record Data

Offset	Name	Size	Contents
4	numIndex	4	Index into series list

SURFACE: Chart Group Is a Surface Chart Group (103Fh)

This record defines a surface chart group.

Record Data—BIFF8

Offset	Name	Size	Contents
4	grbit	2	Option flags

The grbit field contains the following option flags.

Offset	Bits	Mask	Name	Contents
0	0	01h	fFillSurface	1 = chart contains color fill for surface
	1	02h	f3DPhongShade	1 = this surface chart has shading
	7–2	FCh	(reserved)	Reserved; must be zero
1	7–0	FFh	(reserved)	Reserved; must be zero

Record Data—BIFF7 and earlier

Offset	Name	Size	Contents
4	grbit	2	Option flags

The grbit field contains the following option flags.

Offset	Bits	Mask	Name	Contents
0	0	01h	fFillSurface	= 1, chart contains color fill for surface
0	7–1	FEh	(reserved)	Reserved; must be zero
1	7–0	FFh	(reserved)	Reserved; must be zero

TEXT: Defines Display of Text Fields (1025h)

This record is used in conjunction with several child records (which further define the text displayed on the chart) to define the alignment, color, position, size, and so on, of text fields that appear on the chart. The fields in this record have meaning according to the TEXT record's parent (CHART, LEGEND, or DEFAULTTEXT).

Record Data—BIFF8

Offset	Name	Size	Contents
4	at	1	Horizontal alignment of the text (1 = left, 2 = center, 3 = bottom, 4 = justify)
5	vat	1	Vertical alignment of the text (1 = top, 2 = center, 3 = bottom, 4 = justify)
6	wBkgMode	2	Display mode of the background 1 = transparent 2 = opaque
8	rgbText	4	Color of the text; RGB value (high byte = 0)
12	x	4	x-position of the text in 1/4000 of chart area
16	y	4	y-position of the text in 1/4000 of chart area
20	dx	4	x-size of the text in 1/4000 of chart area
24	dy	4	y-size of the text in 1/4000 of chart area
28	grbit	2	Option flags (See following table)
30	icvText	2	Index to color value of text
32	grbit2	2	Option flags (See following table)
34	trot	2	Text rotation: 0dec = Horizontal 90dec = Up 90 180dec = Down 180 -90dec = Down (inverted from 180dec)

The option flags in the grbit field (like the fields themselves) have meaning according to the TEXT record's parent. The grbit field contains the following option flags.

Bits	Mask	Name	Contents
0	0001h	fAutoColor	1 = automatic color 0 = user-selected color
1	0002h	fShowKey	If text is an attached data label: 1 = draw legend key with data label 0 = no legend key
2	0004h	fShowValue	1 = text of label is the value of the data point 0 = text is the category label
3	0008h	fVert	1 = text is not horizontal 0 = text is horizontal
4	0010h	fAutoText	1 = use automatically generated text string 0 = use user-created text string Must be one for fShowValue to be meaningful.
5	0020h	fGenerated	1 = default or unmodified 0 = modified
6	0040h	fDeleted	1= an Automatic text label has been deleted by the user
7	0080h	fAutoMode	1 = Background is set to Automatic
10–8	0700h	rot	0 = no rotation (text appears left-to-right) 1 = text appears top-to-bottom, letters are upright 2 = text is rotated 90 degrees counterclockwise 3 = text is rotated 90 degrees clockwise
11	0800h	fShLabPct	1 = show category label and value as a percentage (pie charts only)
12	1000h	fShowPct	1 = show value as a percent. This bit applies only to pie charts.
13	2000h	fShowBubbleSizes	1 = show bubble sizes
14	4000h	fShowLabel	1 = show label
15	8000h	(reserved)	Reserved; must be zero

The grbit2 field contains the following option flags.

Bits	Mask	Name	Contents
3–0	000Fh	dlp	Data label placement (see text)
15–4	FFF0h	(reserved)	Reserved; must be zero

The dlp field specifies data label placement, as shown in the following table.

dlp	Position	Used on these chart types
1	Outside	Bar, 2d/3d pie
2	Inside	Bar, 2d/3d pie
3	Center	Bar, line, 2d/3d pie
4	Axis	Bar
5	Above	Line
6	Below	Line
7	Left	Line
8	Right	Line
9	Auto	2d/3d pie
10	Moved (user moved the data label)	various

When dlp is equal to 0 (zero), it specifies the following positions:

Chart type	Position
2d/3d pie	Auto
Line	Right
Bar	Outside
Stacked bar	Center

The dlp field will be equal to 0 (zero) for all non-data label text elements.

Record Data—BIFF7 and earlier

Offset	Name	Size	Contents
4	at	1	Horizontal alignment of the text (1 = left, 2 = center, 3 = bottom, 4 = justify)
5	vat	1	Vertical alignment of the text (1 = top, 2 = center, 3 = bottom, 4 = justify)
6	wBkgMode	2	Display mode of the background 1 = transparent 2 = opaque
8	rgbText	4	Color of the text; RGB value (high byte = 0)

Offset	Name	Size	Contents
12	x	4	x-position of the text in 1/4000 of chart area
16	y	4	y-position of the text in 1/4000 of chart area
20	dx	4	x-size of the text in 1/4000 of chart area
24	dy	4	y-size of the text in 1/4000 of chart area
28	grbit	2	Display flags

The option flags in the grbit field (like the fields themselves) have meaning according to the TEXT record's parent. The grbit field contains the following option flags.

Offset	Bits	Mask	Name	Contents
0	0	01h	fAutoColor	1 = automatic color 0 = user-selected color
0	1	02h	fShowKey	If text is an attached data label: 1 = draw legend key with data label 0 = no legend key
0	2	04h	fShowValue	1 = text of label is the value of the data point 0 = text is the category label
0	3	08h	fVert	1 = text is not horizontal 0 = text is horizontal
0	4	10h	fAutoText	1 = use automatically generated text string 0 = use user-created text string Must be one for fShowValue to be meaningful.
0	5	20h	fGenerated	1 = default or unmodified 0 = modified
0	6	40h	fDeleted	1= an Automatic text label has been deleted by the user
0	7	80h	fAutoMode	1 = Background is set to Automatic
1	2–0	07h	rot	0 = no rotation (text appears left-to-right) 1 = text appears top-to-bottom, letters are upright 2 = text is rotated 90 degrees counterclockwise 3 = text is rotated 90 degrees clockwise
1	3	08h	fShLabPct	1 = show category label and value as a percentage (pie charts only)
1	4	10h	fShowPct	1 = show value as a percent. This bit applies only to pie charts.
1	7–5	E0h	(reserved)	Reserved; must be zero

TICK: Tick Marks and Labels Format (101Eh)

This record defines tick mark and tick label formatting.

Record Data—BIFF8

Offset	Name	Size	Contents
4	tktMajor	1	Type of major tick mark 0 = invisible (none) 1 = inside of axis line 2 = outside of axis line 3 = cross axis line
5	tktMinor	1	Type of minor tick mark 0 = invisible (none) 1 = inside of axis line 2 = outside of axis line 3 = cross axis line
6	tlt	1	Tick label position relative to axis line 0 = invisible (none) 1 = low end of plot area 2 = high end of plot area 3 = next to axis
7	wBkgMode	1	Background mode: 1 = transparent 2 = opaque
8	rgb	4	Tick-label text color; RGB value, high byte = 0
12	(reserved)	16	Reserved; must be zero
28	grbit	2	Display flags
30	icv	2	Index to color of tick label
32	(reserved)	2	Reserved; must be zero

The grbit field contains the following option flags.

Offset	Bits	Mask	Name	Contents
0	0	01h	fAutoCo	Automatic text color
0	1	02h	fAutoMode	Automatic text background
0	4–2	1Ch	rot	= 0 no rotation (text appears left-to-right) = 1 text appears top-to-bottom, letters are upright = 2 text is rotated 90 degrees counterclockwise = 3 text is rotated 90 degrees clockwise

Offset	Bits	Mask	Name	Contents
0	5	20h	fAutoRot	Automatic rotation
0	7–6	C0h	(reserved)	Reserved; must be zero
1	7–0	FFh	(reserved)	Reserved; must be zero

Record Data—BIFF7 and earlier

Offset	Name	Size	Contents
4	tktMajor	1	Type of major tick mark 0 = invisible (none) 1 = inside of axis line 2 = outside of axis line 3 = cross axis line
5	tktMinor	1	Type of minor tick mark 0 = invisible (none) 1 = inside of axis line 2 = outside of axis line 3 = cross axis line
6	tlt	1	Tick label position relative to axis line 0 = invisible (none) 1 = low end of plot area 2 = high end of plot area 3 = next to axis
7	wBkgMode	1	Background mode: 1 = transparent 2 = opaque
8	rgb	4	Tick-label text color; RGB value, high byte = 0
12	(reserved)	16	Reserved; must be zero
28	grbit	2	Display flags

The grbit field contains the following option flags.

Offset	Bits	Mask	Name	Contents
0	0	01h	fAutoCo	Automatic text color
0	1	02h	fAutoMode	Automatic text background
0	4–2	1Ch	rot	= 0 no rotation (text appears left-to-right) = 1 text appears top-to-bottom, letters are upright = 2 text is rotated 90 degrees counterclockwise = 3 text is rotated 90 degrees clockwise
0	5	20h	fAutoRot	Automatic rotation
0	7–6	C0h	(reserved)	Reserved; must be zero
1	7 – 0	FFh	(reserved)	Reserved; must be zero

UNITS: Chart Units (1001h)

Microsoft Excel writes this record, but its value is always zero.

Applications writing BIFF do not need to write this record. If your application writes this record, the wUnits field must be zero.

Record Data

Offset	Name	Size	Contents
4	wUnits	2	Always zero

VALUERANGE: Defines Value Axis Scale (101Fh)

This record defines the value axis.

Record Data

Offset	Name	Size	Contents
4	numMin	8	Minimum value on axis
12	numMax	8	Maximum value on axis
20	numMajor	8	Value of major increment
28	numMinor	8	Value of minor increment
36	numCross	8	Value where category axis crosses
44	grbit	2	Format flags

All 8-byte numbers in the preceding table are IEEE floating-point numbers.

The numMin field defines the minimum numeric value that appears along the value axis. This field is all zeros if Auto Minimum is selected on the Scale tab of the Format Axis dialog box. The numMax field defines the maximum value displayed along the value axis and is all zeros if Auto Maximum is selected.

The numMajor field defines the increment (unit) of the major value divisions (gridlines) along the value axis. The numMajor field is all zeros if Auto Major Unit is selected on the Scale tab of the Format Axis dialog box. The numMinor field defines the minor value divisions (gridlines) along the value axis and is all zeros if Auto Minor Unit is selected.

The numCross field defines the value along the value axis at which the category axis crosses. This field is all zeros if Auto Category Axis Crosses At is selected.

The grbit field contains the following option flags.

Offset	Bits	Mask	Name	Contents
0	0	01h	fAutoMin	Automatic minimum selected
0	1	02h	fAutoMax	Automatic maximum selected
0	2	04h	fAutoMajor	Automatic major unit selected
0	3	08h	fAutoMinor	Automatic minor unit selected
0	4	10h	fAutoCross	Automatic category crossing point selected
0	5	20h	fLogScale	Logarithmic scale
0	6	40h	fReverse	Values in reverse order
0	7	80h	fMaxCross	Category axis to cross at maximum value
1	7–0	FFh	(reserved)	Reserved; must be zero

APPENDIX A

Dynamic Data Exchange and XlTable Format

Microsoft Windows provides several methods for transferring data between applications. One way to transfer data is to use Windows dynamic data exchange (DDE). DDE is a message protocol for data exchange between Windows programs. It allows software developers to design applications that share data and thereby provide the user with a more integrated Windows environment.

For complete information about DDE, see the documentation for the Microsoft Windows Software Development Kit (SDK). This appendix describes the DDE formats that Microsoft Excel versions 5.0 and later support, and provides detailed information about the high-performance XlTable DDE format.

DDE Formats

Microsoft Excel supports several DDE formats. The formats are listed in the following table in the order of precedence defined by Microsoft Excel, from highest precedence (XlTable) to lowest precedence (CF_METAFILEPICT). Clipboard formats that begin with CF_ are formats that are already defined in WINDOWS.H. Clipboard formats without CF_ must be registered before use. For more information about registering formats, see "Registering Clipboard Formats" on page 534.

Clipboard format	Description
XlTable	Microsoft Excel fast table format. For more information, see "Fast Table Format" on page 535.
Biff5	Binary interchange file format (BIFF) for Microsoft Excel version 5.0. For more information about the file format, see Chapter 9, "Microsoft Excel File Format."
Biff4	Binary interchange file format (BIFF) for Microsoft Excel version 4.0.
Biff3	BIFF for Microsoft Excel version 3.0.
Biff	BIFF for Microsoft Excel version 2.x.

Clipboard format	Description
CF_SYLK	Microsoft symbolic link (SYLK) format. Microsoft Excel for the Apple Macintosh was originally designed to use SYLK format, and this format is now supported by Microsoft Excel on both Windows and Macintosh platforms.
Wk1	Lotus 1-2-3 Release 2.01 and Release 2.2 formats.
Csv	Comma-separated values format, commonly used in BASIC language I/O. It is similar to CF_TEXT format, except that Csv uses commas to separate fields.
CF_TEXT	The simplest form of clipboard data. It is a null-terminated string containing a carriage return and linefeed at the end of each line.
Rich Text Format	A method of encoding formatted text and graphics for easy transfer between applications. Rich Text Format (RTF) is commonly used by document processing programs such as Microsoft Word for Windows and Microsoft Word for the Macintosh.
CF_DIF	An ASCII format used by the VisiCalc spreadsheet program. The format is under the control of Lotus Development Corporation.
CF_BITMAP	A Windows version 2 compatible bitmap.
CF_METAFILEPICT	A metafile picture structure. For complete information, see the documentation for the Microsoft Windows Software Development Kit.

Registering Clipboard Formats

Whenever an application uses a private clipboard format such as XlTable, Biff5, Biff4, Biff3, Biff, Wk1, Csv, or Rich Text Format, it must register the format before using it. Microsoft Excel registers these private clipboard formats, and your DDE application must also register any of these formats that you want to use to exchange data.

For example, to register XlTable, use the following Windows API function call:

```
wCBformat = RegisterClipboardFormat((LPSTR)"XlTable");
```

If the function call is successful, the return value is equal to the format value for the XlTable format. This format value (type WORD) is between 0xC000 and 0xFFFF, and is equal to the format value that Windows returned to Microsoft Excel when it registered XlTable. If Windows cannot register XlTable, then the function returns zero.

Fast Table Format

The fast table format, XlTable, is designed to maximize the DDE transfer speed of Microsoft Excel. XlTable consists of a sequence of data blocks that represent a rectangular selection of cells (a table). Each data block has three parts:

```
WORD tdt          /* the table data type */
WORD cb           /* the size (count of bytes) of the data */
BYTE data[cb]     /* the data */
```

The first data block is always of type tdtTable, which specifies the number of rows and the number of columns in the table. The data blocks that follow tdtTable represent all the cells in the table. Microsoft Excel renders the reference of the cells in the table (for example, R1C1:R2C4) as the item part of the DDE message.

The cells are always rendered row-wise. In other words, all the cells in the first row of the table appear first, then all the cells in the second row, and so on. To minimize overhead, adjacent cells of the same type (tdt) are represented together in one data block, even if the cells are in different rows. In other words, one tdtFloat can contain several numbers, one tdtString can contain several strings, one tdtBool can contain several Boolean values, and so on. For examples, see the following sections, "XlTable Example 1," and "XlTable Example 2."

The data block types are described in the following table.

Data block type	Value	Description
tdtTable	0x0010	The size of the table. The data (4 bytes, cb=4) consists of two words. The first word is the number of rows, and the second word is the number of columns.
tdtFloat	0x0001	IEEE-format floating-point number. The size of the number is 8 bytes per cell.
tdtString	0x0002	String in st (byte-counted) format. The first byte contains the length of the string (cch). The string is not null-terminated.
tdtBool	0x0003	Boolean value: 1 = TRUE 0 = FALSE The length of the data is 2 bytes per cell.

tdtError	0x0004	Error value: 0 = #NULL!
		7 = #DIV/0!
		15 = #VALUE!
		23 = #REF!
		29 = #NAME?
		36 = #NUM!
		42 = #N/A
		
		The length of the data is 2 bytes per cell.

Data block type	Value	Description
tdtBlank	0x0005	A count of the number of consecutive undefined (blank) cells. The data (2 bytes, cb=2) contains the number of consecutive blank cells.
tdtInt	0x0006	Unsigned integer. The length of the data is 2 bytes per cell. Microsoft Excel can read a number in this format, but it never writes a number in this format.
tdtSkip	0x0007	Number of cells to skip. A skipped cell is a cell that retains its previous value. In other words, a skipped cell is not changed by a WM_DDE_DATA message. You can use tdtSkip to increase DDE performance if your application changes only one or two cells in the middle of a large table. Microsoft Excel does not support tdtSkip when the new cell data is part of a WM_DDE_POKE message. The length of the data is 2 bytes (cb=2).

XlTable Example 1

The following selection of three cells . . .

	A	B	C	D
1	East	West	North	
2				
3				
4				

. . . produces the following XlTable rendering.

Data (hexadecimal)	Description
10 00 04 00 01 00 03 00	tdtTable, cb=4, rows=1, columns=3
02 00 10 00	tdtString, cb=16
04 45 61 73 74	cch=4, East (tdtString continued)
04 57 65 73 74	cch=4, West (tdtString continued)
05 4e 6f 72 74 68	cch=5, North (tdtString continued)

Notice that the table contains three cells, but the XlTable rendering contains only one tdtString data block.

XITable Example 2

The XlTable format uses the tdtBlank data block to represent blank cells in a table. A sequence of several blank cells may be represented by a single tdtBlank data block.

For example, the following table . . .

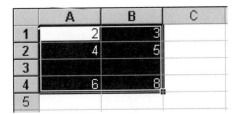

. . . produces the following XlTable rendering.

Data (hexadecimal)	Description
10 00 04 00 02 00 04 00	tdtTable, cb=4, rows=4, columns=2
06 00 08 00 02 00 03 00 04 00 05 00	tdtInt, cb=8, int[0]=2, int[1]=3, int[2]=4, int[3]=5 (Microsoft Excel can read tdtInt as a client, but it would write tdtFloat if it were a server.)
05 00 02 00 02 00	tdtBlank, cb=2, data=2 (2 cells are blank)
06 00 04 00 06 00 08 00	tdtInt, cb=4, int[0]=6, int[1]=8

Biff5, Biff4, Biff3, and Biff Formats

The Biff5, Biff4, Biff3, and Biff clipboard formats contain a variable number of records. The records are identical to the corresponding records in the BIFF file. For more information about the BIFF5 records, see Chapter 3, "File Format." The Biff4, Biff3, and Biff formats are available for backward compatibility with existing applications. The Biff clipboard format corresponds to the BIFF2 file format.

If you implement one of the BIFF clipboard formats, your code should be prepared to receive all BIFF records except the file-specific records such as:

WRITEPROT
FILEPASS
TEMPLATE
WRITEACCESS

FILESHARING
CODEPAGE
PUB
SUB
EDG
INDEX

The minimum BIFF records that your code must provide when it writes to the clipboard are:

BOF
DIMENSIONS
Cell record or records (BLANK, BOOLERR, and so on)
EOF

A P P E N D I X   B

Excel 97 and the Registry

In Microsoft Excel 97, the program preferences are stored in the Windows 95 or Windows NT registry. Microsoft Excel creates a key called Excel under the HKEY_CURRENT_USER key, as shown in the following illustration:

```
HKEY_CURRENT_USER\
    Software\
        Microsoft\
            Office\
                8.0\
                    Excel\
```

Under the Excel key, Microsoft Excel creates a subkey for each category of program preferences.

```
                Add-in Manager\
                AutoSave\
                Converters\
                Delete Commands\
                Init Commands\
                Init Menus\
                Line Print\
                Microsoft Excel\
                Recent File List\
                Spell Checker\
                WK? Settings\
```

Under each section key, the individual settings exist as key=value pairs. Long value settings have type REG_DWORD, binary value settings have REG_BINARY type, and string value settings have type REG_SZ.

Each time you start Microsoft Excel, it checks the registry for startup settings. For example, you can use this file to specify documents that you want opened automatically, whether you want gridlines to appear in new worksheets, or what font you want as the default font.

Editing the Registry

To edit the Windows 95 or Windows NT registry, you use the RegEdit program. This program is located in your Windows directory. You can run RegEdit by choosing Start/Run from the Taskbar menu, and then typing RegEdit into the Run dialog, or by double-clicking RegEdit.exe in the Windows directory from Explorer.

The Add-In Manager Subkey

Values under this subkey are the full file paths for add-ins that are not installed but are shown in the Tools/Addin listbox.

The AutoSave Subkey

This optional subkey is added by the AutoSave add-in.

Entry	Description
Frequency	The number of minutes between saves as an integer.
Options	1 - Save Active workbook only.
	2 - Save all open workbooks.
Prompt	1 - Prompt before saving.
	2 - Don't prompt before saving.
Save	1 - AutoSave enabled.
	2 - AutoSave disabled.

The Converters Subkey

This subkey contains the description and DLL (code resource) location of external file converters such as the Microsoft Multiplan converter that is shipped with Microsoft Excel.

The Delete Commands Subkey

This optional subkey allows you to delete built-in Microsoft Excel commands. The syntax of the line to delete commands is:

```
<Keyword>=<menu_bar_num>,<menu_name>,<command_position>
```

The definitions of <keyword>, <menu_bar_num>, <menu_name>, and <command_position> are the same as those given in the Init Commands subkey.

Caution   Don't delete the Exit command on the File menu unless you've included another way to quit Microsoft Excel!

Defining Custom Menus and Custom Commands

You can use the Init Menus and Init Commands subkeys to define custom menus and commands. These custom menus and commands appear every time you start Microsoft Excel and enable you to load add-ins or standard macro sheets after you choose the custom command.

Note   The Add-In Manager (the Add-Ins command on the Tools menu) reads and writes entries in both the Init Menus and Init Commands subkeys.

The Init Commands Subkey

The syntax for Init Commands subkey entries is as follows:

```
Entry      Value
<Keyword>  <menu_bar_num>,<menu_name>,<command_name>,<macro>,
           <command_position>,<macro_key>,<status_text>,<help_reference>
```

Argument	Description
<keyword>	A unique keyword, such as Scenario, that Microsoft Windows uses to identify commands added by an INI file.
<menu_bar_num>	The number of the built-in menu bar to which you want to add the command.
<menu_name>	The name of the new menu.
<command_name>	The name of the new command.
<macro>	A reference to a macro on an add-in workbook. Choosing the command opens the add-in and runs the specified macro.

Argument	Description
<command_position>	The position of the command on the menu. This may be the name of the command after which you want to place the new command or a number indicating the command's position on the menu. If omitted, the command appears at the end of the menu.
<macro_key>	The key assigned to the macro, if any.
<status_text>	A message to be displayed in the status bar when the command is selected.
<help_reference>	The file name and topic number for a custom Help topic relating to the command.

The following example shows how an Init Commands entry specifies two commands to be added to built-in menu bar number 1.

```
Entry        Value
Views        1, Window, &View...,'C:\EXCEL\LIBRARY\VIEWS.XLA'!STUB,-,,
Show or define a named view,EXCELHLP.HLP!1730
Solver       1, Formula,
Sol&ver...,'C:\EXCEL\LIBRARY\SOLVER\SOLVER.XLA'!STUB
,,,Find solution to worksheet model,EXCELHLP.HLP!1830
```

The Init Menus Subkey

The syntax for Init Menus subkey entries is as follows:

```
Entry        Value
<Keyword>    <menu_bar_num>,<menu_name>,<menu_position>
```

Argument	Description
<keyword>	A unique keyword, such as Custom1, that Microsoft Windows uses to identify menus added by an Init Menus registry entry.
<menu_bar_num>	The number of the built-in menu bar to which you want to add the menu or command.
<menu_name>	The name of the new menu.
<menu_position>	The position of the new menu on the menu bar. This may be the name of the menu after which you want to place the new menu or a number indicating the menu's position from the left of the menu bar. If there is a menu_parent, then menu_position is the position of the new menu on the menu_parent.

Argument	Description
<menu_parent>	Optional. If defining a submenu, this is the menu name or number on the menu bar that will contain this new submenu.
<keyword>	A unique keyword, such as Custom1, that Microsoft Windows uses to identify menus added by an Init Menus registry entry.
<menu_bar_num>	The number of the built-in menu bar to which you want to add the menu or command.
<menu_name>	The name of the new menu.
<menu_position>	The position of the new menu on the menu bar. This may be the name of the menu after which you want to place the new menu or a number indicating the menu's position from the left of the menu bar. If there is a menu_parent, then menu_position is the position of the new menu on the menu_parent.
<menu_parent>	Optional. If defining a submenu, this is the menu name or number on the menu bar that will contain this new submenu.

Note Microsoft Excel doesn't allow more than one new level of submenus.

The following example shows how an Init Menus entry specifies a custom menu to be added to the right of the Window menu.

```
Entry      Value
Custom1    1,Work,Window
```

The Line Print Subkey

The following is a list of entries in a typical Line Print subkey:

```
BotMarg
Comment
LeftMarg
Options
PgLen
RightMarg
Setup
TopMarg
```

This section controls settings used in Lotus 1-2-3 macro line printing. These settings are defined using the various Lotus 1-2-3 Worksheet Global Default Printer (/wgdp) commands and are updated in the Line Print subkey whenever Microsoft Excel encounters a Lotus 1-2-3 Worksheet Global Default Update (/wgdu) command.

The LeftMarg, RightMarg, TopMarg, and BotMarg entries control the respective margin settings. The values for LeftMarg and RightMarg refer to numbers of characters. While these two values can be from 0 to 1000, a standard page is 80 characters wide. The values for TopMarg and BotMarg refer to numbers of lines. While these two values can be from 0 to 240, standard 11-inch paper can accommodate a maximum of 66 lines, as indicated by the PgLen entry.

The Setup entry is equivalent to the Lotus 1-2-3 Worksheet Global Default Printer Settings (/wgdps) command and specifies the printer setup string.

The Options entry controls four global settings using an 8-bit binary number entered in hex format. Each bit is either 0, corresponding to N (no); or 1, corresponding to Y (yes). The following table lists the values used with the Options entry.

Bit	Lotus 1-2-3 /wgdp command
0	Wait
1	Formatted
2	AutoLf
3	Port (0 through 7)
4	(Used for port)
5	(Used for port)

The best way to determine the appropriate decimal number to use with the Options entry is to construct the binary number first and then convert it to a hex value. The default value is `0x00000002(2)` or, in binary, 0000 0010, meaning that bit 1 is set to the value 1 (the Formatted option set to Y) while all others are set to zero (N). For example, the Options entry that is written to the registry when bits 0, 1, and 2 are set to 1 (0000 0111) is the hex value `0x00000007(7)`, meaning that the Wait, Formatted, and AutoLf options are set to Y.

The three bits (3, 4, and 5) that are devoted to the port indicate the setting used by Lotus 1-2-3 to specify the hardware port to be used for printing. With Microsoft Excel, this is interpreted as a logical port. The default port setting is LPT1:, meaning that bits 3, 4, and 5 are all set to zero. The following table shows the binary bit and port settings.

Binary value (bits 3, 4, and 5)	Port
xx00 0xxx	LPT1:
xx00 1xxx	COM1:
xx01 0xxx	LPT2:
xx01 1xxx	COM2:
xx10 0xxx	LPT1:
xx10 1xxx	LPT2:
xx11 0xxx	LPT3:
xx11 1xxx	LPT4:

Note that in the preceeding table, LPT1: and LPT2: are each represented twice. Either combination of bits can be used with equivalent results.

The actual hex value entered in the Options entry depends on the combination of all the values in the preceding table. For example, if both the Formatted and AutoLf settings are turned on (bits 1 and 2 set to 1), and COM2: is the specified port (bits 3 and 4 set to 1), the Options entry value 0x0000001E(30) is written to the Line Print subkey, which is equivalent to the binary number 0001 1110.

Note To assist you in translations between binary and decimal numbers, you can use the BIN2DEC and DEC2BIN add-in functions that are part of the Analysis ToolPak that is shipped with Microsoft Excel 97. To load these functions, open the ADDINFNS.XLA macro sheet, located in the LIBRARY\ANALYSIS subdirectory of the directory where Microsoft Excel is installed.

The Microsoft Excel Subkey

The following is a list of entries in a typical Microsoft Excel subkey:

```
AddIn Path
AltStartup
Asst in Wizard
AutoFormat
AutoFormat Options
Basics
CmdBarData
Comment
Default Chart
DefaultPath
DefFileMRU
Font
GalleryPath
GlDft-HelpType
```

```
GlDft-DemoSpeed
Maximized
MenuKey
MoveEnterDir
MRUFuncs
MsoTbCust
NoPBPAlert
NoXL5ModuleTabsAlert
Options
Options3
Options5
Options6
SavedQueriesFolder
StickyPtX
StickyPtY
TipShown
UndoHistory
UserName
WinCodePage
Wizard Timestamp
```

Specifying the Paths That You Want Excel to Search for Add-Ins

To specify the paths that Microsoft Excel will search for add-ins when the Tools/Add-ins command is invoked, use the AddIn Path entry. The value for this entry is a string of all the paths that Microsoft Excel should search for add-ins. Multiple path entries are delimited by a semicolon. Your custom solution should only append to this string to avoid inadvertently removing a path to other custom solutions.

Specifying an Alternate Startup Directory

The AltStartup entry allows you to specify an alternate directory in which to locate files you want to open each time you start Microsoft Excel. When you start Microsoft Excel, files located in the XLSTART directory are loaded automatically, followed by files located in the alternate startup directory. The General tab of the Tools/Options command lets you modify this setting.

Specifying Automatic Formatting Options

With the AutoFormat and AutoFormat Options entries, you can specify a particular default formatting choice to be used when the AutoFormat tool is clicked. For the AutoFormat entry, the value specifies the format you want. The formats are numbered 1 through 14 according to the order in which they appear in the list in the AutoFormat dialog box.

The AutoFormat Options entry controls which formatting attributes are applied for the format you specified in the AutoFormat entry. The formatting attributes correspond to the options in the AutoFormat dialog box. The values for the formatting attributes are shown in the following table.

AutoFormat Options	Indicates
1	Number
2	Font
4	Alignment
8	Border
16	Patterns
32	Width/Height

For example, set the AutoFormat Options value to 0x0000000a(10) to specify that just the font and border properties of a format are applied. The number 10 is the sum of 2 (font) and 8 (border). The default value for AutoFormat Options is 0x0000003f(63), the sum of all of the numbers, indicating that all of the formatting properties are applied.

Specifying Whether to Run the Online Tutorial at First Startup

Normally, when you start Microsoft Excel for the first time, the online tutorial "Introducing Microsoft Excel" runs automatically. This occurs when the Basics entry is set to 0x00000000(0). After the first startup, the Basics entry is set to 0x00000001(1) and the tutorial no longer runs at startup. If you reset this to 0x00000000(0), the tutorial will run the next time Microsoft Excel is started, after which it will again be reset to 0x00000001(1).

The CmdBarData Setting

The CmdBarData setting stores data for built-in command bars that are shown, hidden, or moved. Once you create a new command bar or customize an existing one, all information is saved in the *.xlb file.

Setting the Default Chart Format

The Default Chart entry specifies the default chart format. You can set this option from the Chart tab of the Tools/Options command.

Setting the Default File Location Path

The DefaultPath entry specifies the default path used by Microsoft Excel for the File Open and File Save As commands. You can set this option from the General tab of the Tools/Options command.

Setting the Number of Files Shown on the Most Recently Used Files List

The DefFileMRU entry specifies the number of files shown on the Most Recently Used Files list. You can set this option from the General tab of the Tools/Options command. Microsoft Excel initially sets this value to 0x00000004(4).

Setting the Number of Sheets in New Workbooks

The DefSheets entry specifies the number of new worksheets in each new workbook. This entry will appear only if the Sheets in New Workbook entry under the General tab of the Tools/Options command has been modified. If the value of the DefSheets entry is 0x00000001(1), when you create a new workbook, the new workbook will contain one worksheet.

Setting the Default Font for Microsoft Excel

To set the default font and font size used for new worksheets, the Font key is used. The syntax of the value setting for the Font key is:

```
font name,font size
```

For example,

```
MS Sans Serif,10
```

The font name you enter must be the name of the font spelled exactly as it appears in the dialog box when you choose the Font tab of the Cells... command from the Format menu. In Microsoft Excel 97, the Font registry entry sets the default font used for the Normal style, for row and column headings, and for text in the Info window. If the default font has not been changed from Arial, this key might not be present.

Specifying the Path to the User-Defined Chart Gallery

The GalleryPath entry is used to specify the path to the xlusrgal.xls file, which contains the user-defined chart gallery.

Specifying Options in Help for Lotus 1-2-3 Users

There are two entries, GlDft-HelpType and GlDft-DemoSpeed, that correspond to options in the Help for Lotus 1-2-3 Users dialog box. The GlDft-HelpType entry indicates whether you want Help for Lotus 1-2-3 Users to display a set of instructions 0x00000000(0) or give a demonstration 0x00000001(1) for the typed-in Lotus 1-2-3 commands.

The GlDft-DemoSpeed entry controls the speed of the demonstration. This entry will appear in the registry only if the GlDft-HelpType value has been set to 0x00000001(1). When 0x00000001(1) (Demo) is indicated as the G1Dft-HelpType entry value, this can be a number from 0x00000001(1) to 0x00000005(5), where 1 is slow and 5 is fast.

Setting the Application Window Size

The Maximized entry indicates the size of the application window and the size of the workbook window when you start Microsoft Excel. The size of the application window and the size of the workbook window are controlled by the value of this entry, as shown in the following table.

Maximized	Indicates
0	Application window is xlNormal; workbook window is xlNormal.
1	Application window is xlMaximized; workbook window is xlNormal.
2	Application window is xlNormal; workbook window is xlMaximized.
3	Application window is xlMaximized; workbook window is xlMaximized.

When the application window is not maximized, the Pos entry sets the size and position of the window. The first two coordinates set the distance in points (1 point = 1/72 inch) from the left and top of the screen to the top left corner of the window. The second pair of coordinates sets the size of the window in points.

Specifying the Transition Menu or Help Key

The MenuKey entry indicates the ASCII value corresponding to the character used to invoke Microsoft Excel menus or Help. The default key is the slash (/) key. For example, if you changed the menu key in the Transition tab of the Tools/Options command to the backslash (\) key, the MenuKey entry recorded in the registry would be 0x0000005c(92).

Specifying the Direction the Cursor Moves After Enter

The MoveEnterDir entry specifies the direction in which the cursor will move after the ENTER key is pressed. You can set this option from the Edit tab of the Tools/Options command.

Value	Indicates
0	Down
1	Right
2	Up
3	Left

Setting the Most Recently Used Functions List

The MRUFuncs entry specifies the functions that appear in the most recently used list in the Function Wizard. In the MRUFuncs value string, they appear in the order in which they were used. In the Function Wizard, they appear in alphabetical order. The complete list of function numbers appears in the XLCALL.H file in the INCLUDE directory on the sample disk. For example, function number 6 is the MIN function (xlfMin in XLCALL.H).

The MsoTbCust Setting

When the 0x04 bit is set, then the old Excel .XLB has been read and converted. When the 0x08 bit is set, then a new .XLB has been created for this user (usually of the form username8.XLB).

Disabling the Welcome to Page Break Preview Dialog

The NoPBPAlert setting determines whether or not the Welcome to Page Break Preview dialog is displayed when entering page break preview mode. When this value is set to 0x00000001(1) the dialog box is not displayed. This is equivalent to checking the option "Do not show this dialog box again." in the Welcome to Page Break Preview dialog.

Disabling the Excel 5/7 Modules Information Dialog

The first time a user opens a workbook containing Excel 5/7 VBA modules, Excel 97 displays a dialog box informing the user of the new VBE editor. The NoXL5ModuleTabsAlert setting determines whether this dialog is displayed. When this value is set to 0x00000001(1), the dialog box is not displayed. This is equivalent to checking the option "Do not show this dialog box again."

Specifying Documents That You Want Opened Automatically

You can use either of the following methods to specify documents that you want opened each time you start Microsoft Excel.

The XLSTART Directory

The first method you can use to specify a document that you want opened automatically is to place the document in the XLSTART directory. During installation, the XLSTART directory was automatically created in the directory in which Microsoft Office was installed.

The OPEN Entry

The second method you can use to specify a document that you want opened automatically is to add an OPEN entry to the Microsoft Excel section of the registry. For example, to open BUDGET92.XLS automatically, add the following value:

```
c:\excel\budget92.xls
```

where \excel is the path to the directory containing the file you want to open.

Option Switches for the OPEN Entry

You can use the /r and /f option switches, alone or together, to modify the behavior of the OPEN entry. The /r option switch opens the file as read-only. The /f (fast load) option switch places template documents in the New dialog box (accessed from the File menu). When used to open a macro sheet containing custom functions, the /f option switch places those functions in the Function Wizard dialog box. When you use one of the custom functions in a specified document, the macro sheet containing the function is opened automatically.

For example, to open the file BUDGET.XLS as read-only every time Microsoft Excel is started, use the following value:

```
/r c:\excel\budget92.xls
```

To enter more than one OPEN entry, you must number them sequentially. For example, OPEN, OPEN1, OPEN2, and so on.

If you have a macro sheet named CUSTOM.XLM that contains function macros, the following value will cause it to open automatically, and the functions it contains will be added to the User Defined function category in the Function Wizard dialog box:

```
/f c:\excel\custom.xlm
```

To use the /f switch with add-in macro sheets (.XLA), you must define the name __*DemandLoad* (the string "DemandLoad" preceded by two underscores) for the workbook. Microsoft Excel checks to see if the name is defined; the actual definition that you use is not important. You can define __*DemandLoad* as the Boolean value TRUE, for example.

When an OPEN entry is used to open an add-in macro sheet on which the name *__DemandLoad* is defined, custom functions are displayed in the Function Wizard dialog box, but the add-in is not actually loaded until one of its functions is recalculated.

Note The Add-In Manager (the Add-Ins command on the Tools menu) reads and writes OPEN entries.

Setting Other Options

There are many other options that can be set using the four Option entries. These entries are Options, Options3, Options5, and Options6.

The Options entry in the registry sets the following options:

Options	Indicates
1	Show scroll bars
2	Show formula bar
4	Show status bar
16	Use A1-style references
64	DDE is enabled
bits 7 and 8	Apple Macintosh command underlines

The Options3 entry in the registry sets the following options:

Options3	Indicates
0	Alternate menu key on
2	Alternate navigation keys on
4	Lotus 1-2-3 help on
8	Cell note indicators off
32	Macros are saved in the Personal Macro Workbook
16384	Gridlines in new sheets off

For example, you set the Option3 entry to:

`0x00000008(8)`

to automatically turn off cell note indicators each time you start Microsoft Excel. To specify more than one of these options, add the numbers for the options you want. For example, an Options3 entry of `0x00000006(6)` turns on both alternate navigation keys (2) and Lotus 1-2-3 Help (4).

The Options5 entry in the registry sets the following options:

Options5	Indicates
Bit 0	Tip Wizard is on
Bit 1	Prompt for Summary Info
Bit 2	Editing directly in cells is not allowed
Bit 3	Status bar is visible in full-screen mode
Bit 4	Formula bar is visible in full-screen mode
Bit 5	Full-screen mode
Bit 6	Most-recently used file list is not displayed
Bit 7	Cut, copy, and sort objects with cells
Bit 8	Tool tips off
Bit 9	Small toolbar buttons
Bit 10	Toolbar auto-sensing
Bit 11	Do not move to next cell after ENTER key is pressed
Bit 12	Do not warn before drag-drop copy or paste
Bit 13	Use black-and-white toolbar buttons
Bit 14	Ask to update automatic links

The Options6 entry in the registry sets the following options:

Options6	Indicates
Bit 0	Show chart tip names
Bit 1	Show chart tip values
Bit 2	Intellimouse roll action. 0 = zoom, 1 = scroll
Bit 3	Set when macro virus warning is enabled

Specifying the Web Queries Directory

The SavedQueriesFolder entry specifies the directory in which Web query (*.iqy) files will be stored.

Setting the Default Display Location for Dialog Boxes

There are two entries, StickyPtX and StickyPtY, that indicate the preferred location where dialog boxes appear on the screen; they are updated every time you exit Microsoft Excel.

StickyPtX and StickyPtY are the x and y coordinates of the current "sticky" point. The sticky point is the point on which dialog boxes are centered when they first appear on the screen. When a user moves a dialog box, a new sticky point is calculated based on the location of the dialog box when it is closed.

The Tip Wizard History

The TipShown setting saves the Tip Wizard tip history. It stores the list of all tips that have been shown so far. Unless the user resets the Tip Wizard, these tips will probably not be shown again.

Specifying Undo Levels

The optional setting UndoHistory determines the number of undo levels to enable. This number can be set anywhere from zero to some number in the 2 billion range. However, it's best to keep the number as small as is practical in order to keep the memory from filling up with Undo information.

Specifying a User Name

With the UserName entry, you can enter a user name for your copy of Microsoft Excel. Then, if you are using a shared document and someone else on the network tries to open it, a message is displayed along with the specified user name.

Specifying the Windows Code Page

The optional setting WinCodePage specifies the Windows code page. The default is WinCodePage=1252 (or omitted). This value may be different in foreign versions of Windows (for example, 1250 for East European Windows). The WinCodePage= statement is directly copied by the Microsoft Excel Setup program from the [Boot] section in the SYSTEM.INI file. WinCodePage is written into the CODEPAGE record of BIFF files so that they can be loaded correctly under different environments.

Setting DDE Advise Format Retention

If the CFDDELink option is set to 1, Microsoft Excel remembers the last clipboard format used for a successful DDE Advise operation; this is used to reduce the time required for future Advise cycles.

The Recent File List Subkey

The Recent File List subkey corresponds to the list of the most recently used files at the bottom of the File menu. This list changes each time the user quits Microsoft Excel. The following is a list of entries in a typical Recent File List subkey:

```
Entry       Value
File1       "C:\ACCTG\CLOSING.XLW"
File2       "C:\MONTHLY\JANSALES.WK3"
File3       "C:\ACCTG\SCRATCH.XLS"
File4       "C:\EXCEL\AMORT.XLS"
File5       ""
File6       ""
File7       ""
File8       ""
File9       ""
```

The Spell Checker Subkey

The following is a list of entries in a typical Spell Checker subkey:

```
Ignore Caps
Speller
Suggest Always
```

Entry	Description
Custom Dict 1	Specifies the name and location of custom dictionaries you want to use with Microsoft Excel. You can specify additional custom dictionaries by sequentially numbering additional entries, such as Custom Dict 2, and so on.
Ignore Caps	Uses a Boolean value (0,1) to indicate the state of the Ignore Caps check box in the Spell Check dialog box.
Speller	Has a value of the form [Number, Word]. The number is a country code, and the word refers to the dictionary type (see the tables later in this section).
Suggest Always	Uses a Boolean value (0,1) to indicate the state of the Suggest check box in the Spell Check dialog box.

Note   Although you can specify the full path for each of several custom dictionaries using *Custom Dict n* entries, all custom dictionaries must be placed in the \MSAPPS\PROOF subdirectory of your WINDOWS directory.

Country Code	Language
1030	Danish
1031	German
1033	U.S. English
1034	Spanish
1036	French
1040	Italian
1043	Dutch
1044	Norwegian
1054	Swedish
2057	British English
2070	Portuguese
3081	Australian English

The Dictionary Type argument refers to five possible types of dictionaries that can be used by the spelling checker. Microsoft Excel always uses Normal. The following table shows the five Dictionary Types.

Dictionary Type
Normal
Concise (subset of Normal)
Complete (includes Medical and Legal)
Medical
Legal

The WK? Settings Subkey

This subkey contains entries that control the settings used for opening and saving Lotus 1-2-3 files. The following is a list of entries in a typical WK? Settings subkey:

```
AFE
Comment
Gridlines
Load_Chart_Wnd
Monospace
WYSIWYG_Save
```

Entry	Description
AFE	Controls whether Transition Formula Entry (AFE) is turned on. A value of 2 is used as the default, indicating that AFE is turned on only if a macro name exists on the Lotus 1-2-3 worksheet. Otherwise, a value of 1 causes AFE to be always turned on, while a value of 0 causes AFE to be never turned on.
Gridlines	Controls the on-screen display of gridlines when a Lotus 1-2-3 worksheet is opened.
Load_Chart_Wnd	Controls whether Lotus 1-2-3 graphs are converted into Microsoft Excel charts.
Monospace	Controls whether Lotus 1-2-3 files are displayed in Microsoft Excel using a monospaced font (10-point Courier). If Monospace=0, then the Normal style is used.
WYSIWYG_Save	Controls whether an FMT or FM3 formatting file is saved along with a Lotus 1-2-3 worksheet.

Miscellaneous Registry Subkeys That Affect Microsoft Excel 97

The following additional registry subkeys may be important to the Microsoft Excel solution provider.

```
HKEY_LOCAL_MACHINE\
    Software\
        Microsoft\
            Office\
                8.0\
                    Common\
```

The Assistant Subkey

Specifies location information for the Microsoft Office Assistant.

Setting	Indicates
AsstPath	The path where the files for the installed assistant are located
AsstSourcePath	The path where the files for additional assistant options are located
OfficeStartupPath	The path where the assistant startup files are located

APPENDIX C

Displaying Custom Help

With Microsoft Excel, you can display Help to provide users with information about the following custom items:

- UserForms
- Commands
- Menus
- Toolbar buttons
- Alert messages displayed in the course of running a macro

Your Help can include powerful and visually interesting features, such as pop-up windows, graphics, the ability to jump from one topic to another, *hypergraphics* (graphics with one or more hot spots assigned to them), and much more.

To create and compile Help files, you will need the Microsoft Windows Help Workshop version 4.0 or greater.

The Microsoft Windows Help Compiler (HCW.EXE) creates Help files; it does not display them. To display Help files, you must use Microsoft Windows Help (WINHLP32.EXE).

Microsoft Windows Help is included with Microsoft Windows and is usually located in your Windows installation directory. You must purchase the Help compiler separately. For information about obtaining the Help compiler, see "Getting More Information About the Microsoft Windows Help Compiler" on page 566.

Reviewing How to Create Help Topics

This appendix explains how to display custom Help topics with Microsoft Excel, not how to create and compile Help topics in general. If you need to review basic procedures for creating Help topics, you can examine the example Help files described in the following table. The example files are in the HELP subdirectory of the directory in which you installed the Microsoft Excel 97 Developer's Kit. If you need more detailed information about creating Help topics or obtaining the Help compiler, see "Getting More Information About the Microsoft Windows Help Compiler" on page 566.

File name	Description
EXAMPLE.HLP	A compiled Help file that explains how to add jumps, graphics, and hypergraphics to your topics and how to use WinHelp macros to add and remove buttons. To display the Help file, see the instructions following this table.
EXAMPLE.DOC	A Microsoft Word for Windows document that contains the source text and *control codes* for the Help topics in EXAMPLE.HLP. Control codes determine how the user can move around the Help system.
EXAMPLE.RTF	The same file as EXAMPLE.DOC, but saved in rich text format (RTF).
EXAMPLE.HPJ	The Help *project file* used to create EXAMPLE.HLP. The Help project file provides information that the Help compiler needs to build the final Help file.
DLG.SHG	A segmented hypergraphics bitmap file used in EXAMPLE.HLP.
ARROWRT.BMP, DLG.BMP, EXCEL.BMP, and PRESS.BMP	Bitmap files used in several topics in EXAMPLE.HLP.

▶ **To display the example Help file in Microsoft Windows Help**

- In the Microsoft Windows Explorer, double-click the file name EXAMPLE.HLP.

Reviewing How to Create a Help System

After you've reviewed how to create Help topics, you're ready to create the Help system for your application in Microsoft Excel. The following list shows the general steps to create a Help system. For specific information about each step, see your Help compiler documentation.

▶ **To create a Help system**

1. After you create the custom commands, dialog boxes, and so on in Microsoft Excel, gather information for the corresponding custom Help topics.

2. Plan the Help system, deciding which items will need custom Help, what type of Help to provide, how to structure your Help files, and how to structure Help topics within each file.

3. Using your word processing program, write the text for the Help topics in the source files.

4. Enter all required control codes into the source files.

5. Save the source files in rich text format (RTF).

6. Create a project file for the build.

   The *build* is the compiled Help file. Similarly, compiling Help is also called *building* Help in some documentation.

7. Compile the Help file.

8. Start Microsoft Excel, run your custom application, and try to display custom Help topics.

The next section explains how to display Help topics with Microsoft Excel.

The Help compiler requires certain settings in the Help project file and enough memory and disk space to compile the files you specify. If you want to make sure that everything is set correctly and that the Help compiler is ready to compile Help files, you can compile the example Help files described in the table on page 560.

▶ **To compile the example Help file**

1. Create a temporary directory on your disk.

2. Switch to the temporary directory.

3. Copy all the files listed in the table on page 560 except EXAMPLE.HLP, to the temporary directory.

4. Start the Help Workshop (HCW.EXE) and open EXAMPLE.HPJ.

5. From the File menu, choose Compile and click the Compile button.

   The compiler should create a new file, EXAMPLE.HLP, in the temporary directory.

Displaying Help Topics with Microsoft Excel

In Microsoft Windows, Help files are displayed using Microsoft Windows Help (WINHLP32.EXE), usually located in the WINDOWS directory.

To display a Help topic in Microsoft Excel, use one of the following:

- The Visual Basic Help method or the HELP macro function
- The Visual Basic MsgBox function or the ALERT macro function
- Help for custom commands and toolbar buttons
- Help for dialog boxes

Displaying Help Topics with the Help Method

When you run the Help method in your Visual Basic code, Microsoft Excel displays the specified Help topic. The Visual Basic Help method has the following syntax:

```
Application.Help "filename", topic_number
```

Here, *filename* is the name of the file containing the topic and can include the full path, and *topic_number* identifies the topic within the Help file. For compiled Help files, *topic_number* is the number you specify in the [MAP] section of the Help project file. The [MAP] section is described on page 565.

For example, in Microsoft Excel for Windows, you might use the following Visual Basic code to display Help topic number 103.

```
Application.Help "C:\REPORTS\REPORTS.HLP", 103
```

Displaying Help Topics with the MsgBox Function

To display Help using the Visual Basic MsgBox function, you must include in its list of arguments a Help file name and topic number. This causes a Help button to be displayed in the message box, and specifies which Help topic will be displayed when the Help button is chosen. For example, in Microsoft Excel for Windows, enter:

```
MsgBox("Delete this item?",vbOKCancel,,"REPORTS.HLP",501)
```

Help topics are assigned to CommandBarControls using the HelpFile and HelpContextID properties. The following example demonstrates how to assign the Help topic number 101 from the custom Help file custhlp.hlp to a custom CommandBarControl.

```
Sub AddHelpToCommandBarControl()
    With CommandBars("MyBar").Controls(1)
        .HelpFile = ThisWorkbook.Path & "\custhlp.hlp"
        .HelpContextID = 101
    End With
End Sub
```

Help for Custom Dialog Boxes

If you are using Visual Basic to create custom dialog boxes (with UserForms), you can use one of two methods for displaying Help for these dialog boxes. The method used is determined by the WhatsThisButton and WhatsThisHelp properties of the UserForm. To use these properties, you must first assign a custom Help file to your VBProject using its HelpFile property. You can do this with code or with the Project Properties dialog box (shown below). The following example demonstrates how to set the custom Help file CustHlp.hlp as the custom Help file for your project.

```
Sub AddCustomHelpFileToProject()
    Dim szHLP as string
    szHLP = Thisworkbook.Path & "\CustHlp.hlp"
    Application.VBE.VBProjects("vbaHelpTest").HelpFile = szHLP
End Sub
```

From the Tools menu, choose the VBAProject Properties menu, and you can set the same property via the following dialog box.

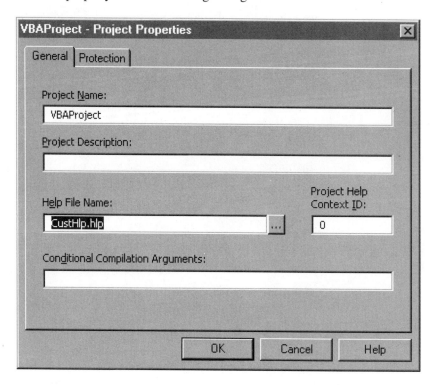

Once you have set a custom Help file for you project, the table below shows the effect of various combinations of the WhatsThisButton and WhatsThisHelp properties of the UserForm.

WhatsThisButton	WhatsThisHelp	Effect
True	True	Displays the WhatsThis icon in the upper right corner of the UserForm. Clicking this icon and then clicking a control displays the Help topic for that control in a control tip-style window.
False	True	No WhatsThis icon is displayed on the UserForm. When the FI key is pressed, the Help topic for the currently active control is displayed in a control tip-style window.
False	False	No WhatsThis icon is displayed on the UserForm. When the FI key is pressed, the Help topic for the currently active control is displayed in a normal help window.

If there is no Help context ID specified for the currently active control when the F1 key is pressed or it is clicked with the WhatsThis cursor, then nothing happens.

Mapping Context Strings to Topic Numbers in Compiled Help Files

When you create source files for custom Help, you must assign a context string to each Help topic. However, when you specify a Help topic to be displayed using any of the methods discussed in this chapter, you must identify the topic using a topic number, not a context string. To map context strings to topic numbers, include a [MAP] section in the Help project file. For more information about the project file, see your Help compiler documentation.

For example, if you have a custom Help file for making reports, with three topics identified by the context strings, Using_Menus, Retrieve_Report_Command, and Open_Any_Command, you might include the following section in the Help project file:

```
[MAP]
Using_Menus 101
Retrieve_Report_Command 102
Open_Any_Command 104
```

To display Help for the Open_Any_Command topic in Microsoft Excel for Windows, you might use the following Visual Basic code.

```
Application.Help "C:\REPORTS\REPORTS.HLP", 104
```

Other Sample Files and Utilities

In addition to the example Help files, the HELP directory also contains sample files for calling Help from a dynamic link library (DLL) or a stand-alone DLL (XLL) and utilities to make creating and displaying Help topics easier.

Calling Help from a DLL or XLL

- HELPCALL.C contains the C source code for CallHelp, a function that could be used in a DLL or XLL to call Microsoft Windows Help, using the Windows API WinHelp function. CallHelp only displays a Help topic, but you can expand it to use the WinHelp API to more fully control Microsoft Help.

- HELPCALL.DEF, HELPCALL.MDP and HELPCALL.MAK are files that, along with HELPCALL.C, you will need if you want to compile your own HELPCALL.DLL file.

- HELPCALL.DLL is the compiled DLL file.
- HELPCALL.XLM contains a two-line macro that calls the CallHelp function (defined in HELPCALL.C) in the compiled DLL. Use this macro to verify that the DLL works.

Also, from a DLL or XLL, you can use the xlfHelp function from the Microsoft Excel C API.

Creating Help Topics Automatically

JUMPS.DOC is the source text of a WordBasic macro that automates creating Help topics. The macro displays a dialog box prompting you for the footnote information (context string, search keywords, title, and so on), creates a skeleton topic, and inserts a page break for the next topic. To use the macro, copy the text into your own WinWord macro template.

Getting More Information About the Microsoft Windows Help Compiler

You can obtain the Microsoft Windows Help Workshop and information about how to use it from any of the following sources:

- The Microsoft Windows Software Development Kit. The Microsoft Win32 SDK includes the Help Workshop. The accompanying documentation assumes you know how to author Help using previous versions of the Help compiler. To obtain the Microsoft Win32 SDK, contact your software vendor or Microsoft Corporation.
- Microsoft Visual Basic, Professional and Enterprise Editions. These versions of Visual Basic include the Help Workshop and documentation explaining how to use it.
- Microsoft Visual C++. This product also contains the Help Workshop and documentation explaining how to use it.
- Your software vendor may know about other products or publications that include the Help compiler or explain how to use it.

Full Code Listing for Wizdemo.xls

Module Code

```
Option Explicit
Const gszEXPLAIN = "The Property Get procedure in" & _
    " the frmWizardDialog allows us to get" & _
    " information from the UserForm."
Const gszADDRESS_R1C1 = "For example: The range" & _
    " selected in step 2 (in R1C1 notation) is: "
Const gszPROPERTY_GET_TITLE = "WizDemo: Getting info" & _
    " from the Object Module"
Const gszSEE_SDK = "See the Wizard section in the" & _
    " Microsoft Excel SDK for details."
''''''''''''''''''''''''''''''''''''''''''''''''''''''''
''' Subroutine: ShowWizard
''' Comments:   Assigned to the Show Wizard Demo command
'''     button. Starts the demo. Calls the
'''     bWizardRun code in the UserForm Object
'''     Module to run the Wizard
''' Date        Developer        Action
''' --------------------------------------------------
'''

Sub ShowWizard(Optional bDeveloper As Boolean = False)
    ''' name of new worksheet
    Dim wksNewSheet As Worksheet
    ''' Add a temporary worksheet for demo
    Set wksNewSheet = ThisWorkbook.Worksheets.Add
    ''' Initialize the appearance of the wizard dialog
    ''' based on whether it's run by user or a developer.
    If bDeveloper Then
        frmWizardDialog.Width = 286.2
        frmWizardDialog.mpgWizardControl.Style = _
        fmTabStyleTabs
```

```
        Else
            frmWizardDialog.Width = 245
            frmWizardDialog.mpgWizardControl.Style = _
            fmTabStyleNone
        End If
        ''' Call Object Module routine to Show the wizard
        If frmWizardDialog.bWizardRun Then
        ''' Wizard was NOT cancelled.
            ''' Procedure continues here...
            ''' Demo the Property Get from the Object Module
            ''' Get the Range user provided in Step 2
            MsgBox gszEXPLAIN & Chr(13) & Chr(13) & _
            gszADDRESS_R1C1 & Chr(13) & _
            frmWizardDialog.szSelectedRangeR1C1 & _
            Chr(13) & Chr(13) & gszSEE_SDK, vbOKOnly + _
            vbInformation, gszPROPERTY_GET_TITLE
            ''' more processing here if needed...
            ''' After your procedure runs, remove the
            ''' UserForm from memory
            Unload frmWizardDialog
        Else    ''' User cancelled the wizard
            ''' don't ask me when deleting the demo sheet
            Application.DisplayAlerts = False
            wksNewSheet.Delete    ''' delete temp worksheet
        End If
End Sub
UserForm Code
Option Explicit
Const miMAX_PAGE_INDEX As Integer = 2
Const mszBASE_DIALOG_CAPTION As String = _
    "Cell Entry Wizard - Step "
Const mszNO_HELP As String = "Sorry - Help is not" & _
    " implemented in the demo but should be in a" & _
    " real Wizard."
Const mszNO_HELP_TITLE As String = "Are you kidding?"
Const mszERROR_TITLE As String = _
    "Wizard Validation Error"
Const mszBAD_SELECTION As String = _
    "Sorry, your selection is not valid."
Const mszNAME_TOO_SHORT As String = _
    "Sorry, your name must be 3 or more characters."
Dim miCurrentStep As Integer
Dim mbUserCancelled As Boolean
```

```
'''''''''''''''''''''''''''''''''''''''''''''''''''''''
''' Property Get: szSelectedRangeR1C1
''' Arguments:  None
''' Comments:   Property Get allows you to get
'''             information from the Object Module in
'''             other modules. This example takes the
'''             range the user selects in step 2 of the
'''             wizard and converts the range to R1C1
'''             notation if needed. This string is
'''             displayed in a message box called in
'''             the mEntry module.
'''
'''             To use this new property, use the
'''             following syntax:
'''                 frmWizardDialog.szSelectedRangeR1C1( _
'''         UserFormName.Property)
'''                 IMPORTANT: This property is NOT available
'''             after the form has been unloaded.
''' Date          Developer          Action
''' -----------------------------------------------------
'''
Property Get szSelectedRangeR1C1() As String
    ''' Create an address string in R1C1 notation.
    With Application
        If .ReferenceStyle = xlA1 Then      ''' convert
            szSelectedRangeR1C1 = .ConvertFormula( _
            refEntryRange, xlA1, xlR1C1)
        Else
            szSelectedRangeR1C1 = refEntryRange.Text
        End If
    End With
End Property


'''''''''''''''''''''''''''''''''''''''''''''''''''''''
''' Function:   bWizardRun
''' Returns:    True if user completes the Wizard
''' Comments:   Shows the Wizard and Unloads it if the
'''         user cancels
''' Date          Developer          Action
''' -----------------------------------------------------
'''
Public Function bWizardRun() As Boolean
    ''' initialize the Wizard assuming user will cancel
    mbUserCancelled = True
    frmWizardDialog.Show
    bWizardRun = Not mbUserCancelled
End Function
```

```
'''''''''''''''''''''''''''''''''''''''''''''''''''''''''''
''' Subroutine: cmdNext_Click
'''
''' Comments:    Moves the wizard one step forward from
'''           the current step.
''' Date         Developer            Action
''' --------------------------------------------------------
'''
Private Sub cmdNext_Click()
    ''' Validate the entries on the current step before
    ''' moving forward.
    If bValidate(miCurrentStep) Then
        ''' Increment the module-level step variable and
    ''' show that step.
        miCurrentStep = miCurrentStep + 1
        mpgWizardControl.Value = miCurrentStep
        ''' Initialize wizard controls for the new step
        InitWizard (miCurrentStep)
    End If
End Sub


'''''''''''''''''''''''''''''''''''''''''''''''''''''''''''''
''' Subroutine: cmdBack_Click
''' Comments:    Moves the wizard one step backward from
'''           the current step.
''' Date         Developer            Action
''' --------------------------------------------------------
'''
Private Sub cmdBack_Click()
    ''' Decrement the module-level step variable and
    ''' display that step.
    miCurrentStep = miCurrentStep - 1
    mpgWizardControl.Value = miCurrentStep
    ''' Initialize the wizard controls for the new step
    InitWizard (miCurrentStep)
End Sub


'''''''''''''''''''''''''''''''''''''''''''''''''''''''''''''
''' Subroutine: cmdCancel_Click
'''
''' Comments:    Dismisses the wizard dialog without
'''              continuing.
''' Date         Developer            Action
''' --------------------------------------------------------
'''
Private Sub cmdCancel_Click()
    ''' Hide the wizard dialog.
    Me.Hide
End Sub
```

```
'''''''''''''''''''''''''''''''''''''''''''''''''''''''''''
''' Subroutine: cmdFinish_Click
'''
''' Comments:   Dismisses the wizard dialog and completes
'''          the task.
''' Date         Developer          Action
''' ------------------------------------------------------
'''
Private Sub cmdFinish_Click()
    ''' Run the validation code. In Demo this is NOT
    ''' needed, but all sheets should run routine
    If bValidate(miCurrentStep) Then
        ''' hide the Wizard, you may need to refer to a
    ''' control from code.
        Me.Hide
        ''' set cancelled flag
        mbUserCancelled = False
        ''' Call routine to do the work of the wizard
        WriteCellEntry
    End If
End Sub


'''''''''''''''''''''''''''''''''''''''''''''''''''''''''''
''' Subroutine: cmdHelp_Click
''' Comments:   In a production app would call the help
'''          system. Not implemented in the demo.
''' Date         Developer          Action
''' ------------------------------------------------------
'''
Private Sub cmdHelp_Click()
    MsgBox mszNO_HELP, vbInformation + vbOKOnly, _
        mszNO_HELP_TITLE
End Sub


'''''''''''''''''''''''''''''''''''''''''''''''''''''''''''
''' Subroutine: txtCellEntry_Change
''' Comments:   Enables the Next button if an entry has
'''          been made in the textbox.
''' Date         Developer          Action
''' ------------------------------------------------------
'''
Private Sub txtCellEntry_Change()
    If txtCellEntry.Text = "" Then
        cmdNext.Enabled = False
        cmdNext.Default = False
    Else
        cmdNext.Enabled = True
        cmdNext.Default = True
    End If
End Sub
```

```
''''''''''''''''''''''''''''''''''''''''''''''''''''''''
''' Subroutine: refEntryRange_Change
''' Comments:   Enables the Next button if the box
'''             contains text (the bValidate
'''             routine validates the range.
''' Date        Developer       Action
''' ------------------------------------------------------
'''

Private Sub refEntryRange_Change()
    If refEntryRange.Text = "" Then
        cmdNext.Enabled = False
        cmdNext.Default = False
    Else
        cmdNext.Enabled = True
        cmdNext.Default = True
    End If
End Sub


''''''''''''''''''''''''''''''''''''''''''''''''''''''''
''' Subroutine: UserForm_Initialize
''' Comments:   Initializes the module-level step
'''             variable and shows the first step.
''' Date        Developer       Action
''' ------------------------------------------------------
'''

Private Sub UserForm_Initialize()
    ''' call common init routine
    InitWizard
End Sub


''''''''''''''''''''''''''''''''''''''''''''''''''''''''
''' Function:   bValidate
''' Comments:   Used to validate a single page or all
'''             pages of the Wizard. In WizDemo the -1
'''             flag (all pages) is NOT used, but would
'''             be if you were validating all pages when
'''             the finish button is chosen. There are 2
'''             major sections:
'''             SECTION 1: Code for All Pages Only
'''             SECTION 2: Code for each page of Wizard.
''' Arguments:  iValidatePage - validate the page passed
'''             (0 based index) If nothing is passed,
'''             default is: validate all pages (-1)
''' Returns:    True if the page validates
''' Date        Developer       Action
''' ------------------------------------------------------
'''
```

```
Private Function bValidate(Optional iValidatePage As _
    Integer = -1) As Boolean
    Dim bIsAllPages As Boolean   ''' true if -1 is passed
    Dim szTrash As String        ''' Holds temp values
    ''' Set function to True. If any validation doesn't
    ''' pass it will be changed to False.
    bValidate = True
    ''' set IsAll flag if -1 is passed.
    bIsAllPages = iValidatePage = -1
    ''' SECTION 1
    If bIsAllPages Then
    ''' placeholder for additional coded needed if
    ''' dialog is being validated as a batch process
    ''' when Finish button is pressed.
    End If
    ''' SECTION 2 if page 1 or all pages (-1)
    If iValidatePage = 0 Or bIsAllPages Then
        If Len(txtCellEntry.Text) < 3 Then
            MsgBox mszNAME_TOO_SHORT, vbOKOnly + _
            vbExclamation, mszERROR_TITLE
            txtCellEntry.SetFocus
            bValidate = False
        End If
    End If
    ''' page 2 or all pages
    If iValidatePage = 1 Or bIsAllPages Then
        ''' Turn off error handling while testing range.
        On Error Resume Next
        With Application
            If .ReferenceStyle = xlR1C1 Then
                szTrash = .ConvertFormula( _
            refEntryRange, xlR1C1, xlA1)
                ''' the next statement will error if the
            ''' selection isn't a valid range
                szTrash = .Range(szTrash).Address
            Else
            ''' the next statement will error if the
            ''' selection isn't a valid range
            szTrash = .Range(refEntryRange).Address
        End If
    End With
    If Err <> 0 Then
        ''' will only happen if range is not valid
        MsgBox mszBAD_SELECTION, vbOKOnly + _
        vbExclamation, mszERROR_TITLE
        refEntryRange.SetFocus
        bValidate = False
    End If
```

```
        ''' reinstate standard error handling
        On Error GoTo 0
        ''' In a production app,
        ''' reinstate custom error handler
        End If
        ''' if page 3 or all pages (-1)
        If iValidatePage = 2 Or bIsAllPages Then
        ''' Page 3 validation goes here...
        ''' no validation needed in WizDemo
        End If
End Function


'''''''''''''''''''''''''''''''''''''''''''''''''''''''''''
''' Subroutine: InitWizard
''' Arguments:  iInitPage - Integer: Page being
'''                 initialized (-1 is special
'''                 case: First time dialog
'''                 displayed)
''' Comments:   Initializes all pages of the wizard
'''             Contains 4 Initialize sections:
'''             SECTION 1: Before initial dialog display
'''                 (iInitPage = -1)
'''             SECTION 2: Before any page is displayed
'''               . EXCEPT the first time
'''             SECTION 3: Common code on any page
'''                 display, no exceptions
'''             SECTION 4: Page specific code
''' Date        Developer           Action
''' -----------------------------------------------------
'''
Private Sub InitWizard(Optional iInitPage As Integer = -1)
    ''' SECTION 1: Before initial dialog display
    If iInitPage = -1 Then
        ''' Set the module-level step variable, set to
    ''' first page of the MultiPage control.
        miCurrentStep = 0
        mpgWizardControl.Value = miCurrentStep
        cmdBack.Enabled = False
        cmdNext.Enabled = False
        cmdNext.Default = False
        cmdFinish.Enabled = False
    ''' SECTION 2: Before any page EXCEPT initial display
    Else
        If miCurrentStep = miMAX_PAGE_INDEX Then
            ''' final page
                cmdFinish.Default = True
            cmdNext.Enabled = False
```

```
            Else
                cmdFinish.Enabled = False
                cmdFinish.Default = False
            End If
            If miCurrentStep > 0 Then
                ''' not first page
                cmdBack.Enabled = True
            Else
                cmdBack.Enabled = False
            End If
        End If
        ''' SECTION 3: Common code for all displays
        ''' Set dialog caption
        Me.Caption = mszBASE_DIALOG_CAPTION & miCurrentStep _
            + 1 & " of " & miMAX_PAGE_INDEX + 1
        ''' SECTION 4: Code for page specific initialization
        ''' if -1 (first time), handled as special case above
        Select Case iInitPage
            Case 0        ''' Page 1
                If txtCellEntry.Text = "" Then
                    cmdNext.Enabled = False
                Else
                    cmdNext.Enabled = True
                End If
            Case 1  ''' Page 2
                If refEntryRange.Text = "" Then
                    cmdNext.Enabled = False
                    cmdNext.Default = False
                Else
                    cmdNext.Enabled = True
                    cmdNext.Default = True
                End If
                    refEntryRange.SetFocus
            Case 2
                ''' Page 3 (none in this example)
        End Select
    End Sub


''''''''''''''''''''''''''''''''''''''''''''''''''''''''''
''' Subroutine: WriteCellEntry
''' Comments:   Enables the Next button if the box
'''             contains text (the bValidate
'''             routine validates the range).
''' Date        Developer           Action
''' -----------------------------------------------------
'''
```

```
Private Sub WriteCellEntry()
    Dim sCellEntry As String
    Dim bBold As Boolean
    Dim bItalic As Boolean
    Dim bUnderlined As Boolean
    Dim rngSelection As Range
    ''' Grab the text entry from the step 1 text box.
    sCellEntry = txtCellEntry.Text
    ''' Create an object reference to the selected range
    ''' from step 2
    With Application
        If .ReferenceStyle = xlR1C1 Then      ''' convert
            Set rngSelection = .Range(.ConvertFormula( _
            refEntryRange, xlR1C1, xlA1))
        Else
            Set rngSelection = .Range(refEntryRange.Text)
        End If
    End With
    ''' Get the font options chosen in step 3.
    bBold = chkBold.Value
    bItalic = chkItalic.Value
    bUnderlined = chkUnderlined.Value
    ''' Error handler here in case of failure
    ''' Make the entry
    With rngSelection
        .Value = sCellEntry
        With .Font
            .Bold = bBold
            .Italic = bItalic
            .Underline = bUnderlined
        End With
    End With
End Sub
```

About the Authors

The Baarns Consulting Group, Inc. (BCGI) has been developing corporate solutions and training with Microsoft Excel since 1987 and was one of the fourteen original Microsoft Excel Consulting Partners, before the Microsoft Solution Provider program started. Today the group specializes in Microsoft Office, BackOffice, and Internet-related technologies. They manage the world's largest third party Web site dedicated to Microsoft Office at http://www.baarns.com. They can also be reached at the following address:

Baarns Consulting Group, Inc.
12807 Borden Ave.
Sylmar, CA 91342
818-362-9235

Co-authors for this book include:

Don Baarns is the President of Baarns Consulting and an internationally known consultant, author, and speaker. Mr. Baarns has been a featured speaker at the Microsoft Excel Developers Conferences (1989-1993), Microsoft Tech Ed and many other industry events. Today he leads a team of highly focused consultants creating high-value solutions for corporations around the world.

Chris Kinsman is the Director of Development for Baarns Consulting and specializes in Microsoft Excel and Internet-related technologies. A highly sought-after speaker, author, and consultant, Mr. Kinsman focuses on maximizing the business value of today's leading technologies.

Rob Bovey is a Senior Consultant with Baarns Consulting and specializes in Microsoft Excel. He has vast experience developing high-value corporate solutions and frameworks for reusable code in Microsoft Office.

Fred Carlsen is the Training Director for Baarns Training and has personally trained over 50,000 students in corporate classrooms over the last 10 years. Today he leads an experienced group of instructors specializing in Microsoft Office and Internet-related technologies.

The most *popular*

office suite *—and the*

top

development *platform.*

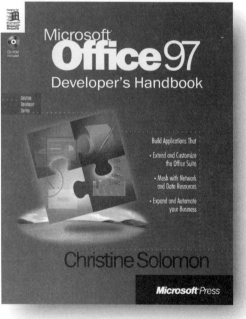

In this thoroughly revised edition, well-known author and experienced consultant Christine Solomon shows systems professionals and developers how to automate and re-engineer a wide assortment of businesses on the powerful Microsoft® Office 97 platform. You'll find plenty of information on new features and technologies. And everything is clarified with detailed explanations, sample applications, anecdotes, examples, and case studies. Plus, the enclosed CD-ROM contains source code and files for sample applications. Get MICROSOFT OFFICE 97 DEVELOPER'S HANDBOOK. And find out why Microsoft Office 97 is a whole new development.

U.S.A.   **$39.99**
U.K.   £37.49 [V.A.T. included]
Canada $53.99
ISBN 1-57231-440-0

Microsoft Press

Blueprint for
excellence.

This classic from Steve McConnell is a practical guide to the art and science of constructing software. Examples are provided in C, Pascal, Basic, Fortran, and Ada, but the focus is on successful programming techniques. CODE COMPLETE provides a larger perspective on the role of construction in the software development process that will inform and stimulate your thinking about your own projects—enabling you to take strategic action rather than fight the same battles again and again.

U.S.A.	**$35.00**
U.K.	£29.95
Canada	$44.95
ISBN 1-55615-484-4	

Winner—
**Software
Development**
Jolt Excellence
Award, 1994!

"The definitive book on software construction. This is a book that belongs on every software developer's bookshelf."
—Warren Keuffel,
Software Development

"I cannot adequately express how good this book really is...a work of brilliance."
—Jeff Duntemann,
PC Techniques

"If you are or aspire to be a professional programmer, this may be the wisest $35 investment you'll ever make."
—*IEEE Micro*

Get all of the *Best Practices* books.

Rapid Development
Steve McConnell
U.S.A. **$35.00** ($46.95 Canada; £32.49 U.K.)
ISBN 1-55615-900-5

"Very few books I have encountered in the last few years have given me as much pleasure to read as this one."
—**Ray Duncan**

Writing Solid Code
Steve Maguire
U.S.A. **$24.95** ($32.95 Canada; £21.95 U.K.)
ISBN 1-55615-551-4

"Every working programmer should own this book."
—**IEEE Spectrum**

Debugging the Development Process
Steve Maguire
U.S.A. **$24.95** ($32.95 Canada; £21.95 U.K.)
ISBN 1-55615-650-2

"A milestone in the game of hitting milestones."
—**ACM Computing Reviews**

Dynamics of Software Development
Jim McCarthy
U.S.A. **$24.95** ($33.95 Canada; £22.99 U.K.)
ISBN 1-55615-823-8

"I recommend it without reservation to every developer."
—Jesse Berst, editorial director, **Windows Watcher Newsletter**

Microsoft Press® products are available worldwide wherever quality computer books are sold. For more information, contact your book or computer retailer, software reseller, or local Microsoft Sales Office, or visit our Web site at mspress.microsoft.com. To locate your nearest source for Microsoft Press products, or to order directly, call 1-800-MSPRESS in the U.S. (in Canada, call 1-800-268-2222).

Prices and availability dates are subject to change.

Microsoft Press

Register Today!

Return this
Microsoft® Excel 97 Developer's Kit
registration card for
a Microsoft Press® catalog

U.S. and Canada addresses only. Fill in information below and mail postage-free. Please mail only the bottom half of this page.

1-57231-498-2A   *MICROSOFT® EXCEL 97 DEVELOPER'S KIT*   *Owner Registration Card*

_____

NAME

_____

INSTITUTION OR COMPANY NAME

_____

ADDRESS

_____

CITY   STATE   ZIP

Microsoft®*Press*
Quality Computer Books

**For a free catalog of
Microsoft Press® products, call
1-800-MSPRESS**